Reprogenetics

Thomas H. Murray, consulting editor in bioethics

Reprogenetics

Law, Policy, and Ethical Issues

Edited by

LORI P. KNOWLES

and

GREGORY E. KAEBNICK

The Johns Hopkins University Press
Baltimore

© 2007 The Johns Hopkins University Press
All rights reserved. Published 2007
Printed in the United States of America on acid-free paper
2 4 6 8 9 7 5 3 1

The Johns Hopkins University Press
2715 North Charles Street
Baltimore, Maryland 21218-4363
www.press.jhu.edu

Library of Congress Cataloging-in-Publication Data

Reprogenetics: law, policy, and ethical issues / edited by Lori P. Knowles and
Gregory E. Kaebnick.
p. ; cm.
Includes bibliographical references and index.
ISBN-13: 978-0-8018-8524-2 (hardcover : alk. paper)
ISBN-10: 0-8018-8524-8 (hardcover : alk. paper)
1. Genetic engineering—Moral and ethical aspects. 2. Genetic engineering—Social
aspects. 3. Reproduction—Moral and ethical aspects. 4. Reproduction—Social
aspects. I. Knowles, Lori P. II. Kaebnick, Gregory E.
[DNLM: 1. Genetic Engineering—legislation & jurisprudence—Canada. 2. Genetic
Engineering—legislation & jurisprudence—Great Britain. 3. Genetic Engineering—
legislation & jurisprudence—United States. 4. Reproductive Techniques,
Assisted—legislation & jurisprudence—Canada. 5. Reproductive Techniques,
Assisted—legislation & jurisprudence—Great Britain. 6. Reproductive Techniques,
Assisted—legislation & jurisprudence—United States. 7. Cross-Cultural
Comparison—Canada. 8. Cross-Cultural Comparison—Great Britain. 9. Cross-
Cultural Comparison—United States. 10. Genetic Engineering—ethics—
Canada. 11. Genetic Engineering—ethics—Great Britain. 12. Genetic
Engineering—ethics—United States. 13. Public Policy—Canada. 14. Public
Policy—Great Britain. 15. Public Policy—United States. 16. Reproductive
Techniques, Assisted—ethics—Canada. 17. Reproductive Techniques, Assisted—
ethics—Great Britain. 18. Reproductive Techniques, Assisted—ethics—
United States. WQ 33 AA1 R4256 2007]
QH442.R472 2007
176—dc22   2006023199

A catalog record for this book is available from the British Library.

Contents

Contributors

Patricia A. Baird, O.C., O.B.C., F.R.S.C., M.D., C.M., F.R.C.P.C., F.C.C.M.G.,
University Distinguished Professor Emerita, Faculty of Medicine,
University of British Columbia, Vancouver, British Columbia

Andrea L. Bonnicksen, Ph.D., Presidential Research Professor, Department
of Political Science, Northern Illinois University, DeKalb, Illinois

Timothy Caulfield, L.L.M., Canada Research Chair in Health Law and
Policy, Professor, Faculty of Law and Faculty of Medicine and Dentistry,
Research Director, Health Law Institute, University of Alberta,
Alberta, Canada

Andrew Grubb, L.L.D., FMedSci, Senior Immigration Judge, Asylum and
Immigration Tribunal, UK; formerly Professor of Medical Law and Head,
Cardiff Law School, Cardiff University, Cardiff, United Kingdom

Kathi E. Hanna, M.S., Ph.D., Science and Health Policy Consultant,
Prince Frederick, Maryland

Suzanne Holland, Ph.D., Associate Professor of Ethics, and Chair,
Department of Religion, University of Puget Sound, Tacoma, Washington,
Affiliate Associate Professor, Department of Medical History and Ethics,
University of Washington School of Medicine, Seattle, Washington

Gregory E. Kaebnick, Ph.D., Editor, *Hastings Center Report*, Director,
Editorial Department and Associate for Philosophical Studies,
The Hastings Center, Garrison, New York

Lori P. Knowles, L.L.B., B.C.L., M.A., L.L.M., Law, Policy and Bioethics
Consultant, Boston, Massachusetts; Research Associate, Health Law
Institute, University of Alberta, Alberta, Canada

Julie Gage Palmer, J.D., Lecturer in Law, University of Chicago Law School,
Chicago, Illinois

Erik Parens, Ph.D., Senior Research Scholar, The Hastings Center, Garrison,
New York

Diane B. Paul, Ph.D., Professor Emerita, University of Massachusetts,
  Boston, Massachusetts
Gladys B. White, Ph.D., R.N., Adjunct Professor of Liberal Studies,
  Georgetown University Washington, D.C.
Alison Harvison Young, Superior Court of Justice, Toronto, Ontario, Canada

Preface

From the cloning of Dolly to the mapping of the human genome and the isolation of human embryonic stem cells, nations around the world continue to grapple with the possibilities posed by new genetic technologies, and especially with the question of how to harness and direct those possibilities for the benefit of humankind. Nowhere is that struggle more necessary and subject to more controversy than in the arena of reproductive genetics, or what the authors of this book call *reprogenetics.* There is an astonishing lack of regulation of reprogenetic technologies in the United States. At the same time, many voices have called for leadership on this issue. It is here that our book enters the fray.

In this book we look at the ethical and public policy issues raised by the burgeoning scientific and commercial enterprise that is reprogenetics. Broadly defined, reprogenetics includes all interventions involved in the creation, use, manipulation, or storage of gametes and embryos. This is a broad yet distinct class of interventions. As we define it, reprogenetics includes procedures such as in vitro fertilization (IVF), the genetic alteration of egg and sperm, and techniques such as research involving the derivation of human embryonic stem cells, including therapeutic or research cloning. Not included are interventions on embryos or fetuses that are *inside* a woman's body. Reprogenetic technologies form an integral part of infertility treatments, from mainstream techniques such as IVF to experimental techniques such as ooplasm transplantation. In addition, much cutting-edge research aimed at curing or treating infertility, but also at addressing some of the most debilitating diseases, uses human embryos, and therefore falls under the rubric of reprogenetics.

There has been a remarkable lack of meaningful moral conversation and public policy concerning the use of reproductive technologies in the United States. As a result, those technologies are subject to no, minimal, or ad hoc regulation. This policy and regulatory void is in sharp contrast to the efforts made in nations such as Canada and the United Kingdom, with which the United States shares cultural, legal, and historical ties. By contrast, genetic technologies have been subject to more formal regulation in the United States, although this regulation tends to isolate the oversight of one technique from another. There are explanations for the historical separation in policy and regulation of reproductive and genetic technologies. Until recently, they were distinct areas of endeavor. Not only have genetic research and reproductive research been conducted in isolation from each other, but genetic science has been considered the purview of molecular biologists, while reproductive science has been conducted by reproductive endocrinologists, obstetricians, and gynecologists. In addition, genetics has offered very few clinical services, while reproductive medicine has offered many. Consequently, the fact that public policy conversations about reproductive technologies and genetic technologies have proceeded on separate tracks has been relatively unproblematic—until now.

We have entered an era in which the possibilities for human reproduction have been expanded by genetic technologies. Together these technologies hold the potential for some wonderful medical advances in disease prevention. However, as we combine genetic technologies with assisted reproduction, we move one step closer to designing the next generation of human beings. The increasing use of reprogenetic technologies challenges our concepts of who we are, who we should be, and what kind of society we want to live in. For example, reproductive medicine, once aimed at helping people overcome infertility, now has the ability to give infertile *and* fertile people the ability to choose the sex and some of the characteristics of a child that will be born to them.

Where an existing child has a disease that requires a transplant or transfusion, finding a suitable donor may lead parents from the family tree to the fertility doctor. It is possible to create embryos in vitro and then choose which will be implanted, stored, or discarded based on each embryo's genetic compatibility with an existing child. Children conceived in this manner are referred to in the media as "designer babies" and "savior siblings." The desire to save an ailing child is laudable and complicates the ethical picture of creating a child for the purpose of providing transplantable blood or tissue for another. While the ethics of creating savior siblings are debatable, sex selection based on parental preference is widely regarded as unethical in the international community. Clearly, sex selection may have profound implications both for the embryos selected and for children already born. Our concept of what it means to be a parent is also challenged when we can select or design children we believe will fulfill *our* needs and desires. And just as sex selection is a reality now, selecting for other traits, such as height, eye color, intelligence, and athletic ability, could also be, at some point in the future. Not only are we moving technically closer to "designer children," but the possibilities for choice and selection will have a profound impact on the relationship between parents and children. These technologies are not regulated in the United States, nor are there guidelines for their ethical use.

In the absence of regulation, reprogenetic technologies are subject only to the limited constraints of the market. Consequently, assisted human reproduction and gene-linked characteristics are becoming commercial commodities in the United States. The market is arguably not an appropriate mechanism by which to regulate the use of technologies that deal in human reproduction and individual genetic composition for another reason. Markets deal in goods or commodities; consequently, once markets are created in human reproduction and genetic composition, both these things become market commodities. Formerly priceless, they gradually become goods that can be bought and sold and subjected to price comparisons. The commercialization of reproduction means that we can answer the questions "How much will it cost to select a little girl?" and "How much are ova from white college women compared to ova from African American women?" In many other countries, reproductive technologies are regulated to respect what they consider a guiding principle: the noncommercialization of human reproduction. In the United States, the lack of regulation of reprogenetic technologies is institutionalizing the opposite principle.

In addition to these questions, which deal with issues of the well-being of individuals and the society in which we live, the overlap between clinical innovation and research in fertility clinics raises issues of safety, as these clinics function free from oversight. For example, research has shown that a technique used to inject sperm directly into eggs in fertility treatments can cause damage to the egg's chromosomes. This technique was used and the resulting embryos implanted in women before rigorous safety testing became commonplace. To use such technologies without thorough animal testing raises serious concerns about the health and safety of women and of any resulting children.

Although we cannot predict the face of the future, these technologies are deployed together in complex ways increasingly frequently, and new applications for human reproduction are inevitable. The absence of integrated moral and policy conversations inhibits our ability to explore the appropriate applications of future technology and to develop policy to control that technology before it hits the market. Rather than wait for the technology to be introduced before engaging in ethical analysis, we must anticipate these developments and begin the process of addressing what they mean for all of us—children, parents, and policymakers alike.

Society's interest in recent reprogenetic developments such as human cloning, embryonic stem cell research, and sex selection have thrown open the doors on the whole enterprise of reprogenetic research and clinical practice. As a result, the question of what we should do with and to embryos is once again front-page news and a burning political issue both in the United States and around the world. Questions this book addresses include the following: How do we understand the background for this policy debate? What are the technologies under discussion? What might we expect to come our way? How do we articulate the concerns that these technologies raise? What is there to fear? What are other countries doing? How do we move forward in the United States? Until very recently, such policy debates were polarized by abortion politics in the United States. For the first time in recent memory, staunch abortion opponents and staunch proponents of choice are rethinking their polarized positions in light of new reprogenetic possibilities—particularly the isolation of human embryonic stem cells. The aim of the book is to take advantage of this opportunity to help define and engage the issues that must be part of any policy conversation.

In Part One, Diane Paul, Julie Gage Palmer, and Andrea Bonnicksen provide the historical and regulatory background necessary to understand what is said and what remains silent in today's public policy discussions about reprogenetics. These chapters allow the reader to understand the historical underpinning for present and future political debates that express caution in regard to regulating reproduction or embracing technologies aimed at "selecting in" or "selecting out" individuals through reproductive means. Chapters on the recent regulation of reproductive medicine and genetic technologies provide the basis for understanding the current regulatory landscape in the United States.

Part Two helps define the issue of what is at stake in an increasingly commercialized world of reprogenetic choices and looks at how policymakers create support for ethically controversial policy decisions in a diverse society. Suzanne Holland explores the need to find other regulatory mechanisms outside the market for reprogenetic technologies. Timothy Caulfield examines how politicians appeal to moral consensus as a means of supporting controversial ethical and policy decisions.

Part Three examines how countries with political, legal, and cultural traditions similar to those of the United States have attempted to govern reprogenetic technologies. Patricia Baird and Andrew Grubb have been involved in the formation and implementation of current policy responses to reprogenetic technologies in Canada and the United Kingdom, respectively. They provide an in-depth understanding of how those countries have addressed the need for regulation of safety and well-being issues and the need for public and policy debate about the implications of reprogenetic technologies. The United Kingdom's system of comprehensive oversight has provided a blueprint for regulatory initiatives by other countries, such as Canada, Australia, and France. In the last chapter in this part, Lori Knowles provides a comparative international perspective that highlights some of the political difficulties countries have grappled with in regulating reprogenetic technologies and the varied responses they have developed. This chapter should help the reader see the similarities and differences in international responses.

In Part Four, three authors look seriously at the possibility of regulating reprogenetic technologies in the United States. Kathi Hanna, a veteran of Beltway politics, provides an insider's perspective on the role of advisory bodies in American reprogenetic policy. Alison Harvison Young looks to existing legal mechanisms of contract and tort law to fill the policy vacuum in the United States. Gladys White looks at the regulation of reprogenetics in the United Kingdom and finds ways to bring some similar, comprehensive regulation to the same enterprise in the United States. Thus, the chapters in this last section of the book illustrate well the differences of opinion about how meaningful reprogenetics policy can be achieved in the United States.

The contributors to this book develop different perspectives and are not all in consensus on the path forward. Nevertheless, the final part of the book, "Reprogenetics and Public Policy," articulates a vision of a specific approach to the regulation of reprogenetic technologies in the United States. In that vision, a body like the U.K.'s Human Fertilisation and Embryology Authority would be established to license the storage, use, and manipulation of gametes and embryos. This is a bold vision, and one that draws both support and criticism from the authors of this book. I invite you, the reader, to enter this debate with us and help us carve a path forward toward meaningful moral debate and responsible public policy bearing on reprogenetics in the United States and abroad.

PART ONE

The Historical and Regulatory Landscape

CHAPTER ONE

On Drawing Lessons from the History of Eugenics

DIANE B. PAUL

Almost every discussion of social issues in reprogenetics identifies eugenics as a central concern. Of course, there are other sources of unease at the prospect of modifying the genome either to treat disease or to enhance physical, mental, or behavioral characteristics. For example, critics also fear that such interventions rest on dubious scientific assumptions, entail unacceptable risks, distort parent-child relations, and exacerbate social inequality. But perhaps their most persistent and passionate accusation is that reprogenetics is a form of eugenics.

A particularly striking feature of such discussions is how often the participants invoke history. The typical analysis of social issues in reprogenetics—irrespective of whether its perspective is optimistic or gloomy—is accompanied by a commentary on the history of the eugenics movement. These accounts tend to be remarkably similar. Despite having widely varying agendas, both celebrants and skeptics tell essentially the same tale. The standard narrative features racists and reactionaries—often Nazis—and policies that are "negative" (that is, they are aimed at preventing or discouraging some people from reproducing), mandated by legislation, and coercively enforced. In these obligatory historical synopses, eugenic policies were based on "pseudo-science." The exemplar of these policies is compulsory sterilization.

Why are the accounts so ubiquitous and uniform? One reason is banal. Those who speak and write on social issues in genetics feel compelled to say something about the history of eugenics, if only to demonstrate that they are aware of it and sensitive to its implications. But few commentators are likely to be specialists in the subject. Indeed, the virtual interchangeability of so many of their accounts suggests that authors often learn from reading each other. The similarity is in any case not explained by the fact that there is only one history to relate, and that the authors are simply faithful to the facts. For the standard account is highly selective. Its particular features are explained by the interests they serve both for admirers and for critics of developments in reprogenetics. But although its appeal is understandable, such a narrow version of the past provides little useful guidance—and indeed, may seriously mislead—as we consider if and how to regulate in this domain.

EUGENICS VOLUNTARY AND UTOPIAN

Although the typical narrative of eugenics emphasizes brutal measures of state control, we could certainly tell another story. After all, most eugenics was not overtly coercive, and some of its leading advocates specifically repudiated compulsory measures. Britain, where the modern movement was founded in the 1860s by Francis Galton, never adopted a mandatory sterilization law, and even the campaigns to legalize voluntary sterilization were defeated. Moreover, Galton himself held that "the possibility of improving the race of a nation depends on the power of increasing the productivity of the best stock. This is far more important than that of repressing the productivity of the worst" (1909, 24). Those who agreed with him tended to favor "positive" eugenics, which, instead of discouraging or preventing reproduction by the wrong people, employed methods, such as propaganda or financial subsidies, to promote reproduction by the right people. After all, the success of efforts to encourage some people to have more children required the subjects' active cooperation.

But even much negative eugenics has relied on education, persuasion, or simply individuals' assumed self-interest. Many birth control advocates argued that middle-class women already had access to contraceptive information and devices, whereas poor women (assumed to be hereditarily inferior) did not. Such leading figures as Margaret Sanger in the United States and Marie Stopes in Britain assumed that if poor women only had the means to do so, they would limit their births for their own social, economic, and health reasons, thus obviating any need for coercion (Gordon 1990; Kline 2001; Paul 1995, 91–96).

Moreover, negative measures aim at preventing further deterioration, not at creating something new. Yet much of the contemporary worry about genetic manipulation focuses on its more ambitious possibilities, especially the potential to transform human nature (for example, Fukuyama 2002; Habermas 2003; McKibben 2003; Sandel 2004; Somerville 2003). That worry has been prompted, or at least intensified, by recent enthusiastic claims that we can and should radically redesign ourselves. Thus, in the last few years, adherents of a movement known as transhumanism have celebrated the coming convergence of cryonics, genetic engineering, nanotechnology, and robotics. (Transhumans are "moderately enhanced humans, whose capacities would be somewhere between those of unaugmented humans and full-blown posthumans," according to Nick Bostrom [2004], co-founder of the World Transhumanist Association in 1998 and one of the movement's most thoughtful exponents.)[1]

The desire to enlarge humans' intellectual, emotional, aesthetic, and physical capabilities is shared by a host of scientists and philosophers associated with more mainstream institutions. Thus Gregory Stock (2002), director of the Program on Medicine, Technology, and Society at UCLA's School of Public Health, has asserted that redesigning humanity is not only a worthwhile but an unstoppable project. (The subtitle of his book, *Redesigning Humans,* is *Our Inevitable Genetic Future*). Lee Silver (1997, 277), professor of molecular biology and public affairs at Princeton, also exhorts us to remake ourselves. Using genetic engineering to this purpose, he suggests, is no different in principle from sending our children to computer camp or providing the multiple other advantages that we generally accept as legitimate (see also Silver 2000, 60). Conceding that the result will be to increase inequality, Silver anticipates that in the distant future, the species will split into "normals" and the "gen-rich," a group that is "as different from humans as humans are from the primitive worms with tiny brains that first crawled along the earth's surface" (1997, 292–93). (He has since somewhat backtracked on this question; see *Liberation Biology,* 1999). German philosopher Peter Sloterdijk's *Regeln für den Menschenpark* (1999) similarly foresees a division of humanity into genetic engineers and the genetically engineered—the zookeepers and the animals in the "human zoo."[2] In Europe, where his work created something of a sensation, Sloterdijk was immediately compared with Hitler. But the real precursors of the transformist vision and the unwillingness to be bound by conventional morality that characterize not only his work but also that of Silver, Stock, and Gregory Pence (2000b), devotees of machine intelligence and nanotechnology such as Hans Moravec (1999), Ray Kurzweil (1999), and Eric Drexler (1986, 1992), and the writings of a host of lesser-known "transhumanists" are the visionary scientific socialists of the 1920s and 1930s. Sloterdijk and his compatriots surely have much less in common with Nazis than with such Marxist scientists as J. B. S. Haldane and J. D. Bernal.[3]

Haldane's paper *Daedalus, or Science and the Future* (1923) describes a future world in which conventional eugenics has been abandoned as too clumsy and slow. Instead, eugenic aims will have been achieved much more efficiently through a combination of directed mutation and "ectogenesis," a process of conceiving and nurturing embryos outside the mother's womb. Because only a tiny proportion of the population is chosen as ancestral material for the next generation, the result is a rapid advance in general intelligence, talent, and character.

To those he knew would find this vision repugnant, Haldane reassuringly notes that eventually our values always adapt to the science. Although every biological invention initially seems "indecent and unnatural," in time it comes to be taken for granted, and what first appeared as a perversion ends "as a ritual supported by unquestioned beliefs and prejudices" (1923, 36–37). That point was recently reiterated by Danny Hillis, the co-founder of Thinking Machines. Commenting on Ray Kurzweil's prediction that humans and robots would merge, Hillis noted that "the changes would come gradually and that we would get used to them" (quoted in Joy 2000).

Inspired by *Daedalus,* the crystallographer J. D. Bernal imagined a future in which the practice of ectogenesis had become routine, resulting in a vastly increased life span and intelligence. *The World, the Flesh, and the Devil* describes a world in which individuals with especially powerful intellects are plugged into an elaborate network of other superior beings. Bernal equably contemplates the possibility that the human race will eventually divide into a race of scientist-rulers and one of controlled and docile masses who are fooled into thinking that they are free (1929, 89).

Haldane, Bernal, H. J. Muller (author of the Haldane-inspired eugenic tract, *Out of the Night*), and other scientific Marxists of the 1920s and 1930s are far closer in spirit to today's genetic techno-utopians than are the racists and reactionaries who play such prominent roles in current commentaries. Despite the fact that, according to Nick Bostrom (2003, 40), Haldane's *Daedalus* was "a significant stimulus in the formation of transhumanism," neither Haldane nor other scientific socialists figure in these critiques. Given the nature of contemporary concerns, why do we hear so much about euthanasia, immigration restriction, and compulsory sterilization and so little about eugenics that was intended to be transformative?

DIVERGENT INTERESTS, INTERSECTING STORIES

As late as the 1980s, many writers took for granted that human genetic engineering either was or would lead to some kind of eugenics—the question was whether it would be the good or the bad kind. That the label, in itself, did not necessarily condemn is reflected in the fact that many enthusiasts unembarrassedly called genetic engineering a "new eugenics." Critics thus had to explain what they thought was wrong with a eugenics that rested on individual choice. Today, by contrast, to label a practice "eugenics" is to denounce it. Thus, when antibiotechnology activist Jeremy Rifkin asserts "Genetic engineering technologies are, by their very nature, eugenic tools" (1998, 116), he takes for granted that the claim is damning. Although it is not always obvious exactly *why* eugenics is wrong, the accompanying histories usually imply that a prime candidate is coercion.

Narratives that equate eugenics with compulsion and jackbooted Nazis allow champions of the new technologies to sharply demarcate their projects from eugenics—to emphasize discontinuity. These stories allow them to say, in effect, "we are obviously *not* Nazis, so this history has nothing to do with us." Indeed, if eugenics is equated with coercion, it allows the enthusiasts to claim either that reprogenetics is not eugenics at all or that it is eugenics of a benign sort. (Both moves are made.)

Moreover, the obvious moral of such histories is that people should be free to reach their own reproductive goals in whatever ways they want. Thus the statement entitled "Eugenics and the Misuse of Genetic Information to Restrict Reproductive Freedom" and issued by the American Society of Human Genetics (1999, 337) discusses immigration restriction, antimiscegenation, and coercive sterilization laws and concludes by condemning all efforts "to restrict reproductive freedom based on genetic information." (The same statement specifically approves laws barring cousin marriages, thus reflecting a common line of demarcation: what we disapprove is eugenics, what we approve is not.)

This kind of history is also easily deployed in support of an antiregulatory agenda, for it explains why, as James Watson succinctly put it, "the state should stay out of it" (Stock and Campbell 2000, 90). Swedish philosopher Torbjörn Tännsjö makes the libertarian moral explicit:

> The important thing to learn from history is that society should not meddle with our reproductive decisions. This does not only imply that no one should be com-

pelled to have an abortion or become sterilised. It implies too that no one should be stopped from becoming a parent in the way he or she sees fit. The use of techniques for assisted reproduction should not be regulated by political authorities (nor by doctors). The decisions about prenatal diagnosis, in vitro fertilization, egg donation, preimplanatory diagnosis, and so forth, should be placed in the hands of prospective parents. The doctors should serve the needs of those prospective parents. The politicians should allow the doctors to do so. (1998, 247–48)

Tännsjö is joined by such reprogenetic enthusiasts as John Robertson (1994), John Harris (1998), Leroy Hood (2000, 80), Silver, Pence, and Stock in arguing that we all have the right to seek to achieve our reproductive goals, whatever they may be.

The principle of respect for autonomy is thus employed to distinguish these current and impending reproductive possibilities from past eugenics. After admonishing us not to forget the Nazi concentration camps, Stock (2002, 198–99) asserts that the lesson to be derived from the history of the first half of the twentieth century is "Governmental abuse is what we must fear, not germinal choice technology." Severino Antinori, the Italian fertility specialist who with Panos Zavos is attempting human cloning, similarly observes that Josef Mengele was a "government doctor" in arguing against legislation or regulation of the enterprise (2001, 3). In response to the question, "Do transhumanists advocate eugenics?" Nick Bostrom (2003, 21) notes that they condemn the coercion, as well as race and class biases associated with pre-World War II eugenics. "Transhumanists uphold the principles of bodily autonomy and procreative liberty," he writes. "Parents must be allowed to choose for themselves whether to reproduce, how to reproduce, and what technological methods they use in their reproduction." Mindful of the historical lessons of Nazi eugenics and Stalinism, "transhumanists are often deeply suspicious of collectively orchestrated change, arguing instead for the right of individuals to redesign themselves and their own descendants" (40). Philosopher Gregory Pence (2000a, 113) is exceptionally blunt:

> Some day soon, when the opportunities arise, we will see the wisdom of allowing parents maximal choice about their future children. This is not state-controlled eugenics (which attempted to take away such choices from parents) but its opposite. If a child can be given an extra decade of life by an artificial chromosome, or 50 percent more memory through a therapy in utero, then I personally would feel *obligated* to give my future child such benefits. I believe that my child would be grateful to have been deliberately given such a benefit.

Others might disagree and choose not to do so for their children—a decision I would respect. What I fail to understand is how other people—or the federal government—could think it just to prevent a parent from benefiting her future children in this way—for example, by banning such enhancements (perhaps from a misplaced concern for equality and social justice). I see no difference between such a ban and a similar ban on parents sending their children to computer camps in the summer: both are intended to better children, both will be done most by people with money, and both are not the business of government.

It is easy to see how a laissez-faire agenda is served by a particular version of the history of eugenics. But why do critics so often tell the same simplistic story? The answer seems to be that, for them, a history that focuses on compulsory sterilization and the killing of mental patients serves to associate current and prospective genetic manipulations with practices that we now find odious. It serves to stress the continuity of new technologies with ugly past events, thus investing arguments with emotional charge.

HISTORICAL NARRATIVES AND CONTEMPORARY CHOICES

But for critics, the version of history that serves this interest is in tension with another. For they rarely wish to draw an antiregulatory moral—except in relation to coerced sterilization and abortion. From their standpoint, eugenics that is private is not thereby benign. In fact, voluntary, market-driven eugenics is the kind they most fear.

The view that contemporary eugenics arises from our increased capacity to choose the kind of children we want, and thus will be hard to resist, was first articulated by Rollin Hotchkiss in the essay in which he coined the term "genetic engineering." Recognizing that a eugenics requiring state action was no longer acceptable, Hotchkiss (1965, 198) noted that the interventions made possible by advances in molecular biology "could be practiced in private and in secret on individual genes of individual persons." He also presciently observed: "It will be much more difficult to regulate, and legislation *against* it will seem like the same invasion of personal rights that legislating *for* eugenic measures appears to be."

The association of a new eugenics with choice was actually a common theme in the writings of early molecular biologists, who were generally enthusiastic about the potential of their science to improve humanity, and was only later taken up by detractors. Thus, Caltech molecular biologist Robert Sin-

sheimer, who famously termed genetic engineering a "new eugenics," emphasized that this kind would be accomplished by individuals acting voluntarily
in their own interests. "The new eugenics," he claimed, "would permit in
principle the conversion of all of the unit to the highest genetic level. The old
eugenics was limited to a numerical enhancement of the best of our existing
gene pool. The horizons of the new eugenics are in principle boundless—for
we should have the potential to create new genes and new qualities yet
undreamed" (1969, 13).

As Daniel Kevles has noted (1985, 267), that prediction occurred before the
development of recombinant DNA technology, which promised to overcome
the difficulty of isolating specific human genes, which could then in principle
be identified and replicated. It also occurred before the development of reproductive technologies such as in vitro fertilization. Today, genetic manipulations are entering clinical practice in the context of the nearly unregulated fertility industry. As a consequence of the de facto ban on federally funded
embryo research in the United States, no federal laws regulate what services
may be offered or monitor their efficiency or safety. Enthusiasts tend to
approve this lack of regulation. Thus, Gregory Pence (2000b, 74) attributes the
"rapid, creative innovation" in assisted reproduction to the federal funding
ban, since research in fertility clinics has not been hampered by the National
Institutes of Health or by the local institutional review boards, whose approval
would have been required for proposals receiving federal funds.

But for critics, lack of regulation virtually guarantees fulfillment of Sinsheimer's prediction, which they find repugnant. Their worry is not that parents will be forced by the state to genetically engineer their progeny. It is
rather the opposite: that individuals responding to social norms of health,
attractiveness, intelligence, and so forth will *want* to alter the characteristics
of their offspring, and even demand the right to do so, a practice variously
labeled "back-door" (Duster 1990), "laissez-faire" (Kitcher 1996), "do-it-your-
self" (Morton 1998), and "user-friendly" (Rifkin 1998) eugenics. Like Hotchkiss, those fearful of privatized eugenics know that it will be much harder than
its precursors to counter.[4]

Why do critics think it *should* be resisted? If coercion is not the issue, what
makes the new eugenics insidious? Included in a wide array of actual or
potential dangers would be a widening of already immense social inequalities, given that a sixth of Americans have no health insurance, and standard
policies do not pay for high-technology reproductive services, which would
be available only to individuals with costly private insurance or the wealth to

pay for them (Frankel and Chapman 2000, 36–37); reinforcement of assumptions about the contribution of genes to differences in human mentality and behavior, with a consequent shift away from more effective medical, social, and environmental means to improve human health and well-being; a related concern that decisions about what enhancements to offer would be made by and thus embody the values of scientists and biotech entrepreneurs (see Darnovsky 2001a; 2001b, 1; Hubbard and Wald 1999, 116); a negative impact on parent-child relationships in cases where efforts to produce a child meeting certain specifications disappointed (Elshtain 1998, 184–85; Rothman 2001, 204–5), and a negative effect on children, who might feel even more constrained by parental expectations than they do now (Darnovsky 2001b, 13; Frankel and Chapman 2000, 31–32; Sandel 2004); and the fostering of an unhealthy preoccupation with perfection, and consequent prejudice against people with disabilities (Andrews 2001, 97–106; Parens and Asch 2001; Saxton 2001; Silvers, Wasserman, and Mahowald 1998).

MANAGING TENSIONS: BEING FOR PROCREATIVE LIBERTY AND AGAINST GENETIC MANIPULATION

It might seem that such perceived risks would prompt calls for curbs on consumer sovereignty. But proposals to limit procreative liberty in the service of other values are rare on the political left, even among those critics of genetic manipulation who identify with the disability rights movement. The entanglement with abortion politics has made candid discussions of solutions to the problems posed by private eugenics extremely difficult. Especially in the United States, access to abortion has been defended on the principle that women have an absolute right to control their own bodies, and on that basis, the procedure is permitted for any reason at all. To argue that some genetic grounds should not be respected is implicitly to limit the scope of the principle that has underpinned access to abortion.

But the discourse of rights is employed on every side of the issues. Opponents of abortion invoke the rights of the fetus, while defenders invoke the rights of the pregnant woman. Champions of the new reproductive technologies appeal to the right to choose, while the Council on Responsible Genetics, which is highly skeptical, has issued a "Genetic Bill of Rights" that asserts: "All people have the right to have been conceived, gestated, and born without genetic manipulation" (GeneWatch, April 2000, 3).

Some feminists have argued that we should abandon the language of "choice," along with rights arguments in general, both because such arguments inevitably generate rival claims and because they are embedded in a framework of liberal assumptions about the asocial and self-interested nature of individuals, assumptions that they deem both conceptually inadequate and contrary to women's lived experiences (e.g., Fox 1998; Himmelwait 1988).

But the political risks such a move entails have made such proposals unpalatable. The more typical stance, at least on the part of critics of human genetic modification, is to assert the compatibility of being *for* choice and *against* tampering with the human genome. Thus the director of the Center for Genetics and Society writes, "Advocates of women's health and choice will need to develop a voice for women's reproductive rights that is firmly pro-choice and firmly opposed to the modification of human beings" (Darnovsky 2001b, 14). But if "firmly pro-choice" implies that reproductive autonomy is an absolute right, it is unclear how both those demands could be met. After all, these modifications will be chosen by individuals exercising their reproductive rights.

A common response to this dilemma is to implicitly suggest that choices about the use of genetic technologies are not really autonomous—that women are not after all "free to choose" (a phrase that often appears in scare quotes). In a passage typical of this line of argument, David King (2001, 175) maintains that "structural factors and social pressures guarantee that allowing parents a 'free choice' results in a systematic bias against the birth of genetically disabled children that can only be called eugenic," while Ruth Hubbard and Elijah Wald (1999, 27) assert that norms pertaining to reproductive responsibility convert "the so-called choices of future parents, especially of mothers, into obligations to make a socially approved choice."

That women are pressured by economic circumstances and social expectations to make certain choices is undoubtedly true. The provision of reproductive genetic services implies that some conditions are insupportable, and the success of such programs is often measured by the extent of reduction in the births of children with expensive disorders (Paul 1998). Risk information may be misleading or otherwise inadequate, and genetic counseling in practice (as opposed to theory) is sometimes directive (Michie et al. 1997). The costs of caring for a severely disabled child are large, and the fate of the child after the parents are no longer able to provide care is a source of great anxiety, even in systems with national health insurance. There do exist social norms regarding what constitutes reproductive responsibility, attractiveness, and health; social attitudes about gender, sexual orientation, and race; and views about what life is like for disabled people and their families (Kerr and Shakespeare 2002, 125–27; Saxton 2001, 11). These norms will influence individual decisions in respect to reprogenetic technologies, and some attitudes and opinions will be superficial or wrong.

But discussions of this issue often imply that a choice influenced by social expectations or trends is not free—as though a world in which people failed to be influenced by the views of their family, communities, and larger society were somehow possible (and desirable). Thus Gregor Wolbring makes explicit a point tacitly implied in the statements by King and by Hubbard and Wald when he writes that "there is no free choice and autonomy regarding eugenic practices: the decisions are all embedded in the society surrounding the person" (1999, 10). But as feminists in particular have stressed, our choices—including reproductive choices—are always embedded in a social context, which inevitably includes the expectations of others (Kerr and Shakespeare 2002, 120; for a sensitive anthropological account of reproductive decision making see Rapp 1999). If an "autonomous" decision is defined as one independent of social norms, no decision on any matter—including whether to terminate a pregnancy for personal reasons—could possibly count as free. But that implication cannot be intended, for the discussions implicitly contrast the lack of genuine autonomy in the realm of reprogenetics with its ostensible existence elsewhere. It seems rather that choices the authors approve of are "free" and "autonomous," whereas those they dislike are not.[5]

Perhaps what is meant is not that people influenced by social forces are unfree but rather that in choosing to use these particular technologies, they are influenced to take action that is contrary to their interests or fundamental values. After all, we think quite differently about parental teaching and example that leads children to be kind to others, take their studies seriously, and generally flourish, and peer-group influences that lead them to drive recklessly, drink excessively, and shoplift, even though in both cases the subjects are only partly the author of their own plans for living. In the case of potentially foolish or self-destructive behavior, we at least try to ensure that choices are made thoughtfully and knowledgeably before supporting individuals' insistence on being left alone.[6]

With respect to the use of reprogenetic technologies, the risk is not to the values and interests of the influenced individuals—that is, the prospective parents. Rather, such choices undermine important social values and interests. It is therefore reasonable to argue that we should try to dissuade people from making them, if not for their own, then for society's sake—to convince them that most children with disabilities in fact do much better than we think, that "disability, vulnerability, dependency on the care and protection of others are not to be willed but are to be accommodated and accepted into the proper realm of human experience" (Jennings 2000, 144), and that the Olympian athlete ideal of a human life free of frailty and disability is both a will-o'-the-wisp and injurious to the structures of support on which we will all at some point depend.

CONCLUSION

A communal conversation about these matters is ultimately undermined by an assumed dichotomy between choices that are "free" and those that are influenced and hence "unfree." All decisions are influenced, for better or worse. The concept of unencumbered individuals free to choose their own obligations, values, and ends—a core assumption of classical liberalism—is congruent with a laissez-faire approach to the new technologies. It is therefore not surprising that the writings of John Robertson, Gregory Pence, Gregory Stock, John Harris, Lee Silver, and other champions of the free market are permeated by an assumption of sovereignty over our own values. But that is hardly a promising starting point for those who would argue the need for social oversight of technologies now being developed, marketed, and used in a regulatory vacuum.

Neither is a simplistic historical narrative that equates eugenics with state-sponsored brutality. What united eugenicists was not agreement on any particular policy or method. Some eugenicists favored compulsory sterilization while others fervently opposed it, and the same is true for every eugenic policy and practice. The proponents of eugenics were not necessarily racist, nor were they all filled with hate toward the working class. What they had in common was an attitude toward people with physical or mental disabilities linked to a fetish for efficiency. One might say that they despised dependency. They did not see that the category of "dependents" eventually includes almost everyone. As Hubbard and Wald (1999, 31) rightly note, "all of us can expect to experience disabilities—if not now, then some time before we die, if not our own, then those of someone close to us." It is therefore in our own best interest to acknowledge the inevitability of our temporary or permanent dependence on others and consequent reliance on networks of social support (MacIntyre 1990; see also Gaylin and Jennings 2003, 251–68; Kaplan and Saxton 1999, 6).

The standard eugenics narratives do nothing to advance discussion of that need. On the contrary, they point us in just the opposite direction. As a guide to future action, they are therefore profoundly deficient. It is time to be more sophisticated in our accounts of eugenics, not just for the sake of fidelity to the historical record but of a more adequate public policy.

ACKNOWLEDGMENTS

Some of the arguments advanced in this chapter were originally developed for the conference entitled "Genetic Engineering and the Future of Human Nature" at the University of Scranton, April 6–8, 2001. A version of the chapter that is more historically focused (and that includes an extended discussion of utopian and Marxian schemes for the biological transformation of humanity and of debates about the morality of genetic engineering in the 1960s to 1980s) was published in a volume of conference papers; see Paul 2005. I am grateful to Harold Baillie and Tim Casey for organizing that stimulating meeting, Lori Knowles for her infinite patience in editing this volume, and Daniel Wikler for very helpful comments on a draft of the chapter.

NOTES

1. "Posthumans" are possible future beings whose physical, intellectual, psychological, emotional, aesthetic, and other capacities have been enhanced through technological modification to the point that they "so radically exceed those of present humans as to be no longer unambiguously human by current standards" (Bostrom 2003, 5–6).

2. Pessimists often accept at face value the optimists' assumptions about the power of genes to shape mentality and behavior. Thus physicist Freeman Dyson warns that, in the absence of regulation, human germline engineering "could cause a splitting of humanity into hereditary castes" (cited in *Techno-Eugenics Email Newsletter,* June 12, 2000, 4); equally credulous are political scientist Francis Fukuyama (2002) and ecology author Bill McKibben (2003).

3. A more detailed discussion of Haldane, Muller, Bernal, Leon Trotsky, and other scientifically oriented marxists of the 1920s and 1930s can be found in Paul 2005.

4. Other examples: Andrew Kimbrell (1997, 147): "We no longer have Nazi or racial eugenics. We have instead a 'commercial' eugenics peddled by clinics and biotechnology companies"; Jeremy Rifkin 1998, 128): "The old eugenics was steeped in political ideology and motivated by fear and hate. The new eugenics is being spurred by market forces and consumer desire"; Mae-Wan Ho (2000, 222): "Genetic discrimination and eugenics are being privatised and depersonalised and are therefore much more insidious than the state-sanctioned forms, because they cannot be effectively opposed."

5. Willard Gaylin and Bruce Jennings (2003, 174) remark: "When we perceive that one person's will is being bent by the force of another's and judge it a good thing, we tend to say that it's not 'really' coercion. On the other hand, when we do not approve of a power relationship between two people, we label it 'coercive,' as if that alone were enough to condemn it morally."

6. I am grateful to Daniel Wikler for suggesting this reading of the critics' argument.

REFERENCES

American Society of Human Genetics, Board of Directors. 1999. ASHG Statement: Eugenics and the misuse of genetic information to restrict reproductive freedom. *American Journal of Human Genetics* 64:335–38.

Andrews, L. B. 2001. *Future Perfect: Confronting Decisions about Genetics.* New York: Columbia University Press.

Antinori, S. *Genetic Crossroads,* April 1, 2001, 3.

Bernal, J. D. 1929. *The World, the Flesh, and the Devil: An Inquiry into the Three Enemies of the Human Soul.* London: Kegan Paul.

Bostrom, N. 2003. *The Transhumanist FAQ: A General Introduction—Version 2.1.* World Transhumanist Association. www/transhumanism.org/resources/faq.html#32.

———. 2004. A transhumanist perspective on human genetic engineering. *Journal of Value Inquiry,* www.nickbostrom.com/ethics/genetic.html.

Darnovsky, M. 2001a. The case against designer babies: The politics of genetic enhancement. In *Redesigning Life? The Worldwide Challenge to Genetic Engineering,* ed. B. Tokar, 133–49. London: Zed Books.

———. 2001b. Human germline engineering and cloning as women's issues. *GeneWatch* 34:13–14.

Drexler, K. E. 1986. *Engines of Creation: The Coming Age of Nanotechnology.* Garden City, NY: Anchor Press/Doubleday.

———. 1992. *Nanosystems: Molecular Machinery, Manufacturing, and Computation.* New York: John Wiley and Sons.

Duster, T. 1990. *Backdoor to Eugenics,* London: Routledge.

Elshtain, J. B. 1998. To clone or not to clone. In *Clones and Clones: Facts and Fantasies about Human Cloning,* ed. M. S. Nussbaum and C. R. Sunstein, 181–89. New York: W. W. Norton.

Fox, M. 1998. A woman's right to choose? A feminist critique. In *The Future of Human Reproduction: Ethics, Choice, and Regulation,* ed. J. Harris and S. Holm, 77–100. Oxford: Oxford University Press.

Frankel, M. S., and A. R. Chapman. 2000. *Human Inheritable Genetic Modifications: Assessing Scientific, Ethical, Religious, and Policy Issues.* Washington, DC: American Association for the Advancement of Science.

Fukuyama, F. 2002. *Our Posthuman Future: Consequences of the Biotechnology Revolution.* New York: Farrar, Straus and Giroux.

Galton, F. 1909. The possible improvement of the human breed, under the existing conditions of law and sentiment. In *Essays in Eugenics*. London: Eugenics Education Society.

Gaylin, W., and B. Jennings. 2003. *The Perversion of Autonomy: Coercion and Constraints in a Liberal Society*. Rev. ed. Washington, DC: Georgetown University Press.

Gordon, L. 1990. *Woman's Body, Woman's Right: A Social History of Birth Control in America*. 2nd ed. New York: Penguin.

Habermas, J. 2003. *The Future of Human Nature*. Cambridge: Polity Press.

Haldane, J. B. S. 1923. *Daedalus, or Science and the Future. A paper read to the Heretics, Cambridge, on February 4th, 1923*. In *Haldane's* Daedalus Revisited, ed. K. R. Dronamraju. Oxford: Oxford University Press (reprinted 1995).

Harris, J. 1998. Rights and reproductive choice. In *The Future of Human Reproduction*, ed. J. Harris and S. Holm, 5–27. Oxford: Oxford University Press.

Himmelwait, S. 1988. More than "a woman's right to choose"? *Feminist Review* 29: 38–56.

Ho, M.-W. 2000. *Genetic Engineering: Dream or Nightmare? Turning the Tide on the Brave New World of Bad Science and Big Business*. 2nd ed. New York: Continuum.

Hood, L. 2000. Comments in The road ahead: A panel discussion. In *Engineering the Human Germline: An Exploration of the Science and Ethics of Altering the Genes We Pass on to Our Children*, ed. G. Stock and J. Campbell, 73–95. New York: Oxford University Press.

Hotchkiss, R. D. 1965. Portents for a genetic engineering. *Journal of Heredity* 56: 197–222.

Hubbard, R., and E. Wald. 1999. *Exploding the Gene Myth: How Genetic Information Is Produced and Manipulated by Scientists, Physicians, Employers, Insurance Companies, Educators, and Law Enforcers*. Boston: Beacon Press.

Jennings, B. 2000. The liberalism of life: Bioethics in the face of biopower. *Raritan* 22:132–46.

Joy, B. 2000. Why the future doesn't need us. *Wired* (April). www.wired.com/wired/archive/8.04/joy_pr.html.

Kaplan, D., and M. Saxton. 1999. Disability, community, and identity: Perception of prenatal screening. *GeneWatch* 12:4, 6–8.

Kerr, A., and T. Shakespeare. 2002. *Genetic Politics: From Eugenics to Genome*. Cheltenham, UK: New Clarion Press.

Kevles, D. J. 1995. *In the Name of Eugenics: Genetics and the Uses of Human Heredity*. Cambridge, MA: Harvard University Press.

Kimbrell, A. 1997. *The Human Body Shop: The Cloning, Engineering, and Marketing of Life*. 2nd ed. Washington, DC: Regnery.

King, D. 2001. Eugenic tendencies in modern genetics. In *Redesigning Life? The Worldwide Challenge to Genetic Engineering*, ed. B. Toklar, 171–81. London: Zed Books.

Kitcher, P. 1996. *The Lives to Come: The Genetic Revolution and Human Possibilities*. New York: Simon and Schuster.

Kline, W. 2001. *Building a Better Race: Gender, Sexuality, and Eugenics from the Turn of the Century to the Baby Boom*. Berkeley and Los Angeles: University of California Press.

Kurzweil, R. 1999. *The Age of Spiritual Machines: When Computers Exceed Human Intelligence.* New York: Viking.

Liberation biology. (Interview with Lee Silver). 1999. *Reason Online*, May. http://reason.com/9905/fe.rb.liberation.shtml.

MacIntyre, A. 1999. *Dependent Rational Animals: Why Human Beings Need the Virtues.* Chicago: Open Court.

McKibben, B. 2003. *Enough: Staying Human in an Engineered Age.* New York: Henry Holt.

Michie, S., F. Bron, M. Bobrow, and T. M. Marteau. 1997. Nondirectiveness in genetic counseling: An empirical study. *American Journal of Human Genetics* 60:40–47.

Moravec, H. P. 1999. *Robot: Mere Machine to Transcendent Mind.* New York: Oxford University Press.

Morton, O. 1998. Overcoming yuk. *Wired* (January): 44–48.

Parens, E., and A. Asch, eds. 2001. *Prenatal Testing and Disability Rights.* Washington, DC: Georgetown University Press.

Paul, D. B. 1995. *Controlling Human Heredity: 1865 to the Present.* Amherst, NY: Prometheus.

———. 1998. Genetic services, economics, and eugenics. *Science in Context* 11:481–91.

———. 2005. Genetic engineering and eugenics: The uses of history. In *Is Human Nature Obsolete? Genetic Engineering and the Future of the Human Condition,* ed. H. W. Baillie and T. K. Casey, 123–51. Cambridge, MA: MIT Press

Pence, G. E. 2000a. Maximize parental choice. In *Engineering the Human Germline: An Exploration of the Science and Ethics of Altering the Genes We Pass to Our Children,* ed. G. Stock and J. Campbell, 111–13. Oxford: Oxford University Press.

———. 2000b. *Re-Creating Medicine: Ethical Issues at the Frontiers of Medicine.* Lanham, MD: Rowman and Littlefield.

Rapp, R. 1999. *Testing Women, Testing the Fetus: The Social Impact of Amniocentesis in America.* New York: Routledge.

Rifkin, J. 1998. *The Biotech Century: Harnessing the Gene and Remaking the World.* New York: Penguin Putnam.

Robertson, J. A. 1994. *Children of Choice: Freedom and the New Reproductive Technologies.* Princeton, NJ: Princeton University Press.

Rothman, B. K. 2001. *The Book of Life: A Personal and Ethical Guide to Race, Normality, and the Implications of the Human Genome Project.* Boston: Beacon Press.

Sandel, M. J. 2004. The case against perfection. *Atlantic Monthly* 293:51–62.

Saxton, M. 2001. Why members of the disability community oppose prenatal diagnosis and selective abortion. *GeneWatch* 14:10–12.

Silver, L. M. 1997. *Remaking Eden.* New York: Avon.

———. 2000. Reprogenetics: How reprogenetic and genetic technologies will be combined to provide new opportunities for people to reach their reproductive goals. In *Engineering the Human Germline: An Exploration of the Science and Ethics of Altering the Genes We Pass on to Our Children.* New York: Oxford University Press, 57–71.

Silvers, A., D., Wasserman, and M. B. Mahowald. 1998. *Disability, Difference, Discrimination: On Justice in Bioethics and Public Policy.* Lanham, MD: Rowman and Littlefield.

Sinsheimer, R. L. 1969. The prospect of designed genetic change. *Engineering and Science* 13:8–13.

Sloterdijk, P. 1999. *Regeln für den Menschenpark: Ein Antwortschreiben zu Heideggers Brief den Humanismus.* Frankfurt am Main: Suhrkamp.

Somerville, M. 2003. How perfect do we want to be? *Globe and Mail*, August 29. http://www/theglobeandmail.com/servlet/ArticleNews.

Stock, G. 2002. *Redesigning Humans: Our Inevitable Genetic Future.* Boston: Houghton Mifflin.

Stock, G., and J. Campbell, eds. 2000. *Engineering the Human Germline: An Exploration of the Science and Ethics of Altering the Genes We Pass on to Our Children.* New York: Oxford University Press.

Tännsjö, T. 1998. Compulsory sterilisation in Sweden. *Bioethics* 12:236–49.

Wolbring, G. 1999. Eugenics, euthenics, euphenics. *GeneWatch* 12 (June): 8–10.

CHAPTER TWO

Governmental Regulation of Genetic Technology, and the Lessons Learned

JULIE GAGE PALMER

For thousands of years, human beings have both deliberately and unintentionally changed the genetic composition of their world. By selectively breeding plants and animals to enhance desired characteristics, by extinguishing species, and even by simply choosing mates, humans have been "tampering" with the "genetic landscape" (President's Commission for the Study of Ethical Problems in Medicine 1982, 8). Oswald Avery, Maclyn McCarty, and Colin MacLeaod's 1944 proof that genes were made of DNA, and the rapidly ensuing development of techniques for working directly with DNA, accelerated the pace at which humans could accomplish genetic change. In 1953, informed and inspired by Rosalind Franklin's x-ray photographs and data, James Watson and Francis Crick published their discovery of the double-helical structure of DNA. Less than twenty years later, scientists had already figured out how to join DNA fragments from two separate species. By 1973, recombinant DNA molecules were being duplicated and grown in bacteria (U.S. Congress, Office of Technology Assessment [OTA] 1984, 3). An array of new scientific endeavors, variously known as "recombinant DNA," "genetic engineering," "biotechnology," "gene splicing," "gene therapy," "inheritable genetic modification (or IGM)," and now "reprogenetics," grew from these discoveries.

The explosive pace of development of genetic technologies has inspired fear of their potential "malevolent use" and of the social risks they pose. In some respects, this concern has been healthy and useful. The history of governmental regulation of genetic engineering illuminates how collective concern led to thoughtful, unprecedented study and guidelines, even in advance of the technological maturity of the new field. Scientists and regulators have cooperated to establish a fruitful conversation about the ethical implications of human genetic engineering. This conversation has developed earlier than comparable conversations in other scientific fields. However, in any context, fear can lead to wise or foolish choices. The challenge posed by the potentially revolutionary scientific methods for manipulating human genes is to make the wise choices and avoid the foolish ones.

In this chapter, I examine the history of governmental regulation of genetic technology. That history offers several lessons for avoiding unwise choices in the future, as information continues to be generated by the Human Genome Project and other biological research. I argue first that past experience shows us we should not center our regulatory scheme on transient technological limitations. Second, during the current research phase, governmental regulation plays an important role in promoting public review and input and in protecting the human subjects of genetic engineering research. Finally, we should resist the urge to design static regulatory models that extend beyond the research phase of this new medical technology. That is, we should not establish long-term regulatory bureaucracies based on early fears. Fixed, fear-inspired bureaucracies could impose the closely held "notions of well-being" of a small group on many diverse individuals who might benefit from genetic technology, thereby interfering with innovations in medical practice and with important individual freedoms.

HISTORY OF THE REGULATION OF GENETIC TECHNOLOGY
Planning to Regulate Human Genetic Engineering

The fast pace of research and development in the changing field of genetic engineering first captured public attention in the early 1970s, when scientists imposed a moratorium on themselves by agreeing not to do recombinant DNA experiments they feared might prove hazardous (Berg 1974; Palmer and Cook-Deegan 2003, 283). By 1974, the National Institutes of Health (NIH) had established the Recombinant DNA Advisory Committee (RAC) to formulate safety guidelines for recombinant DNA research (Palmer and Cook-Deegan 2003, 283). The RAC was seated within the U.S. Department of Health and Human Services (DHHS) and charged with advising the director of the National Institutes of Health (NIH 2005, Charter). The scientific self-imposed moratorium was lifted for most recombinant DNA research, subject to specific containment measures, following the Asilomar Conference in 1975 (President's Commission 1982, 11). Recombinant DNA research proceeded.

After the U.S. Supreme Court issued its decision in *Diamond v. Chakrabarty*,[1] allowing a scientist to patent a living, genetically engineered microorganism, public concerns about the implications of genetic engineering intensified. In July 1980, three general secretaries of Jewish, Catholic, and Protestant associations joined in a letter to President Jimmy Carter expressing concern over the "fundamental danger triggered by the rapid growth of genetic engineering" (President's Commission 1982, 94).[2]

In response, the existing President's Commission for the Study of Ethical Problems in Medicine and Biomedical and Behavioral Research added a study of genetic engineering to its agenda.[3] After a two-year study, the commission issued *Splicing Life: A Report on the Social and Ethical Issues of Genetic Engineering with Human Beings*. In *Splicing Life*, the commission wrote:

> Beyond any fear of the malevolent use of gene splicing, attention must be paid to a more basic question about the distribution of power: who should decide which lines of genetic engineering research ought to be pursued and which applications of the technology ought to be promoted?
>
> This question is not ordinarily raised about medical technology in general. When it is, the assumption is that for the most part the key decisions are to be made by the relevant experts, the research community, and the medical profession, guided by the availability of research funds (which come predominantly from Federal agencies) and by the dictates of medical malpractice law and of state and Federal regulatory agencies designed to protect the public from very tangible, unambiguous harms. Yet genetic engineering is more than a new medical technology. Its potential uses, as discussed, extend far beyond intervention to cure or prevent disease or to restore functioning. This more expansive nature makes it unlikely that decisions about the development of gene splicing technology can be made appropriately within institutions that have evolved to control medical technology and the practice of medicine. (1982, 73)[4]

The commission recommended the institution of a new oversight mechanism for human genetic engineering.

In the final chapter of *Splicing Life*, entitled "Protecting the Future," the commission set out several objectives that should guide the design of an oversight group. First, it directed that the oversight group "should regard education as a primary responsibility. It is necessary to educate the scientific community about the social and ethical implications of its work as well as to educate the public about science." Second, the commission recommended that the group "have roles of both general oversight and of leadership within the Federal government." Third, it recommended that the group have a diverse membership that would enable it to both lead and reflect public thinking. Fourth, it found that the group should have a mechanism for seeking scientific advice and explanation without being dominated by the scientific community. Fifth, the commission said the oversight group "should treat—in as unified a framework as possible—all the issues raised by genetic engineering: laboratory and industrial safety, environmental hazards, agricultural and commercial opportunities and pitfalls, international ramifications, biomedical benefits and risks, and social and ethical implications." Sixth, the commission insisted that oversight functions be separated from sponsoring functions to avoid conflicts of interest (President's Commission 1982, 82–84).

The commission further recommended several concrete alternatives for overseeing genetic engineering, including options that involved revisions of the RAC to serve that purpose. At that time, the RAC had a successful history of interdisciplinary oversight of recombinant DNA laboratory research, but it had become less active because laboratory biohazards were no longer considered urgent.[5]

In April 1983, the RAC established the Working Group on a Response to the *Splicing Life* Report. When the working group recommended that the RAC declare its readiness to review gene therapy proposals, if they should be propounded, the RAC responded by asking the working group to suggest guidelines for gene therapy. Following a series of meetings and discussions, a new, interdisciplinary, fifteen-member Working Group on Human Gene Therapy was formed. This working group, composed of medical clinicians, laboratory scientists, ethicists, and lawyers, prepared a set of guidelines for gene therapy research entitled "Points to Consider in the Design and Submission of Human Somatic-Cell Gene Therapy Protocols." These were published in the *Federal Register*, revised after public comment, and adopted by the RAC in September 1985.[6]

"Points to Consider" poses more than one hundred questions to investigators who submit protocols for approval. These questions relate to the consequences of a disease, alternative treatments, and the proposed genetic intervention, as well as fairness and research subject autonomy. They have been summarized as the following seven central questions:

1. What is the disease to be treated, and why is it a good candidate for gene therapy?

2. What alternative treatments are available for this disease?
3. What is the potential harm associated with the genetic intervention?
4. What is the potential benefit associated with the intervention?
5. What steps will be taken to ensure that participants in the study are selected in a manner that is fair to everyone who wants to take part in the study?
6. What steps will be taken to ensure that the consent of study participants is both informed and voluntary?
7. What steps will be taken to protect the privacy of participants and the confidentiality of medical information about them? (Walters and Palmer 1997, 149)

The "Points to Consider" document states in the second paragraph that RAC will not "entertain proposals for germ line alterations." The RAC was unwilling to consider research in germline cells (reproductive cells and other undifferentiated cells that could give rise to reproductive cells) because research in germline cells could result in inheritable genetic changes. The RAC distinguished somatic cell gene therapy (involving nonreproductive, differentiated cells) because it saw somatic cell gene therapy "as an extension of present methods" of therapy (first paragraph of the document).

While the RAC worked on its "Points to Consider," the federal government made additional plans for regulating genetic engineering. The executive branch published a document entitled "Coordinated Framework for Regulation of Biotechnology" (the Framework) in the *Federal Register* in November 1985. According to the Framework, five federal bodies—the NIH, Food and Drug Administration (FDA), U.S. Department of Agriculture (USDA), Environmental Protection Agency (EPA), and the National Science Foundation (NSF)—had jurisdiction over biotechnology research. The Framework proposed the formation of a Biotechnology Science Coordinating Committee (BSCC) to coordinate questions and issues addressed by the five federal agencies, promote consistency, facilitate cooperation, and identify gaps in scientific knowledge.[7] In June 1986, the major agencies involved in reviewing research and products of biotechnology published their policies under this framework.[8]

Although both the FDA and the NIH claimed jurisdiction over gene therapy research under the Framework, for many years the NIH RAC was the only agency that proposed new regulations governing gene therapy. During the 1980s, the FDA proposed no new procedures or requirements for medical applications of genetics. Instead, the FDA asserted that its existing requirements and review procedures would apply, and that "nucleic acids used for human gene therapy trials [would] be subject to the same requirements as other biological drugs." The FDA recognized the possibility that there would "be some redundancy between scientific reviews of these products performed by the National Institutes of Health and FDA."[9] Likewise, the NIH RAC's 1985 revised "Points to Consider" acknowledged that the FDA had jurisdiction over drug products intended for use in human gene therapy trials.[10] As described below, for several years, most gene therapy researchers submitted their research proposals, or protocols, to both the NIH RAC and the FDA.

While the executive branch sorted out responsibilities among its many agencies and actors, the legislative branch also studied genetic engineering. Following the issuance of *Splicing Life,* then congressman Albert Gore Jr., chairman of the U.S. House of Representatives' Subcommittee on Investigations and Oversight of the Committee on Science and Technology, convened hearings on human genetic engineering. During those hearings, in November 1982, Alexander Capron, then executive director of the President's Commission, testified about scientists' concern that the public had "many misconceptions about, as I said, the scientists dipping into some genetic soup and creating a mixture in one way or another that could be frightening." Congressman Gore responded, "I think science would be ill-advised to dismiss the concerns of the American people, because they may . . . be grasping some truths that the specialists are not." Capron returned, "I think your comments are likely to spread some fear and trembling to the scientific community when they hear you saying that the public's concern that this line of research ought not be pursued should be heeded" (U.S. Congress 1982). The controversy, fueled by the public's fear of genetic engineering and the scientific community's fear that the public would overreact, did not end with the hearings. Indeed, public concern about human genetic engineering gave rise to a request for a research ban.

On June 8, 1983, a coalition of religious leaders, ethicists, and biologists, led by Jeremy Rifkin of the Foundation on Economic Trends, asked Congress to ban genetic engineering experiments that make it possible to "design and program specific physiological characteristics . . . into the sperm, egg or embryo of a human being." The coalition, which included Moral Majority leader Jerry Falwell, National Council of Churches President James Armstrong, and Harvard biologist Dr. George Wald, asserted that if the price for medical advances such as gene therapy "mean[t] accepting the idea of reducing the human species to a technologically designed product, then it [was] too dear a price" (*Detroit Free Press* 1983).

Congress did not impose a ban, but Congressman Gore did request that the Congressional Office of Technology Assessment prepare a background paper on "human applications of recombinant DNA technology." The report identified human gene therapy as "preeminent among the topics of concern" (U.S. Congress 1984, iii). OTA published its Background Paper on Human Gene Therapy in December, 1984 (U.S. Congress 1984).[11] The background paper concluded that although somatic cell gene therapy could be seen as an extension of other types of medical therapy,

> the consensus about the propriety of somatic cell therapy does not extend to treatment for traits that do not constitute severe genetic diseases, and does not encompass germ line gene therapy in humans. The question of whether germ line gene therapy should ever begin is now highly controversial. The risk to progeny, relative unreliability of the techniques for clinical use, and ethical questions about when to apply it remain unresolved. The question of whether and when to begin germ line gene therapy must therefore be decided in public debate informed by technological developments. (U.S. Congress 1984, 47)

The background paper was distributed widely to the public and to the NIH, FDA, and all members of the RAC.

Not long after the OTA background paper appeared, in 1985, Congress established a Congressional Biomedical Ethics Board for the purpose of studying and reporting

> to Congress on a continuing basis on the ethical issues arising from the delivery of health care and biomedical and behavioral research, including the protection of human subjects of such research and developments in genetic engineering (including activities in recombinant DNA technology) which have implications for human genetic engineering. (Health Research Extension Act of 1985)

There were no plans to coordinate any congressionally mandated oversight that might arise from the board's work with the BSCC's work on behalf of the executive branch. Although the possibility of conflicting or even inconsistent oversight seemed large, it was mitigated by the likelihood that the advisory committee to the ethics board might include individuals with strong ties to the RAC, because the family of gene therapy experts was very small in 1985. As it worked out, the Biomedical Ethics Board never studied anything or produced any advice to Congress. By March 1987, it had not even chosen its scientific advisory committee.[12] Mired in disputes over "sanctity-of-life issues"—abortion, euthanasia, and others—the board never completed its work.

Beginning in the mid-1980s, the RAC took the lead in establishing a public conversation about and regulation of human gene transfer research. The RAC, an executive branch committee, advisory to the NIH director and seated within the Department of Health and Human services, was perhaps relatively insulated from some of the political disputes that stalled the Biomedical Ethics Board and any other potential congressional response to the burgeoning new genetic technologies.

Federal Regulation in Practice

The RAC's "Points to Consider" were adopted in 1985, but there was some delay before the new regulatory system was put to use. In April 1987, W. French Anderson and others at the NIH submitted a prototype gene therapy protocol to the RAC in the spirit of conducting a kind of test run of the "Points to Consider" and RAC review. The RAC Working Group on Human Gene Therapy (now called the Human Gene Therapy Subcommittee) reviewed the document, called "Human Gene Therapy: Preclinical Data Document," as if it were a real clinical protocol (Walters and Palmer 1997, 149–50). In April 1988, Steven Rosenberg submitted the first protocol for a real human experiment involving gene transfer into humans. Although this protocol did involve transfer of genetic material into human cells, it did not propose a gene *therapy* experiment. Rather, the Rosenberg protocol was designed to use gene transfer to mark cancer-fighting cells so that they could be identified and followed in the bodies of cancer patients. After debate, some extended procedural jockeying, approval by the RAC, FDA, and NIH, and the settlement of a lawsuit by Jeremy Rifkin's Foundation on Economic Trends, this gene marking study began in May 1989 (Walters and Palmer 1997, 150).

On March 30, 1990, the first true gene therapy protocol was submitted to the RAC by R. Michael Blaese, W. French Anderson, and NIH colleagues. Their somatic cell gene therapy protocol proposed to treat children who suffered from adenosine deaminase (ADA) deficiency, a type of severe combined immune deficiency (SCID). ADA deficiency is a rare genetic disease that arises from the malfunction of a gene expressed in bone marrow stem cells and the infection-fighting white blood cells they produce. Normally, ADA metabolizes a compound called deoxyadenosine. Absent ADA, toxic levels of deoxyadenosine build up inside the infection-fighting blood cells, destroying these cells and leaving the patients prey to infections. Most devastated are the important infection-fighting T cells. Unless a bone marrow donor can be found and a transplant performed, ADA-deficiency can be life-threatening (Walters and Palmer 1997, 17).[13] The protocol proposed drawing blood from the research subjects, isolating the subjects' own T cells, delivering properly functioning copies of the ADA gene into the T cells, and transfusing them back into the subjects. By adding a functioning copy of the ADA gene to as many T cells as possible, researchers hoped to increase the blood levels of ADA in the subjects, thereby improving their immune system function. The Human Gene Therapy Subcommittee reviewed this protocol in June and July of 1990, approving it at the end of July. The first research subject received an infusion of genetically modified T cells in September 1990 (Walters and Palmer 1997, 150–51).

Additional research protocols followed the approval of the ADA deficiency research. In 1991, the FDA's Center for Biologics Evaluation and Research (CBER) formally issued its own "Points to Consider" document governing human somatic cell and gene therapy, based on its experience regulating gene transfer and gene therapy under investigational new drug (IND) rules and draft versions of points to consider.[14] For a while, the FDA and the NIH RAC continued to exercise their regulatory oversight concurrently. Protocols subject to the jurisdiction of both entities were submitted to both.[15]

From autumn of 1990 to July 1995, more than one hundred protocols were submitted to the RAC and the FDA concurrently for review.[16] Of the first hundred gene therapy protocols approved by the RAC, the target diseases were the following:

Cancers: 63
HIV infection/AIDS: 12
Genetic diseases: 22
Other diseases: 3

The genetic diseases addressed by these protocols included cystic fibrosis (twelve protocols), Gaucher disease type 1 (three protocols), and several others (Walters and Palmer 1997, 151).[17]

Some in the biotechnology industry found the dual FDA/NIH oversight too burdensome. The dual oversight was not entirely redundant, however. While the NIH RAC reviewed protocols publicly according to the many concerns identified in the RAC's "Points to Consider," the FDA conducted confidential reviews, focusing on compliance with safety rules, compliance with human subjects protections, efficacy, and product manufacturing and quality control. Nevertheless, in 1995, a committee advising NIH director Harold Varmus recommended that the FDA take over most of the responsibility for reviewing gene transfer protocols.

In 1996, Varmus reduced the size of the RAC and curtailed its functions. The RAC relinquished its function as primary reviewer of gene transfer experiments to the FDA and changed its focus to gene therapy policy. The RAC's newly limited roles and responsibilities included (1) "identifying novel human gene transfer experiments deserving of public discussion," (2) "identifying novel scientific, safety, social, and ethical issues relevant to specific human applications of gene transfer" that would inform recommendations to the NIH Director regarding modifications of the "Points to Consider," (3) publicly reviewing human gene transfer clinical trial data, and (4) identifying "broad scientific, safety, social, and ethical issues relevant to human gene transfer research" as potential Gene Therapy Policy Conference topics.[18]

From July 1995 through September 8, 2003, approximately 485 protocols were submitted for review. Of these, sixty-eight protocols were reviewed by RAC under its new mandate. The FDA reviewed the remainder alone.[19] Also as of September 2003, the RAC Web site listed a total of 588 protocols as having been submitted. Of those, 65 percent were aimed at treating cancer, approximately 10 percent were directed toward single gene disorders, such as cystic fibrosis and SCID, about 7 percent targeted HIV and other viral diseases, and 11 percent addressed other disorders, such as peripheral artery disease, coronary artery disease and arthritis. The rest of the protocols were nontherapeutic (or marking) studies.[20]

The RAC continues to meet quarterly, reviewing novel protocols, not for approval but for advice and public discussion. Materials provided by the NIH's Office of Biotechnology Activities (OBA), which, among other things, oversees the RAC, state:

> This open discussion has two important benefits. First, it disseminates this information to scientists who can then incorporate new scientific findings and ethical considerations into the design of trials they may be conducting or planning. The efficiency of the research system is improved by allowing scientists to build on a common foundation of new knowledge emanating from this ongoing process of analysis and assessment. Second, it creates enhanced public awareness and allows for a public voice in the review of the safety and ethics of gene transfer research. This helps assure the public that scientists are attending to these important matters and sustains confidence in the enterprise. Finally, as the major funder of human gene transfer research and the basic science that underpins it, the

NIH has an important responsibility for the appropriate stewardship of this area of scientific activity. This stewardship role is both an ethical obligation and a public mandate associated with the tax-derived research funds appropriated to the agency by Congress.[21]

In addition to reviewing novel protocols, as of September 2003, the RAC had convened three Gene Therapy Policy Conferences since 1998.[22]

Despite scattered reports of successful "cures" in gene therapy trials,[23] the field has suffered some setbacks. These have led to regulatory responses designed to enhance protections for human subjects of gene transfer research. In September 1999, gene therapy resulted in its first widely reported iatrogenic death. Jesse Gelsinger, a nineteen-year-old man who had a nonfatal, mosaic version of a normally fatal disease called ornithine transcarbamylase deficiency (OTC), died while participating in a Phase I clinical trial of gene therapy at the University of Pennsylvania.[24] Researchers were attempting to determine the appropriate dose of an adenoviral vector carrying the gene for the missing OTC protein. They infused the vector directly into the patients' livers. The gene transfer vector itself caused Gelsinger to suffer a systemic inflammatory response, which led to adult respiratory distress syndrome and, ultimately, multi-organ failure (Woo 2000). Following Gelsinger's death, the FDA cited the researchers for multiple regulatory violations and suspended all gene transfer research at the University of Pennsylvania.

Additional investigations revealed that fewer than 6 percent of adverse events in gene transfer studies across the United States had been reported to the NIH as required. Researchers cited confusion about the differing reporting requirements of the FDA and NIH, along with confidentiality, as justifications for not reporting serious complications and deaths associated with gene therapy trials. The FDA had received an average of 1,000 adverse event reports per year, including some reports of research subject deaths, but had not made the adverse events reports public. Instead, the FDA had protected these reports as confidential trade secrets. The need to promote open discussion of issues and reporting of risk information to prospective research participants has continually conflicted with confidentiality claims due to commercial concerns and patient privacy concerns. This conflict has been an obstacle to the establishment of clear reporting requirements for adverse events in gene therapy research (Palmer and Cook-Deegan 2003, 279–80).

In November 1999, a few months after Gelsinger's death, the FDA's CBER sent a letter to gene therapy researchers outlining the processes for submitting gene transfer protocols and adverse event reports to both the FDA CBER and the NIH RAC. The letter reminded researchers that the submission process had been established since 1994. Included in the November 1999 letter was a statement that the "FDA will notify NIH/ORDA[25] of the receipt of an adverse event report on a gene therapy IND to enhance investigator compliance with the *NIH Guidelines*" (CBER Letter 1999).

In March 2000, the FDA and NIH announced new initiatives to protect participants in gene therapy trials (DHHS 2000). These included the Gene Therapy Clinical Trial Monitoring Plan, which required sponsors of gene therapy trials to routinely submit their monitoring plans to the FDA. Under this initiative, clinical trial monitors are responsible for verifying that the "rights and well-being" of human subjects are protected and that data reporting, including safety reporting to the NIH, is accurate. Addressing conflict of interest problems that had come to light during the Gelsinger case, the FDA and NIH also announced that "in some gene therapy trials, one or more of the investigators is also the sponsor [of the research]. . . . NIH will work to develop procedures to further assure appropriately independent oversight of the conduct of such trials" (DHHS 2000).

Following a model safety symposium in December 1999, the NIH and FDA announced an additional new program of Gene Transfer Safety Symposia. These symposia were intended as a mechanism to "enhance patient safety by providing critical forums for the sharing and analysis of medical and scientific data from gene transfer research" (DHHS 2000). The first symposium was held during the week following the announcement and addressed the safety of adenoviral vectors, the same type of vector used in the Gelsinger OTC trial. Since March 2000, NIH has convened two more Gene Transfer Safety Symposia.[26]

In 2001, the FDA published proposed rules that would, for the first time, provide for public disclosure by the FDA of certain safety data and information related to gene transfer and xenotransplantation (transplantation into humans of nonhuman tissue).[27] Prior to the proposal of these new regulations, the FDA had treated gene transfer as just one more regulated product, as noted above. The proposal explicitly justifies the change in treatment as follows:

Human gene therapy and xenotransplantation investigative approaches individually pose: (1) Risks that extend beyond the individual (e.g., public health risks, including the potential for the transmission of infectious agents from the recipient to the public at large); and (2) risks of inadvertent modification of the germline (alterations of the genetic material of the progeny). Moreover, these

approaches may also be used in combination (e.g., xenotransplantation products genetically modified before implantation), resulting in complex questions
and issues for consideration and discussion prior to and during human clinical
trials. . . .

Information of the kind FDA proposes to disclose concerning clinical trials
on human gene therapy and xenotransplantation is already widely disclosed.
This disclosure has not impeded commercial development of these products. In
addition, the agency considers public disclosure of data and for [sic] information
from human gene therapy or xenotransplantation clinical trials essential for public education, and for informed discussion and consideration of the public health
and safety risks associated with the use of these investigational therapies.[28]

These proposed rules recognize that gene therapy and xenotransplantation
pose "complex" questions requiring more than traditional attention.

Also in response to Gelsinger's death and the subsequent discovery of the
failure to report serious adverse events, NIH modified its requirements for the
reporting and analysis of serious adverse events in human gene transfer
research. The four main objectives of the NIH's action were to:

1. harmonize NIH requirements for expedited reporting of serious adverse
   events in gene transfer trials with those of FDA;
2. clarify how claims that annual and safety reports contain confidential
   commercial or trade secret information will be resolved, given the need
   for disclosure of information to ensure broad public knowledge of issues
   raised by gene transfer research;
3. maintain the privacy of individuals participating in gene transfer research;
   and
4. develop a new mechanism for the analysis and dissemination of adverse
   event information with the goal of enhancing knowledge about scientific and safety trends.[29]

The action changed the requirements for expedited reporting of serious
adverse events and established a new working group of the RAC, to be known
as the NIH Gene Transfer Safety Assessment Board, that would be responsible
for reviewing, analyzing, and disseminating adverse events reports and other
safety information.[30]

In June 2002, the FDA finalized a Gene Therapy Patient Tracking System
(GTPTS), rationalizing that "[t]hrough experience in the review and regulation of gene therapy products, FDA has identified several concerns and issues

raised by gene therapy products that differ from those typically raised by more traditional products."[31] The GTPTS identifies five areas of improvement over preexisting FDA safety systems, including collection of information regarding long-term safety outcomes.[32] The GTPTS also reports efforts to harmonize FDA and NIH adverse events reporting requirements.[33]

Just as Jesse Gelsinger's death inspired regulatory revisions, more recent problems in gene transfer research have stimulated FDA action. First, gene therapy research enjoyed some promising achievements. In early 2000, French researchers reported success in a gene therapy trial designed to treat X-linked SCID. Nine children were able to live at home normally after beneficial gene therapy treatments of their immune deficiencies, which could have been fatal without treatment.[34] American researchers also reported successful gene therapy in hemophilia patients treated with a viral vector containing the gene for Factor IX (Thompson 2000).

However, gene therapy's prospects plunged again shortly after these promising triumphs. Two of the nine "cured" French children developed T-cell acute lymphoblastic leukemia (T-ALL) almost three years after their treatment. The leukemias in both children appeared to be caused by the gene therapy itself. The viral vector, this time a retrovirus used to carry the properly functioning gene into the children's bone marrow stem cells, caused insertional mutations in both children, leading to their leukemias.[35] The FDA put twenty-seven similar U.S. gene therapy trials on clinical hold, determining that leukemia was an inherent risk of the study design.[36] Nevertheless, a review of U.S. gene therapy trials using similar viral vectors found no evidence of leukemia. In February 2003, the FDA announced that it would still "actively consider specific requests for retroviral gene therapy trials involving fatal or life-threatening disorders for which there currently are no viable alternative treatments."[37]

The brief history outlined above explains how both the FDA and the NIH RAC came to have detailed regulatory requirements for human somatic cell gene therapy research. "Fear of the malevolent use of gene splicing" has thus far proved unfounded. While some ethical norms have been violated by genetics researchers (as in the Gelsinger case), the violations have been of human research norms, rather than malicious uses of gene splicing for evil purposes. In response to violations, both the FDA and the RAC have responded promptly. Proposals for additional improvements of the genetics research regulatory scheme have been described elsewhere (Palmer and Cook-Deegan 2003, 275–99). These include improvements in managing violations of the regulatory process, avoiding conflicts of interest within the regulatory system, and extending jurisdiction for public review of protocols. Establishing a mechanism for referring alleged violations of the regulatory process to a credible, independent government organization with the capacity to investigate these violations could go a long way toward improving the process for investigating violations and making it more responsive. Conflicts of interest or the appearance of them could be better avoided by removing the responsibility for public review of research to a location outside of NIH. NIH funds human genetic research and has a potential interest in promoting its success. Its ability to review the research it funds (or competing research) objectively may appear compromised.[38] Finally, and most significantly, public review of research protocols should be extended to all protocols, as will be further addressed below.

Other Sources of Genetics Regulation

In addition to the regulatory limits explicitly established for human genetic engineering research by the NIH and the FDA, other federal and state limits potentially apply to human genetic research. These include the federal government's human research subject protections and federal and state common law.[39]

The DHHS regulations protecting human research subjects cover institutions that have a formal agreement with the federal government binding them to abide by Title 45, Section 46 of the *Code of Federal Regulations,* otherwise known as the "common rule." Any institution that receives federal funds from one or more of seventeen federal departments and agencies must have a "federalwide assurance" that commits the institution receiving federal funds to abide by the federal human subject protections. These protections include a requirement that the institution set up an institutional review board (IRB) that will review and approve research protocols involving human subjects, monitor those protocols, and report violations of human subjects protections (Palmer and Cook-Deegan 2003, 284–85). Parallel regulations cover private firms and institutions that submit data to FDA for approval for testing and marketing drugs, biologics, or devices, even if they do not use federal funds for research (Palmer and Cook-Deegan 2003, 285; these parallel regulations can be found in Title 21, Parts 50 and 56 of the *Code of Federal Regulations*). Federal human subjects protections cover most medical research in the United States. A few areas are not covered by these regulations, including studies considered "innovative therapy" or "experimental treatment" rather than "research." If an institution does not use federal funds and does not have a federalwide assurance, and if its research does not involve an unapproved drug, device, or biological subject to FDA jurisdiction, then it may pursue that research out-side of IRB review and it is not subject to federal human subject regulations.

In addition to federal human research protections, state and federal com-mon law—the body of law developed through successive court decisions—may set limits for genetic engineering. Common law principles that might apply to gene therapy include negligence precedents developed in the context of medical malpractice or other tort cases, decisions that have interpreted or augmented guidelines, regulations or statutes, and contract doctrines (Palmer and Cook-Deegan 2003, 282). In order to determine the standard to which gene therapy researchers would be held, a court would probably look to RAC guide-lines, "Points to Consider," and human subjects protections, among other things.[40]

Inheritable Genetic Modification and Embryo Research Laws

Embryo research laws indirectly affect genetic research because they limit research in the cells or tissues that might be the targets of gene transfer. It is the intersection of genetic engineering and embryo-related technologies that gives rise to the subject of this book. In their thoughtful and thought-provoking report, "Reprogenetics and Public Policy," Erik Parens and Lori Knowles pro-posed a new oversight board with "significant discretion" to address issues raised by "reprogenetics." Parens and Knowles have defined "reprogenetics" as "all interventions involved in the creation, use, manipulation, or storage of gametes and embryos" (2003, S4). Thus defined, "reprogenetics" includes genetic manipulation of gametes and embryos.

Why would anyone propose genetic manipulation of gametes and embryos? Gene transfer into gametes or embryos has been proposed theoreti-cally for treatment of rare genetic diseases affecting many cell types or leading to irreversible damage early in embryonic development (Walters and Palmer 1997, 78–80). It has also been considered for male infertility that might be treated by genetic correction of spermatogonia (Culver 2003, 77–92). While these aforementioned gamete or embryonic gene transfers could correct defects in the first generation, gene transfers into gametes or embryos could also result in inheritable changes in DNA, if the transferred genes integrated into the host cell genomes.[41]

It is possible that much early IGM research will involve the manipulation of embryos because embryos offer scientists access to the germline.[42] Federal law forbids the use of federal funds for "research in which a human embryo or embryos are destroyed, discarded, or knowingly subjected to risk of injury or death greater than that allowed for research on fetuses in utero."[43] This provision, known as the Dickey-Wicker amendment and included in the annual Health and Human Services appropriations law, prevents embryo-based genetic research in most major academic research institutions. It does not prevent embryo research in private institutions (Palmer and Cook-Deegan 2003, 289).

Several states have enacted laws prohibiting or regulating embryo research.[44] These laws apply to the private as well as the public sector. Some of these state statutes explicitly apply to research in pre-embryos (usually defined as embryos no older than fourteen days) or early embryos.[45] Many are directed at cloning, fetal experimentation, or abortion, but apply to IGM research in pre-embryos expressly or by implication.[46] Many of the state statutes that prohibit embryo research make exceptions for research that is intended to be therapeutic either for the mother or for the individual resulting from the procedures.[47] Presumably, then, IGM research beyond early Phase I–type safety trials would be allowed under many of these statutes. How IGM research could proceed to the therapeutic stage without passing through a safety phase is an unanswered question.

The state statutes are inconsistent in their terminology and substance. For example, a New Hampshire surrogacy statute provides that "I. No preembryo shall be maintained ex utero in the noncryopreserved state beyond 14 days postfertilization development. II. No preembryo that has been donated for use in research shall be transferred to a uterine cavity."[48] This New Hampshire statute has the effect of disallowing IGM research involving preembryos. A Rhode Island law prohibiting human cloning, on the other hand, provides that "nothing in this section shall be construed to restrict areas of biomedical, microbiological, and agricultural research or practices not expressly prohibited in this section, including research or practices that involve the use of . . . gene therapy."[49] The Rhode Island law explicitly allows gene therapy research involving pre-embryos. Given the inconsistencies in language and content of the embryo research rules from one state to the next, existing limits will not provide coherent treatment of IGM research protocols that involve embryo transfer of DNA.

Without running afoul of any embryo research laws and regardless of any regulatory guidance (such as the statement that the RAC will not "entertain proposals for germ line alterations"), human IGM has occurred already (Parens and Jeungst 2001). Since 1997, researchers have reported several ooplasm transfers carried out in an attempt to treat infertility. In these attempts, which were not submitted to FDA or NIH review, fertility specialists injected ooplasm from healthy donor oocytes into the compromised oocytes of women undergoing in vitro fertilization for fertility problems. It has been reported that almost thirty children were born following the use of this procedure (Barritt et al. 2001, 513). It is possible that each of these children carry mitochondria, and concomitantly mitochondrial DNA, from both the donor ooplasm and the mother's own ooplasm. While ooplasm transfer does not involve recombinant DNA, it does involve the transfer of outside genes into a gamete.

In response to these reports of ooplasm transfer, the FDA asserted jurisdiction over ooplasm transfer, along with cloning.[50] In a letter to sponsors and researchers, the FDA announced that it has

> jurisdiction over human cells used in therapy involving the transfer of genetic material by means other than the union of gamete nuclei. Examples of such genetic material include, but are not limited to: cell nuclei (e.g., for cloning), oocyte nuclei, ooplasm, which contains mitochondrial genetic material, and genetic material contained in a genetic vector, transferred into gametes or other cells. The use of such genetically manipulated cells (and/or their derivatives) in humans constitutes a clinical investigation and requires submission of an Investigational New Drug application (IND) to FDA.[51]

FDA's assertion of jurisdiction has been criticized for ignoring the Administrative Procedure Act's rulemaking requirements, calling into question the legality of FDA's authority over cloning and ooplasm transfer.[52]

THOUGHTS ABOUT THE FUTURE
Transient Technological Limitations—Regulating Genetics and Reproductive Technologies Separately

Heretofore, the government regulation of genetic engineering has had little to do with assisted reproductive technologies (ARTs) or corresponding government oversight. Aside from the NIH and FDA admonitions that germ line therapy research will not be considered and the FDA's assertion of jurisdiction over ooplasm transfer and cloning, genetics oversight has remained separate from ART oversight.[53] Most of the regulation of human genetics research has been directed at somatic cell gene therapy.

Regulating human genetics research and reproductive technologies separately makes sense. A closer look at the relevant technologies reveals that although some individuals may seek genetic modification in conjunction with ARTs, most individuals who use genetic technologies in the future will likely use them outside of the ART context. Ooplasm transfer makes an interesting first example of human IGM, but it is not likely to be the paradigm example.[54] Where the mother's oocytes do not develop normally because of mitochondrial deficiencies, ooplasm transfer may prove useful as an enhancement of assisted reproduction. But that usefulness does not appear likely to apply to treatment of other diseases or to genetic enhancement.

Embryo-based IGM itself will probably not become widespread. Most couples seeking to avoid genetic disease in their offspring would choose less risky, less complicated methods, such as selective pregnancy termination or preimplantation genetic diagnosis followed by selective implantation. The availability of selective implantation of unaffected embryos makes IGM in embryos unnecessary except in cases where couples are morally opposed to discarding or donating affected embryos or where all embryos will be affected (for example, in couples both homozygous for a monogenic disorder).[55]

It is unlikely that IGM accomplished via embryos or gametes in vitro will be widespread enough to cause social changes that give rise to concerns about the "well-being" of society. As long as IVF is involved, few fertile couples will choose IGM. Reproductive technologies, especially those involving the relatively invasive and risky procedures of superovulation and egg harvesting (as IVF does), though much sought after by those desperate to give birth to genetically related children, are not likely to be popular methods for producing children with particular characteristics.[56] Choosing a partner with whom to reproduce the traditional way will likely predominate for the foreseeable future.

Nevertheless, the use of IGM to treat multifactorial diseases or for enhancement could become widespread if technologies were developed to accomplish modifications in gametes in vivo rather than through IVF or other reproductive technologies. Fertile couples are more likely to use genetic technologies to prevent certain traits or to enhance others if the genetic treatments they seek can be administered in a way that is not labor intensive and intrusive. One can imagine that a technology like "injectable gene repair" would experience great demand.[57] If a less invasive delivery system were developed, reproductive technologies would not be required for human genetic modifications. Therefore, looking at IGM scenarios beyond ooplasm transfer and even further into the future, reproductive technologies and genetics ought to be regulated separately.

Proposing that reprogenetics ought to be the subject of governmental regulation, Parens and Knowles report that "genetic and reproductive technologies are converging. A new system to oversee reprogenetic research and services is needed, therefore, for functional reasons, since the old categories of 'genetics' and 'reproductive' research do not reflect the new technological realities" (2003, S9). But any convergence of these two fields is incidental and probably temporary. Reproductive technologies are about fertility.[58] The theoretical goal of IGM is to cure disease, or possibly to enhance traits in particular individuals and their descendants. The expected use of embryos and reproductive technologies to accomplish this goal is contingent on the limitations of currently available methods for delivering genetic modifications to reproductive cells.

While reproductive technologies are here to stay, and IGM may be inevitable, history teaches that regulating them together does not make good sense.[59] The technological limitations that marry IGM with reproductive technologies will ultimately be surmounted. Therefore, reprogenetics does not establish a good foundation for governmental regulation as a field unto itself. One can draw an analogy here. When RAC guidelines were first proposed, they seemed thorough and well-founded. Twenty years later, they no longer fit the technology. That ill fit has created gaps that could have been avoided had the regulations been designed around outcomes or principles rather technology. Parens and Knowles themselves have disapproved:

Unfortunately, . . . RAC's guidelines describe its mandate in terms of the technology that was around in the 1980s; it considers only those interventions that involve recombinant DNA (rDNA). Thus the ooplasm transplantation protocol technically fell outside of RAC's purview, even though it involved inheritable genetic modifications, because the protocol employed cellular surgery rather than recombinant DNA. It was only that detail that kept the protocol, which the researchers themselves called the first successful 'human germline genetic modification,' from being subject to RAC scrutiny. And thus that research was conducted without public conversation, under the supervision only of the researchers and of their institution's IRB. (2003, S10)

Setting up a regulatory scheme that anticipates covering IGM but is focused on reproductive technologies would repeat the mistake made by the current regulatory scheme, which anticipated proscribing IGM research but focused on recombinant DNA.[60] IGM protocol review should be triggered by substantive ethical issues such as risk to research participants and implications for society rather than by the use of either recombinant DNA or ART.[61]

During the experimental phase, some risks and concerns related to genetic and reproductive technologies may be coincident. But imagine a world where both genetic technologies and ART were relatively risk-free. Reproductive technologies would present issues about reproductive privacy, and about relationships among a variety of potential parents and children, while IGM would probably not. Genetic technology would present issues about justice, fairness in sports, and a "level playing field," while ARTs would probably not. Reprogenetics technologies will call into play two separate sets of regulation. But this is preferable to setting up a new scheme that might sweep regulation of genetic technologies into a maelstrom of abortion issues and other political hot buttons that are not related to genetic modifications.

Public Input and Review in Research and Human Subjects Protections

IGM research protocols, whether accomplished using reproductive technologies or not, should be subject to prospective public review. Public review will keep IGM researchers accountable to human research subject protections, to conflicts of interest concerns, and to the diverse interests of a variety of players in the research process. Public review enhances the credibility of the research, promotes public education, and permits informed public conversation about risks and implications of research. Moreover, in the words of NIH OBA, "the efficiency of the research system is improved by allowing scientists to build on a common foundation of new knowledge."[62] The 1982 *Splicing Life* report insisted that public education should be the "primary responsibility" of a genetic engineering oversight group. This admonition is no less important today than it was then, when the President's Commission stated, "It is necessary to educate the scientific community about the social and ethical implications of its work as well as to educate the public about the science" (1982, 82–83).

Although the existing regulatory scheme for gene transfer research has holes and inefficiencies, it has worked relatively well. It has created some of the interdisciplinary, open public discussion promoted by *Splicing Life* and longed for most recently by critics of the FDA's assertion of jurisdiction over cloning. The FDA's recent proposed rules providing for public disclosure of information relating to gene therapy "essential for public education, and for informed discussion and consideration of the public health and safety risks" are an additional step in the right direction.[63] By clarifying and strengthening the adverse events reporting requirements, the FDA has reinforced the call for accountability and credibility in human gene transfer research. More regular adverse events reporting will also contribute to the "common foundation of new knowledge." The federal government has addressed the basic issues around gene transfer research that warrant public participation and review. Still, especially for inheritable genetic manipulation research, the current regulatory scheme could be improved by extending public review to all IGM research protocols, whether they are conducted in institutions that receive public funds or not.

Distinction between IGM Research and Practice

It is important to draw a distinction between IGM research and practice. The Belmont Report, the 1978 document prepared by the National Commission for the Protection of Human Subjects of Biomedical and Behavioral Research, set up the distinction between research and accepted therapy as the guiding distinction for determining which activities are subject to regulation.

> The term "practice" refers to interventions that are designed solely to enhance the well-being of an individual patient or client and that have a reasonable expectation of success. . . . By contrast, the term "research" designates an activity designed to test a hypothesis, permit conclusions to be drawn, and thereby to develop or contribute to generalizable knowledge. . . . the general rule is that if there is any element of research in an activity, that activity should undergo review for protection of human subjects.[64]

Although the distinction is subject to confusion in particular clinical settings,[65] it offers an operative basis for distinguishing between IGM regulatory policies.

Human IGM research protocols, if (or when) they are proposed, will be intended to contribute to "generalizable knowledge." Each proposal will require coordinated efforts and effective information distribution among a variety of players. Genetic scientists, who control information and esoteric expertise, are not on a level playing field with human subjects, who often approach gene "therapy" research protocols in desperation, as potential life-saving treatments. IGM researchers' career aspirations and financial objectives, combined with their control of information and expertise, could put individual human subjects of IGM research at risk.[66] In this context, government has an important role in establishing appropriate incentives for IGM researchers and research sponsors. Government vigilance will be required to protect individual research subjects and to promote the flow of information about research risks and adverse events. Regulating IGM research will set up the necessary incentives to protect human subjects and the fruits of the research. On the other hand, skipping ahead to the distant future, once IGM is no longer an experimental research project, centralized review of IGM procedures will no longer be necessary to protect human *research* subjects. Then, regulation of IGM will present an inappropriate intrusion into the practice of medicine and on individual choice.

Reasons to Avoid Central Regulation of IGM Practice in the Distant Future

A national reprogenetics technologies board? "Even if all the safety concerns were addressed," Parens and Knowles argue, "other vital concerns would remain," necessitating systematic regulation of the practice of reprogenetics even after it moves out of the research context (Parens and Knowles 2003, S6). Knowles and Parens propose a national reprogenetics technologies board (RTB) that would "make policy regarding the things that people can do with gametes and embryos," set standards by creating a code of practice, and "engage in public consultation and promote public conversation" about reprogenetics (2003, S19). In calling for oversight of both research and practice, the RTB proposal goes too far. When various reproductive technologies and IGM are no longer considered research, when these have been fully reviewed for safety and efficacy, government should step back from regulation just as it does for other medical advances. Too much oversight of the practice of reprogenetics and IGM threatens individual liberty.

In his book, *What Sort of People Should There Be?* Jonathon Glover sets up the issue:

> The central line of thought is that we should not start playing God by redesigning the human race. The suggestion is that there is no group (such as scientists, doctors, public officials, or politicians) who can be entrusted with decisions about what sort of people there should be. And it is also doubted whether we could have any adequate grounds for basing such decisions on one set of values rather than another. (1984, 46)

It is theoretically possible that at some time in the distant future, parents may be able to specify genes for height or eye color, or (if they ultimately prove subject to genetic manipulation) athleticism or intelligence, for their children. While the prospect of parents being able to make such choices may be unprecedented and alarming, having a group of "experts" decide what parents may choose is unwise. Who is best positioned to make appropriate choices for each family about which familial traits ought to be subject to genetic manipulation? When the research phase is complete (that is, when group consensus finds IGM technology safe and effective), decisions about what is best for each family should be left to each family. Robert Nozick, author of *Anarchy, State, and Utopia*, writes that biologists

> do not tend to think, perhaps because it diminishes the importance of their role, of a system in which they run a 'genetic supermarket,' meeting the individual specifications (within certain moral limits) of prospective parents. . . . This supermarket system has the great virtue that it involves no centralized decision fixing the future human types(s). (1974, 315)

Centralized decisions fixing the future human types are worrisome because they impose social notions of well-being and unproven mechanisms for achieving justice on individuals in restraint of their liberty.

Social notions of well-being. Parens and Knowles want the RTB to consider "well-being" issues raised by IGM, along with reproductive technologies. In the interest of promoting public conceptions of "well-being" as determined by the members of the RTB, they want this board to engage in licensing that will limit the types of genetic modification and reprogenetics that individuals can seek from their medical providers.

Knowles and Parens justify their call for centrally imposed notions of well-being by pointing to the primacy of community notions of social well-being over individual decisions about genetic modification. "The decision to make inheritable genetic modifications in the human genome should not be left to individuals. It should be made at a policy level after public discussion about both safety and well-being concerns," they argue. They recognize that some believe regulations "informed by a particular conception of well-being could threaten the liberty of those who hold different beliefs about human well-being." But they think that reprogenetic technologies "might transform the meaning of having a child, being a member of a family, and being a member of a community." Therefore, they reason, social notions of well-being predominate over individual ones. In service of promoting the "public" notions of meaning, they have proposed their regulatory scheme (Parens and Knowles 2003, S10–S13).

Parens and Knowles think that the best way to determine public notions of well-being is to convene a group of thinkers who will lead a public conversation and then distill the wishes of the public into policy. The RTB will make policy and establish a code of practice that will then limit individuals' ability to choose reprogenetic technologies.[67] Parens and Knowles reject the concept of accrued individual choice as a measure of the public notion of well-being. They ask: "Are we in danger of allowing the market mentality to colonize childbearing, as it has already colonized so much of our lives?" They do not see the market as a measure of collective mores.

In the penultimate paragraph of their report, Parens and Knowles recall the concern of ART pioneer Robert Edwards that establishing a British authority to govern reproductive technologies would "bring 'Nazism and Stalinism into the bedroom.'" Parens and Knowles report that the British authority was established despite this warning and reply that "civilized societies have always exerted some control over reproduction, whether by crafting rules to govern incest, or the appropriate age of marriage, or abortion, or contraception, or adoption" (Parens and Knowles 2003, S20). But Edwards's concern is not trivial, especially as it applies to IGM.

When worrying about the dangers of centralized notions of well-being, we need fear not only evil giants who play on the world stage, but also well-meaning bureaucrats and thinkers, who impose their own ideas of well-being on others.[68] In early twentieth-century America, many states enacted compulsory, eugenic sterilization laws for the "good of society." Indiana's 1907 sterilization law allowed a panel of experts to review whether it was advisable for inmates in state institutions to procreate, and if not, to order them sterilized to protect society. By 1931, twenty-eight states had enacted involuntary sterilization laws (Reilly 2000, 204–8).

In the 1927 U.S. Supreme Court case *Buck v. Bell*, Justice Holmes allowed the forced sterilization of a young institutionalized woman on the grounds that she and her mother were both "feeble minded" and likely to produce "inadequate offspring." He announced, "It is better for all the world, if . . . society can prevent those who are manifestly unfit from continuing their kind."[69] In their excellent casebook *Genetics: Ethics, Law and Policy*, Lori Andrews, Maxwell Mehlman, and Mark Rothstein note that the outcome in *Buck v. Bell* "was embraced by such progressives of the time as Clarence Darrow, Helen Keller, and Margaret Sanger (who started Planned Parenthood as a pro-eugenics organization)" (2002, 54) To justify his decision in *Buck v. Bell*, Justice Holmes extended the reasoning of a Massachusetts court that had upheld compulsory smallpox vaccinations. The Massachusetts court had found:

> In every well-ordered society charged with the duty of conserving the safety of its members the rights of the individual in respect of his liberty may at times, under the pressure of great dangers, be subjected to such restraint, to be enforced by reasonable regulations, as the safety of the general public may demand.[70]

Presumably, Holmes thought the "great danger" to society from Carrie Buck was the risk that she would produce "inadequate offspring." The decision to restrict Carrie Buck's reproduction based on the possibility that her reproductive choices would have undesirable social repercussions is analogous to a decision to restrict reproductive choices of couples choosing to use reprogenetics based on potential social repercussions.[71]

Andrews, Mehlman, and Rothstein question whether the enforced sterilization in *Buck* met the standard that "'the means prescribed by the State to that end [must have a] real and substantial relation to the protection of the public health and safety'" (Andrews, Mehlman, and Rothstein 2002, 55).[72] One should question as well whether the regulatory scheme proposed by Parens and Knowles goes too far beyond protecting public health and safety into the realm of imposing the well-being notions of a few on the rights of many. The dangers to society from individual reprogenetic decisions are not analogous to the dangers to society of unchecked virus transmission. They are more analogous to the dangers Justice Holmes thought he saw in Carrie Buck's reproduction. No real and substantial danger to public health and safety can be identified sufficient to justify imposing centralized notions of well-being to limit the serious parenting decisions that must be made when considering reprogenetics or IGM. The dangers postulated by advocates of social control of these technologies are speculative and deferred.

The new choices offered by genetic technologies present social risks. But "choice is fraught with risk."[73] Those who advocate centralized decision-making argue that the social risks are so grave that IGM and reprogenetic decisions ought not be left to individuals; the individual good, as determined by the individual himself, must be subsumed to the good of society, as determined by a group of regulators. This argument sounds very much like the advice given by Screwtape, the senior devil, to the junior devils in C. S. Lewis's *Screwtape Letters:*

> I would not—Hell forbid! encourage in your own minds that delusion which you must carefully foster in the minds of your human victims. I mean the delusion

that the fate of nations is *in itself* more important than that of individual souls. The overthrow of free peoples and the multiplication of slave states are for us a means (besides, of course, being fun); but the real end is the destruction of individuals. (1978, 170)

The idea that the fate of society is more important than the collective fates of individuals is a delusion, further compromised by the mistaken notion that a group of "experts" can determine best what are the social mores that ought to be imposed on individuals. Centralized notions about having children, the meaning of family, and belonging to a community (those notions of "well-being" identified by Knowles and Parens) do not exist separate and apart from individual notions about children, family, and community. Rather than ask whether the "market mentality" will "colonize childbearing," we should ask whether a regulatory board could possibly provide a more sensitive measure of collective mores than accrued individual choice. The answer is "no." These individual mores should not be subsumed to a conjectural "public" notion, determined by a board of regulators.

Just distribution. Parens and Knowles believe that centralized control of the practice of IGM and reprogenetics is necessary because they worry that unequal access to reprogenetic technnologies will increase "the gap between the haves and have-nots."

> Parents who already purchase social advantages will be able, in effect, to purchase genetic capacities to use those advantages . . . Imagine that the teenager already blessed with social advantages like Stanley Kaplan prep courses has already been outfitted at birth with a reprogenetic form of Ritalin—with the capacity to be especially good at exploiting social advantages like the prep courses. That children with advantages are already using psychopharmacological agents in just that way is hardly an argument for permitting reprogenetic means to achieve more of the same. Nor can we regard the decision to use reprogenetic means as a 'private choice' since such choices would generate pressures on others to follow suit. (2003, S7)

Others have used similar arguments to advocate government control of genetic technology. They fear that, given free choice, parents will use IGM to have children who exceed norms of height, strength, longevity, or other traits. They reason that free choice will aggravate existing inequalities in contravention of egalitarianism, which they believe requires equal distribution of genetic advantages (Parens 1999, 401).[74]

The notion that enhancement IGM or reprogenetics would aggravate existing inequalities relies on pure speculation. For starters, there is no one definition of success, and no one knows which traits ensure it. In addition, enhancement could have the opposite effect, leveling the playing field over time because people might choose to use it only when they suspected that a pre-embryo would end up below the curve. Why bother with IGM or reprogenetics if one expects one's child to be a successful person without the technology? Accordingly, if the technology grew affordable, enhancement IGM might in fact serve to reduce inequalities.

Tight government control of IGM and reprogenetics could stifle the development of the technologies and keep prices artificially high, making them less available for distribution. On the other hand, one could make a plausible prediction that allowing market forces to work on IGM enhancement would (1) bring more resources to bear on the development of the technology, (2) lead to developments in IGM technology, (3) drive the cost of IGM down, and (4) ultimately make the technology cheaper and more accessible to all. If instead IGM were restricted by government to uses deemed "acceptable" by a committee, the resources brought to bear on the development of the technology would be fewer, the cost of IGM would remain higher, and the technology would be less accessible to everyone, including the disadvantaged.

Still, for the sake of argument, let us assume that uncontrolled IGM would remain expensive and enhancement IGM would increase inequalities. Is an increase in inequality always bad? It is possible that IGM enhancement might benefit the least advantaged sufficiently to justify unequal distribution, even based on modern egalitarian principles.[75] In some distant future, if IGM could be used to help parents raise one hundred new Mozart-like musical prodigies, these musicians might indeed have natural advantages that would bring them great wealth and other social advantages. However, these "music gene" recipients might also benefit others, enriching lives by their art and by teaching. Or imagine an IGM enhancement that improves concentration. While this might give a competitive advantage to those who come to society with the enhancement, it might also decrease the common car accidents, workplace accidents, and medical mistakes that result in death or disability in bystanders. In other words, something that confers a competitive advantage on one person is not always a problem for others.[76] IGM enhancement could confer a competitive advantage to its user and also offer some benefit to others. In a society that relies on technological advances to support its economy, that result appears likely.[77]

Furthermore, even if one grants for argument's sake that IGM would promote a gap between the haves and the have-nots, and that increasing that gap
is morally wrong, it is not clear that government control would prevent the
growth of the gap. To observe what happens when government makes allocation decisions, one need only compare the health benefits that legislatures provide for themselves with those that are available to others. Government is
made up of people who have the same self-interest and lack of access to
"truth" as the rest of us. Add in the inefficiencies and instances of corruption
common in government, and it becomes clear that distributive justice cannot
be achieved through government control. Richard Epstein puts it best:

> Most people know their own preferences better than other people do. Accord-
> ingly, people are better able to act in order to protect themselves and advance
> their own interests if given the legal power to do so. The complexity of legal rules
> tends to place the power of decision in the hands of other people who lack the
> necessary information and whose own self-interest leads them to use the infor-
> mation that they do have in socially destructive ways. (1995, xi–xii)

Those who face decisions about reprogenetics and IGM can make better decisions for themselves than a regulatory body could make for them. In the aggregate, these self-regarding decisions could lead to a more just distribution of
IGM than an appointed group of "experts" could accomplish.

Distributive justice concerns do not justify governmental control of IGM or
reprogenetics because they mistakenly assume (1) that genetic enhancement
will lead to inequalities that do not benefit the least advantaged and (2) that
governmental control will provide the best mechanism for achieving just distribution. Denying individual liberty in order to prevent a gap between the
haves and the have-nots is not justified theoretically or empirically.

Treating new technologies differently. Although IGM and reprogenetics are
new technologies, associated issues about distribution of access and social
notions of well-being are not new. These issues arise in other medical and
non-medical contexts. As already mentioned, social notions of well-being
have been imposed on individual decisions about childbearing in the form of
forced sterilization of those considered "unfit." Yet we no longer consider
such forced sterilization appropriate.[78] Distribution of access to preventative
medical care such as Pap smears is already uneven. Enhancement technologies, such as cosmetic dental work, that might lead to real economic advantages, are available primarily to those who can afford them, potentially leading to greater economic gaps between the haves and the have-nots. Even

low-tech enhancements like piano lessons are distributed unequally in our society.[79] Nevertheless, prohibiting these more traditional enhancement choices would be preposterous. Parents may choose cosmetic orthodontia or piano lessons on behalf of their children. The state no longer forces people to be sterilized to prevent social harm. The burden rests on those who would deny similar choices to individuals seeking IGM to explain why IGM should be treated differently.

No compelling argument justifies restricting IGM or reprogenetic technologies based on social notions of well-being or inequalities of access in a society where other medical developments and new technologies are not similarly restricted. Without a viable reason for treating genetic technology differently from other new medical technologies, the justification for restricting access to it fails. Using the same arguments employed by Parens and Knowles, one could demand that distributive justice be achieved and social notions of well-being be satisfied before access to any new medical technology is allowed. Extending the logic applied by those who would restrict access to IGM, one is forced to reach the absurd conclusion that society will permit no new medical technologies until distributive justice in our health care system is achieved.

Similar arguments could have been employed to justify government control of computer technology. A group of regulators could have restricted the growth, sale, or use of computer technology on the basis that people who had access to (then expensive) computers thereby had greater ability to compete in school and business, exacerbating the differences between the "haves" and "have-nots." Yet it is difficult to deny that people are better off now than if the government had attempted to control computer technology. If government had controlled computer technology and had restricted the market, computer prices would likely have remained artificially high, resulting in market restrictions on access, along with government restrictions.

It is possible that the primary motivation for treating IGM differently is fear. Choice is fraught with risk, but a measured response to the risk is necessary to prevent the construction of a system under which the new choices offered by genetic technologies are controlled by a bureaucracy rather than affected individuals themselves. We should have humility about our ability to predict the future. We must use restraint in establishing regulatory systems and ensure that regulations are wise in light of history. The principal decision makers ought to be the users of the IGM themselves.

Final thoughts on government's role. An important function of government as it relates to IGM is to distribute information, educate the public, and ensure that people understand their choices well enough to make informed decisions. *Splicing Life* identified education as the primary obligation of a group overseeing human genetic engineering (President's Commission 1982, 82–83). Looking toward a distant future when IGM is no longer experimental, government should be responsible for educating the public and distributing comparative information about available nonexperimental technologies, along with protecting the public from adulteration of products and false claims. The ability of individuals to make their own decisions will be thereby enhanced. When potential users can receive complete information about IGM (that is, when the technology is no longer experimental), then they ought to have the freedom to decide for themselves and their children.

Of course, there are moral limits on the choices parents ought to make on behalf of future children and other descendants. These are analogous to the limits placed on parenting in general. A parent may discipline a child but may not cross the line and commit child abuse. A parent may arrange for her child's cosmetic orthodontic treatments, for example, but not for cosmetic treatments that might cripple the child or impinge on his freedoms. Likewise, a parent ought to be able to choose IGM or reprogenetic treatments on behalf of a potential child, but not to produce a child whose ability to enjoy the rights promised to all in our society is compromised.

One way to strike a balance between individual freedoms and appropriate legal limitations on IGM would be to focus on the rights invested in citizens of the United States by the Constitution. That is, we should promise to future generations the basic goods and rights we now promise to existing human beings. Under this formulation, government should step in to prevent IGM where the proposed genetic procedure would violate the constitutional rights of an existing or future individual. Then, for example, people would not be allowed to design genetically limited descendants for the purpose of their exploitation. Legal restrictions would prevent the creation of human beings who would be genetically unable to enjoy the liberty promised by the Constitution. But people could choose brown-eyed boys over blue-eyed girls, given safe technology. Governmental prohibitions would be limited to ensuring that the future person was able to enjoy his or her constitutional rights. This approach would minimize problems associated with centralized decisions fixing future human types.

How ought these regulatory limits be imposed? Not by a board of experts held over from regulating IGM research or set up to ensure information distribution. This government veto should be exercised in the form of legislative criminal sanctions against those who seek or perform IGM intended to create humans who cannot exercise their constitutional rights.[80] Doctors who administer IGM and who supervise IGM programs could be entrusted with reporting requirements analogous to those imposed on pediatricians who suspect child abuse.

Within moral limits and with the limited help of government as collector and distributor of information, we can leave the decision making about non-experimental IGM to individuals. We should avoid centralized decisions fixing future human types, because we should have the humility to recognize that we do not have the answers for society or for other individuals about what sort of human types ought to be allowed. In the words of C. S. Lewis,

> The real reason for democracy is . . . no man can be trusted with unchecked power over his fellows. Aristotle said that some people were only fit to be slaves. I do not contradict him. But I reject slavery because I see no men fit to be masters. (1986, 17)[81]

Each individual must choose for himself and for his descendants. No man is fit to choose for another.

This lesson of humility is taught in the classic Talmudic story about two men walking in the desert.[82] One man carries a flask of water, enough to keep only one man alive until he reaches civilization. If the men share the water, both will die. What ought to be done with the water? Should we observers of this moral dilemma allocate the water based on the quality of the two men's lives, based on whose life has more value? If one man is a great surgeon and one man a lowly lawyer, should we choose the surgeon because he is able to save more lives in the future? If we impose hierarchical value judgments on this scenario, how can we be sure we choose correctly? We cannot. The surgeon may change careers; the lawyer may beget a great national leader who saves her country from poverty or war. A fortiori, what we consider valuable to society may not represent absolute value in a broader universe whose purpose we do not fully comprehend. Although the Talmudic sages disagree about the outcome, they do not resolve the dilemma in favor of the more "deserving" man getting water. The wisest and most cherished sage is Rabbi Akiva. In his view, the man who is holding the flask should drink the water.[83] According to this view, there is no moral principle that can justify compelling a man to give up his life-saving water.

Likewise, we should not compel individuals to give up free choice in determining genetic modifications because of notions of speculative social utility.

Choice is indeed fraught with risk, and risks rightly inspire fear and concern. But the choice about what sort of children to bear belongs to parents. Taking this choice from parents and giving it to a committee of experts that determines which sort of people there should be is like choosing which man should drink the water based on a committee's decision about whose life is more valuable. No committee of humans is in a position to know enough about the future to make these decisions for others.

NOTES

1. *Diamond v. Chakrabarty,* 447 U.S. 303 (1980) (holding that "the patentee has produced a new bacterium with markedly different characteristics from any found in nature and one having the potential for significant utility. His discovery is not nature's handiwork, but his own; accordingly it is patentable subject matter"). The Chakrabarty patent involved but more traditional methods for selecting genetic traits rather than recombinant DNA. Also in 1980, a patent was granted to Stanley Cohen and Herbert Boyer for the process of making recombinant DNA. See U.S. Congress, Office of Technology Assessment 1984, 3.

2. While the public conversation was beginning in the United States, one researcher was already performing unauthorized human gene therapy experiments abroad. Martin Cline, chairman of the UCLA Hematology-Oncology Department, performed experiments on human subjects from Israel and Italy without informed consent and without authorization from his local IRB. The NIH subsequently stripped Cline of some of his grants, and UCLA removed him from the chairmanship of his department. Still, the scientific community continued to invite him to speak at gene therapy conferences and to respect him as a leader in the field. Esmail D. Zanjani, personal communication, 1986.

3. For a more detailed history of this period, see Walters and Palmer 1997.

4. Note that the "more expansive" nature cited by the President's Commission refers to uses beyond disease cure or prevention. But enhancement uses can also be found for conventional medical technologies, as will be further discussed below. Note also that it is no longer true that genetic research funds come predominantly from Federal agencies. See Palmer and Cook-Deegan graph. Although the commission stated that "genetic engineering is more than a new medical technology" and declared that it had a "more expansive nature," the commission ultimately concluded otherwise. In the cover letter accompanying the report, the commission concluded that the genetic engineering applications being planned in humans were "analogous to other forms of novel therapy."

5. It is interesting that, also by the time *Splicing Life* was issued, the departments of agriculture, defense, and energy, the Environmental Protection Agency, the National Institutes of Health, and the National Science Foundation were all conducting, sponsoring, or studying recombinant DNA research.

6. A current version of "Points to Consider" can be found at http://www4.od.nih .gov/oba/rac/guidelines_02/Appendix_M.htm. For an earlier version, see Walters and

Palmer 1997, 147–48. Subsequent revisions to the "Point to Consider" included an amendment providing for expedited review in certain cases.

7. 50 *Fed. Reg.* 47,176 (1985).

8. 51 *Fed. Reg.* 23,302 (1986).

9. 49 *Fed. Reg.* 50,878 (1984).

10. 50 *Fed. Reg.* 33,462, n.2 (1985).

11. By 1984, more than 200 commercial firms had been founded to exploit new biotechnologies. See U.S. Congress, Office of Technology Assessment 1984, 3.

12. Julie Gage, "Gene Therapy Decisions: How They Are Made Now and How They Might Be Made in the Future," unpublished externship paper, University of Michigan Law School, April 22, 1987, 11–13. The board operated from December 1988 to September 1989. Robert Cook-Deegan, personal communication.

13. For more on ADA deficiency, see F. S. Arredondo-Vega, I. Santisteban, S. Daniels, S. Toutain, and M. S. Hershfield, "Adenosine Deaminase Deficiency: Genotype-Phenotype Correlations Based on Expressed Activity of 29 Mutant Alleles," *American Journal of Human Genetics* 63 (1998): 1049–59.

14. The FDA issued an addendum to this document in 1996. In 1998, the FDA issued "A Guidance for Human Somatic Cell Therapy and Gene Therapy," http://www.fda.gov/cber/gdlns/somgene.htm.

15. Both the FDA and the NIH RAC review follow local IRB review according to federal human subject protections.

16. For a current list of protocols, see http://www4.od.nih.gov/oba/rac/clinical-trial.htm.

17. Note that the number of protocols designed to treat genetic diseases is small. When the OTA report was issued in 1984, it defined gene therapy as the "ability to insert human genes into human patients to treat specific genetic diseases." The OTA report cited "the number and severity of genetic diseases—i.e., diseases whose roots can be traced to specific genes or known inheritance patterns" as the primary justification for attempting human gene therapy (OTA Report, 1). Ultimately, hereditary diseases have not proved to be the most popular targets of gene therapy research. Rather, as researchers have learned more about DNA's involvement in more common illnesses, many have shifted their attention to these. The OTA report's inability to predict the trajectory of the technology is a worthy reminder of our limitations now as we choose oversight mechanisms for reprogenetics. We must be mindful that developments in genetic technology will not necessarily continue accelerating along the lines they currently traverse.

18. 62 *Fed. Reg.* 59,032 (October 31, 1997). As will be further discussed below, regulatory control of genetic engineering should be curtailed eventually, after the technology is established and no longer considered research. Varmus's decision to remove approval authority from the RAC happened too soon, however. Gene therapy is still highly experimental and unproven. Public discussion and review of protocols is still vital.

19. See protocol list at http://www4.od.nih.gov/oba/rac/documents1.htm.

20. See protocol list at http://www4.od.nih.gov/oba/rac/documents1.htm.

21. http://www4.od.nih.gov/oba/RAC/RAC_FAQs.htm.

22. See OBA Web site, http://www4.od.nih.gov/oba/rac/meeting.html.

23. The ADA deficiency trial, identified above as the first true gene therapy trial, resulted in success for its subjects, but could not be called a gene therapy achievement because the patients in that trial continued to take enzyme replacement therapy in addition to gene therapy. The level of protein produced by the inserted genes was not enough to justify discontinuing the [peg-ADA therapy]. Also cited as successes have been a hemophilia B trial at the Children's Hospital of Philadelphia and Stanford University, a French X-linked SCID trial using (transduced) bone marrow stem cells (both cited in Woo 2000), an ADA replacement therapy trial at Hadassah Hospital in Israel (*North Shore Chapter of Hadassah Bulletin*, Great Plains Region, Winter 2002–2003), and gene therapy using a gene for vascular endothelial growth factor, delivered in an adenoviral vector, used to restore blood flow to areas of the heart where the blood supply has been blocked (Ron Winslow, *Wall Street Journal*, November 21, 2002, D3, column 1). See also fn. 1 in Evans 2003, 101.

24. Phase I is a designation based on the type of questions a research trial is addressing. Phase I trials evaluate safety, determine safe dosage range and identify side effects.

25. Office of Recombinant DNA Activities, or ORDA, is the administrative office for the RAC.

26. See http://www4.od.nih.gov/oba/RAC/meeting.html.

27. http://www.fda.gov/cber/rules/frgene011801.htm.

28. "Proposed Rules on Availability for Public Disclosure and Submission to FDA for Public Disclosure of Certain Data and Information Related to Human Gene Therapy or Xenotransplantation," http://www.fda.gov/cber/rules/frgene011801.htm.

29. "Notice of Actions Under the NIH Guidelines for Research Involving Recombinant DNA Molecules (NIH Guidelines)," 66 FR 57970 (November 19, 2001), http://www4.od.nih.gov/oba/rac/frnotices/11-19-01act.htm.

30. Ibid.

31. "Gene Therapy Patient Tracking System," June 27, 2002, http://www.fda.gov/cber/genetherapy/gttrack.htm

32. http://www.fda.gov/cber/genetherapy/gttrack.htm. pp. 1–2.

33. http://www.fda.gov/cber/genetherapy/gttrack.htm. p. 24.

34. Children affected by X-linked SCID usually die from overwhelming infection. Larry Thompson, "Human Gene Therapy Harsh Lessons, High Hopes," *FDA Consumer Magazine*, September–October 2000.

35. OBA, NIH, "Memorandum to Principal Investigators for Human Gene Transfer Trials Employing Retroviral Vectors," March 20, 2003, http://www4.od.nih.gov/oba/rac/XSCID_letter2.pdf.

36. Ronald Kotulak, "FDA Calls a Halt to Gene Therapy as Child Falls Ill," *Chicago Tribune*, January 14, 2003, 1, 7.

37. "FDA Advisory Committee Discusses Steps for Potentially Continuing Certain Gene Therapy Trials That Were Recently Placed on Hold," http://www.fda.gov//bbs/topics/ANSWERS/2003/ANS01202.html.

38. Even back in 1980, *Splicing Life* called for the "next generation" RAC to be "independent of Federal funding bodies such as NIH, which is the major Federal sponsor of gene splicing research, to avoid any real or perceived conflict of interest." President's Commission 1982, 4.

39. Institutional Biosafety Committees (IBCs), required by NIH's first guidelines for recombinant DNA research, still oversee the biohazard aspects of safety in recombinant DNA experiments.

40. For more on common law's application to IGM, along with the other legal limits on IGM, see Palmer and Cook-Deegan 2003, 281–90.

41. Gametes and embryo cells differentiate into other cells in a growing organism, including the reproductive cells that could lead to genetic inheritance in the next generation. When an embryo (or a gamete, upon fertilization) develops into a fetus and ultimately into a baby, its genome is transferred during cell division from these early precursor cells to the daughter cells they engender. Likewise, genetic changes in a gamete (sperm or egg cell) can be transferred after fertilization as the resulting embryo develops. Depending on the stage of development at which the genetic change is made, the DNA alteration may be passed along during cell division to some or all of the resultant individual's cells. If the genetic alteration is conveyed to the individual's reproductive cells, then the change can be passed on again to the next generation. For this reason, gene therapy performed at the gametic or embryonic stage would be considered germline gene therapy, or to use more current terminology, inheritable genetic modification (IGM). Candidates for inheritable genetic *enhancement* are more numerous than candidates for inheritable genetic therapy.

42. It is also true that researchers might choose embryos or gametes as target cells because they wish to reach all the cells of the developing first-generation individual, in which case germline consequences would be foreseeable, but not the subject of the primary intention.

43. The current (2004) version of this provision is found at 108 P.L. 199, 118 Stat. 3, sec. 510 (January 23, 2004). See also Palmer and Cook-Deegan 2003, 289.

44. See, for example, *La. Rev. Stat. Ann.* sec. 9:121-122 (2001); *Mass. Gen. Laws Ann.* Ch. 112, sec. 12J (2001); *Mich. Comp. Laws Ann.* sec. 333.2685-.2692 (2001); *Minn. Stat.* sec. 145.421-.422 (2001); *N.D. Cent. Code* sec. 14-02.2-02 (2002); *N.H. Rev. Stat. Ann.* sec. 168- B:14 (2002); 18 *Pa. C. S.* sec. 3216 (2002); *R.I. Gen. Laws* sec 11-54-1 (2001). Three state statutes banning fetal research have been challenged in court. and in all three challenges the statutes have been struck down as unconsitutionally vague. See *Jane L. v. Bangerter,* 61 F.3d 1493, 1499–1502 (10th Cir. 1995), rev'd on other grounds sub nom *Leavitt v. Jane L.,* 518 U.S. 137 (1996); *Lifchez v. Hartigan,* 735 F.Supp. 1361, 1364–67 (N.D. Ill. 1990), aff'd mem., 914 F.2d 260 (7th Cir. 1990); *Margaret S. v. Edwards,* 794 F.2d 994, 999 (5th Cir. 1986). Note that this material and the following two paragraphs are reprinted with permission of the authors from Palmer and Cook-Deegan 2003, 289–90.

45. See, for example, *Mass. Gen. Laws Ann.* Ch. 112, sec. 12J (2001); *N.H. Rev. Stat. Ann.* sec. 168-B:15 (2001); *La. Rev. Stat. Ann.* sec. 9:121-122 (2001).

46. See. for example, *R.I. Gen. Laws Ann.* Ch. 112, sec. 12J (2001); *Mich. Comp. Laws Ann.* sec 333.2685-.2692 (2001).

47. See, for example, *Mass. Gen. Laws Ann.* Ch. 112, sec. 12J (2001); *R.I. Gen. Laws* sec. 11-54-1 (2001).

48. *N.H. Rev. Stat. Ann.* sec. 168-B:15 (2002).

49. *R.I. Gen. Laws* sec. 23-16.4-2 (2001).

50. "Letter to Sponsors / Researchers: Human Cells Used in Therapy Involving the Transfer of Genetic Material By Means Other Than the Union of Gamete Nuclei," http://www.fda.gov/cber/ltr/cytotrans070601.htm.

51. Ibid.

52. FDA did not give researchers and sponsors advance notice or opportunity to comment on its determination that these materials were subject to agency regulation. Commentators presume that the agency's assertion of jurisdiction was intended to discourage cloning experimentation and to forestall restrictive legislation. These critics claim that the assertion of jurisdiction without public discussion inhibited creative legislation and regulatory solutions that might have followed an open, democratic process for developing national policy on cloning research. See Merrill and Rose 2001.

53. Questions like those found in the "Points to Consider" could have been posed for ARTs, just as they were for gene therapy. Why genetics and not reproductive technologies? Perhaps the fear associated with the new genetic technologies was stronger. Or the privacy/abortion-related issues associated with ARTs might have derailed any efforts to establish a regulatory system for ART research.

54. On the other hand, ooplasm transfer does provide an example of the future of the technology in one respect: no viral vector is involved in ooplasm transfer because the ooplasm and the mitochodria carried within it are the delivery vehicles for the transferred genes. The regulatory sequences that go with those genes come in along with the whole package.

In the wake of the Gelsinger and X-linked SCID leukemia somatic gene therapy cases, it is easy to see why viral vectors make poor candidates for IGM. Viral vectors carry exogenous DNA into host cells and integrate into the host cell genomes, transferring additional genetic material along with the desired gene. During development, as a gamete goes from zygote to embryo to fetus, added genetic material may disrupt cell differentiation and tissue development. Therefore, research into methods of nonviral gene delivery hold the most promise for the type of gene therapy that would be considered "reprogenetics."

While many researchers are still working to develop safe viral vectors for delivering genes into somatic cells, others are working on non-viral gene delivery or gene correction methods. See Gorman 2003, 43–44.

55. Ken Culver, Global Head of Translational Medicine at Novartis Oncology, Novartis Pharmaceutical Corporation, has described a scenario in which mutation correction technologies could be used for IGM in germ cells themselves, rather than in embryos (Culver 2003, 87). Culver identifies new oligonucleotide-based repair technologies as promising candidates for the future of IGM. Gene repair methods do not require viral vectors or the insertion of active genetic elements into the host genome. Using oligonucleotide transfections to accomplish gene repair in cells in vitro has not resulted in adverse molecular consequences. Theoretically, these techniques, using transient molecules that are degraded within hours, would induce endogenous DNA repair enzymes to correct mutations. The technologies described by Culver make use of host cells' own DNA repair machinery to correct genetic mutations. Still, Culver has pointed out that *any* method of genetic alteration, even via germ cells, has the potential to mutate the

genome, resulting in adverse inheritable consequences. Scientists need to know how genes function during development in order to be sure that successful correction of a gene would not cause harm. As Culver explains, "A detailed understanding of the effects of any IGM procedure on the genome is essential. Satisfactory resolution of these key scientific issues must be achieved before intentional IGM is attempted in the human germ line" (Culver 2003, 78).

Gene repair methods in gametes have not yet been proven safe or efficient. If they were and if technologies were developed that could screen for potential deleterious effects caused by gene repair methods, then Culver argues that a logical place to begin using them would be in spermatogonia cells for the treatment of male infertility. Spermatogonia cells make sense as targets of IGM for several reasons. First, correcting the genetic defect requires treating only the spermatogonia cells themselves rather than the whole person or even an embryo. Second, successful correction of spermatogonia would lead to motile sperm that could be analyzed before use in fertilization. High efficiency of mutation correction would not be necessary because only the corrected cells would be used in combination with established IVF techniques. Genetic analysis of the embryo during IVF is available, making it possible to double-check the correction (Culver 2003, 78–88). Culver further suggests that repair technologies, used first to treat male infertility in spermatogonia, might one day form the basis for gene repair technologies that could be used to treat other diseases (Culver 2003, 89).

Harvard Professor Chris Evans agrees that, along with gene therapy in IVF embryos for couples who are both homozygous for a monogenic disease, gene repair of male spermatogonia presents a possible early IGM scenario. On the other hand, Evans predicts that more common, complex polygenic disorders might prove to be the best targets for IGM. One approach would be to direct gene therapy toward disease susceptibility genes. Another would be "to provide individuals with extra copies of inducible genes encoding therapeutic products." Evans acknowledges that "considerable technical limitations need to be resolved before any of this can take place," but he believes that IGM "is increasingly suffused by an air of inevitability" (Evans 2003, 93–100).

56. Of course, others may disagree. See Cohen and Kristol 2004, 25–29.

57. If IGM could be accomplished with "injectable genes," or by some other method, with gametes in vivo, IGM and ARTs would use separate providers. Even now, how many gene therapy researchers are working with fertility researchers?

58. Parens and Knowles present embryo stem cells as an example of the convergence of reproductive and genetic technologies and worry that embryo stem cells could be used to create genetically enhanced children. See Parens and Knowles 2003, S12. While it is possible to imagine a futuristic scenario where many fertile parents will choose to use invasive technologies to design enhanced children à la GATTACA, even in that scenario, parents prefer to have genetically related children. Embryo stem cells, unless selected from the embryos of the parenting couple themselves, will contain hereditary material from others rather than the prospective parents, making the use of embryo stem cells to create "designer children" relatively less likely.

59. Parens and Knowles look to the British HFEA as a model for their regulatory proposal. See Parens and Knowles 2003, fn. 118. But they acknowledge that the HFEA

worked together with the Human Genetics Advisory Committee to act on issues around embryo stem cell isolation. The two separate groups worked together on a technology that involved issues subject to the jurisdiction of both (Parens and Knowles 2003, S15).

60. As noted above in note 17, original predictions about which diseases would be targeted by gene therapy proved inaccurate as well.

61. For more on this, see Palmer and Cook-Deegan 2003, 275–78.

62. http://www4.od.nih.gov/oba/RAC/RAC_FAQs.htm (see second Q and A).

63. Proposed Rule 2001, http://www.fda.gov/cber/rules/frgene011801.htm.

64. Belmont Report (1979) Part A.

65. For more on this confusion and the associated dangers, see Churchill et al., "Genetic Research as Therapy: Implications of 'Gene Therapy' for Informed Consent," *Journal of Law, Medicine and Ethics,* 26 (1998): 38-47.

66. The unauthorized Cline research illustrates this point. See note 2, above. Cline was censured by the public but continued to be a leader in the scientific community, pointing out how important a variety of viewpoints are in the conversation about research ethics.

67. How would this regulatory scheme apply, for example, where two very short parents sought either preimplantation genetic diagnosis or IGM to ensure the birth of a child who did express the inherited trait of extreme short stature? The use of growth hormone therapy to treat non-growth hormone-deficient children has generated similar issues in this country but has not led to the sort of regulatory restrictions envisioned by Parens and Knowles. In part, this is because of a recognition that the line between disease treatment and enhancement is ambiguous and difficult to draw. The paradigm case of Johnny and Billy has been posed to highlight the inequity of placing growth hormone-deficient children and short children of the same expected height on opposite sides of an arbitrary allowable treatment line (Allen and Fost 1990). In part, these restrictions have been avoided because of respect for the autonomous decisions of parents and medical providers on behalf of specific children, with whom they are familiar.(Also, we don't regulate the practice of medicine or off-label uses of drugs.) Even if the technology to accomplish this goal (or some other that ethicists might criticize as compromising social utility) were proved safe, the RTB's policies or code of practice presumably would forbid the parents or their medical providers from choosing to use that safe technology on the basis of the RTB's conception of social well-being. If, on the other hand, the use of nonexperimental technology remained unregulated, parents and their medical providers could make such decisions together, based on their own mores and notions of well-being.

68. For a brief history of eugenics in the United States, see Everett Mendelsohn, "The Eugenic Temptation," *Harvard Magazine* March–April (2000): 39–41,105–106, 39–40. The American eugenics movement itself informed Hitler's racial purity policies.

69. *Buck v. Bell,* 274 U.S. 200, 207 (1927).

70. *Jacobson v. Massachusetts,* 197 U.S. 11, 29 (1905).

71. Admittedly, a forced sterilization is more physically invasive than a restriction from use of technology. Nevertheless, limiting a person's reproductive choices for the sake of promoting public notions of well-being, as determined by a small group of

"experts," crosses the boundary of appropriate government intervention. These issues are related to but not the same as abortion issues. The arguments in favor of and opposed to abortion rights call into play an already existing fetus and the rights of the mother to self-determination. The reprogenetic IGM issues do not involve already existing fetuses (except from the perspective of those who consider pre-embryos to carry the same moral weight as fetuses) or the rights of mothers to bodily integrity and self-determination.

72. *Jacobson v. Massachusetts*, 197 U.S. 11, 25, 29, 31 (1905), excerpted and questioned in Andrews, Mehlman, and Rothstein 2002, 55.

73. I owe this wise point to Rabbi Irwin Groner (March 12, 2004).

74. Some have suggested that disease treatment uses of IGM ought to be forbidden because the line between IGM treatment will lead to enhancement, and there is no just way to distribute enhancements.

75. Some have used an egalitarian application of the Rawlsian difference principle to argue that IGM enhancement should be forbidden entirely or rationed by the federal government to ensure equal distribution. John Rawls's "difference principle" holds that, along with equalities in the assignment of basic rights and duties, inequalities should be permitted only if they "result in compensating benefits for everyone, and in particular for the least advantaged members of society" (Rawls 1999, 13). Other conceptions of justice do not focus on end-state equal distribution of goods. For example, Robert Nozick's principle of "distributive justice" focuses on the mechanism by which people acquire holdings and says "simply that a distribution is just if everyone is entitled to the holdings they possess under the distribution" (Nozick 1974, 151). According to Nozick, a principle of justice that requires a particular end-state pattern requires "continuous interference with people's lives" (163). Nozick points out that "when people force you to do certain work . . . decide what you are to do and what purposes your work is to serve apart from your decisions . . . This process whereby they take this decision from you makes them a *part-owner* of you; it gives them a property right in you" (172). In other words, a principle of justice that requires equal distribution of goods may violate such important norms as freedom of transfer, freedom of choice, and self-determination.

76. Rawls makes a similar point in the context of education. He points out that although the difference principle "gives some weight" to considerations mandating spending more money on the education of less intelligent than is spent educating the more intelligent, "the difference principle would allocate resources in education, say, so as to improve the long-term expectation of the least favored. If this end is attained by giving more attention to the better endowed, it is permissible; otherwise not" (Rawls 1999, 86–87).

77. Indeed, Rawls supports the notion that earlier generations owe it to later generations to pursue policies that ensure better genetic endowments for them:

We should note, though, that it is not in general to the advantage of the less fortunate to propose policies which reduce the talents of others. Instead, by accepting the difference principle, they view the greater abilities as a social asset to be used for the common advantage. But it is also in the interest of each to have greater natural assets. This enables him to pursue a preferred plan of life. In the original position, then, the parties want to insure for their descendants the best genetic endowment (assuming their own to be fixed). The pursuit of reasonable policies in this regard is something that earlier generations owe to later ones, this being a question that arises between generations. Thus over time a society is to take steps at least to preserve the general level of natural abilities and to prevent the diffusion of serious defects. These measures are to be guided by principles that the parties would be willing to consent to for the sake of their successors. I mention this speculative and difficult matter to indicate once again the manner in which the difference principle is likely to transform problems of social justice. We might conjecture that in the long run, if there is an upper bound on ability, we would eventually reach a society with the greatest equal liberty the members of which enjoy the greatest equal talent. (Rawls 1999, 92–93)

78. *Skinner v. Oklahoma*, 316 U.S. 535, 62 S.Ct. 1110 (1942) (invalidating on equal protection grounds a state statute that allowed the sterilization of some convicted criminals). See also regulations prohibiting the use of federal funds for sterilization of institutionalized persons, 42 C.F.R. sections 441.254 (Medicare and Medicaid reimbursement is not available "for the sterilization of a mentally incompetent or institutionalized individual") (1978); 42 C.F.R. 50.206.

79. From the point of view of social justice, there is no difference between arranging for piano lessons for a child and enhancing his piano playing talent genetically (if proven safe), except for the questionable perception that the genetic method will be more successful. There is certainly no proof that IGM will work better than piano lessons. Even if IGM were proved more successful, would that make IGM for piano skill wrong?

80. The existing web of property, contract, and tort law, in combination with private litigation, could provide additional protections. For more on this, see Julie Gage Palmer, "Human Gene Therapy: Suggestions for Avoiding Liability," *Annals of the New York Academy of Sciences* 716 (1994): 294–306.

81. Lewis pairs this strong statement in favor of democratic equality with a claim that humans have a spiritual need for inequality. One need not accept Lewis's view of spiritual inequality in order to recognize the wisdom of his elucidation of democratic equality.

82. This story has been used to illustrate a variety of principles, including Good Samaritan rules, universal love, the ethics of self-sacrifice, social utility, and values more important than life, among others. The story is instructive here as an analogy.

83. Knowing both men will die, Ben Petura says the men should divide the water because it is unjust for one man to live while the other dies. Rabbi Akiva's view is the more widely accepted.

REFERENCES

Allen, D., and N. Fost 1990. Growth hormone therapy for short stature: Panacea or Pandora's box? *Journal of Pediatrics* 117:16–21.

Andrews, L., M. Mehlman, and M. Rothstein. 2002. *Genetics: Ethics, Law and Policy.* St. Paul, MN: West Group.

Barritt, J. C., S. Brenner, S. Willardson, and J. Cohen. 2001. Spontaneous and artificial changes in human ooplasmic mitochondria. *Human Reproduction* 6:513–16, 513.

Berg, P. 1974. Letter. *Science* 185:303.

Buck v. Bell. 1927. 274 U.S. 200 (1927).

Center for Biologics Evaluation and Research, Food and Drug Administration. 1999. Letter to sponsors / researchers. Human cells used in therapy involving the transfer of genetic material by means other than the union of gamete nuclei. http://www.fda .gov/cber/ltr/cytotrans070601.htm (accessed September 2, 2005).

———. 1999. Dear gene therapy IND sponsor / principal investigator letter. November 5. http://www.fda.gov/cber/ltr/gt110599.htm (accessed September 2, 2005).

———. 2002. Gene Therapy Patient Tracking System. June 27. http://www.fda.gov/cber/ genetherapy/gttrack.htm (accessed September 2, 2005).

Churchill, L., M. Collins, N. King, S. Pemberton, and K. Wailoo. 1998. Genetic research as therapy: Implications of "gene therapy" for informed consent. *Journal of Law, Medicine and Ethics* 26:38–47.

Cohen, E., and W. Kristol. 2004. The politics of bioethics. *Weekly Standard,* May 10, 25–29.

Culver, K. 2003. Gene repair, genomics, and human germ-line modification. In *Designing Our Descendants: The Promises and Perils of Genetic Modifications,* ed. A. Chapman and M. Frankel, 77–92. Washington, DC: American Association of the Advancement of Science.

Department of Health and Human Services. 2000. New initiatives to protect participants in gene therapy trials. Press release, March 7. http://www.hhs.gov/news/press/2000 pres/20000307A.html (September 2, 2005).

Detroit Free Press. 1983. Coalition asks for ban on genetic experiments. June 9, 14.

Diamond v. Chakrabarty. 1980. 447 U.S. 303 (1980).

Epstein, R. 1995. *Simple Rules for a Complex World.* Cambridge, MA: Harvard University Press.

Evans, C. H. 2003. Germ-line gene therapy: Can we do it, do we need it, where do we start, and where might it lead? In *Designing Our Descendants:The Promises and Perils of Genetic Modifications,* ed. A. Chapman and M. Frankel, 93–101. Washington, DC: American Association for the Advancement of Science.

Food and Drug Administration. 2003. FDA Advisory Committee discusses steps for potentially continuing certain gene therapy trials that were recently placed on hold. Talk paper. February 28. http://www.fda.gov//bbs/topics/ANSWERS/2003/ANS012 02.html (accessed September 2, 2005).

Glover, J. 1984. *What Sort of People Should There Be? Genetic Engineering, Brain Control, and Their Impact on Our Future World.* Harmondsworth, Middlesex, UK: Penguin Books.

Gorman, J. 2003. Delivering the goods: Gene therapy without the virus. *Science News* 163:43–44.

Health Research Extension Act of 1985. 1985. P.L. No. 99-158, sec. 381(c)(1).

Lewis, C. S. 1978. Screwtape proposes a toast. In *The Screwtape Letters: How a Senior Devil Instructs a Junior Devil in the Art of Temptation*. London: Macmillan,

———. 1986 [1943]. Equality. In *Present Concerns: Essays by C. S. Lewis*. London: Fount Paperbacks.

Mendelsohn, E. 2000. The eugenic temptation. *Harvard Magazine*, March–April, 39–41, 105–6.

Merrill, R., and B. Rose. 2001. FDA regulation of human cloning: Usurpation or statesmanship? *Harvard Journal of Law & Technology* 15 (1): 85 (Fall).

National Commission for the Protection of Human Subjects of Biomedical and Behavioral Research. 1979. *The Belmont Report: Ethical Principles and Guidelines for the Protection of Human Subjects of Research*. April 18. http://ohsr.od.nih.gov/guidelines/belmont.html.

National Institutes of Health. Frequently asked questions (FAQs) about the NIH review process for human gene transfer trials. http://www4.od.nih.gov/oba/RAC/RAC_FAQs.htm (accessed September 2, 2005).

———. 2001. Notice of actions under the NIH Guidelines for research involving recombinant DNA molecules (NIH Guidelines) 66 FR 57970 (November 19, 2001). http://www4.od.nih.gov/oba/rac/frnotices/11-19-01act.htm (accessed September 2, 2005).

———. 2002. Guidelines on Recombinant DNA Research. Appendix M. Points to consider in the design and submission of protocols for the transfer of recombinant DNA molecules into one or more research participants. http://www4.od.nih.gov/oba/rac/guidelines_02/Appendix_M.htm (accessed September 2, 2005).

———. 2005 (April). Charter, Recombinant DNA Advisory Committee. http://www4.od.nih.gov/oba/rac/documents1.htm (accessed September 2, 2005).

National Institutes of Health, Office of Biotechnology Activities. 2003. Memorandum to principal investigators for human gene transfer trials employing retroviral vectors, dated March 20, 2003. http://www4.od.nih.gov/oba/rac/XSCID_letter2.pdf.

Nozick R. 1974. *Anarchy, State, and Utopia*. New York: Basic Books.

Palmer, J. 1994. Human gene therapy: Suggestions for avoiding liability. *Annals of the New York Academy of Sciences* 716:294–306.

Palmer, J., and R. Cook-Deegan, R. 2003. National policies to oversee inheritable genetic modifications research. In *Designing Our Descendants: The Promises and Perils of Genetic Modifications,* ed. A. Chapman and M. Frankel, 275–295. Washington, DC: American Association for the Advancement of Science.

Parens, E. 1999. Review of Resnik, Steindraus, and Langer *Human Germline Gene Therapy: Scientific, Moral and Political Issues. Theoretical Medicine,* 21:399–403.

Parens, E., and E. Juengst. 2001. Inadvertently crossing the germ line. *Science* 292:397.

Parens, E., and L. Knowles. 2003. Reprogenetics and public policy. *Hastings Center Report* 33, no. 4: S1–24.

President's Commission for the Study of Ethical Problems in Medicine and Biomedical and Behavioral Research. 1982. *Splicing Life: A Report on the Social and Ethical Issues of Genetic Engineering with Human Beings*. Washington, DC: President's Commission.

Public Law 108-199 [H.R. 2673]. 2004. 108 P.L. 199, 118 Stat. 3, sec. 510 (January 23, 2004). Food and Drug Administration. Proposed Rule on Availability for Public Disclosure and Submission to FDA for Public Disclosure of Certain Data and Information Related to Human Gene Therapy or Xenotransplantation. 21 CFR Parts 20, 312, and 601. http://www.fda.gov/cber/rules/frgene011801.htm.

Rawls. J. 1999. *A Theory of Justice.* Rev. ed. Cambridge, MA: Belknap Press of Harvard University Press.

Reilly, P. R. 2000. Eugenics, ethics, sterilization laws. In *Encyclopedia of Ethical, Legal, and Policy Issues in Biotechnology* 204, 204–208.

Skinner v. Oklahoma. 1942. 316 U.S. 535, 62 S.Ct. 1110 (1942).

Thompson, L. 2000. Human gene therapy: Harsh lessons, high hopes. *FDA Consumer Magazine,* September–October.

U.S. Congress, House Committee on Science and Technology. 1982. *Human Genetic Engineering, Hearings Before the Sub-committee on Investigations and Oversight of the Committee on Science and Technology,* 97th Congress, 2d Session; 182.

U.S. Congress, Office of Technology Assessment. 1984. Human Gene Therapy: A Background Paper. Report no. DC. OTA-BP-BA-32 December. Washington, DC.

Walters, L., and J. Palmer. 1997. *The Ethics of Human Gene Therapy.* New York: Oxford University Press.

Woo, S. 2000. The last word: Researchers react to gene therapy's promises and pitfalls. *FDA Consumer Magazine.* U.S. Food and Drug Administration. September–October.

CHAPTER THREE

Oversight of Assisted Reproductive Technologies

The Last Twenty Years

ANDREA L. BONNICKSEN

Assisted reproductive technologies (ARTs) refer to in vitro fertilization (IVF) and its variations, such as embryo freezing, gamete and embryo donation, intracytoplasmic sperm injection (ICSI), and preimplantation genetic diagnosis (PGD). Oversight falls into two general and sometimes overlapping categories. In public oversight, governmental officials weigh the scientific, legal, societal, and ethical dimensions of ARTs to craft rules and regulations enforceable by the government. In private oversight, professionals in the private sector weigh similar dimensions to develop voluntary guidelines for the application of new technologies. For the purposes of this chapter, four groups of public and private policymakers are identified: the U.S. Congress, state legislatures, the Food and Drug Administration (FDA), and professional societies.

Oversight of ARTs extends beyond the practice of ARTs in fertility clinics to include developments arising before and after clinical practice. As such, this chapter divides ART development and practice into three stages: innovation, clinical practice, and assessment. The first, innovation, involves the process by which prospective ART procedures move from the preclinical setting, where animal or human cells and tissues are studied, to the clinical setting, where procedures are used with small and later larger numbers of patients. For example, ICSI was introduced clinically without systematic experiments using animal models (Leese and Whittall 2001; Powell 2003). Although ICSI has come to be generally regarded as safe and effective, its nearly serendipitous first use has raised concerns about the premature use of ARTs and the prospect of experimentation taking place in the clinic rather than the laboratory. Some oversight issues thus address the adequacy of criteria and guidelines for determining when it is appropriate to offer ARTs to patients.

The use of ARTs in the clinical setting comprises a second stage of oversight. One aspect of oversight at this stage is the scientific concern for quality control, which mirrors oversight of the practice of medicine generally. A second aspect involves questions geared to the ethics of ART practices. For example, if egg donation is safe and efficacious for recipients and offspring and is performed under rigorous quality control, questions still arise about the ethics of the practice, such as what level of compensation is appropriate for egg donors and what information must be conveyed to the donor for her to make an informed decision about proceeding.

A third stage of ART development and practice involves assessment. Here, short- and long-term data collection and analysis allow ARTs to be monitored over time for safety and efficacy. The Fertility Clinic Success Rate and Certification Act of 1992 (FCSRCA) has facilitated collection of pregnancy success rates and other data by professional associations. Although FCSRCA's primary purpose is to inform patients who are deciding whether to try ARTs and where, the data can also be used to assess the frequency and outcomes of reproductive technologies. Other data gathering is conducted by researchers who conduct controlled studies for analysis and publication in professional journals.

In reviewing the forms and conduct of oversight over the past twenty years in this chapter, I use these three stages as an organizing device to suggest ways in which the nature of oversight varies across stages and among groups of policymakers. This approach helps to identify areas of oversight that are carefully covered by existing regulatory mechanisms and those that are less fully covered. Moreover, the historical oversight patterns in ART yield some implications for future reprogenetic technologies, which I take up at the end of the chapter.

U.S. CONGRESS

When one thinks of policymaking, it is natural to look to the U.S. Congress. As the nation's central legislative body, Congress is a potential location for constructing a uniform approach to issues of public interest such as ART oversight. Yet the past twenty years of ART oversight reveal a distinctly different pattern. Divisive politics relating to abortion and fundamentally different views about the moral status of the human embryo have contributed to a Congress unable to forge the consensus needed for substantive policy relating to ART research and practice. The tenacious disputes over abortion, which reflect conflicts over the moral and legal status of fetuses and embryos, have led members of Congress to avoid ART policy initiatives and the attendant political pitfalls.

Congress has been less reticent in its attempts to pass laws with the advent of somatic cell nuclear transfer (SCNT) and human embryonic stem (ES) cell research as political issues. Members of Congress have sponsored numerous hearings and introduced a variety of bills related to SCNT and ES cell research, although to date, Congress has not passed substantive new laws relating to either reproductive SCNT or human ES cell research. Arguably, these issues relate only tangentially to ARTs, however. For one thing, few if any ART practitioners support reproductive SCNT (cloning); indeed, their main professional association, the American Society for Reproductive Medicine, endorses a ban on the transfer to a woman's uterus of an embryo created through SCNT. For another, ES cell research relates to ARTs only indirectly, through informed consent procedures for couples to donate spare embryos for research; it does not touch on embryos to be used for reproduction.

Innovation

Ideally, innovative technologies are introduced in the clinical setting after preliminary studies using animal or analogous models, human cells and tissues, and experimental use with a small number of patients following review by an institutional review board (IRB). Governmental funding is one avenue for ensuring that clinical trials are well-designed and protective of the interests of participants. In the funding process, peer review of proposals focuses attention on the merits of the study, probable safety and efficacy, and provisions for the well-being of participants. The funding process asserts control over the pace and nature of innovation, and it confers legitimacy on the research. Both the executive and legislative branches of the U.S. government, however, have foreclosed the oversight that comes with public funding in the area of ARTs. At present and in the past, Congress has barred funding for research in which human embryos are harmed or destroyed. As a consequence, Congress has not exercised oversight of ART innovation.

The federal policy of not funding research in which embryos are injured or destroyed dates from the 1970s. Shortly before the first baby was born through IVF in 1978, then Department of Health, Education, and Welfare (DHEW) developed a policy to prepare for the possibility it would receive proposals regarding human IVF research. As part of this policy, the DHEW secretary was to set up an ethics advisory board to review IVF for its ethical acceptability. The National Institutes of Health (NIH) received its first proposal in 1977, and the secretary set up the Ethics Advisory Board (EAB), which solicited public comments and testimony. It issued a report in 1979 concluding that IVF was ethical for married couples and that research was acceptable under certain conditions. The publication of the report in the *Federal Register* met with many critical responses, and, reflecting the political volatility of the issue, the then DHEW secretary Joseph Califano tabled the EAB's recommendations (Ethics Advisory Board 1979). The next DHEW secretary, Patricia Harris, disbanded the EAB altogether. None of the EAB's recommendations, such as the recommendation that the government fund IVF data gathering, was enacted, and the original research proposal was implicitly rejected. The EAB report, four years in the making, was ignored.

Following the EAB's disbanding, investigators who conducted research using human embryos did so on an ad hoc basis in IVF clinics using private funds, but it was not known how much research was under way. Congress attempted to establish a bipartisan ethics advisory board in 1985, but the board never got off the ground because Congress was unable to agree on its topics and membership. In 1987, researchers from Washington University submitted a proposal to study nonviable fertilized and unfertilized human eggs, which was the first proposal sent to the NIH since the proposal from ten years previously. Officials from NIH proposed in the *Federal Register* the establishment of a new EAB, but no action was taken (U.S. Department of Health and Human Services 1988).

Another attempt to change the funding policy occurred during the transition from the presidency of George H. W. Bush to that of Bill Clinton. During that time Congress lifted the EAB requirement for IVF research in a "barely noticed" section of the NIH Revitalization Act of 1993 (P.L. 103-43) (Gianelli 1994, 3). With this proviso, Congress intended for embryo research to proceed, as indicated in the Senate report that accompanied the bill to the floor: "Section 492A will permit the funding of peer reviewed and approved research proposals involving assisted reproductive technologies including in vitro fertilization (IVF)." Similarly, the House report stated that "Subsection c nullifies the de facto moratorium currently in place on federal support for research on human in vitro fertilization" (U.S. Department of Health and Human Services [DHHS], NIH 1994, 14).

To guide the allocation of research funds, the acting director of the NIH set up a Human Embryo Research Panel (HERP) to review issues raised by embryo research, solicit public comment, and make recommendations about the ethical acceptability of various kinds of research using human embryos. After a series of public meetings, the panel in 1994 issued its report, which regarded some forms of research as ethically acceptable if, among other things, the studies promised significant benefit, the objectives could not be met through research using animals or human gametes, researchers kept the number of embryos to a minimum, and donors were informed about the nature and purpose of the research (U.S. DHHS, NIH 1994, 14). HERP regarded the generation of embryos for research as ethically acceptable, within limits, as well as the use of embryos donated by couples in IVF programs. It proposed a three-stage review process.

Before the end of the first day after the report's publication, however, President Clinton had issued an executive order rejecting the most controversial part—funding to create human embryos for research—and directing the NIH director not to allocate money for projects involving the creation of embryos for research. In the ongoing legislative session, opponents of embryo research amended the NIH appropriations bill to bar funding for projects in which embryos were created or harmed. Similar riders have been added to all subsequent NIH appropriations bills. Congressional policy does, however, allow funding of projects related to ART that do not injure embryos, such as those examining female health or the physiology of human eggs (Tasca 2002).

In recent years, the issue of research funding reemerged with the ability to isolate and derive human ES cells. Members of Congress introduced bills to forbid funding for research in which ES cells have been derived from human embryos and for the use of biological products developed from these cell lines. After months of intense political activity on behalf of and in opposition to human ES cell research, President George W. Bush authorized research funding for a limited number of cell lines that had been derived by the date of his August 9, 2001, policy announcement. The concession was not sufficient to challenge the conclusion that the federal government has refrained from using the power of the purse to shape expectations about when it is appropriate to move innovative ARTs from the laboratory to the clinic.

In a different strategy for restricting research on human embryos, DHHS in 2002 formed a new committee, the Secretary's Advisory Committee on Human Research Protections. The committee was authorized to "provide advice relating to the responsible conduct of research involving human subjects with particular emphasis on . . . pregnant women, embryos, and fetuses" (Weiss 2002).

The addition of embryos to a list of human subjects could eventually set the stage for a policy change in which Congress or DHHS officials amend the law to protect embryos as research subjects. Doing so would shift policy from the present passive position (not funding research) to a more active position (protecting human embryos) that would, in the process, restrict studies involving human embryos.

Congress has attempted in another way to regulate reproductive technologies by proposing to ban reproductive SCNT. If enacted into law, this proposal would set a precedent for innovation by forbidding a prospective technology altogether. Two types of bills have been introduced in Congress. One would forbid anyone from transferring an embryo created through SCNT to a woman's uterus (a narrower restriction) and the other would forbid anyone from using SCNT to create an embryo (a broader restriction). A broad bill passed the House of Representatives in 2001 and again in 2003. As of 2003, however, no equivalent bill had passed the Senate. Neither chamber has voted on a narrower restriction, largely because those opposed to cloning appear to prefer no law over a law banning only reproductive SCNT.

Clinical Practice

The U.S. Congress does not traditionally regulate the practice of medicine, and that includes the practice of ARTs. Consequently, congressional oversight of ARTs takes the indirect form of regulations affecting medicine generally, such as the Clinical Laboratory Improvement Act of 1967, as amended in 1988. This law set standards for clinical laboratories that conduct tests whose results are reported to patients. This category includes andrology laboratories, where tests such as semen analysis are conducted in the diagnosis of infertility. Indirect oversight also stems from Federal Trade Commission regulation of truth in advertising and the regulation of working conditions mandated by the Occupational Safety and Health Act (Adamson 2002, 933–34). Periodically, members of Congress attempt to require insurance coverage of infertility treatment in selected situations. If passed, these bills would require the reimbursement of patients only if they sought treatment at laboratories or clinics that met core standards. Generally, these standards would be established by the American College of Obstetricians and Gynecologists (ACOG) and the American Society for Reproductive Medicine (ASRM).

Congress has not imposed substantive restrictions on the practice of ART, in large part because doing so would confront constitutionally based procreative liberty. For example, if Congress were to limit the number of embryos to be transferred in an IVF cycle or bar cross-generational gamete donation, it would need to show a compelling interest in doing so. Congress could, however, pass laws facilitating ARTs, such as allocating funds to publicize ART procedures. In 2002, DHHS officials did the latter, by setting aside $900,000 to make the public aware that spare embryos could be donated for use by other couples wanting to conceive. No allowance was made to publicize the option of donating embryos for research.

Assessment

In regard to assessment, in 1992 Congress passed what has been called the "most visible and important ART-specific regulation" in the United States, the Fertility Clinic Success Rate and Certification Act of 1992 (FCSRCA) (Adamson 2002, 933). This law dates from the 1980s, when members of the American Fertility Society (now the ASRM) organized the Society for Assisted Reproductive Technology (SART) to respond to concerns about inconsistent reporting of pregnancy and birth rates in ARTs. After surveying its members to accumulate success rates and other data for annual reports, in 1989 SART published the first of what were to become annual reports designed to protect patients by revealing differences in success rates among clinics (Garcia 1998, 634). As the only congressional statute initiated with ARTs in mind, the FCSRCA directed the DHHS, through the Centers for Disease Control and Prevention (CDC), to develop a model certification program for fertility laboratories where eggs, spermatozoa, and embryos are handled, and to make the program available to the states to consider adopting. It also directed clinics to report pregnancy rates annually to the DHHS through the CDC, and it obligated the DHHS Secretary to publish pregnancy and live birth rates according to age, diagnosis, and other factors. The published data would include the certification status of embryology laboratories used by programs and the names of programs that did not provide data. The annual publication of data was designed to be easy for prospective patients to understand, and it was available at no cost (Stolberg 1997).

Congress passed this law with the sponsorship of the then representative Ron Wyden (D-OR), who worked with SART, ASRM, the infertility support group RESOLVE, and experts in ART procedures to frame the bill and work for its passage. With this law, Congress acted in an affirmative sense to encourage uniform procedures for ART data gathering and assessment. The law highlighted a private-public partnership in which professionals assumed primary responsibility for the mechanics of oversight. The CDC published its first report in 1997, covering data collected for 1995. More than 95 percent of ART programs comply by providing data to the CDC. Programs that do not report data are identified as such in the annual report. The act provides for validation of reported findings too, and in each year of 1999, 2000, and 2001, thirty programs were randomly selected for validation visits (Adamson 2002, 936). In addition to advising prospective patients, the data in these reports can be used in assessment studies.

STATE LEGISLATURES

As in all areas of medicine, physicians who specialize in one or more aspects of ARTs must be licensed to practice in their states, according to standards set by state medical boards. Beyond that, states have passed a variety of laws with both restrictive and affirmative impacts on ARTs. Although laws passed in one state can serve as models for other states to adopt, the idiosyncratic pattern of most state laws directed at ARTs reduces their significance for overall ART oversight.

Innovation

States have passed various laws designed to regulate research involving human embryos. Twenty-six states have laws relating to research on fetuses or embryos. Nine of these states ban embryo research directly or indirectly by forbidding research on the product of conception, variously called a conceptus, embryo, fetus, or unborn child. A tenth state, New Hampshire, allows research on embryos within fourteen days after fertilization, provided the embryos are not transferred for pregnancy. Federal courts have struck down other state laws for vagueness. For example, in *Lifchez v. Hartigan* (735 F.Supp. 1361 [N.D.Ill.1990]), a federal district court struck down an Illinois abortion law that provided no person may "experiment upon a fetus produced by the fertilization of a human ovum by a human sperm unless such experimentation is therapeutic to the fetus." Although the law was not intended to forbid IVF, the law did interfere with IVF, the court concluded, because techniques in IVF are experimental and are not necessarily therapeutic, even though they are done to achieve a pregnancy. Thus, the law interfered with a woman's "cluster of constitutionally protected" reproductive choices that included "the right to submit to a medical procedure that may bring about, rather than prevent, pregnancy." Moreover, by not defining "experimentation" or "therapeutic," the law left researchers and practitioners guessing at the law's meaning, and this led to the court's decision that the law was unconstitutionally vague, in violation of Fifth Amendment due process.

More recently, a number of states have made reproductive SCNT illegal, including Arkansas, California, Michigan, North Dakota, Rhode Island, Louisiana, Missouri, and Virginia. These states vary in how they define SCNT, the punishments they set up, and whether or not the legislation includes a research protection clause (Bonnicksen 2002, 137–40). For example, in 1997 California forbade for a five-year period nuclear transfer "from a human cell from whatever the source" to an enucleated human egg for the purpose of implanting the resulting embryo for pregnancy. It later made its anticloning law permanent (Holden 2002). Louisiana's anticloning law has this same language. In 1998, Michigan made "human somatic cell nuclear transfer to produce an embryo" a felony, with a prison sentence or fine (or both) for violation. Rhode Island forbids SCNT to attempt a pregnancy, and also the twinning of embryos. Louisiana bars state funding for human cloning. Missouri in 1988 provided that no state funds may be allocated for research on cloning human beings, where cloning is the replication of a human person by cultivating "a cell with genetic material through egg, embryo, fetal and newborn stages of development into a new human person."

Several states have responded to controversies over ES cell research by passing laws (Aldhous 2005). South Dakota passed a prohibitive law in 2000 making it a misdemeanor to "knowingly conduct nontherapeutic research that subjects a human embryo to substantial risk of injury or death" (Bonnicksen 2002, 140). On the other hand, California passed a law affirming the state legislators' support of ES cell research, including SCNT for research purposes, and stating that "publicly funded research will be essential to realizing the promise of stem cell research" ("California passes" 2002). In 2004, California voters approved Proposition 71, the Stem Cell Research and Cures Bond Initiative, which provided for $3 billion from state-backed funds over a ten-year period to fund stem cell research (California Health and Safety Code, 2004). New Jersey enacted a stem cell research bill (S1909) into law in 2004. The law was designed to assure researchers that the state would not interfere with ES cell, embryonic germ cell, and adult stem cell research, including cells developed from SCNT. The governor set aside $6.5 million in the state budget to establish a stem cell institute to be administered by Rutgers University and the University of Medicine and Dentistry of New Jersey and funded by state and private money (Kocieniewski 2004).

Clinical Practice

Medical licensing is generally a province of the states, which regulate medicine through licensing and the enforcement of tort law. In addition, some states have introduced new regulations that require such things as certification of laboratories performing diagnostic tests, licensing of gamete storage banks (California, Georgia, Maryland, New York), minimum personnel qualifications at ART clinics (Virginia), disclosure of success rates (Pennsylvania, Louisiana), and the meeting of ASRM standards by ART clinics (Louisiana, New Hampshire). County medical societies are also involved in the oversight of clinical practice (Adamson 2002, 933).

Following a case of unauthorized use of patients' eggs, California passed a law requiring physicians who remove sperm or eggs to obtain written consent from patients before using the spermatozoa or eggs for any purpose other than implantation into the patient or the patient's spouse. It passed a second law making it a crime knowingly to use spermatoza, eggs, or embryos for purposes other than those specified on the consent form (Angergame and Tierney 1996).

Thirteen states have supportive laws that require some degree of insurance coverage for infertility treatment: Arkansas, California, Connecticut, Hawaii, Illinois, Maryland, Massachusetts, Montana, New Jersey, New York, Ohio, Rhode Island, Texas. These laws generally require eligible clinics to meet professional standards. For example, New Jersey passed a law in 2001 requiring categories of insurers to cover "medically necessary expenses incurred in the diagnosis and treatment of infertility." Among the stipulations is one requiring that the services be provided at facilities that follow the standards of the ASRM or ACOG. The states have not been actively engaged in assessment activities.

FOOD AND DRUG ADMINISTRATION

The FDA is a relatively new participant in ART oversight. The Public Health Service Act and the Federal Food, Drug, and Cosmetic Act give the FDA the authority to oversee the development of drugs, devices, and biological products that fit into a relevant product category and are part of interstate commerce. The FDA ensures that enough evidence to assess safety and efficacy exists for clinical trials to begin and later for products to be released to the public for marketing. Until fairly recently, the FDA regarded ART as part of the practice of medicine, which was beyond FDA purview, but over time it has expanded its definition of biological products to include "more than minimally manipulated" embryos. The agency can also regulate human cellular and tissue-based products to prevent the spread of infectious disease, where these products are defined as "medical products derived from the human body and used for replacement, reproduction, or therapeutic purpose."

Innovation

An early indication that the FDA intended to assert discretionary judgment to oversee reproductive cells and tissues arose after the onset of animal cloning through SCNT. Facing concerns that scientists would attempt human reproductive SCNT, FDA officials sent a letter to members of Congress asserting the agency's authority to oversee clinical studies using cloning technology (Bonnicksen 2002, 109). Specifically, they announced that the FDA would allow clinical studies to proceed only with evidence from preclinical research that the technique was safe and effective. Because cloning had not been shown to be safe or very often successful with animals, the FDA would not be likely to allow an Investigational New Drug (IND) application to proceed, if one were submitted.

FDA officials later sent similar notices to IRB chairs asserting the agency's authority over "clinical research using cloning technology to create a human being" (Nightingale 1998). After human ES cells were isolated in 1998, officials submitted a memorandum to the National Bioethics Advisory Commission and testified before Congress that the agency's authority was broad enough to cover human clinical studies involving human cloning and human ES cells. According to the memorandum, "the definitions for somatic cell and gene therapies are sufficient to cover not only 'conventional' cell and gene therapy, but also human cloning and human embryonic pluripotent stem cells" (Bonnicksen 2002, 110).

Thus, the FDA used its discretionary judgment to broadly interpret somatic cell and gene therapies to include reproductive SCNT, therapeutic SCNT, ES cell therapies, and other forms of nuclear transfer. A cell subject to more than minimal manipulation and created to cure or treat a disease or condition was a biological product subject to the expectations related to an IND. Concerned about premature clinical use of innovative techniques, the

FDA in 2002 convened a public workshop designed in part to "assess the usefulness of animal models in evaluating the safety and efficacy of human ART" (U.S. DHHS, FDA 2002).

The FDA also has claimed authority over ooplasm transfer (OT), in which ooplasm from a donor egg is injected into the ooplasm of the egg of a woman whose embryos had previously failed to develop (Barritt et al. 2001). The agency notified researchers that it would require an IND before OT could be used with human patients, which in effect amounted to a clinical hold on the procedure (Zoon 2001). Researchers had been criticized for proceeding with OT before preliminary data had shown OT's safety and efficacy. Two fetuses conceived after OT were found in utero to have Turner syndrome. Although this chromosomal abnormality was not conclusively linked to OT, it evoked suspicion and underscored the importance of adequate preliminary work before introducing novel techniques to the clinical setting (Hawes, Sapienza, and Latham. 2002). Some clinicians also argued that the use of OT was premature because practitioners had not clarified which criteria were used to select patients for OT and because data had not established that OT was, in fact, responsible for the pregnancies that followed the procedure (Hawes, Sapienza, and Latham. 2002; Templeton 2002). On a different level, OT was criticized for introducing an inheritable genetic modification (mitochondrial DNA from the donor egg) without public deliberations (Frankel and Chapman 2001; Parens and Juengst 2001). The FDA's responses to SCNT and OT reveal FDA involvement in innovation, in which the agency uses its existing regulatory framework based on INDs to prevent what it regards as premature clinical use.

Clinical Practice

The FDA regulates medicine in general through its premarket oversight of drugs, biologicals, and medical devices. Regarding ARTs in particular, the FDA's Center for Biologics Evaluation and Research (CBER) proposed in the 1990s a "single regulatory program" for regulating cellular-and tissue-based products in order to prevent the spread of infectious diseases (U.S. DHHS, FDA 1997). The program relied on a tiered-risk approach. Assuming that products pose differing risks of communicating disease, the approach stipulated that the greater the risk, the greater the regulation. Tissues and cells that are more than minimally manipulated and that pose a higher risk are more extensively regulated than tissues and cells with lesser manipulation and posing a lower risk. Products that are less risky do not need premarket approval, although they must meet minimum standards for infectious disease testing and processing.

The first part of the new approach was introduced in 1998 and made final in 2001 (U.S. DHHS, FDA 2001). It requires manufacturers of human cellular and tissue-based products to register with CBER so that a database of the names, addresses, and products of manufacturers can be set up. The database lets officials inform manufacturers about policies and risks and to conduct inspections. The second part, introduced in 1999 and made final in 2005, requires testing of cell and tissue donors, including gamete and embryo donors, for communicable diseases when they contribute biological products for transfer or transplantation (U.S. DHHS, FDA 2005). The policy stipulates that egg donors will be screened for communicable diseases up to thirty days before the planned donation. Frozen embryos may be donated if it is shown that steps were taken, when possible, to test the couple before transferring the embryos to recipient couples. Recipients must be advised that the screening took place after the embryos were frozen. If no screening took place, the recipients must be told of this and of the possibility of infectious disease. This rule for the first time brings gametes and embryos under the agency's purview on the grounds that infectious disease can be spread by donating, processing, or storing reproductive cells and tissues.

The third stage, made final in 2004, requires manufacturers of human cellular-and tissue-based products to follow current good tissue practice, which includes handling, processing, storage, and labeling of the products. Surveying 330 ART facilities and 110 sperm banks in the country, the FDA concluded that 80 percent of ART facilities already conformed to these practices as a result of standards within the industry, accreditation programs, state licensing, and ASRM guidelines. The FDA does not enact assessment policies for ARTs, but certain postmarket studies of biologicals and other products can be used for this end.

PROFESSIONAL SOCIETIES

Professional societies and health care providers in the private sector have played a central role in ART oversight in the past twenty years. By tradition, physicians engage in self-regulation against the backdrop of the state licensing authority and malpractice concerns. Substantive decisions, especially those involving ethical acceptability of certain practices, have largely been the province of medical personnel. This is especially true for ARTs, where reproductive liberty and free scientific inquiry work against governmental restrictions. In addition, the absence of significant public health crises in ART practice leaves ART oversight for the most part outside the government's agenda. Of note is that professional societies, in particular the ASRM, have developed policy for all stages of ART development—innovation, practice, and assessment. The activities of the professional associations are an example of private sector self-regulation.

Innovation

An infertility treatment is regarded by the ASRM as experimental until scientific evidence indicates that the treatment yields a higher pregnancy rate than nontreatment. In addition, the safety and efficacy of the treatment must be corroborated by "at least two appropriately designed, peer-reviewed, published studies by different investigator groups" (ASRM 1993). Beyond this, however, professional associations, like governmental entities, have little specific guidance for when it is appropriate to try new technologies on human participants. Instead, oversight of innovative technologies has been informal, with primary attention given to guidance standards and quality control in the laboratories. In addition, it is important for patients in the consent process to be informed of the experimental status of the procedure.

Clinics affiliated with academic centers receiving federal funds have IRBs to review experimental procedures before they are used in patients. Clinics without these affiliations technically need not go through IRB review, although some do voluntarily. Others have their own IRBs or ethics boards. Although the independence of IRBs can be questioned when they review protocols developed in their own institutions, the system of IRB oversight is generally relied on in the research process to ensure that the consent process is open and informed. There are concerns, however, about whether couples intent on having a baby are truly aware of the experimental status of the technologies they see as treatments. Professional societies have addressed this issue in part by publishing guidelines about the essential elements of informed consent in ART procedures.

Clinical Practice

ASRM oversight of clinical practice covers three key areas: practice standards, laboratory certification and quality control, and ethics guidelines. The society published at least twenty-four practice standards between 1984 and 2001, which are available as guides for practitioners. Examples of practice standards include assisted hatching (2000), ICSI (2000), PGD (2001), and gamete and embryo donation (2002) (Adamson 2002, 936). Regarding laboratory oversight, the society oversees the inspection and accreditation of embryology laboratories in conjunction with the College of American Pathologists (CAP)/ASRM Reproductive Laboratory Accreditation Program. Under the auspices of this program, more than 200 infertility clinics had been accredited by 2003, and accreditation is now required for SART membership (Adamson 2002, 935). The program also validates IVF programs independently of the CDC and requires evaluation of programs with low success rates (Ory 2002). Other professional associations participating in oversight include the American Association of Tissue Banks, which accredits semen banks, and the American Board of Bioanalysis, which certifies ART laboratory personnel.

The ASRM Ethics Committee issues periodic reports relating to problematic ethical issues to its members and to the general community through the society's journal, *Fertility and Sterility,* and over the ASRM Web site. The society published reports on the ethical considerations of ARTs in 1988, 1990, and 1994. Beginning in 1997, it has produced individual Ethics Committee reports on topics that include informed consent for gametes and embryos for research (1997), sex selection and PGD (1999), human reproductive SCNT (2000), financial incentives for oocyte donors (2000), infertility treatment and HIV (2002), human ES cell research (2002), and fertility preservation in cancer patients (2005).

In another move aimed at oversight, in 1996 the ASRM formed the National Coalition for Oversight of Assisted Reproductive Technologies (NCOART) to identify issues in ARTs and to develop plans for addressing them. It consists of a core group (SART, ASRM, RESOLVE) and liaison groups (CDC, FDA, Federal Trade Commission). One purpose is to provide a forum for discussion of ART oversight.

Assessment

The ASRM has been actively involved in ART data collection for more than years. In 1988, SART published the first of what were to become annual reports on data voluntarily collected by infertility programs (SART and ASRM 2002, 918). After Congress passed the FCSRCA in 1992, which required the CDC to publish success rates from infertility programs, the CDC and SART collaborated to publish the first of these reports in 1995. The CDC also randomly selects clinics for data validation visits by members of the SART Validation Committee.

The 1999 report, published in *Fertility and Sterility* in 2002, reported data from virtually all (95 percent) of the 370 programs in the United States (SART 2002). Programs that did not respond were labeled "non-reporters" (Adamson 2002, 933). The reporting system collected data on the background characteristics, history, and diagnosis for patients and for the treatment and outcomes for all cycles initiated. Outcome data included numbers of cycle starts, cancellations, oocyte retrievals, embryo transfers, clinical pregnancies, pregnancy loss, total deliveries, deliveries per retrieval and per transfer, and ectopic pregnancies. In 1999, more than 63,000 IVF cycles were initiated using fresh embryos generated from the patients' own oocytes (variations led to a total of more than 88,000 initiations). From basic IVF (fresh, no donors), 22,000 deliveries resulted in the birth of nearly 31,000 infants, which was a delivery rate per embryo transfer of 31.6 percent. The overall delivery rate per transfer was 29.9 percent in 1998 and 30.3 percent in 1999, reflecting an increase over previous years as well.

The voluntary reporting plan of the CDC and SART gains strength through the idea that consumers will expect infertility programs they select to be members of SART. Virtually all U.S. IVF clinics are members of SART, and programs that do not report data face expulsion, which would lessen a program's legitimacy. SART guidelines require all members to report outcomes data to the CDC, allow laboratory inspections and run accredited embryology laboratories, and follow ethical and practice committee guidelines of ASRM. SART also requires the medical directors of new programs to be reproductive endocrinologists. It remains true, however, that some stand-alone clinics either are not members or do not report data following the SART model. In its 2004 report, the President's Council on Bioethics urged professional societies to institute more rigorous enforcement of their oversight policies. It also recommended federal funding for longitudinal studies of the impact of ARTs on the health and development of offspring and on the health of women.

SUMMARY AND CONCLUSIONS

Several observations can be made about the oversight of ARTs for the past twenty years. First, oversight has been decentralized, incremental, pluralistic, and shared by private and public decision makers. This pattern is not inconsistent with that of policy in general in the United States, where the balance of powers and federal system are designed to distribute rather than consolidate power. Change takes place gradually, across many access points, and divided among the legislative, executive, and judicial branches of government. Thus, the pattern of ART oversight is what might be expected for areas of emerging technologies. Because the health and safety of children are at issue, however, critics of this traditional approach contend that it is inadequate and that a more comprehensive oversight model is needed (Annas 1998; ISLAT Working Group 1998).

Second, some stages of oversight have received more attention and been subject to more guidance than others. The categories used to organize this chapter can be visualized as a table with twelve cells, in which four columns on the horizontal axis correspond with categories of decision makers (Congress, states, FDA, private associations) and the three rows on the vertical axis correspond with stages of ART practice and development (innovation, clinical practice, and assessment). As the preceding discussion has suggested, oversight is more focused on clinical practice and assessment than on innovation. Clinical practice is regulated along the same model as medicine in general, with licensing and other provisions in place to protect public health. Assessment receives considerable public attention because of concerns about ART safety and the potential exploitation of vulnerable patients. The combined public and private commitments to assessment, as reflected in the SART/CDC partnership, helps establish assessment as an important and legitimate goal.

Innovation is less clearly regulated, which in itself is not unusual, given the blurred transition between experimentation and practice for the practice of medicine in general, as when surgeons try new techniques without systematic experimental studies. What is unusual is the prohibition of government funding, which shifts the oversight of innovative procedures away from the public sector and into the less visible private sector. In addition, the lack of funding withholds legitimacy from the importance of preclinical research.

Third, some categories of decision makers are more involved than others. The federal government is not actively involved in ART development and practice. Although the FDA has taken a role in innovation, its role is limited, and its statutory authority to regulate innovative ARTs has been questioned. The state governments play an important role in medical licensing and quality control measures, but not for ART practice in particular. The professional sector takes a relatively active role across all stages, with most attention to practice, including ethics review and assessment.

The evaluation of today's decentralized and incremental policy is the sub-ject of numerous inquiries. It is easy to target this untidy framework, espe-cially when it is contrasted to the United Kingdom's comprehensive and well-functioning model administered by the Human Fertilisation and Embryology Authority (Parens and Knowles 2003). Yet if one compares the United States with other nations in which ARTs are practiced, it is evident that the United States is not alone in its inclination to private policy. When ART practitioners in thirty-eight nations were contacted in a cross-national survey, twenty responded that their nations did have a national statute setting forth a frame-work for ARTs (Jones and Cohen 1999). Over half, however, responded that they had no national legislation. Eleven nations, including the United States, relied on voluntary adherence to guidelines, and seven had neither framework nor guidelines. Even in nations without comprehensive laws, practitioners have incentives for following their profession's standards. The desire to be part of a rewarding and safe endeavor helping people to have children is a positive inducement. Negative inducements include the threat of lawsuits, sanctions by professional associations, and the desire to avoid governmental regulation through self-monitoring.

Discussions about the adequacy of existing policy benefit from an exami-nation of the outcomes of ART procedures over the past twenty or more years, namely the industry's efficacy and safety. While this is not the place for a detailed review of ongoing studies, it appears that ARTs are efficacious in that the key outcome, the take-home baby rate, has steadily improved for most fer-tility programs (Toner 2002), and new procedures have improved the success rates for specific groups of people. For example, ovum donation has signifi-cantly improved birth rates for women more than forty years old, and ICSI has had a major impact on conception in the face of male factor infertility.

Studies on safety point for the most part to the basic safety of assisted reproduction. One long-term study revealed "no detectable increases in health problems in the offspring born as a result of ART" (Leese and Whittall 2001, 173), and SART data showed a comparable rate of major birth defects (1.9 per-cent) between 134,985 infants conceived with ART between 1996 and 2000 and all infants born in Europe and North America (Steinkampf and Grifo 2002). Investigators in a study of 1,000 infants born following assisted repro-duction concluded, however, that these infants had lower birth weights than those conceived without assisted reproduction (Schieve et al. 2002). Members of SART countered that the study did not control for the nature of infertility, maternal age, or paternal age, all of which affect the incidence of anomalies

(Steinkampf and Grifo 2002). Other safety issues relate to multiple pregnancies as a risk factor for fetal and neonatal health (Lambert 2002).

Concerns have been raised about the safety of ICSI. It is known that chromosomal anomalies due to male factor infertility can be passed to male children through ICSI, but this outcome is not a major birth defect, and it is a known risk that ought to be conveyed to IVF patients in the consent process. Other concerns about ICSI's safety are still under investigation (see, e.g., Hansen et al. 2002).

Also of interest in the evaluation of ART oversight is the presence of forums for deliberating about what procedures should be offered to whom, when, and why. Such questions go beyond safety to encompass questions about the daily application of ART innovations. For example, what ethical issues arise when eggs from younger women are donated to older women, allowing even post-menopausal women to become pregnant? What issues arise when couples ask practitioners to transfer only female or only male embryos to them for reasons of preference rather than for medical reasons? What financial compensation is appropriate to acknowledge the risk, time, and inconvenience assumed by egg donors? Are practitioners obligated to provide ART assistance to families that appear dysfunctional or to couples or singles who have serious personal problems? What should be done with excess embryos (Hoffman et al. 2003)?

Over the past twenty years, questions of ethics have been raised by academics, ethicists, practitioners, policymakers, policy advisory groups, and others in conferences, workshops, publications, and in the ethics committees of professional societies. President Bill Clinton formed the National Bioethics Advisory Commission primarily to examine ways of protecting participants in human research. The commission issued several reports, including one on reproductive SCNT and another on ES cells, but its charter (initially three years, later extended) expired in 2001. President George W. Bush formed the President's Council on Bioethics in 2001, but it, too, is limited in the number of issues it can review. Thus, the identification of and deliberation about the ethics of ARTs is ad hoc and pluralist rather than systematic and centralized.

What are the implications of ART oversight history for future reprogenetic innovation and practice? The history of ART oversight suggests that the existing decentralized private-public framework, with its attention to autonomous reproductive choice, is firmly in place. The traditional framework may be troublesome if the federal government carries over its hostility to embryo research by refusing to consider issues related to inheritable genetic modifications. On the other hand, the framework is adaptable to policy mechanisms developed in response to advances in genetic medicine. Various policy advisory groups have contributed to advance thinking about potential policy change in response to genetic innovation, including the American Association for the Advancement of Science (2000) and the Genetics and Public Policy Center (2004, 2005).

Genetics policy reflects norms and traditions different from those of ART policy. With somatic cell gene therapies, for example, the government actively encouraged open research. With grants earmarked for studies of the ethical, legal, and social implications of the human genome project, it also encouraged public deliberation about ethical issues. Early in the history of recombinant DNA research, the NIH set up the Recombinant DNA Advisory Committee (RAC), which later served as a forum for exploring the societal, ethical, and clinical issues raised by somatic cell gene therapies.

Although oversight of genetic and reproductive therapies has taken separate paths to date, one might expect greater overlap in the future, as with PGD and other interventions involving genetic tests. For example, the DHHS oversees genetic tests through the CDC, FDA, Centers for Medicare and Medicaid Services, and Office for Human Research Protection, among other agencies (Adamson 2002, 934-35). If these tests relate to assisted reproduction, they open the door for new patterns of ART oversight. Still to be seen is the direction of influence for reprogenetics policy. On the one hand, private patterns of ART oversight may become more public if blended into genetics policies; on the other hand, public patterns of genetics oversight may become more private if blended into the ART model. Patterns of funding will provide direction: the more active the governmental funding, the more public and refined the oversight.

REFERENCES

Adamson, D. 2002. Regulation of assisted reproductive technologies in the United States. *Fertility and Sterility* 78:932–42.

Aldhous, P. 2005. After the Gold Rush. *Nature* 434:694–96.

American Association for the Advancement of Science. 2000. Human inheritable genetic modifications. Washington DC: AAAS.

American Society for Reproductive Medicine. 1993. Practice Committee Opinion. www.asrm.org/media/practice/opinion_experimental.html (accessed August 29, 2002).

Angergame, L., and J. S. Tierney. 1996. California enacts "Fertility Fraud" laws." *Fertility News* 30, no. 4: 24.

Annas, G. J. 1998. The shadowlands: Secrets, lies, and assisted reproduction. *New England Journal of Medicine* 339:935–39.

Barritt, J. A., C. A. Brenner, H. E. Malter, and J. Cohen. 2001. Mitochondria in human offspring derived from ooplasmic transplantation. *Human Reproduction* 16, no. 3: 513–16.

Bonnicksen, A. L. 2002. *Crafting a Cloning Policy: From Dolly to Stem Cells.* Washington, DC: Georgetown University Press.

California passes groundbreaking ES cell law. 2002. *Nature Biotechnology* 20:1073.

California Health and Safety Code, Section 125291.10-125291.85, California Stem Cell Research and Cures Bonds Act of 2004.

Ethics Advisory Board, Department of Health, Education, and Welfare. 1979. *Report and Conclusions: HEW Support of Research Involving Human In Vitro Fertilization and Embryo Transfer.* Washington, DC: U.S. Government Printing Office.

Frankel, M. W., and A. R. Chapman. 2001. Facing inheritable genetic modifications. *Science* 292:1303.

Garcia, J. E. 1998. Profiling assisted reproductive technology: The Society for Assisted Reproductive Technology Registry and the rising costs of assisted reproductive technology. *Fertility and Sterility* 69:624–26.

Genetics and Public Policy Center. 2004. *Reproductive Genetic Testing: Issues and Options for Policymakers.* Washington, DC: Genetics and Public Policy Center.

———. 2005. *Human Germline Genetic Modifications: Issues and Options for Policymakers.* Washington, DC: Genetics and Public Policy Center.

Gianelli, D. M. 1994. Embryo research approved—with a catch. *American Medical News* 37:3.

Hansen, M., J. J. Kurinczuk, C. Bower, and S. Wess. 2002. The risk of major birth defects after intracytoplasmic sperm injection and in vitro fertilization. *New England Journal of Medicine* 346:725–30.

Hawes, S. M., C. Sapienza, and K. E. Latham. 2002. Ooplasmic donation in humans: The potential for epigenic modifications. *Human Reproduction* 17:850–52.

Hoffman, D. I., G. L. Zellman, C. C. Fair, J. F. Mayer, J. G. Zeitz, W. E. Gibbons, et al. 2003. Cryopreserved embryos in the United States and their availability for research. *Fertility and Sterility* 79:1063–69.

Holden, C. 2002. California flashes a green light. *Science* 297:2185.

ISLAT Working Group. 1998. ART into science: Regulation of fertility techniques. *Science* 281:651-53.

Jones, H. W., Jr., and J. Cohen, eds. 1999. IFFS Surveillance 98. *Fertility and Sterility* 71, no. 5: Suppl. 2.

Kocieniewski, D. 2004. McGreevey signs bill creating stem cell research institute. *New York Times*, May 13, A23.

Lambert, R. D. 2002. Safety issues in assisted reproduction technology. *Human Reproduction* 17: 3011–15.

Leese, H. J., and H. Whittall. 2001. Regulation of the transition from research to clinical practice in human assisted conception. *Human Fertility* 4:172–76.

Nightingale, S. L. 1998. [Associate Commissioner for Health Affairs, Public Health Service, Food and Drug Administration, Department of Health and Human Services]

Letter to institutional review board chairs, October 28. Photocopy. Andrea Bonnicksen, private collection, DeKalb, IL.

Ory, S. J. 2002. The practitioners' perspective. Comments at Workshop on Evidence Based Assisted Reproductive Technologies (ART). Bethesda, MD: National Institutes of Health. September 18.

Powell, K.. 2003. Seeds of doubt. *Nature* 442:6933.

Parens, E., and E. Juengst. 2001. Inadvertently crossing the germ line. *Science* 292:397.

Parens, E., and L. P. Knowles. 2003. Reprogenetics and public policy: Reflections and recommendations. *Hastings Center Report* 33:S1–S24.

President's Council on Bioethics. 2004. *Reproduction and Responsibility: The Regulation of New Biotechnologies.* Washington, DC. www.bioethics.gov.

Schieve, L. A., S. F. Meikle, C. Ferre, H. B. Peterson, G. Jeng, and L. S. Wilcox. 2002. Low and very low birth weight in infants conceived with use of assisted reproductive technology. *New England Journal of Medicine* 346:731–37.

Society for Assisted Reproductive Technology and the American Society for Reproductive Medicine. 2002. Assisted reproductive technology in the United States: 1999 results generated from the American Society for Reproductive Medicine/Society for Assisted Reproductive Technology Registry. *Fertility and Sterility* 78:918–31.

Steinkampf, M. P., and J. Grifo. 2002. Major birth defects after assisted reproduction. Letter to editor. *New England Journal of Medicine* 347:1449.

Stolberg, Sheryl Gay. 1997. U.S. publishes first guide to treatment of infertility. *New York Times,* December 19, A14.

Tasca, R. J. 2002. Methods of supporting research in this area. Comments at Workshop on Evidence Based Assisted Reproductive Technologies (ART). Bethesda, MD: National Institutes of Health. September 18.

Templeton, A. 2002. Ooplasmic transfer: Proceed with care. *New England Journal of Medicine* 346:773–75.

Toner, J. 2002. Progress we can be proud of: U.S. trends in assisted reproduction over the first twenty years. *Fertility and Sterility* 78:943–50.

U.S. Department of Health and Human Services. 1988. Ethics Advisory Board; Notice of establishment. *Federal Register* 53:35232–33.

U.S. Department of Health and Human Services. Food and Drug Administration. 1997. A proposed approach to the regulation of cellular and tissue-based products. *Federal Register* 62, no. 42: 9721–22.

———. 2001. Human cells, tissues and cellular and tissue-based products: Establishment registration and listing. Final rule. *Federal Register* 66, no. 13: 5447–69.

———. 2004. Current good tissue practice for human cell, tissue, and cellular and tissue-based product establishments: Inspection and enforcement. Final rule. *Federal Register* 69:68612.

———. 2005. Human cells, tissues, and cellular and tissue-based products: Donor screening and testing, and related labeling. *Federal Register* 70, no. 100: 29949–52.

U.S. Department of Health and Human Services. Food and Drug Administration. Center for Biologics Evaluation and Research. 2002. Evidence based assisted reproductive technologies (ART): Public workshop. *Federal Register* 67:46196.

U.S. Department of Health and Human Services. National Institutes of Health. 1994. *Final Report of the Human Embryo Research Panel.* Bethesda, MD: National Institutes of Health.

Weiss, R. 2002. New status for embryos in research. *Washington Post,* October 30, A1.

Zoon, K. C. 2001. *Letter to Sponsors / Researchers. Human Cells Used in Therapy Involving the Transfer of Genetic Material By Means Other Than the Union of Gamete Nuclei.* www.fda.gov/cber/ltr/cytotrans070601.htm.

PART TWO

Ethical Issues in Reprogenetics

CHAPTER FOUR

Market Transactions in Reprogenetics

A Case for Regulation

SUZANNE HOLLAND

In a nation as pluralistic as the United States, establishing a case for the regulation of reprogenetic technologies is no easy task. Nonetheless, I argue here (as I have elsewhere; see Holland 2001a, 2001b) not for outlawing market transactions in reprogenetics but for regulating them in accordance with what I believe are shared, if often subterranean, commitments to the notion of a good society. While I do not mean to imply that most Americans are closet Aristotelians, I do maintain that if you ask the "average American" what his or her ideal is of a good society, you will get something like an Aristotelian rendering: a society that promotes decency, a sense of the good, the virtuous; one that treats its citizens humanely and justly, and one in which all citizens can flourish equally, to the best of their capacities. In a sense, this is what we mean when we profess liberty, justice, and equality.

A good society posits some notion of the "good life," and for the purposes of this chapter, it is my contention that whatever else the good life means, it will not be fostered by extending the reaches of the laissez-faire market to technologies that intimately affect reproduction and future generations. Nor can the good life mean extending a doctrine of personal autonomy, uncritically, to the uses of such reprogenetic technologies that have far-reaching social implications. It is rather through public dialogue about regulation that we can best safeguard freedom of choice, economically and personally. Freedom of choice is itself a contextual right, tied to a larger sense of social flourishing, as I will proceed to show.

A CENTRAL QUESTION AND THREE OBSERVATIONS

To make the case for regulation, I pose a central question, out of which emerge three sets of observations. What does it mean for society to commercialize, and not to regulate, the technologies of reproduction and genetics? My first observation is that most of us would find ourselves at a loss in approaching an answer, because most Americans do not have access to information by which we can comprehend these technologies and their implications. This problem has deep and longlasting consequences for a democratic society and is one that the average education has not prepared us to approach. Hence, most U.S. Americans, including, of course, most lawmakers, do not know how to navigate their way around issues like somatic cell nuclear transfer, embryonic stem cells, oocyte transplantation, genetic modifications of the germline, and preimplantation genetic diagnosis, to list only a few of the dizzying technologies of the emerging field of reprogenetics.[1] And most do not know that reprogenetics is a burgeoning growth industry, estimated at $2–$4 billion annually,[2] and an integral part of our complex health care economy.

Second, I observe that when you call Americans' attention to it, they tend to express an aversion to, or at least a hesitation about, commercializing anything to do with reproduction, children, and families. For example, the rhetoric we use to speak of reproduction, family, and children is quite distinct from the rhetoric we use to describe the products of the marketplace. Our experience of children—having them, raising them, loving them—is connected to a deep sense of respect for the human person and the sense that such experiences are priceless beyond commodities. We do not speak of our children and the families we love in the language of property, and most of us would be offended to read, for example, economist Gary Becker's analysis of why people have children in the first place. He writes, "The demand for children would depend on the relative price of children and full income. An increase in the relative price of children . . . reduces the demand for children and increases the demand for other commodities (if real income is held constant)" (quoted in Radin 1996, 7). The average person simply finds it distasteful to conceive of children in terms of market transactions and as fungible with other "commodities," as Becker does. Yet in a sense, children have become part of the marketplace of goods. Even adoptions are bought and paid for, as are all of the technologies of reproduction. Indeed, the field of reprogenetics augurs a heretofore unimagined marketplace for offspring.

My third observation is that middle-class Americans, whether conservative or liberal, are not so very different on two fundamental issues: both embrace individual rights and negative liberty,[3] and both are wary of government intrusion into our lives. Sociologist Alan Wolfe's landmark study of the 1990s demonstrated that the great American middle class was not involved in a culture war at all, and in fact shared more commonalities than differences on cultural values (Wolfe 1998). Interestingly, exit polling data from the 2004 elections showed that the majority of Americans (across party lines) identified "moral values" as being of primary concern to them in casting their presidential votes, which tends to support Wolfe's earlier findings. Classically, of course, the distinction between liberals and conservatives is that liberals fear government intrusion into the realm of privacy (the home, personal liberties, sexual expression), while conservatives fear not so much intrusion into personal privacy as governmental interference with business, the economy, and the private sector in general. In short, both mistrust government, but for different reasons.

Insofar as government makes laws that appear to uphold "family values," conservatives can seem quite sanguine about government regulation. Examples of this include the Federal Defense of Marriage Act, signed into law by President Clinton, the Bush administration's policy of extending health care benefits to unborn fetuses (but not prenatal care to pregnant, poor women), the curtailing of federal funding for population control and family planning efforts at the United Nations, support for the Faith-Based Initiative Program, and so on. We might say that American conservatives actually have a "pro-choice" position: they advocate for market choice for consumers and economic freedom for business. It is axiomatic to free-market conservatives that the American laissez-faire market is a cornerstone of democracy itself. As Margaret Jane Radin puts it, "For one who is willing to conceive of everything (corneas for transplant, sexuality, babies for adoption) in market rhetoric, the only explanation for why some things might be held out of the market is market failure" (1996, 7).

The cornerstone of democracy for American liberals, however, is expressed differently: preservation of personal freedoms. Their pro-choice issue is, of course, reproductive freedom for women. In general, liberals want their government to take a laissez-faire approach to the realm of personal morality, which includes sexual mores as well as personal privacy issues. For example, liberals may not approve of homosexuality any more than conservatives do (Wolfe's study shows that they do not), but it is a bedrock issue for them that government not attempt to legislate behavior that liberals regard as liberty of choice. On this view personal and civil liberties are sacred choices, and it is the duty of government to protect these freedoms by not interfering in them. I do not think that liberals really want governmental regulation of the free market any more than conservatives do, but they will support regulation where it appears to protect the personal freedoms they value. (That is why liberals tend to want governmental regulation of the environment, of food processing, of pharmaceuticals, and so on.)

It is ironic that in the realm of reprogenetics, neither liberals nor conservatives appear to be aware that the regulation they fear is actually likely to protect the values that each champions—family values mores for conservatives and reproductive autonomy for liberals. The further irony is that for each group to get what it values, it must be prepared to move slightly away from its ideological center. Liberals will have to cede some territory on the hallowed ground of reproductive autonomy, while conservatives will have to accept some amount of market regulation. Unless each does this, they risk further erosion of the fundamental values each claims to hold so dear (family values, freedom of choice), as my analysis of reprogenetics will attest.

REPROGENETICS AS A RIGHT?

It has been argued that Americans have a fundamental right to bear children (Roberston 1994); thus the use of technological means to do so would be, in this view, fully in accord with that right.[4] Whether or not one agrees with the argument concerning procreative liberty, it might be useful to look at the logic behind it: The right to procreate has historical precedent and therefore ought to be preserved as a legitimate aim for individuals in this society who are desirous of that end. In other words, because the end is legitimate, historically, the means are also legitimate. Is it therefore appropriate that society should uphold whatever means are at its disposal to reach that desired end? Strictly as a matter of logic, we would have to answer in the affirmative, so long as the means employed do not involve harm or undue burden to others.

This is where each ideological position (liberal or conservative) becomes self-contradictory. What if the means employed involve the destruction of embryos, which conservatives (and many other Americans) view as the moral equivalent of human beings? Unquestionably, a consequence of the techniques of assisted reproduction is the destruction of embryos—whether through the creation of them in excess for implantation or through the freezing and thawing of them for disposal. What if the means employed involved a technique that called into question the very meaning of family? This is already the case, of course, with the use of sperm and egg donors, whose genetic material adds another genetic parent to any child conceived from someone else's gametes. Thus one would expect to see conservatives en masse objecting to in vitro fertilization (IVF) altogether, since it employs means that alter the nature of the family and destroys embryos in the process. But such protests are rare. Neither do we hear objections from liberals, but they are silent for different reasons: these technologies heighten reproductive choice. Let us push the point a bit further by probing a specific application of reprogenetic technology.

REPROGENETIC CHALLENGES

Today we have a dizzying array of technologies that make it possible for an infertile couple to conceive a child, and all are commodified: intracytoplasmic sperm injection (ICSI), preimplantation genetic diagnosis (PGD), and IVF and its variants gamete intrafallopian transfer (GIFT) and zygote intrafallopian transfer (ZIFT), to cite a few. Historically, IVF was the first of these technologies, and that is how the so-called test-tube baby ("Baby Louise") was conceived in 1978. Nearly thirty years ago, the world was aghast at the thought of such an "unnatural" means of conception; today, many of us know children who have been conceived using assisted reproduction and most of us do not find anything particularly unnatural, freakish, or morally reprehensible about that. In fact, estimates are that in 1999, some kind of assisted reproduction was responsible for one out of every 150 children born in the United States; worldwide, one million children have been conceived through assisted reproductive technologies (ARTs) since Baby Louise (Schultz and Williams 2002, 2188). What we ought to be aghast at instead is the lack of oversight for these new technologies of reproduction.

Amazingly, science is progressing so rapidly that as you read this chapter, the technologies I am describing may have already been eclipsed by something new. That is part of the point: new technologies are moving from the research bench to the marketplace of assisted reproduction clinics with a rapidity that is both exciting and frightening, because there are no regulatory bright lines in the United States. Even in Britain, where reprogrenetics is regulated, fertility expert Lord Robert Winston has critiqued the fertility industry for its inadequate testing before commercial use, saying, "Many of these things have not been tested properly using animal models, or more importantly, using spare embryos." According to *BBC News*, Winston "blamed the commercial focus of many IVF clinics for the lack of funding for IVF research outside humans," and said "If you are using treatments that might damage somebody—such as an unborn child—then you have a duty to tell people" (*BBC News* 2003). Winston raises a key issue: for the better part of the last fifteen years, developments in science (genetics and cell biology in particular) have outstripped our capacity as a society to know how to think about them ethically. Yet think about them ethically we must. In the new field of reprogenetics, we have both an opportunity and an obligation to consider the ethical implications of what lies before us—perhaps while it is still possible to set directions that could make a positive contribution to our collective futures. Enter oocyte transplantation.

The arrival of reprogenetics has brought with it, among other scientific wonders, a technology known as oocyte transplantation. As the name implies, the procedure entails transplantation of the cytoplasm and some of the mitochondria of a donor's egg cell into the egg of an otherwise infertile woman. The egg is then fertilized in vitro, where it retains the DNA of the mother-to-be and allows her to become pregnant using the cytoplasm from another woman. In this case, the goal is to make it possible for a woman who wishes to conceive, and whose eggs are either too old or damaged, to conceive by using eggs from a younger woman. A consequence of this procedure is that it introduces three genetic parents into the offspring's genes, which now have mitochondrial DNA from the ooplasm donor, the DNA of the mother, and the DNA of the father. The risks of this procedure, as with many reprogenetic technologies, are unknown (as of this writing, ooplasm transfer has not been subjected to long-term clinical trials), although there is the risk that activation of abnormal oocytes could lead to abnormal embryos. An associated condition would be aneuploidy; this condition of having too few or too many chromosome numbers results in a variety of diseases from Down syndrome to Turner syndrome.

Surprisingly, however, there is no history of regulated clinical trials of oocyte transplantation because assisted reproduction clinics in the United States are not federally regulated and thus have not been subject to the same kinds of standards that the Food and Drug Administration (FDA) applies to other industries that affect consumer health and safety, including pharmaceuticals and many types of genetic tests.[5] The issue of regulation over the reprogenetics industry was considered by the Genetics and Public Policy

Center at Johns Hopkins University. A recent report from the center concluded that

> Without new authority from Congress, it could be difficult for FDA to assert jurisdiction over IVF and PGD. The agency's only option might be to argue that an embryo created by IVF meets its existing definition of a biological "product" and a laboratory test used to test the embryo's DNA constitutes a "medical device," since it will be used to treat or prevent a medical condition (e.g., infertility, genetic disease). Some are skeptical that FDA could lawfully extend existing authority to cover PGD and others are simply offended by the notion of calling an embryo a "product. (Genetics and Public Policy Center 2004)

Such a view highlights the difficulties in the American regulatory schema and the ambivalences Americans have toward these technologies.

An issue related to ooplasmic transfer is alteration of the germline. Because the children born of this process carry the genes of three distinct individuals, any resulting genetic modification could be passed along to future generations. As of 2001, thirty babies had been born worldwide using this reprogenetic technique, and although early reports are that the children are normal and healthy, the long-term effects of such a technique cannot be known (Barritt et al. 2001). In the United States, the FDA responded by declaring oocyte transfer to be a form of gene therapy (over which it does have control), though whether or not such protocols are acceptable is a matter of debate (Zoon 2001). (It should be noted, however, that the purview of the FDA is the safety and efficacy of "products"; ethical ramifications are outside its scope.) Altering the germline is illegal in many countries, including Britain, and although it is not expressly outlawed in the United States, federal funding is precluded for germline alteration. Private funders, however, are not precluded from this or any such research, and this takes us back to the problem of the unregulated and commodified nature of the assisted reproduction industry in the United States, which has the potential to undermine both liberal and conservative values.

IS THE ALLOWABLE NECESSARILY ETHICAL?

Should Americans, liberal or conservative, be concerned about the fact that scores of children have already been born who possess the DNA of three distinct individuals? Does such a thing alter the nature of the traditional family? Is it acceptable to pursue such a form of reprogenetic technology because of a perceived right to procreate? Are individual liberties sacred in themselves, or are there other ends of society that ought to be considered? In the United States, that which is not expressly forbidden by law is allowable—but of course, the allowable is not necessarily ethical, as the following scenarios illustrate.

The liberal's worst nightmare might be the kind of portrait painted by novelist Margaret Atwood in *The Handmaid's Tale*—a society in which some women were used as breeders for upper-class infertile women, whose husbands impregnated the surrogates in a bizarre ritual involving the man and both women. In neither case do women have any real choice or personal liberty about reproductive issues and their bodies, and the end result is that some women are reproductively exploited for the "benefit" of other women. While Atwood's tale is pure fiction, its real-life parallel might be the unregulated use of egg donors or surrogates to fulfill the reproductive "needs" of some couples who can afford to have genetically related children in the unregulated marketplace of ARTs.

The conservative's worst nightmare, on the other hand, might be one in which fertility clinics harvested embryos, destroyed those that were not viable, and performed genetic alterations on those that were viable to create desirable children for parents who wanted to pay for them. That there are 400,000 embryos in storage in U.S. clinics does lend some bit of credence to this scenario (Weiss 2003).

Consider a different scenario in which a group of entrepreneurs opens a series of financially profitable fertility clinics. The clinics are successful at helping couples to become pregnant using a variety of reprogenetic technologies that increase the likelihood not just of pregnancy but also of desirable children—a noteworthy distinction between older forms of IVF and reprogenetics. The former simply meant using technology to conceive a child, while reprogenetics means opening the door to choosing the *kind* of child you want to have (Parens and Knowles 2003). In any case, these fertility clinics in our scenario attract investors, and before long a public stock offering is made, allowing the initial investors to reap a great return on investment and the public to trade in a successful business. Helping couples conceive children is a socially constructive business endeavor that also happens to be lucrative. The fact that it is a largely unregulated industry would likely be appealing to conservative economic libertarians. Liberal investors might find it attractive as well; arguably such an industry offers women unprecedented reproductive choices.

None of these scenarios, however fantastic in narration, would be illegal in the United States today, and thus each of them is theoretically permissible. I do not really believe that liberals, in seeking to preserve reproductive choice and personal liberties, actually intend to support technologies that lead to the commercialization (and hence possible exploitation) of reproduction itself. Nor am I persuaded that most conservatives, in seeking to preserve market efficiency, intend to bring about a system in which reproduction and its processes are for sale to potential parents as well as to potential investors. Surely neither group intends to support technologies in which paying for the kinds of children we will have becomes a normative practice. Erik Baard's interview with a Manhattan father illustrates my point:

> The trade-offs and ethical conundrums are enough to tie an anti-quota Republican parent like Steve Sanford in knots. He's a successful commercial artist and credits genetics for much of his ability . . . His daughter, Emily, recently won admission to two prestigious New York City institutions . . . But what if she couldn't get into Harvard because its ranks were filling with the offspring of parents who could afford million-dollar enhancements?
>
> "I'd say that's not fair—it's like being able to buy your way out of conscription in the Civil War," her father says. "There could be riots, I think. Things could get out of control." Then again, if he were having a new child in an era when designer babies were common, he'd opt for enhancement if he knew it was safe and a competitive necessity. (Baard 2003)

In the world of reprogenetics, Steve Sanford's hypothetical moral quandary could cease to be hypothetical. I use this interview to illustrate that few people (even anti-quota Republicans!) have an intention to participate in the commodification of our children and their futures. Intentional or not, however, we may end up becoming complicit in perpetuating normative assumptions that we instead ought to call into question, and perhaps mean to call into question, if we understood them. What are those assumptions? A list might include the following: that an unregulated market in a democracy is some kind of good in itself; that all commercial transactions belong in the laissez-faire market; that technologies of reproduction and genetic manipulation (reprogenetics) are morally equivalent to other technologies; that having a genetically related child is an unquestioned right; that it is appropriate to commodify reproduction. Are these assumptions that we mean to support? The absence of a movement to regulate (let alone public conversation about regulation) is a de facto indication of societal agreement with the current structural arrangement.

QUESTIONING NORMS

When market norms that celebrate lack of regulation as an inherent good are applied to the realm of technologies that are used to produce offspring, I argue that the application (and perhaps the content) of such norms is morally suspect. In other words, the laissez-faire market is perhaps neither good nor bad in itself, but when it is applied wholesale to technologies that are not equivalent to silicon chips or automobiles *because* of their connection to human reproduction, then we must question the assumptions behind that application. And if we do not question the assumptions, we are tacitly supporting their perpetuation, a perpetuation that itself supports a false moral dichotomy: withholding federal funding from morally objectionable enterprises somehow absolves the public from moral complicity. This is a false dichotomy that ought not receive further legitimation from the federal government and its taxpayers. Indeed, it is the unquestioned legitimation of market norms that makes us cooperative with an unjust set of normative assumptions—unjust because they entail favoring some over others, particularly Caucasians with enough discretionary income to purchase competitive genetic advantages for their children, just as they purchase other advantages (prestigious preschool admissions, for instance).

While there is no denying the great pluralism that exists in the United States in this era of postmodern thought, the problem of ethical inconsistency I have outlined must be solved on the basis of shared values or it will not be solved at all. Thus, the neo-Aristotelian values I referred to at the outset of this chapter and that I maintain have a subterranean place in American middle-class morality might themselves be the grounding of a positive solution For if we do share common assumptions about the good society and human flourishing (even if we restrict the application of those values to reprogenetics and commodification), then a case can be made for regulation on the basis of this appeal.

A CASE FOR REGULATION

How, then, might we begin to regulate the legally allowable but ethically problematic technologies of reprogenetics? Though it might be tempting to do so, there are a variety of reasons why we cannot simply turn everything over to the FDA, perhaps the most important of which is that its purview is limited to safety and efficacy. Safety and efficacy are necessary but not sufficient criteria for technologies of reproduction precisely because reproduction gets at the larger ethical issue of well-being and human flourishing. We need to create a regulatory policy for this field on the basis of the social good, and not on the basis of private profit. In their article on genetic testing and PGD, Hudson and colleagues (2005) identified five basic approaches to regulation approaches, ranging from banning PGD at all levels to federal control, state control, or nongovernmental approaches, all of which should stimulate discussion about the regulation of the reprogenetics industry as a whole. It is my view that public policy that allows the maximization of private profit in this arena runs two risks: seeing our children as commodities that can be enhanced and built to suit, and seeing our children as mechanistic means in the perpetuation of unjust norms: private profit and individual liberties at the expense of the common good, genetic values over larger bonding values, standardized norms of appearance and intelligence, and so on (Parens and Knowles 2003).

Regulation of reprogenetic technologies is a *public* policy issue, and as such, it needs to be guided by normative principles that reflect a balance of American concerns for equality, justice, and liberty. In the current market of assisted reproduction, a market that is entirely privatized, the normative principles that undergird this industry are the principles of the unregulated market and personal liberty, not those of social justice. This is evidenced by the fact that only those who can afford the market prices for these technologies are able to use them to have a genetically related child; the rest of us who might need assisted reproduction must be content with adoption or infertility. It is interesting to think about the fact that many people who can afford it prefer to conceive through the use of assisted reproduction rather than risk adopting a child with an unknown genetic heritage that might later become problematic. We might call this the "damaged goods" fear of adoption: we simply can't know about the health, intelligence, and traits of the parents who put a child up for adoption. Yet it is ironic that reprogenetics carries with it very much the same kinds of risks. We do not know the long-term health effects of the children who have been conceived using reprogenetic technologies; we do not even know the long-term health effects of children conceived using some of the more "conventional" forms of assisted reproduction because the industry is not regulated and such studies are not mandated. This raises questions (which I will not answer here) of whether childbearing and the genetic tie is an appropriate model for the good life, whether it is good *in se*, and whether it is the only worthy conception of the good life.

In any case, under the current system of privatized reprogenetics, the American value of personal liberty appears to have trumped the equally important values of equality and justice. I submit, however, that when we are dealing with the issue of progeny we cannot sublimate equality and justice to personal liberty and the private sector. To do so reflects a priority for commodification and risks conflating progeny with property, something I do not think we really want to do (see also Knowles 1999). On the other hand, if commercializing assisted reproduction can be seen as promoting human flourishing then from a social ethics point of view, it must be offered equitably to all in society who need it. In other words, if it can be shown that having a genetically related (and perhaps enhanced) child via reprogenetics adds to the sum total of human flourishing, then public policy must make it publicly available. If, however, it merely increases competitive advantage, then it reflects market values, and, as I have said, market values are inappropriate as the primary guides for public policy on technologies of reproduction.

We could, of course, decide not to have a public policy in this arena, which is really the current state of affairs in the United States. Lack of a thoughtful public policy is the consequence of the ethically incoherent principle that says we should not give public funding to technologies that deal with embryos. It is ethically incoherent because it does not keep people in the private sector from doing research on embryos or creating embryos for any purpose whatsoever. On the contrary, it simply keeps public monies away from embryo research and thus drives all the research and the products from it into the private and unregulated sector for the benefit of some—though not most—persons. This may be the result we are after, but I think that if Americans had a chance to weigh in on the matter after being fully informed, this is not the public policy they would choose.

LEARNING FROM CANADA AND BRITAIN

The regulatory schema I propose for reprogenetic technologies is one in which we take a page from our Canadian and British cousins—but only a page, for the policy must fit the U.S. situation. The page I would take is the establishment of a new and centralized regulatory body that would not be dependent on annual congressional or presidential approval so that it could withstand the vicissitudes of electoral politics, provide consistent and long-term oversight, and adapt to technological developments. It would need to be created by an act of Congress, but membership should be selected neither by Congress nor by the president. Both the Assisted Human Reproduction Agency of Canada (AHRAC) and the British Human Fertilisation and Embryology Authority (HFEA) are quasi-governmental entities, and both are comprised of an interdisciplinary group of experts as well as laypersons. The HFEA is structured as a body "in an arm's-length relationship to the government that is housed outside the Department of Health yet is accountable to the Secretary of State" (Parens and Knowles 2003).

While Canada has taken a "blocked exchange" approach to payments for certain forms of assisted reproduction (it bans commerce in reproductive tissues and surrogacy),[6] I do not favor categorically removing all ARTs from the market. Instead, I advocate regulation that would "incompletely commodify" this industry in the United States. Incomplete commodification is a theory advanced by Stanford law professor Margaret Jane Radin that seeks a middle ground between taking something off the market entirely (a blocked exchange) and allowing all things to be commodified (complete commodification) (Radin 1996). In the U.S. context, which is so thoroughly grounded in the free market, I think it would be wiser to place modest capitations on charges and payments for reprogenetic technologies, for example, than to eliminate the industry altogether. This might be part of the charter of the central regulatory body.

It is critical that neither Congress nor the president tie the hands of this new regulatory body because it will be developing and acting from expertise that we cannot expect members of Congress or the president to have. In fact, it seems to me that part of the reason we have such a problematic situation on our hands with respect to regulating reprogenetics is precisely because we have been looking both to Congress and the president to set policies in an area where neither has the expertise to do so. The present system subjects specialized science and ethics to political pandering, special interests, and regulation by those who know least about it. To continue down this path is by any standard as foolish as it is dangerous. Further, it no longer makes any sense to maintain an outright ban on federal funding for embryo research because it goes on regardless in the private sector, as we have seen. As Parens and Knowles have put it, "If we do not forthrightly acknowledge that fact by allowing the federal government to oversee research and practice involving embryos, then the market will be the only mechanism that will distinguish between the acceptable and unacceptable purposes of those activities" (Parens and Knowles 2003, S18). In the United States today, we have been given more than enough reasons to conclude that we ought not leave it to the market to determine the ethics of its activities. Since others have articulated a well-developed set of recommendations for the kind of regulatory body I am proposing, I will spare the reader a reinvention of the proverbial wheel here (see Parens and Knowles 2003; Genetics and Public Policy Center 2004).

CONCLUSION

At the outset of this chapter I made three observations: (1) that most U.S. Americans, including congresspersons, do not know how to approach thinking through the ethics of technologies of reprogenetics because most Americans do not have access to comprehensible information on the subject; (2) that Americans tend to have an aversion to the commercialization of anything to do with reproduction, children, and families, and that inferences to some kind of shared commitments to human flourishing may be drawn from this; and (3) that both conservatives and liberals embrace negative liberty and governmental noninterference, but for different reasons, and that each needs to move off its ideological center and toward its antithesis so as to preserve the very things each claims to value.

With respect to the first observation, I conclude that we need an independent regulatory body, as discussed. With respect to the second observation, I conclude that people in the United States would indeed favor such a body if they knew the realities of the commodification of reproduction. In fact, they may find such a body desirable simply because there would be a group of people with the appropriate expertise to guide sensible policy in this complex and confusing area. With respect to number three, I conclude that conservatives and liberals will have an incentive to move off their respective ideological dimes to demand as an aggregate the kind of central regulation that will clearly cohere with the ideological impulses of each. By this I mean that conservatives are likely to favor an independent regulatory body insofar as it becomes clear that such an entity will be more likely to promote the kind of "family values" commitments conservatives hold dear than will simply leaving reprogenetics to the unregulated private sector. Liberals will likely favor an independent regulatory body because it is the best means of removing debates about choice from the halls of Congress and ensuring equality of access. Thus, liberals would be more likely to realize the preservation of reproductive autonomy with a regulatory body of experts than by leaving it to the ideological pandering of partisan politics. And finally, I have maintained throughout this chapter that middle-class Americans, liberal and conservative, share subterranean commitments to values that can provide the content for social flourishing and well-being—equality, justice, and liberty—though it is the *balance* of these core values that we will want to see reflected in public policy on reprogenetics. We should insist on it.

NOTES

1. Reprogenetics is defined as the practical confluence and application of genetic technologies and reproductive technologies, an emerging field of its own.

2. It is difficult to get a precise figure for this. In 1997, *US News* called it a "rapidly expanding $4 billion industry" (Leo 1997), and in 1998, a columnist in *Science* cited $2 billion for the ART industry ("Art into science"). One conservative measure of annual expenditures can be obtained by calculating the number of ART treatment cycles performed in one year (88,000 in 1999 and 100,000 in 2000) and multiplying this by the average cost per cycle, $10,000 (though some couples report having spent $20,000 per cycle). This would mean that almost one million dollars was spent in one year by couples using assisted reproduction. This appears to be a conservative estimate: "According to the 1999-2000 *Dorland Biomedical Healthcare Marketplace Guide*, the annual expenditures relating to fertility services are approximately $2 billion" (Integramed America, 2003). See also Weiss 2003 and ASRM/SART 2002.

3. By negative liberty I mean the right to freedom from interference in one's personal liberties, but not the corresponding sense of positive obligations.

4. Even Robertson, however, draws boundaries around this right (*Children of Choice*, 41).

5. We may see a slight change in the direction of regulation. In 2002, the FDA determined that "a small clinical trial" for oocyte transplantation could go forward under its Investigational New Drug protocol (BRMAC 2002).

6. Assisted Human Reproduction Act (AHRA), Bill C-13, House of Commons, Canada. First Session, Thirty-seventh Parliament, 2002.

REFERENCES

American Society for Reproductive Medicine and Society for Assisted Reproductive Technology (ASRM/SART). 2002. Assisted reproductive technology in the United States: 1999 results generated from the American Society for Reproductive Medicine/Society for Assisted Reproductive Technology Registry. *Fertility and Sterility* 78, no.5: 918–31.

Atwood, M, E. 1986. *The Handmaid's Tale* Boston: Houghton Mifflin.

Baard, E. 2003. Supertots and Frankenkids. *The Village Voice*, April 23–29.

Barritt, J. A., C. A. Brenner, H. E. Malter, and J. Cohen. 2001. Mitochondria in human offspring derived from ooplasmic transplantation. *Human Reproduction* 16:513–16.

BBC News. 2003. Test tube pioneer research call. September 11. http://news.bbc.co.uk/2/hi/health/3099698.stm.

Biological Response Modifiers Advisory Committee (BRMAC), Food and Drug Administration, Center for Biologics Evaluation and Research. 2002. Summary minutes, May 9. http://www.fda.gov/OHRMS/DOCKETS/ac/02/questions/3855g1_draft.doc.

Holland, S. 2001a. Contested commodities at both ends of life: Buying and selling of gametes, embryos and body tissues. *Kennedy Institute of Ethics Journal* 11, no. 3: 263–84.

———. 2001b. To market, to market: Cloning as ART? *Second Opinion* 6: 5–22.

Hudson, K., S. Baruch, and G. Javitt. 2005. Genetic testing of human embryos: Ethical challenges and policy choices. In *Expanding Horizons in Bioethics*, ed. A. Galston and C. Peppard, 103–22. Dordrecht: Springer.

Integramed America, Inc. 2003. *Annual Report 2002*, 2. U.S. Securities and Exchange Commission Document 10-K, filed on March 27, 2003. Washington, DC: SEC.

ISLAT Working Group. 1998. Art into science: Regulation of fertility techniques. *Science* 281:651–52.

Knowles, L. P. 1999. Property, patents and progeny: Selling our selves. *Hastings Center Report* 29, no. 2: 38–40.

Leo, J. 1997. A new medical skill: Counting. *U.S. News & World Report* 132, no. 22: 20.

Parens, E., and L. P. Knowles. 2003. Reprogenetics and public policy: Reflection and recommendations. *Hastings Center Report* 33, no. 4: S1–S24.

Radin, M. J. 1996. *Contested Commodities*. Cambridge, MA: Harvard University Press.

Robertson, J. A. 1994. *Children of Choice: Freedom and the New Reproductive Technologies*. Princeton, NJ: Princeton University Press.

Schultz, R. M., and C. J. Williams. 2002. The science of ART. *Science* 296:2188–2190.

Weiss, R. 2003. 400,000 Human embryos frozen in U.S. *Washington Post*, May 8, A10.

Wolfe, A. 1998. *One Nation, After All : What Americans Really Think About God, Country, Family, Racism, Welfare, Immigration, Homosexuality, Work, the Right, the Left and Each Other*. New York: Viking.

Zoon, K. 2001. *Letter to Sponsors / Researchers—Human Cells Used in Therapy Involving the Transfer of Genetic Material By Means Other Than the Union of Gamete Nuclei* (July 6). http://www.fda.gov/cber/ltr/cytotrans070601.htm.

Stem Cells, Clones, Consensus, and the Law

TIMOTHY CAULFIELD

The introduction of new technologies often forces us to reevaluate our moral convictions and ethical norms, but rarely do they invoke a completely uniform social response. The area of reproductive genetics stands as an example of the challenges associated with regulating an area where there is little or no social consensus about benefits and risks. Though most in the public may be uncomfortable with the idea of reproductive cloning, other techniques have produced very different social reactions, ranging from almost complete acceptance, in the case of sperm donation and in vitro fertilization (IVF), to areas where the public seems relatively divided, such as embryonic stem (ES) cell research. For policymakers, this lack of consensus makes reproductive genetics a particularly challenging area to regulate.

In this chapter, I explore some of the available evidence on public perceptions and consider how public opinion relates to legal policy. Much of the chapter will focus on stem cell research, reproductive cloning, and "therapeutic cloning"—that is, the use of the "Dolly" technique to produce stem cell lines for research or therapy. These topics have been the subject of a good deal of social controversy and policymaking activity. There is also a significant amount of evidence about public opinion in these areas.

The chapter is not meant to be a comprehensive analysis of the complex relationship between public opinion and law-making, nor do I consider the many factors relevant to the shaping of public perceptions, including the media, education and cultural differences. Rather, I seek to highlight the often divergent nature of public opinion and what this lack of consensus means to policy development. I argue that though a lack of consensus should not necessarily stop the development of policy, it does, at a minimum, have implications for the type of regulatory tool to be used. For example, it calls into question the appropriateness of the use of criminal prohibitions.

AVAILABLE EVIDENCE REGARDING PUBLIC PERCEPTIONS

While few would disagree with the idea that there is little social agreement about the harms and benefits associated with many forms of reproductive genetics, it is instructive to review some of the relevant evidence.

Available Data

There has been a great deal of both qualitative research, such as with focus groups, and quantitative research on the public perceptions of the risks and benefits associated with cloning technologies. Much of this research has been done because of the ongoing controversies associated with reproductive cloning and the close ties between cloning technology and the politically charged area of stem cell research. Indeed, some of the studies have been done with the explicit purpose of informing regulatory policy. In Canada, for example, the federal government sponsored a number of surveys, some referred to below, as part of the deliberations surrounding a recently enacted national law, the Assisted Human Reproduction Act of 2004.

In general, the available data paint a picture of a public that is generally supportive of stem cell research, divided over "therapeutic cloning," and strongly opposed to reproductive cloning.

To cite just a few examples, a 2002 Gallup poll of 1,012 Americans found that 90 percent thought cloning an entire human was morally wrong. However, that same survey found that 59 percent approved of the "cloning of human organs," and 34 percent approved of cloning embryos for research purposes (Saad 2002). A recent study by the Genetics and Public Policy Center found clear opposition to reproductive cloning (88 percent against) and a relatively strong negative attitude toward research cloning (76 percent of the respondents thought research cloning "should not be allowed at all") (2005, 52). However, other studies have found more support for research cloning. A survey of 1,022 citizens sponsored by the Coalition for the Advancement of Medical Research found strong, though not overwhelming, support (68 percent) for "government allowing scientists to do therapeutic cloning research to produce stem cells for treating life-threatening diseases" (2002). A 2005 survey by the same research group found even higher support (72 percent) for somatic cell nuclear transfer stem cell research. Similarly, a 2001 poll found that 88 percent "disapproved" of "cloning that is designed specifically to result in the birth of a human being" and 54 percent approved of cloning "designed to aid medical research" (*USA Today*/CNN/Gallup 2001).

When the question is worded in the context of regulatory policy, the public seems to become even more divided. For example, a Canadian Ipsos-Reid (2001) poll found that of those surveyed, 21 percent opposed any law that restricts research into human cloning; 39 percent supported a ban on human cloning while allowing research on cloned embryos; and only 33 percent supported a complete ban on all human cloning.

In Canada, survey research has consistently shown public support for ES cell research, and even a degree of support for the concept of therapeutic cloning. In fact, a 2002 poll found that six in ten Canadians approved of the creation of cloned human embryos for collecting stem cells (Ipsos-Reid 2002). A poll of 1,500 Canadians taken shortly after the Raelians claimed the first human clone was born found that 84 percent of those surveyed were against human cloning, but 53 percent supported cloning human embryos to create stem cells (Canadian Press 2003). The same study found that only 30 percent believed a ban on all types of human cloning was required. An early study that related cloning to potential treatments, specifically to cloning human organs for transplant, found that three-quarters of respondents said it was either very or somewhat acceptable (CRT 2001).

Focus group data from the University of Calgary also found strong support for therapeutic cloning, although these data are preliminary (Reid 2003). The research found that twenty-three out of twenty-seven participants supported the use of cloning for research purposes, while only two participants felt it should be banned. A content analysis of the focus group data found that the participants believed that the benefits outweighed the risks by a three-to-one ratio. There was, however, almost uniform condemnation of reproductive cloning.

Public opinion surveys and focus groups are, of course, inherently limited methods. A great deal depends on how the questions are asked and the context within which they are placed (Nisbet 2004). Survey questions about cloning that emphasize potential therapeutic benefit, for example, seem to elicit a more positive response. Likewise, when the potential benefits are left out of the relevant survey question, studies have found a lower level of support for therapeutic cloning (Genetics and Public Policy Center 2005). And at least one study, done for the U.S. Civil Society Institute, found that support for embryonic stem cell research grows with the provision of information about the science (Civil Society Institute 2004). However, research by Einsiedel (2000) found that scientific knowledge did not necessarily affect the public view of reproductive cloning. This conclusion is supported by recent work by Nisbet who found that "although an increase in awareness leads to an increase in support for research, both religious and ideological value predispositions strongly moderate the impact of awareness" (Nisbet 2005, 90).

Taken as a whole, however, the data paint a fairly consistent picture. There appears to be a clear desire to stop reproductive cloning, but there is little public consensus on other techniques, such as creating embryos for research purposes and conducting "therapeutic cloning." Though the public in some jurisdictions, such as Canada, is tentatively supportive of such techniques, few jurisdictions have a strong and clear public mandate to guide policy and lawmaking (Genetics and Public Policy Center 2005, 53).

Religious Perspectives

This lack of consensus about how to address reproductive genetic technologies is also reflected in the diverse responses of religious organizations (Cole-Turner 1997; National Bioethics Advisory Commission 1997). Many religious organizations have well-known policies against stem cell research and human reproductive cloning—positions that are often closely related to views about the use of human embryos for research purposes. The Catholic Church, for example, has stated that it opposes therapeutic cloning because of its beliefs about the embryo's moral status. Evangelical Protestant groups also have policies against human cloning. As noted by Evans, "the Southern Baptist Convention, meeting in 2001, passed a resolution claiming concerns with safety, the destruction of human embryos in research, and that through cloning procreation will become manufacture" (2002a, 749).

In the United States, these Christian perspectives have played a significant role in policy development in this area. As noted by Donley Young, "Religious influences also play a part in the regulation of stem cell research. In the United States, religion is a pervasive factor in many of our laws—examples include prohibitions of and limitations on the use of contraceptives, same-sex marriages, and abortion" (2002, 854). In addition, some have speculated that a religious agenda has played a role in the tone of the national bioethics discourse, skewing it toward a neo-conservative ethos (Charo 2004). Though not as dominant as in the United States, religion has also played a role in the direction of policy development in Canada and the United Kingdom (Plomer 2002). Often, the religious elements of the debate are reflected in a strong antiabortion or pro-life lobby (*Edmonton Journal* 2002). This was a clear theme in the Canadian parliamentary debates in the spring of 2003 surrounding the enactment of the new assisted reproduction law. Indeed, politicians from various political parties professed their concerns about cloning and stem cell research with religious references. Jocelyn Girard-Bujold, a member of Bloc Quebecois, the Quebec separatist party, condemned such research in an address on January 28: "I am very religious and, according to my principles, human beings are created by God. He gives us the ability to give birth to other human beings." In the same debate, Philip Maryfield, a member of the conservative Canadian Alliance said on January 30, "Life is a precious gift. That is the basis of many of the great religions of the world and certainly of the religion of Christianity, of which I am a part." Other politicians, such as Progressive Conservative Elsie Wayne, simply framed the concern, as many do, in relation to the moral status of the embryo. "When I see these tiny babies, I ask myself how could they take a cell and stop the birth of that child," she said on February 29.

While such religiously infused political statements may be commonplace in the United States, Canadian political discourse usually has a much more secular tone. The use of religious arguments to justify a particular policy position is relatively rare. Their presence in the stem cell research and cloning debates highlights both the source of the various perspectives and the degree to which these controversial technologies engage strongly held values.

It should not be forgotten, however, that other religious organizations explicitly support research involving embryos and therapeutic cloning. For example, Malaysia's highest religious authority, the National Fatwa Council, supports most forms of ES cell research because, as explained by its chair, Ismail Ibrahim: "Before 120 days, the embryo has not yet been infused with a soul [*roh*]" (Islamic Republic News Agency 2003; see also Abraham 2002). Likewise, the Organization of the Islamic Conference issued a fatwa in January 2003 asserting that "early embryos and five-day-old blastocysts created through nuclear transfer are not human subjects deserving protection, but are instead undifferentiated bearers of potentially beneficial cells from donors to recipients" (Walters 2004, 6). Indeed, it has been noted that for some within the Islamic community, even reproductive cloning may be permissible so long as it is used to help infertility and occurs within a "lawful male-female relationship" (Evans 2002b).

Although it is difficult to draw generalizations about how the Jewish community views cloning and research involving embryos, Evans (2002b) suggests it is likely to be supportive, even in the context of "therapeutic cloning" (see also Traubman 2002). This is because "in the Jewish tradition a fetus has no status during the first 40 days. More to the point, an embryo existing outside of a woman has no legal status in the Jewish tradition. Therefore, there is no intrinsic objection to embryo research" (Evans 2002b, 10). Indeed, a number of Jewish scholars have taken strongly supportive stances (Greenway 2004). For example, Rabbi Yigal Shafran, who heads the Department of Jewish Medical Ethics in the Chief Rabbinate of Jerusalem, has suggested that "cloning is part of science's desire to benefit the human race" (Traubman 2002). Likewise, Rabbi Moses Tendler of Yeshiva University has been quoted as saying that a ban on therapeutic cloning would be a "travesty of justice launched on humanity" (Evans 2002b, 10).

Naturally, there are also diverse views within a particular religious perspective, even within those religious communities that have traditionally argued against research involving embryos. This fact is nicely highlighted by the differing positions of U.S. senators Orrin Hatch and Sam Brownback, both Christian conservative Republicans with a history of advocating pro-life policies. Hatch has become an advocate of stem cell research and even therapeutic cloning, arguing that he believes "human life begins in the womb, not in a petri dish" (Suh 2003). Brownback, who staunchly supports a total ban on all forms of cloning, has suggested that "there's only one type of human cloning and it always results in the creation of a human being" (Suh 2003).

It is far from clear what role religious organizations and religious perspectives should have in the development of social policy (Skene and Parker 2002), particularly in liberal democracies that have an established separation between church and state. However, an understanding of the diverse faith-based perspectives in reprogenetics again highlights both the severity and, to some degree, the source of the lack of consensus. One study found that 36 percent of Americans felt that religious beliefs "had the most influence on [their] opinion on the issue of cloning" (Sussman 2001). The next highest ranked influences were "non-religious beliefs (17 percent) and "education" (16 percent).

Of course, there are countries where cultural and religious perspectives form a unifying force such that public consensus seems a political possibility. For example, Ireland's restrictions on research involving human embryos is obviously informed by the country's strong Catholic tradition (Regnier and Knoppers 2002). Likewise, in Israel, the government's support of ES cell research and therapeutic cloning flows, in part, from the Jewish perspective as described by Rabbis Tendler and Shafran. For most countries, however, religion is not a source of social consensus. Canada and the United States, for example, are pluralistic societies with no one dominant religious voice (although the Christian view admittedly remains the most influential from a political perspective). As such, policymakers cannot rely on religious doctrine as a means of building even the appearance of public consensus.

Finally, there remains little agreement in the academic community about the benefits and risks of many of these technologies. Although a detailed discussion of how various legal, ethical, and social science academics have responded to reproductive genetics is beyond the scope of this chapter, it is fair to say that here too we find little consensus that would meaningfully guide policymakers (Caulfield 2003; Knowles 2004). Indeed, even reproductive cloning, safety issues aside, is the subject of much debate (McGee 2000; Pattinson 2002b). Stephen Marks, for instance, has noted that the "ethical pros and cons of human cloning . . . are sufficiently balanced and uncertain that there is not an ethically decisive case either for or against permitting it or banning it" (2002, 93).

In the end, policymakers are left with little concrete direction. For some sectors, reproductive genetics, and cloning technology in particular, pose a grave threat to the embryo. This has led to strong and vocal opposition that may have had a disproportionate impact on policy development and likely does not reflect broader public opinion. However, even if policymakers had access to a more dispassionate view of public opinion, its value to policymaking in this context remain vague.

THE RELEVANCE OF PUBLIC OPINION

What does this lack of social consensus mean in the context of policymaking (Condit 2001)? Policies and laws do not necessarily flow from social consensus. Nor should social consensus always be a required element in the lawmaking process (Turner 2003). It is entirely possible that a strictly moral or ethical argument against a particular technology could support a restrictive policy, even in the face of a promotive or ambivalent public. Indeed, some of the most important legal reforms, such as the human rights movement in the United States, faced a degree of public opposition. Other important scientific ideas, such as those of Newton and Galileo, were hardly part of the popular consensus and were viewed as a threat to the existing moral framework. Other commentators have warned against a simplistic reliance on public opinion surveys as a means of making laws (Ahlers 2002, 681).

Despite these legitimate reservations about the role of social consensus to this policy debate, I believe the great divergence in views has a number of important implications. For many in the public, the lack of consensus reflects deeply differing views on critical moral issues, such as the status of the early-stage embryo and the role and meaning of fundamental concepts like human dignity. Though a lack of consensus should not result in a policymaking road-block, the lack of consensus has relevance to the nature of the justifications used to support a given policy approach and, more important, the type of legal tool used to regulate the technology.

A "Critical Moral Background"?

Without a clear and consistent public mandate, it is essential that the relevant "fundamental values" and philosophical foundations for a particular regulatory response be articulated and have an enduring relevance (such as the belief that all humans should be treated as equals) (Caulfield, Knowles, and Meslin 2004). This is especially true in the regulation of science, where so many of the relevant variables—considerations of safety, the state of the science, and public opinion—are in a state of flux. In such a situation, as argued by Dworkin, "we must rely on a more critical and abstract part of our morality. We must try to identify what we might call a critical moral background: a basic set of convictions that we hope can guide when the moral practices and assumptions that we took for granted have been challenged" (Dworkin 2000, 448).

But in the context of reproductive genetics, is there a critical moral background we can refer to? The relationship between public opinion as revealed in opinion research, be it qualitative or quantitative, and core values or moral positions is complex and contested. Beyleveld and Brownsword note:

> To be sure, philosophers continue to debate the details of the list of formal conditions (universalizability, categoricality, impartiality, and so on) but it is common ground that there is something distinctive about having a moral position— there is more to it than having a practical attitude (positive or negative) towards some matter or making a practical judgment in relation to some action (for it or against it). (2001, 45)

Unfortunately, because the moral ambiguity cuts so deeply in this area, there are few core values we can turn to in order to guide policy development. That is, the lack of social consensus is about more than the appropriate application of the technology, an intuitive response to a practice, the nature of the safety issues, or the value of the relevant science. There also appears to be little or no agreement about the role or relevance of many core values and ethical principles, such as the role of human dignity.

There is, no doubt, agreement on the "intrinsic dignity and worth of human nature" (Polkinghorne 1997; Wright 2000). But the application of this value in the context of, for instance, cloning and stem cell research remains uncertain (do early-stage embryos have dignity worth protecting?). Indeed, though concerns for human dignity have been used to justify a variety of cloning policies, the debate over whether reproductive cloning infringes human dignity continues. For example, the UNESCO Universal Declaration on the Human Genome and Human Rights recommends a ban on "practices which are contrary to human dignity, such as reproductive cloning" (1997, 4, art. 11; see also Pattinson 2002a). However, as noted by numerous commentators (Marks 2002), this is far from a universally accepted conclusion. Shalev argues, for instance, that "aside from the moral debate on whether the embryo is a human being arguments about human dignity do not hold up well under rational reflection" (2002, 149). And one scholar has gone so far as to suggest that reproductive cloning may actually promote human dignity: "Human cloning may well serve to highlight, to emphasize, and to set off with greater clarity, quite apart from anyone's intentions, the mysterious capacities that comprise and express our human dignity" (Wright 2000, 31).

On an intuitive level, reference to respect for human dignity evokes impressions of a universally accepted and unifying social value. This is undoubtedly why policymakers often use the term. It creates the impression that there is, at a minimum, agreement about what is at stake. But in the context of reproductive genetics, available evidence suggests that there is often no such agreement (Caulfield 2003; Ries 2004). In large part, this is because human dignity means different things to different people. It is not a unifying concept but instead one that may change meaning, depending on an individual's or community's worldview. As a result, the concept of dignity "cannot represent any particular set of values or meaning that 'naturally' stem out of it" (Shultziner 2003, 5). This, in turn, makes it difficult to (legitimately) rely on dignity as a primary justification for the regulation of reproductive genetics, particularly in pluralistic liberal democracies that strive to respect a diversity of cultural views. As noted by Beyleveld and Brownsword: "The practical problem with the conception of human dignity as constraint is that modern societies are often pluralistic societies" (2001, 45). Indeed, without a clear, agreed-upon normative role, an appeal to the concept of human dignity may obscure the real rationales for, and the lack of consensus about, a given policy approach (Schachter 1983, 849). As I have argued elsewhere (Caulfield 2003), it becomes little more than shorthand for general social unease, an unease that may not reflect social consensus and may flow from very different sources, such as religious conviction or simple unfamiliarity with the technology.

Likewise, though the sanctity of human life is certainly part of our "moral background," its application in the context of reproductive genetics is hardly a unifying value. On the contrary, the moral and legal status of the embryo is arguably the single most divisive issue in the area of reproductive genetics. "In brief, no consensus exists among religious traditions—or secular moral traditions—about the moral status of the extra-corporeal embryo" (Childress 2001, 161). So, though we all may agree on the value of human life, there is great difference of opinion regarding the degree to which early stage embryos should be treated as human life.

In the context of reproductive genetics, then, there appears to be a relationship between the diversity of views found in the survey work about the acceptability of a given technology and the diversity of views about the role of core moral concepts. One is, to some degree, the result of the other. Individuals who feel strongly about the moral status of the human embryo, for example, undoubtedly have strong views about the appropriateness of ES cell research. Likewise, those who feel that an early-stage human embryo does not have the same moral standing as a human after birth are undoubtedly more likely to be supportive.

Given the lack of agreement on the role of core values, it becomes more difficult for policymakers to provide a principled justification for a given law. There is no "critical moral background" on which all agree. To make matters worse, there are reasons to believe that public perceptions will change (a fact that further emphasizes that for many individuals, these technologies do not engage an immutable moral concern). Whereas the initial reactions to a particular technology or scientific advance may be marked by skepticism, even fear, with the passage of time these concerns often dissipate. This seems particularly true in the context of reproductive technologies. Gamete donation and IVF were once viewed as tremendously controversial practices. There were calls to criminally prohibit sperm donation and the announcement of

Louise Brown, the first "test tube baby," was met with a degree of revulsion (Andrews and Elster 2000). Though both practices are still associated with a variety of social and scientific controversies (Margues et al. 2004), such as the appropriateness of anonymous donation, they have become commonplace. Indeed, since the birth of Louise Brown in 1979, IVF has been responsible for more than 100,000 babies in the United States alone (CNN 2003). Could the same social accommodation happen with cloning technology? Possibly. "Medical advances often have been greeted initially with the same fear and trepidation that the new cloning technology has raised" (Shapiro 2003, 396). At a minimum, the changing nature of social attitudes should remind us to question our reactions to new technologies. Is our intuitive response based on a lack of familiarity or on ethical concerns that may have enduring relevance?

Policy Roadblock?

In some jurisdictions, the lack of social consensus has, not surprisingly, had a practical impact on the ability of policymakers to provide concrete recommendations with long-term relevance. Some policymakers have suggested that definitive regulatory steps should follow an effort to build social consensus. This was explicitly recognized in the 2002 report of the President's Council on Bioethics, *Human Cloning and Human Dignity: An Ethical Inquiry.* The council stated that there was a lack of moral consensus and that therefore a ban on all forms of human cloning was not justified. Instead, it recommended a moratorium be imposed to give time "to seek moral consensus." Some members of the council felt that even this relatively moderate recommendation was inappropriately restrictive, and they published an editorial in *Science* calling for an approach that would allow "therapeutic cloning" to move forward (Rowley et al. 2002).

Of course, moral consensus is often an unattainable policy goal, as highlighted by the shifting nature of the U.S. political landscape in the area of stem cell research (Stolberg 2005). One commentator has suggested that, in the context of bioethics, consensus is a "utopian fantasy." "If we think that society must reach a full consensus before legislation is legitimated, we generate insurmountable roadblocks to policy making" (Turner 2003, 1433). Social consensus appears especially unlikely on cloning. In 1997, the National Bioethics Advisory Council's report on human cloning came to a similar conclusion as the one provided by Bush's council, and seven years later we are no closer to finding a moral consensus. If the enactment of a relevant legal framework must await true social consensus, it will never happen.

The lack of consensus has also affected the development of international policies, such as attempts by the United Nations to create an international treaty against human reproductive cloning (a history of the debate is available at the referenced Web site: United Nations Ad Hoc Committee 2005). In December 2001, the General Assembly established an ad hoc committee to consider the development of a convention addressing reproductive cloning. Since then, different proposals have been put forward. Some countries favor the adoption of a convention, proposed by France and Germany, that would ban only reproductive cloning. Other countries support a proposal, submitted by Spain, that would ban all forms of human cloning, including therapeutic cloning. More recently, Costa Rica has submitted a proposal to require states to create criminal offences relating to any type of human cloning. The preamble to the Costa Rican proposal declares that all cloning "is morally repugnant, unethical and contrary to respect for the person and constitutes a grave violation of fundamental human rights" (Walters 2004, 5). Despite such strong and definitive language, there remains a deep lack of consensus on the moral and legal basis for a comprehensive ban (Caulfield and von Tigerstrom forthcoming). In fact, it has been suggested that there is a "deep and seemingly irreconcilable division among member states over how far the [cloning] ban should reach" (Aschwanden 2004, 76). On November 19, 2004, the UN General Assembly gave up on the development of a cloning treaty by agreeing to develop a nonbinding declaration that could be used to guide the development of national laws. This declaration, which was adopted in March 2005, suggests that member states "prohibit all forms of human cloning inasmuch as they are incompatible with human dignity and the protection of human life." The ambiguous nature of the language seems capable of accommodating a broad range of policy positions.

The Regulatory Approach: Statutory Criminal Prohibitions?

One of the most significant implications of the lack of public consensus relates to the type of regulatory tool that ought to be used. For example, in Canada, the 1982 Law Reform Commission suggested that statutory criminal law should be an instrument of "last resort" and should be used only for "conduct which is culpable, seriously harmful, and generally conceived of as deserving of punishment" (Law Reform Commission of Canada 1982;

Caulfield 2001). Because so many of these activities remain morally ambiguous, many reproductive genetic activities seem likely to fail this test, and as such, they should not be addressed by means of the criminal law (Caulfield, Knowles, and Meslin 2004). For example, available evidence indicates that most in the public do not regard therapeutic cloning as "seriously harmful" and generally deserving of punishment. All may agree that some form of oversight is required, but outside reproductive cloning, the lack of consensus among the public and in the academic, religious, and scientific communities makes it difficult to justify the use of statutory criminal prohibitions, the most severe regulatory tool available to liberal democracies.

In Canada, policymakers are clearly aware of the political value of a perceived social consensus in this context. Social consensus is one of the primary explicit justifications for Canada's criminal prohibition in the Assisted Human Reproductive Act of a variety of reproductive genetic activities, including reproductive and therapeutic cloning. A Health Canada document that accompanied the release of an early draft of the law stated "there is a broad consensus that the activities that would be banned under the proposed legislation are not acceptable in Canada" (Health Canada 2001, para. 9). Later, a report by the Parliamentary Standing Committee on Health argued that "the use of the statutory ban also signals that these activities are of such concern to Canadians that their status as a prohibited activity may not be altered except with the approval of Parliament" (2001, sec. 4).

But, as highlighted by the opinion research cited earlier in the chapter, there is simply no evidence of a "broad consensus." Indeed, most available evidence suggests Canadians support the concept of therapeutic cloning. To be fair, the Canadian government is likely relying on criminal law because it is one of the only regulatory tools they have clear jurisdiction to apply in this context (in Canada, health policy is generally left within provincial jurisdiction) (Jackman 2000). Nevertheless, in Canada and for that matter in many other countries, policymakers cannot honestly rely on social consensus as a major justification for the use of a given regulatory framework. And given the lack of consensus about the application of foundational values such as human dignity, policymakers are left with few legitimate justifications for the use of the heavy hand of criminal bans.

More important, however, criminal law seems a poor way to handle an area with such a high degree of moral ambiguity. Criminal prohibitions are a blunt and relatively inflexible regulatory tool, a point noted by a variety of commentators (Caulfield, Knowles, and Meslin 2005). For example, Harvison Young and Wasunna argue that "criminal law, in itself, is an inadequate tool with which to address the complex issues raised by [new reproductive technologies]. It is a blunt instrument that is ill-suited to both the nuances and subtleties that pervade the area, and to the realities of rapid change" (1998, 276).

In addition, the use of statutory prohibitions seems unlikely to stimulate the open public discourse so essential to the continued examination of the complex moral issues surrounding cloning technologies. A criminal law is among the harshest formal action a society can take against a particular activity. As a result, criminal laws imply a degree of consensus and closure to the debate. While there may be an emerging public consensus regarding reproductive cloning, many other reproductive technologies remain surrounded in moral ambiguity.

CONCLUSION: DEALING WITH DISAGREEMENT

Future developments might help to foster more social consensus on stem cell research and cloning. The development of a beneficial therapeutic intervention based on ES cell research would undoubtedly bolster support for the research. Indeed, there is already evidence that information about benefits can have a profound impact on public perception. Likewise, controversial events, such as the Raelian announcement that the first cloned human was born, encourage support for a more cautious regulatory approach. However, regardless of what the future holds, it is safe to say that there will never be a high degree of social consensus in many areas of reproductive genetics. Regulatory frameworks need to be designed to reflect this reality.

This is not to say that regulators should always strive for a compromise position that tries to balance all the diverse perspectives. Indeed, some commentators have suggested we need to be careful not to produce policies based on "a hypothetical judgement suffering from the pathology of a pooling of public opinions" (Ahlers 2002, 684). Likewise, we should not let the lack of consensus paralyze policy development. As suggested by Turner:

> Many of us inhabit societies containing multiple cultural, philosophical and religious traditions. We should spend less time pining for the utopian ideal of society's reaching consensus about biomedical technologies. We should recognize that citizens and advocacy groups will generate different ethical analyses of such topics as ES cell research, therapeutic cloning and xenotransplantation. (2003, 1433)

However, the lack of consensus should raise questions about how and why we seek to regulate a given reproductive technology. First, policymakers should not use social consensus as a justification for regulatory action if no consensus exists, as was recently done in Canada. By doing so, the law's legitimacy is put into question and the true justifications for the law are obscured. The plurality of views needs to be explicitly recognized (though not necessarily balanced). It must be explained how the choice of regulatory instrument relates to public views. If the law conflicts with a given public perspective, this should also be explicitly addressed. This approach will facilitate transparency and ongoing public debate about the government's rationales for a given regulatory approach.

Second, and perhaps more important, we need to recognize the depth of disagreement. For many (but not all), cloning technologies implicate strongly held views about, for example, the moral status of the embryo and notions of human dignity. However, these views are not shared by all. Indeed, there is evidence that in some countries, such as Canada, they are not even shared by the majority. In such an environment, we should not use moral concepts like respect for human dignity (a concept that often seems to imply consensus), without explaining how and why it is implicated by the technology in question. Again, if this information is not provided, decision-making transparency is lost. "Without a reasonably clear general idea of its meaning, we cannot easily reject a specious use of the concept, nor can we without understanding its meaning draw specific implications for relevant conduct" (Schachter 1983, 849).

Third, though the lack of social consensus should not necessarily stand as a policymaking roadblock, it does have implications for deciding on a regulatory approach. Criminal law should be an instrument of last resort. It seems an inappropriate first response to moral ambiguity and public uncertainty. As suggested by Alta Charo: "Moral angst is one thing; federal criminalization of research or medical practice is another" (2004). The use of criminal prohibitions is particularly problematic when there are other regulatory tools available. Indeed, a flexible, regulatory approach, one that can respond to changes in science and emerging social concerns, seems more appropriate to the complex area of reproductive genetics (Caulfield et al. 2005; Gogarty and Nicol 2002). While a description of the elements of a suitable regulatory regime is beyond the scope of this chapter, there are existing models, like the licensing scheme in the United Kingdom, that provide a balanced approach. Such schemes provide the oversight necessary to address issues associated with human safety, research ethics, and the commodification of human reproductive material, while not foreclosing continued public debate on the intractable moral issues.

ACKNOWLEDGMENTS

I thank Nola Ries, Lori Knowles, and Eric Meslin for their insights, and the Stem Cell Network, Genome Prairie, and the Alberta Heritage Foundation for Medical Research for their continued support.

REFERENCES

Abraham, C. 2002. Stem-cell study to begin soon in Saudi Arabia. *Globe and Mail*, June 13.

Ahlers, R. 2002. Biotech and theodicy: What can and what ought we to do in procreative technology? *Albany Law Review* 65:679–700.

Andrews, L. B., and N. Elster. 2002. Regulating reproductive technologies. *Journal of Legal Medicine* 21:35–65.

Aschwanden, C. 2004. UN to vote on cloning in one year, not two. *Bulletin of the World Health Organization* 82:76.

Assisted Human Reproduction Act. 2004. R.S.C. 2004, c. 2.

Beyleveld, D., and R. Brownsword. 2001. *Human Dignity in Bioethics and Biolaw*. Oxford: Oxford University Press.

Bonnicksen, A. 2002. *Crafting a Cloning Policy: From Dolly to Stem Cells*. Washington, DC: Georgetown University Press.

Canada Bill C-13. 2002. *An Act Respecting Assisted Human Reproduction*. 2nd Sess., 37th Parl.

Canadian Press. 2003. Most Canadians oppose human cloning. *CTV News Net*, January 20. www.ctv.ca/servlet/ArticleNews/story/CTVNews/20030120/cloning_poll_030 119 / (accessed June 25, 2004).

Caulfield, T. 2001. Controversy and criminal law: A comment on the proposal for legislation governing assisted human reproduction. *Alberta Law Review* 39:335–45.

———. 2002. Politics, prohibitions and the lost public perspective: A comment on Bill C-56: The Assisted Human Reproduction Act. *Alberta Law Review* 40:451–63.

———. 2003. Human cloning laws, human dignity and the poverty of the policy making dialogue. *BMC Medical Ethics* 4:3–10.

Caulfield, T., L. Knowles, and E. Meslin. 2005. Law and policy in the era of reproductive genetics. *Journal of Medical Ethics* 30:414–17.

Caulfield, T, and von Tigerstrom B. Forthcoming. Globalization and biotechnology policy: The challenges created by gene patents and cloning technologies.

Charo, R. A. 2004. Passing on the right: Conservative bioethics is closer than it appears. *Journal of Law, Medicine and Ethics* 2:307–14.

Childress, J. F. 2001. An ethical defense of federal funding for human embryonic stem cell research. *Yale Journal of Health Policy Law and Ethics* 2:157–65.

Civil Society Institute. 2004. *Survey: Expanded Cell Research Backed by Strong Majority of Voters in 18 States.* Washington DC: Civil Society Institute. http://www.results foramerica.org/calendar/files/stemcellsurvey.pdf (accessed June 25, 2004).

Cloning conundrums. 2002. Editorial. *Nature Medicine* 8:1331.

CNN. 2003. Test tube babies, 25 years later. Health, July 28. http://www.cnn.com/2003/HEALTH/parenting/07/25/ivf.anniversary/ (accessed June 25, 2004).

Coalition for the Advancement of Medical Research. 2002. New poll shows more than two thirds of Americans support therapeutic cloning research to produce stem cells. April 24. http://www.camradvocacy.org/fastaction/arc_news.asp?id=250 (accessed June 25 2004).

———. 2005. Survey conducted March 18–21, 2005. http://www.camradvocacy.org/fast action/news.asp?id=1326 (accessed August 8, 2005).

Cole-Turner, R. 1997. *Human Cloning: Religious Responses.* Louisville, MO: Westminster / John Knox Press.

Condit, C. 2001. What is "public opinion" about genetics? *Nature Reviews Genetics* 2:811–15.

CRT. 2001. Canadians support cloning of human organs, new survey suspects. February 22. www.crt_online.org/022201.html.

Dworkin, R. 2000. *Sovereign Virtue: The Theory and Practice of Equality.* Cambridge, MA: Harvard University Press.

Edmonton Journal. 2002. Anti-abortion march focuses on stem cell bill. May 11.

Einsiedel, E. 2000. Cloning and its discontent: A Canadian perspective. *Nature Biotechnology* 18:943–44.

Evans, J. H. 2002a. Religion and human cloning: An exploratory analysis of the first available opinion data. *Journal for the Scientific Study of Religion* 41:747–58.

———. 2002b. *Cloning Adam's Rib: A Primer on Religious Responses to Cloning.* Washington, DC: Pew Forum on Religion and Public Life.

Genetics and Public Policy Center. 2005. *Cloning: A Policy Analysis.* Washington, DC: Genetics and Public Policy Center.

Gogarty, B., and D. Nicol. 2002. The UK's cloning laws: A view from the Antipodes. *Murdoch University Electronic Journal of Law* 9, no. 2, para.32. http://www.murdoch.edu.au/elaw/issues/v9n2/gogarty92.html (accessed June 25, 2004).

Greenway, N. 2004. Jewish, Islamic faith support controversial stem cell research. *Edmonton Journal,* February 29.

Harvison Young, A., and A. Wasunna A. 1998. Wrestling with the limits of law: Regulating reproductive technologies. *Health Law Journal* 6:239–77.

Health Canada. 2001. Assisted Human Reproduction: Frequently Asked Questions. *Health Canada online,* May. http://www.hc-sc.gc.ca/english/media/releases/2001/2001_44ebk3.htm (accessed June 25, 2004).

Ipsos-Reid. 2001. Stem cell research debate last summer paved the way for greater acceptance of human cloning research today. News release. Ipsos News Center,

December 3. www.ipsos-na.com/news/pressrelease.cfm?id=1368&content=full (accessed June 25, 2004).

———. 2002. Six in ten Canadians approved creation of cloned embryos for collecting stem cells. Press release, October 22. www.ipsos-na.com/news/pressrelease.cfm ?id=1650.

Islamic Republic News Agency. 2003. Malaysia's Fatwa Council bans cloning, okays embryonic stem cell research. News release. January 7.

Jackman, M. 2000. Constitutional jurisdiction over health in Canada. *Health Law Journal* 8:95.

Knowles, L. 2004. A regulatory patchwork: Human ES cell research oversight. *Nature Biotechnology* 22:157–63.

Law Reform Commission of Canada. 1982. *The Criminal Law in Canadian Society.* Ottawa, ON: Law Reform Commission of Canada.

Marks, S. 2002. Human rights assumptions of restrictive and permission approaches to human reproductive cloning. *Health and Human Rights* 6:81–100.

Marques, C. J., F. Carvalho, M. Sousa, et al. 2004. Genomic imprinting in disruptive spermatogenesis. *Lancet* 363, no. 9422: 1700–2.

McGee, G., ed. 2000. *The Human Cloning Debate.* Berkeley, CA: Berkeley Hills Books.

National Bioethics Advisory Commission. 1997. *Cloning Human Beings.* Rockville, MD: National Bioethics Advisory Commission.

Nisbet, M. 2004. The polls—trends: Public opinion about stem cell research and human cloning. *Public Opinion Quarterly* 68:131–39.

———. 2005. The competition for worldviews: Values, information, and public support for stem cell research. *International Journal of Public Opinion Research* 17:90–112.

Pattinson, S. D. 2002a. *Influencing Traits before Birth.* Aldershot, U.K.: Ashgate Publishing.

———. 2002b. Reproductive cloning: Can cloning harm the clone? *Medical Law Review* 10:295–307.

Plomer, A. 2002. Beyond the HFE Act 1990: The regulation of stem cell research in the UK. *Medical Law Review* 10:132–63.

Polkinghorne, J. 1987. Cloning and the moral imperative. In *Human Cloning: Religious Responses,* ed. R. Cole-Turner, 35–42. Louisville: Westminster John Knox Press.

President's Council on Bioethics. 2002. *Human Cloning and Human Dignity: An Ethical Inquiry.* Washington, DC: President's Council on Bioethics. www.bioethics.gov/ reports/cloningreport/pcbe_cloning_report.pdf (accessed June 25, 2004).

Regnier, M. H., and B. M. Knoppers. 2002. International initiatives. *Health Law Review* 11, no. 1: 67–71.

Reid, G. 2003. Representation of ? in the Public Sphere. Montreal, PQ: GELS Winter Symposium, 6; February 8.

Ries, N. 2004. Human dignity and biotechnology. *Journal of the Centre for International Studies* 5:49–55.

Rowley, J. D., E. Blackburn, M. S. Gazzaniga, et al. 2002. Harmful moratorium on stem cell research. *Science* 297(5589): 1957.

Saad, L. 2002. Cloning of humans is a turn off to most Americans. Gallup Organization. May 16. www.gallup.com/content/login.aspx?ci=6022 (accessed June 25, 2004).

Schachter, O. 1983. Comment: Human dignity as a normative concept. *American Journal of International Law* 77:848–54.

Shalev, C. 2002. Human cloning and human rights: A commentary. *Health and Human Rights* 6:137–51.

Shapiro, R. S. 2003. Legislative research bans on human cloning. *Cambridge Quarterly of Healthcare Ethics* 12:393–400.

Shultziner, D. 2003. Human dignity: Functions and meanings. *Global Jurist Topics* 3, no. 3: 1–21.

Skene, L., and M. Parker. 2002. The role of the Church in developing the law. *Journal of Medical Ethics* 28:215–18.

Standing Committee on Health. 2001. *Assisted Human Reproduction: Building Families.* Ottawa: House of Commons. http://www.parl.gc.ca/InfoComDoc/37/1/HEAL/Studies/Reports/healrp01-e.htm (accessed June 25, 2004).

Stolberg, S. 2005. Senate's leader veers from Bush over stem cells. *New York Times,* July 29. www.nytimes.com/2005/07/29/politics/29stem.html?th&emc=th (accessed August 2, 2005).

Suh, C. 2003. Hearing on cloning examines what is human. *United Press International Science News,* March 19. http://www.upi.com/view.cfm?StoryID=20030319-032318-3673r> (accessed June 25, 2004).

Sussman, D. 2001. Majority opposes human cloning. *ABC News,* August 16. http://abc news.go.com/sections/scitech/DailyNews/poll010816_cloning.html and http://www.pollingreport.com/science.htm (accessed June 25, 2004).

Traubman, T. 2002. Leaps of faith: Dolly the kosher camel. *Tishrei/Israeli Times,* September 16.

Turner, L. 2004. Time to drop the language of "consensus." *Nature Biotechnology* 21:1433.

USA Today/CNN/Gallup Poll Results. 2001. *USA Today,* November 28 http://www.usatoday.com/news/sept11/2001/11/28/poll-results.htm (accessed June 25, 2004).

UNESCO. 1997. *Universal Declaration of the Human Genome and Human Rights.* Sess. 29 of the General Conference. November 11. http://unesdoc.unesco.org/images/0010/001096/109687eb.pdf

United Nations, Ad Hoc Committee on an International Convention against the Reproductive Cloning of Human Beings. 2005. Update of May 18. www.un.org/law/cloning (accessed September 16, 2006).

Walters, L. 2004. The United Nations and human cloning: A debate on hold. *Hastings Center Report* 34, no. 1: 5.

Wright, T. G. 2000. Second thoughts: How human cloning can promote human dignity. *Valparaiso University Law Review* 35:1-35.

Young, C. D. 2002. A comparative look at the US and British approaches to stem cell research. *Albany Law Review* 65:831-55.

PART THREE

International Regulation
of Reprogenetics

CHAPTER SIX

The Governance
of Reprogenetic Technology

International Models

LORI P. KNOWLES

Recently, American bioethics committees have begun to examine foreign models of biotechnology governance in order to develop their own domestic policy advice. President Clinton's National Bioethics Advisory Committee (NBAC, 1999) and President Bush's Council on Bioethics (2002, 2004) invited presentations from experts on international regulation of assisted reproductive technology (ART), stem cell, and embryo research policy. In large part, the interest in other countries' approaches to biotechnology governance stems from recent developments in reprogenetics, primarily the possibility of human reproductive cloning raised by the cloning of Dolly, and the continued intense interest in human embryonic stem (ES) cell research. These developments have reinforced the international nature of biotechnology initiatives, both in development and in implementation. This is certainly the case for reprogenetic technologies.

A vast body of political, scientific, and public opinion data and analysis informs the policy and regulatory decisions of foreign governments concerning new biotechnological developments. Understanding and building on that body of work makes sense in striving to develop domestic policy. The strengths and weaknesses of foreign systems offer lessons for future policy initiatives. Keeping in mind that reprogenetic technologies are defined as technologies involving the use, manipulation, and storage of gametes and embryos, in this chapter I examine how selected foreign models of technology governance address the use of human embryos in research and treatment.

These models suggest how such policy might be created in the United States, backed by trends that inform that endeavor.

Although the range of policy responses to reprogenetic technologies is wide, a distinction can be made between those countries in which all research involving human embryos is prohibited and those in which it is not. For example, through legislation passed over the last twenty-five years, Ireland, Austria, Norway, Italy, Poland, and Germany prohibit all embryo research, and consequently reprogenetic research and treatment are practically nonexistent in those countries.[1] In countries that permit such research, regulation of reprogenetic technologies falls primarily within the scope of embryo research regulation. Embryo research regulation is often part of a comprehensive ART regulatory scheme, as in the United Kingdom (*Human Fertilisation and Embryology Act* 1990), Canada (*Assisted Human Reproduction Act* 2004), and France (*Loi Relative à la Bioethique* 2004); however, it may also be covered in part by human subjects research regulation or by specific legislative initiatives, as has happened in Australia and Germany (*Research Involving Human Embryos Act* 2002; *Prohibition of Human Cloning Act* 2002).[2] Several countries have recently enacted reprogenetic regulation, as the therapeutic possibilities that may flow from human ES cell research have helped galvanize or reshape efforts to create reprogenetic policy. This is the case in France, Australia, and Canada.

Because most reprogenetic interventions with people happen in infertility clinics, how those clinics are regulated affects the success of human research protections as a means to govern the use of reprogenetic technologies. In the field of reproductive medicine, there is a historical and ongoing overlap between infertility treatment involving clinical innovation and experimentation on human subjects. Many of the newest techniques that offer hope to infertile couples, such as ooplasm transplantation, have clearly involved human experimentation at the initial stages but have not always been regulated as such (Barritt et al. 2001; U.S. FDA 2002). Consequently, how regulations define what activities constitute research determines whether women are research subjects or patients or both. Absent a comprehensive scheme that oversees appropriate uses of human embryos, the enforcement of human subjects research protections and of important safeguards such as informed consent depends on the individual clinician-researcher's perceptions of the nature of the intervention as mere treatment, as innovative treatment, or as research. Although many clinician-researchers are motivated by deep concern for the well-being of their patient clients, their knowledge may not always lead to clarity on where the line between innovation and experimentation lies.

In many countries, legislators have attempted to create a broader regulatory structure that recognizes cloning and human ES cell research as embryo research and encompasses the larger reprogenetic enterprise. This is a daunting task, however, especially in the United States, which remains so divided by the abortion issue that all human embryo research is seen as a political and moral battleground in the abortion wars. In addition, since the practice of medicine is largely self regulating, attempts by others to regulate in the field are rare. Consequently, in contrast to the trend toward comprehensive ART regulation elsewhere in the Western world, the U.S. response to reprogenetic developments continues to be a piecemeal response to each new technology or application. For example, embryo research, already subject to a ban on federal funding, is further constrained by a limitation of federal funding to research on human ES cell lines derived by August 9, 2001, as announced in President Bush's *Address to the Nation* (Bush 2001). This situation has prompted some states—California and New Jersey in 2004, Massachusetts, Connecticut, Illinois, and New York in 2005—to create or consider state-funded stem cell research initiatives to ensure that human ES cell research continues within their borders.[3] A patchwork of state initiatives could lead to myriad and conflicting policy and regulatory approaches to the same technology within one country and no clear nationwide standards for appropriate uses of human embryos (Knowles 2005). Alternatively, should attempts be made to harmonize standards for such research, they could provide a de facto national standard. Steps in this direction have been taken by the National Academy of Sciences with its *Guidelines for Human Embryonic Stem Cell Research* (2005).

COMPREHENSIVE ART POLICY

International trends toward a comprehensive ART policy that encompasses reprogenetic regulation are often based on the blueprint for such a regulatory scheme created by the United Kingdom more than a decade ago. The Warnock Report, as it became known, was the first reprogenetics policy statement of any European country. It led in turn to the passage of the *Human Fertilisation and Embryology Act* (HFEA) of 1990. That act is the enabling legislation for a licensing scheme the purview of which is the use of human embryos and gametes in research, storage, and treatment.

The central component of the HFEA is its establishment of the Human Fertilisation and Embryology Authority, a nondepartmental, multidisciplinary public body that functions through several committees to monitor and inspect licensed facilities, review research protocols using human embryos, and make policy when faced with novel issues. The HFEA act is characterized by purposive language. That is, rather than enumerating permitted and prohibited uses of human embryos and gametes, it establishes the purposes for which a license may be granted and leaves open the means by which those purposes will be achieved. By so structuring the act, the legislative drafters enabled it to respond to almost any change in the dynamic area of reprogenetic research and treatment.[4]

The HFEA also provides for a code of practice and an information registry of children born of ART, and it includes limits that circumscribe the use of human embryos in research and prohibit some activities outright. While the HFEA prohibits the use of human embryos in reproductive cloning, Parliament felt it necessary to pass the *Human Reproductive Cloning Act* (2001) to clearly underline the prohibition.

Under the provisions of the act, it is possible to create embryos for research purposes, and it is possible to use cloning technology to do so—an issue of great disagreement internationally (Research Purposes Regulation 2001). In the United Kingdom, where scientific freedom is valued highly, to date a handful of licenses have been granted to permit research protocols that include the creation of human embryos by the process of cloning (HFEA 2004, 2005).

Canada, too, has a comprehensive ART regulatory scheme. The Canadian system is new, however, Parliament having enacted the *Assisted Human Reproduction Act* (AHRA) in March 2004 after more than a decade and a half of attempts to create national ART policy. Like the HFEA, the AHRA covers treatment, storage, and research related to human embryos and gametes used in both public and private research and practice. The AHRA has three stated objectives: it delineates a set of prohibited activities, establishes a means of protecting the health and safety of ART patients, and establishes oversight by creating a controlled environment for ART-related research. The latter is accomplished by establishing an oversight body called the Assisted Human Reproduction Agency (AHRA). Once established, the agency, like the U.K. HFEA authority, will be responsible for licensing, inspection, and enforcement of a set of controlled activities.

Unlike the HFEA, the AHRA does not follow a purposive approach. Instead, it delineates the activities that would be permissible yet subject to licensing and restrictions. The creation of this list is being prepared pursuant to regulations to the AHRA and is currently in formation. The challenge to this approach is to keep the list of controlled activities framed in broad, general, and, if possible, purposive terms to avoid a laundry list of specific techniques and technological applications. Such a list would rapidly become outdated and incomplete.

The AHRA incorporates several other elements that also distinguish it from the HFEA. First, it sets out a list of guiding principles in section 1 of the act, rather than in a legislative preamble, where they then provide only interpretative background to the act. This is an important point, for embedding the principles within the act itself means that decisions of the agency can be reviewed or challenged by invoking the principles as part of the enabling legislation. This gives the principles greater legal force and provides a strict ethical backdrop against which to examine or challenge administrative decisions about particular research protocols, licensing decisions, or regulations pertaining to controlled activities. Second, the ARHA prohibits human cloning for either reproductive or research purposes. The prohibition of the latter was particularly contentious in the debates preceding the passage of the legislation. In addition, the AHRA puts considerable emphasis on legislating a principle of noncommercialization of human reproduction, including prohibitions against the sale of ova and sperm and against commercial surrogacy arrangements. Finally, the AHRA establishes a legislative review period for three years after the act came into force. Given the swift pace of change and development in reprogenetics, this is a particularly appropriate mechanism to review the effects of regulation, and it is a relatively common provision in more recent regulatory initiatives worldwide.

Like Canada, France has struggled to update its bioethics law in light of developments in cloning and stem cell science. Traditionally a conservative nation when faced with human embryo research, France has changed its policy significantly, adopting a more comprehensive approach to regulating the use of embryos in treatment and research. Although passed in mid-2004, the new bioethics law, *Loi Relative à la Bioethique* 2004, did not come into effect until mid-2005. The law updates previous bioethics legislation passed in 1994 and creates an agency, l'Agence de la biomédecine, that oversees infertility treatments, prenatal diagnostics, and embryo research. As is the case in Canada, embryo research is limited to the use of surplus embryos from fertility treatments, and cloning for both reproduction and research is prohibited. Research on human ES cells will be permitted for a period of five years so long as it is in pursuit of developing treatments for serious diseases. France's dramatic change from no embryo research to national ART oversight and stem cell research reflects awareness that human ES cells and other reprogenetic research is now a global scientific enterprise, one that, in the words of François Aubert, deputy minister for research, "it would not be realistic to prevent" (quoted in Burgermeister 2004).

TARGETED EMBRYO RESEARCH LEGISLATION

Legislation that aims to regulate the use of human embryos only in reprogenetic research (and not in treatment) generally takes two forms. The first is a blanket prohibition on embryo research, such as the German *Embryo Protection Act* (1990), and the second is a regulatory scheme aimed solely at delineating research uses of human embryos. An example of the latter is Australia's 2002 *Research Involving Human Embryos Act* (RIHEA). Passed simultaneously with the *Prohibition of Human Cloning Act,* these two Australian Acts prohibit reproductive and research cloning and the creation of embryos for research purposes. The RIHEA addresses only the use of surplus embryos establishing a licensing scheme directed by a committee of the National Health and Medical Research Council, which is the body that oversees the practice of medicine on a national level. Additional uses of embryos in ART are regulated by state legislation to varying degrees. In keeping with review provisions found in many of the more recent reprogenetic acts, both Australian statutes are subject to periodic review of their operation, the first review having been completed in December 2005.

Technology-specific regulation is another means of governing reprogenetic technologies. For example, nations around the world have acted swiftly to create human cloning policy. Many nations have specific legislation prohibiting human reproductive cloning, while others include such a provision in existing legal frameworks. Human ES cell science has also prompted the creation of ad hoc policy responses. Even where the derivation of stem cells is covered under comprehensive ART regulations, actual uses of stem cells, once derived, may not fall under the purview of ART regulations. This is the case for the HFEA. In response to this lacuna the United Kingdom has created a national stem cell bank, with its own steering committee, that is responsible for guidelines and oversight of research using banked stem cell lines (http:// ukstemcellbank.org.uk).

International human ES cell policy is a regulatory patchwork that includes a number of countries with specific human ES cell policy that is not part of broader reprogenetic regulation (Knowles 2004). Israel, a world leader in stem cell research, has restrictive embryo research laws dating from 1998 (which are being revisited), but it also has a more liberal attitude toward the creation of embryos by cloning for research, as evidenced by a recommendation to permit the technique by the Bioethics Advisory Committee of Israel Academy of Sciences and Humanities (*Use of Embryonic Stem Cells for Therapeutic Research* 2001). In Asia, several countries have either no formal ART regulation or restrictive regulations concerning embryos, yet they also have liberal attitudes toward human ES cell research or research cloning. In China, Japan, Singapore, and South Korea, reproductive cloning is prohibited but research cloning either is being conducted, or is permitted, or is supported by policy bodies such as bioethics advisory committees (Knowles 2004; Régnier and Knoppers 2002).

COMMONALITIES IN REPROGENETICS POLICY DEVELOPMENT

Although the discussion to this point has focused on the wide variety of policy responses to reprogenetic developments, there are also similarities, both in policy development experience and in regulatory content, that are informative for future reprogenetic policy development. Almost every nation that regulates reprogenetics has struggled to develop clear policies with respect to embryo research, and in many cases the road to policy implementation has been long and tortuous.

The question of whether or not to permit embryo research is characterized everywhere by a tension between the desire for therapeutic benefits from that research and the need to prevent abuses. Internationally accepted norms have force not only because they are widely endorsed but also because the reputation of human embryo research depends on the standards under which it is performed. Countries in which there is little regulation of embryo research, such as China, often face an uphill battle gaining recognition and respect for their research results. In addition, as research is increasingly conducted in multicenter trials and with international cooperation, harmonization of standards becomes increasingly important.

UNDERLYING MORAL CONTROVERSY

The task of developing reprogenetics policy is fraught with difficulty, primarily because of the great diversity of opinions on the moral status of the human embryo.[5] The determination of moral status requires certain responses to questions about the permissibility, restrictions, and prohibitions of embryo research. Despite cultural, social, and religious differences within and among the nations examined, it is possible to find commonalities in guiding principles, limitations on permissible research, and prohibited uses of embryos.

The central finding from public consultation about reprogenetic research is that there is a great diversity of opinion on the acceptability of that research, which reflects a lack of consensus on the moral status of the embryo (*Proceed with Care: Final Report of Royal Commission on New Reproductive Technologies* 1993; *Report of the Committee of Enquiry into Human Fertilisation and Embryology* 1984). Two slightly different formulations of the conflict over the status of the embryo and its deserved legal protection in scientific research can be gleaned. The first formulation describes the conflict as follows: either human embryos have the same moral status as human persons and consequently deserve equal protection, or they have a lesser moral status and consequently are not deserving of the same level of protections. A more extreme formulation of these two irreconcilable positions turns to the concept of potentiality. The first position here is that human embryos have the same status as human persons by virtue of their potential for human life, and consequently they too must be protected from research that is not for their benefit, and certainly from research that could harm or kill them. The argument on the other side posits that human embryos are not persons or even potential persons but are simply a form of human tissue and therefore do not deserve protected status. In the face of this fundamental disagreement, science fails. It is not possible to resolve this issue using scientific tools, something acknowledged in several policy documents.

Despite the impossibility of resolving this seemingly threshold issue, a majority of nations adopt a position that elects to permit embryo research within limits. This pragmatic approach seeks to balance the scientific, medical, and moral costs of not pursing embryo research with the moral cost of permitting such research. Although a decision to pursue embryo research within limits is often cast as a compromise, it is actually a choice to reject the position that human embryos have the same status and rights of full human beings. Similarly, countries that prohibit embryo research are choosing in favor of the former position—that embryos have the same moral weight as full human persons, entitled to the same protections against harmful research.

Where the opinions of a population are divided between the extreme positions, some regarding embryos as human persons and others seeing them as mere collections of cells, the intermediate position is a true compromise. Such a dichotomy permits a compromise that rejects both extreme positions and holds that the embryo must have special status—less than full personhood and more than simply a mass of cells. Interestingly, in reaching this decision, many countries appeal to the legal status of the human embryo, which in nearly every country in the Western world is less than that of a juridical person. This fact is used to bolster the argument that embryos are not moral persons, but without much explanation as to why the legal interpretation informs the question of moral status. It would seem that widespread legal agreement that embryos ought not to be accorded the same rights as children and adults could be used as evidence of an international norm; however, this is not explicitly stated.

COMMON PRINCIPLES GUIDING REPROGENETICS POLICY

Diverse nations adopt common principles to guide the formation of reprogenetic governance. Chief among these is respect for human life and dignity. The concept of human dignity is widely accepted and understood outside the United States, but it is hard to define, and it remains controversial in the United States (Caulfield and Chapman 2005). Despite U.S. resistance to the concept and a corresponding resistance to formalizing the language of human rights, respect for human dignity informs other internationally shared principles, such as that reproduction should not be commercialized. Not surprisingly, this is another controversial idea in the United States. Other guiding principles seek to ensure the high quality and safety of medical treatments, safeguard respect for free and informed consent of individuals, minimize the harms and maximize the benefits of reprogenetic interventions, relieve human suffering, protect the freedom of scientific research, and promote the health and well-being of women and children. These principles are not controversial and respond to several closely held values in the United States. How one balances these principles in designing specific legislation is the heart of the challenge in creating reprogenetic policy.

Finding that balance is challenging, as some of the guiding principles point in different directions with respect to the constraints that should be placed on scientific investigation and market exploitation of reprogenetic technology applications. For example, respect for scientific freedom and the relief of human suffering suggest that constraints on developing treatments or applications of reprogenetic technology should be applied in the least invasive way. A principle of noncommercialization of reproduction, however, mandates strict limitation on market exploitation of reprogenetic applications. This principle is part of the Canadian, Australian, and continental European approach to reprogenetic technology applications. By contrast, the United States has an embedded tradition of commercialization that already applies to many realms of human reproduction, from sales of ova and commercial surrogacy to sales of gender selection technologies and parental DNA testing. Restrictions on commercialization in the United States are viewed with suspicion, as is much government regulation. Current government restrictions on funding of human ES cell research continue to be controversial. Despite differing emphases on principles that should guide the regulation of reprogenetic technologies, there is widespread agreement that some regulation of these technologies is needed. What remains controversial is the scope and content that reprogenetic policy should take.

COMMON LIMITS IMPOSED ON REPROGENETICS REGULATION

Although there is no consensus about the moral status of the embryo, there is agreement that if embryo research is permissible, limitations are necessary and appropriate. Such limitations reflect a compromise view about the acceptability of research using human embryos and are a means of addressing concerns about inappropriate uses of reprogenetic technologies. Legislated limits represent an acknowledgment that public fears are respected and recognition that human embryos are distinct from other human tissue—a distinction that merits special treatment. Support for oversight of reprogenetics is in part a desire to ensure that objectionable scientific research is not being conducted out of sight. Many of the fears about abuse in embryo research are widely shared and have resulted in considerable consensus about what uses should be prohibited. There is less consensus, although some commonality, about the limitations that should be imposed on the use of human embryos in order to strike a balance between allaying public concerns, promoting beneficial research and respecting the connection between human embryos and the rest of the human community.

Limitations commonly imposed in creating reprogenetic policy include the need to obtain specific informed consent from the sources of the gametes or embryos before use in treatment or research unrelated to the source. Such a policy would recognize not only that the embryo originates from two people, but also that those people might have specific wishes with respect to its disposition or might have attachments to the embryo that might be deeply held and should be respected. Although informed consent with respect to research using all human tissue has become the standard of care, gametes and embryos are often imbued with hopes and life plans by the tissue sources, which results in a different sort of connection between source and tissue.[6] Given the possible choices for the disposition of gametes and embryos, including donation, indefinite storage, destruction, and "adoption," most agree that consent to use them in reprogenetic research is appropriate and should show the source's understanding of the nature of the research (Lo et al. 2003).

Other common limits on embryo use in research include limits on the time during which an embryo may be used in research (generally not after fourteen days of development, not including time in cryopreservation) and a requirement for peer review to determine whether use of embryos in a particular protocol is necessary and appropriate. If the work can be conducted using animal models, then human embryos should not be used. Most reprogenetics policy, even in very laissez-faire systems, still incorporate protocol review. The more decentralized the policy, the greater the likelihood that protocol review will be local rather than national. The existence of regulatory oversight also represents a limit on the use of human embryos in research.

Finally, one limit about which there is disagreement is restricting the use of embryo research to those embryos that are surplus to reproductive projects—surplus in vitro fertilization (IVF) embryos created in pursuit of infertility treatment. Many countries—Canada, France, Australia, and the seventeen European countries that have ratified the Council of Europe Convention on Human Rights and Biomedicine—limit embryo research to only those embryos (*Additional Protocol to The Convention for the Protection of Human Rights* 1998). Because much of the benefit of human ES cell research is potentially from the ability to create embryos using cloning technology to enable autologous transplantation, the issue of creating embryos for research purposes is a major dividing line among countries with regulation of reprogenetic technology.

The primary objection to creating embryos specifically for research is based on both the intentions of the person creating the embryo and, related to that, the chance that embryo might be implanted. The argument is that there is a qualitative difference between creating an embryo in a reproductive project, leaving a chance that it could be implanted in a woman, and creating an embryo specifically for use in a research project, where both intention and chance of implantation are absent. Objections to the creation of embryos for research appeal to notions of respect for human dignity and avoidance of instrumental use of human embryos. Some believe that the creation of embryos without the intention of implantation does not show adequate respect for the potential of the human embryo or its connection to the rest of the human community. Others deny that there is a difference between creating embryos for the purposes of reproduction and creating them for research, as in the former situation there is still a significant chance that the embryos will not be implanted.

Because this is becoming a major issue in the regulation of human ES cell research, particularly with respect to creating embryos by means of cloning technology (research cloning), a few points should be kept in mind. First, the creation of embryos provides the only way to conduct some crucial and basic research, such as research on the process of human fertilization. Second, as techniques for IVF improve, it is possible that the need to create surplus embryos will be significantly reduced or even eliminated; one of the frequently approved uses of embryo research is the improvement of IVF techniques. At the same time that legislation permits embryo research, it is advocating that research improve IVF techniques and that fertility specialists attempt to reduce the surplus of embryos created for infertility treatment. As this happens, and if embryo research is dependent on the existence of spare embryos donated with informed consent, it is possible that the supply of embryos for research will dwindle, although not likely in the next few years given existing surpluses.

Alternatively, if the research supply is limited to surplus embryos from IVF, two other results are possible. First, in light of the tremendous interest in human ES cell research, there is little doubt that demand for embryos and ova for research will increase. Increased demand will only augment incentives for infertility clinics and researchers to ensure a supply of ova is available. This is particularly true where physicians and clinics are conducting embryo research themselves, and if ova and embryos can be bought and sold between clinics and research institutions. Clearly, one solution to this last issue is to institute clear conflict of interest guidelines that ensure that infertility clinics cannot benefit financially for providing surplus embryos to other researchers. However, where the research is conducted on site, conflict of interest problems will continue to exist. There are a number of safeguards that impose distance between scientific benefit, procurement, and consent procedures with respect to tissue collection and use in research. These might provide a good template for policy development in this area.

Demand for ova or embryos could translate into pressure on women undergoing IVF to "donate" ova or embryos specifically for research when undergoing infertility treatments that already involve invasive removal of ova for IVF. Relationships between doctors and patients are notoriously prone to imbalances in power, and this is especially true in infertility clinics. Mix in a real desire and enthusiasm on the part of the clinician-researcher for research that will alleviate infertility issues, and the patient's desire to be compliant and agreeable, and it may not be possible to refuse consent to obtain extra ova or embryos for research. Unfortunately, while it might be tempting to regulate a maximum number of embryos that can be created, or ova that can be retrieved, doing so would not benefit the many women who try to get pregnant through several cycles of IVF. In fact, establishing a maximum could increase the number of surgeries women would need to retrieve ova for subsequent treatments of IVF.

In light of the foregoing, a country attempting to draft ART regulation ought to consider endorsing the use of spare embryos where possible and permitting the creation of embryos for research where necessary to achieve the objectives of research, or in situations in which access to spare embryos is not possible. This does not fully address the concerns over possible coercion of infertility patients; these concerns require greater analysis and specific guidelines or recommendations.

COMMON PROHIBITED PRACTICES IN REPROGENETICS POLICY

While limits on the use of embryos in research differ to greater and lesser degrees, there are several commonly prohibited reprogenetic practices. The chief challenge with respect to defining prohibited practices is that the more comprehensive the list of prohibited activities, the more difficult it is to get public and political agreement. For this reason it is tempting to draft a response to a particular practice on which there is widespread agreement. For example, there is remarkable consensus that research and clinical attempts aimed at reproductive cloning should be prohibited. But though it is generally easier to get agreement with respect to a specific technique, this leads to a regulatory patchwork with respect to different technologies that does not aid the development of comprehensive, dynamic, adaptive regulation of a field of scientific endeavor.

International condemnation of human reproductive cloning stands as one of two examples of international accord. There is agreement among most nations that the practice of reproductive cloning should be not only prohibited but also criminalized. Similarly, the creation and implantation of human-animal hybrid embryos has been widely condemned, although Asia tends to be more permissive regarding chimeric embryos. South Korea and China have used animal ova and human sperm to create embryos that can be used in stem cell research. This would be unacceptable in most other countries in which there is human embryo regulation. Other widely prohibited practices include the introduction of inheritable genetic modifications (also known as germline interventions) and the use of fetal eggs. Outside the United States, there is agreement on the noncommercializability of human reproduction and on prohibiting the use of genetic sex selection for nonmedical purposes (Convention on Biomedicine 1997; UNESCO 1997).

CONCLUSION

Regulation of reprogenetic technologies runs the gamut from minimal regulation, with reliance on market forces, to comprehensive ART regulation governing the use of embryos and gametes in research and treatment. Between these extremes there are models of reprogenetic governance that are more and less restrictive. Differences in regulation are not limited to the form (national oversight or technology-specific legislation) but also depend on the principles that guide the development of national policy. While the newly formed regimens in Canada and France adopt a model similar to that of the United Kingdom by requiring licenses for reprogenetic activities and endowing an agency with administrative and policymaking powers within the scope of the enabling legislation, the scope of permissible reprogenetic activities in those countries is vastly different. These differences within similar regulatory structures show that a comprehensive regulatory strategy need not be overly restrictive, but that it ensures awareness and vigilance of ongoing research protocols. By contrast, a seemingly laissez-faire system that leaves private enterprise largely unregulated, as in the United States, may in fact be more restrictive if government funding is withheld for human embryo research.

Despite differences in scope and content of reprogenetic technology governance, there are important lessons to be learned. First, both the form and substance of policy initiatives are important. Policy should be drafted in general terms with a reliance on purposive language where possible. Avoidance of overly specific descriptions of technologies and practices that are subject to regulation will provide a more dynamic and adaptable regulatory scheme in the face of rapidly developing science and technology. Second, the creation of reprogenetics policy has proven publicly contentious, politically controversial and extremely time-and-resource-consuming. Despite this, the need to engage in the process becomes more pressing with each new technological and scientific development.

As tempting as it is to develop an ad hoc response to each new controversial reprogenetic application, there are some common guiding principles and clearly unacceptable uses of human embryos that need to be publicly discussed and debated. Failure to define the ethical commitments that underlie even the most basic attempts at reprogenetic regulation makes future policy exercises reactive in nature and can result in potentially incoherent or inconsistent policy. The need to engage in developing reprogenetic policy is only becoming more apparent. Looking to foreign models of reprogenetic technology governance provides fertile ground to begin that process.

ACKNOWLEDGMENTS

The author gratefully acknowledges the research assistance of Laura Inglis, Health Law Institute, University of Alberta, made possible through funding by StemCellNet.

NOTES

1. The relevant legislation is Ireland (*Constitution Act,* 1983), Austria (*Austrian Reproductive Medicine Act* 1992), Norway (*Law No. 100 of 5 December 2003*), Italy (*Law 40/2004*), Poland (*Law of 7 January 1993*), and Germany (*Embryo Protection Act of 1990*).

2. While permitting no embryo research, Germany passed a law in 2002 that permitted the importation of human ES cell lines for the purposes of research.

3. The relevant legislation is California (*California Stem Cell Research and Cures Act* 2004), New Jersey (*New Jersey Act Concerning Human Stem Cell Research* 2004), Massachusetts (*An Act Enhancing Regenerative Medicine in the Commonwealth* 2005), Connecticut (*An Act Permitting Stem Cell Research and Banning the Cloning of Human Beings* 2005), Illinois (*Executive Order Creating the Illinois Regenerative Institute for Stem Cell Research* 2005), and New York (*New York State Institute for Stem Cell Research and Regenerative Medicine Act* 2005).

4. An amendment to the act was necessary to include research purposes leading to the treatment of diseased or damaged tissues. This amendment was specifically inserted to provide for human ES cell research and the possibility of research cloning.

5. This section draws on an article I wrote on international stem cell regulation for the *Journal of Women's Health and Law* in 2000.

6. I use "tissue" here as a description, not to indicate any judgment about moral status.

REFERENCES

Additional Protocol to The Convention for the Protection of Human Rights and Dignity of the Human Being with Regard to the Application of Biology and Medicine, on the Prohibition of Cloning Human Beings. 1998. Paris: Council of Europe, December. http://conventions.coe.int/treaty/en/treaties/html/168.htm (accessed August 8, 2005).

Assisted Human Reproduction Act. 2004. Canada (c. 2).

Barritt et al. 2001. Mitochondria in human offspring derived from ooplasmic transplantation. *Human Reproduction* 16:513–16.

Burgermeister, J. 2004. France green lights stem cells. *The Scientist,* October 11.

Bush, G. W. 2001. *Address to the Nation on Stem Cell Research. Public Papers of the Presidents,* 953–956. *www.whitehouse.gov/news/releases/2001/08/20010809-2.html.*

Caulfield, T, and A. Chapman. 2005. Human dignity as a criterion for science policy. *PLoS Medicine* 2(8): e244.

Committee on Guidelines for Human Embryonic Stem Cell Research, National Research Council. 2005. *Guidelines for Human Embryonic Stem Cell Research.* Washington, DC: National Academies Press.

Convention on Human Rights and Biomedicine. 1997. *Convention for the Protection of Human Rights and Dignity of the Human Being with regard to the Application of Biology and Medicine.* Council of Europe. http://conventions.coe.int/treaty/en/treaties/html/164.htm (accessed August 8, 2005).

Embryo Protection Act. 1990. Germany.

Human Fertilisation and Embryology Act. 1990. United Kingdom (c. 37). www.opsi.gov.uk/acts/acts1990/Ukpga_19900037_en_1.htm.

Human Fertilisation and Embryology Authority. 2004. HFEA grants first therapeutic cloning license for research. London: HFEA, August 11. www.hfea.gov.uk/PressOffice/Archive/1092233888 (accessed August 5, 2005).

———. 2005. HFEA grants embryonic stem cell research license to study motor neuron disease. London: HFEA, February 8. www.hfea.gov.uk/PressOffice/Archive/110786 1560.

Human Fertilization and Embryology (Research Purposes) Regulation. 2001. S.1 2001/188.

Human Reproductive Cloning Act. 2001. United Kingdom (c. 23). www.opsi.gov.uk/acts/acts2001/20010023.htm.

Knowles, L. P. 2004. A regulatory patchwork: Human ES cell research oversight. *Nature Biotechnology* 22, no. 2: 157–63.

———. 2005. Stem cell research policy: Where do we draw the lines? *New England Law Review* 39:623.

———. 2006. State-sponsored human stem cell research: Regulatory approaches and standard setting. In *States and Stem Cells: Policy and Economic Implications of State-Sponsored Stem Cell Research,* ed. A. D. Levine, 75-111. Princeton, NJ: Policy Research Institute for the Region.

Lo, B., V. Chou, M. I. Cedars, et al. 2003. Consent from donors for embryo and stem cell research. *Science* 301:921.

Loi Relative à la Bioethique. 2004. France: *Law no. 2004-800,* effective May 5, 2005, p. 9872. www.sante.gouv.fr/adm/dagpb/bo/2004/04-32/a0322316.htm (accessed August 5, 2005).

National Academy of Sciences. 2005. *Guidelines for Human Embryonic Stem Cell Research.* Washington, DC: National Academies Press.

National Bioethics Advisory Committee. *Ethical Issues in Human Stem Cell Research.* www.georgetown.edu/research/nrcbl/nbac/execsumm.pdf (accessed August 8, 2005).

Office of Governor Jim Doyle. 2004. Governor Doyle outlines Wisconsin's strategy to remain at the forefront of biotechnology, health sciences, and stem cell research. www.wisgov.state.wi.us/journal_media_detail.asp?prid=832 (accessed August 8, 2005).

Office of Governor M. Jodi Rell. 2005. Governor Rell signs law establishing stem cell research fund, ban on human cloning. www.ct.gov/governorrell/cwp/view.asp?Q= 294840&A=1761 (accessed August 8, 2005).

President's Council on Bioethics. 2002. *Human Cloning and Human Dignity: An Ethical Inquiry.* 2002. Washington, DC. www.bioethics.gov/reports/cloningreport/pcbe_ cloning_report.pdf (accessed August 8, 2005).

———. 2004. *Reproduction and Responsibility: The Regulation of New Biotechnologies.* Washington, DC. www.bioethics.gov/reports/reproductionandresponsibility/_pcbe_ final_reproduction_and_responsibility.pdf (accessed August 8, 2005).

Proceed with Care: Final Report of Royal Commission on New Reproductive Technologies. 1993. Ottawa: Canada Communications Group-Publishing.

Régnier, M. H., and B, M. Knoppers. 2002. International initiatives. *Health Law Review* 11, no. 1: 70.

Report of the Committee of Enquiry into Human Fertilisation and Embryology. 1984. London: HMSO.

Research Involving Human Embryos Act. 2002. Australia.

UNESCO. *Universal Declaration on the Human Genome and Human Rights.* 1997. Paris. http://unesdoc.unesco.org/images/0011/001102/110220e.pdf#page=47 (accessed August 8, 2005).

U.S. Food and Drug Administration. 2002. CBER, Biological Response Modifiers Advisory Committee meeting, hearings, May 9-10. www.fda.gov/phrms/dockets/ac/ cber02.htm.

Walters, L. 2004. The United Nations and human cloning: A debate on hold. *Hastings Center Report* 34, no. 1 (January–February): 5–6.

CHAPTER SEVEN

Regulating Reprogenetics in the United Kingdom

ANDREW GRUBB

In 1978 the first test-tube baby, Louise Brown, was born in the United Kingdom. At that time there was no regulation or control of assisted reproductive technologies (ARTs) or embryo research in the United Kingdom. The technology was in its infancy, but it was clear that in vitro fertilization (IVF) and future developments in the technology would present challenges for established social and ethical thinking. State control and regulation of ART and embryo research seemed inevitable, but until 1991 and the coming into force of the Human Fertilisation and Embryology Act of 1990, no formal, statutory regulation existed.

Between 1985 and 1991, professional self-regulation existed through a body set up jointly by the Medical Research Council and the Royal College of Obstetricians and Gynaecologists. Known at first as the Voluntary Licensing Authority and subsequently as the Interim Licensing Authority, this body issued licenses for embryo research and ART procedures. It had no teeth, and its only sanction in removing a license was to shame (or generate peer pressure on) clinicians and scientists into conforming with its licensing requirements.

In the light of public concerns about the new technologies, in particular embryo experimentation, the British government was not complacent in pursuing public policy formation, but it was undoubtedly cautious in moving forward, as the subsequent history of the resulting legislation shows. In 1982, it set up a multidisciplinary Committee of Inquiry chaired by Baroness Warnock, a distinguished moral philosopher. In 1984, a document that came to be known as the Warnock Report (*Report of the Committee of Inquiry into Human Fertilisation and Embryology*) recommended a statutory framework for the regulation of ART and embryo research in the United Kingdom. In 1986 the government produced a consultative document entitled *Legislation on Human Infertility Services and Embryo Research*. This was followed in 1987 by a white paper, *Human Fertilisation and Embryology: A Framework for Legislation*, which set out the government's proposals for future legislation and in large part enacted the recommendations of the Warnock Committee. At the center of these proposals was the creation of a statutory licensing authority with powers to license ART and embryo research. In 1989, the government introduced the Human Fertilisation and Embryology Bill, which, after protracted and sometimes acrimonious parliamentary debate, became an Act of Parliament on November 1, 1990. The Human Fertilisation and Embryology Act of 1990 came fully into force on August 1, 1991. It covers ART and embryo research in the United Kingdom as a whole.[1]

THE HUMAN FERTILISATION AND EMBRYOLOGY ACT OF 1990

The 1990 act created a complex regulatory framework dealing with licensing of ART procedures (section 11 and schedule 2), control over embryos and gametes (section 12(c) and schedule 3), disclosure of information (sections 33–35), and parentage of children (sections 27–29).[2] The regulation is intrusive and the scheme is virtually comprehensive, covering everything except research on gametes or treatment with gametes that are not donated. Surrogacy is also not directly regulated, except to the extent that IVF procedures are used.

At the focus of the legislative framework is the Human Fertilisation and Embryology Authority (HFEA). The principal functions of the HFEA are:

- To license treatment services and the storage of gametes and embryos (sections 11–14);
- To license research on embryos (sections 11–12 and 15 and schedule 2);
- To monitor and inspect premises and activities carried out under a license (section 9);
- To maintain a register of information about donors, treatments, and children born from those treatments (section 31);
- To produce a "Code of Practice" as guidance for clinics about the conduct of licensed activities (section 25);

- To publicize its role and provide relevant advice and information to patients, donors, and clinics (section 8); and
- To submit an annual report to the secretary of state on its activities (section 7).

The 1990 act divides ART into three categories, according to whether those procedures are (1) illegal, as with keeping or using embryos after fourteen days (sections 3(3)(a) and 3(4)); (2) permitted with a license from the HFEA, as is the creation and use of embryos up to fourteen days for treatment or research (sections 3(1)(a)) and the storage of embryos and gametes (sections 3(1)(b) and 4(1)(a)); or (3) unregulated, as with GIFT and IUI. The legislative framework remains virtually unaltered eleven years later.[3]

To carry out a licensable treatment procedure or to conduct research on embryos without a license from the HFEA is a criminal offense, with a maximum sentence of two years' imprisonment (sections 41(2) and (4)). Licensing procedures include annual inspection of clinics and research facilities, together with monitoring of their activities.

Licenses are subject to statutory conditions relating to such matters as record keeping, supplying information to the HFEA, payment for gametes or embryos, welfare of the child, counseling, providing information to donors or patients, and the maximum storage periods and disposal of gametes and embryos after storage (sections 12–15). In addition, further standard license conditions or ones specific to a particular clinic are imposed by the HFEA.

REPROGENETICS AND THE 1990 ACT

The main thrust of the 1990 act, and the motivation behind it, was to regulate reproductive technologies and embryo research, not genetic technologies. The HFEA has no general remit over genetic issues as such; that is a matter for a number of other genetics-oriented public bodies,[4] in particular the Human Genetics Commission, created in 2000 (replacing the Human Genetics Advisory Commission and the Advisory Committee on Genetic Testing).

However, the 1990 act brings reprogenetics within the HFEA's jurisdiction in two ways. First, some genetic issues were explicitly dealt with in the act. For example, some prohibitions on genetic manipulations were written into the act: certain (but not all) cloning procedures were made illegal (section 3(3)(d)); treatment and research licenses cannot authorize altering the genetic structure of a cell while it forms part of an embryo (schedule 2, paragraphs

1(3) and 3(4)); and the creation of human-animal hybrids is illegal unless for diagnostic fertility testing (schedule 2, paragraphs 1(1)(f) and 3(5)). Also, Parliament specifically contemplated research on embryos in order to develop preimplantation genetic diagnosis (PGD), and this is one of the five specific purposes for which a research (schedule 2, paragraph 3(2)(e)) or treatment (schedule 2, paragraph 2(1)(d)) license may be granted by the HFEA.

Second, the broad "regulatory net" of the 1990 act catches most reprogenetic developments so far. For example, PGD treatment involves the "creation" and "use" of an embryo and therefore requires a license (section 3(1)(a) and (b)). The HFEA has developed a specific licensing procedure to deal with PGD treatments (see below). Likewise, cloning by "cell nuclear replacement" (CNR) requires a license from the HFEA to be carried out lawfully (and it can be carried out only for research, not for treatment). The extraction of embryonic stem cells for research purposes also requires a license from the HFEA, and the scope for granting such licenses has recently been extended by Parliament (although the regulation does not cover subsequent storage or use of the cells). As a result, the HFEA has become the United Kingdom's regulator of reprogenetics.

THE REGULATORY SCHEME
The Human Fertilisation and Embryology Authority

The HFEA is constituted as a nondepartmental public body (NDPB), independent of the Department of Health, although it works closely with the department. It has legal personality as a body corporate (section 5). It has eighteen members (including a chairman and deputy), a substantial executive arm, including a chief executive, and it is accountable to Parliament through the minister for public health.

Members of the HFEA are appointed by the health ministers for terms of three years. (schedule 1, paragraphs 4(1) and 5). Applications for vacancies are invited by advertisement in the national press. The government is committed to making public body appointments following a fair procedure and on the basis of merit following the so-called Nolan Principles for conduct in public life, comprising selflessness, integrity, objectivity, accountability, openness, honesty, and leadership (Committee on Standards in Public Life 1995). The Nolan Principles inform both the conduct of the process of appointment and the essential qualities of appointees. Potential appointees are interviewed by a panel, including Department of Health officials and the chair of the authority, after which recommendations are made to the ministers. Some names of suitable appointees may be held on a "reserve list," should vacancies occur in the coming two years. There is no evidence, nor any suggestion, that appointments are influenced by political considerations or individuals' value systems, although there is probably one exception to this rule: it is difficult to see how an individual who objected to embryo research in principle could function as part of a body that regulates and licenses that activity. But this exception is not a political matter; rather, it is a legal one. Given that embryo research is lawful in appropriate circumstances, a person who held this view could not fairly consider, for example, whether to grant a license for embryo research, and his or her involvement would open up the HFEA to legal challenge.

The appointments to the HFEA must accord with a number of features. First, there must be gender diversity, as appointments must reflect the need that the HFEA's proceedings be "informed by the views of both men and women" (schedule 1, paragraph 4 (2)). Second, there must be a mix of "expert" and "lay" members, and the latter must be in the majority. Hence, the chairman, deputy chairman, and a majority of the other members must not be doctors, scientists, or clinicians involved in ART or embryo research (schedule 1, paragraph 4(3)). However, to retain the necessary professional expertise required in the HFEA's work, at least a third of its members must be scientists or clinicians (schedule 1, paragraph 4(4)). There are (or have been) lawyers, counselors, theologians, and individuals with personal experience of infertility on the HFEA, as well as clinicians and research scientists. There has also apparently been a practice of making at least one appointment each from Northern Ireland, Scotland, and Wales.

As regards the HFEA's work, there has been a steady and substantial increase since 1991. In August 1991, fifty-four centers were providing IVF treatment, twenty of which also carried out embryo research (Interim Licensing Authority for Human In Vitro Fertilisation and Embryology 1991). In addition, three centers carried out embryo research alone. As of August 31, 2002, there were 115 licensed centers, nineteen of which carried out embryo research (Human Fertilisation and Embryology Authority 2002a). At that date, there were twenty-eight licensed research projects on human embryos. To give an overall sense of the scale of ART in the United Kingdom, in 2000–2001, 23,737 patients received IVF treatment, and there were 4,621 singleton births, 1,579 twin births, and 109 triplet births. In the same period, 3,438 patients underwent donor insemination (DI), and there were 746 singleton births, 49 twin births, and five triplet births. Average success rates of live births per treatment cycle are 21.8 percent (for IVF), 25.7 percent (for ICSI), and 11.0 percent (for DI). (Contrary to the usual position for medical care in the United Kingdom, most infertility treatment is paid for through the private sector. IVF and DI are not widely provided by the National Health Service.)

There are three aspects to the regulatory process to notice here: first, the regulatory mechanism (the licensing process); second, the formulation of policy that may inform regulatory behavior; and third, the overlap between the two processes.

The Licensing Process

The 1990 act locates the licensing process primarily within the remit of license committees of the HFEA (section 9; HFEA 1991). These consist of five members of the HFEA (one of whom must be a lay member), who decide whether to grant, vary, revoke, suspend, or renew licenses for treatment or research (sections 16 and 18–19). (Recently, the HFEA has set up a single Research Licence Committee chaired by, and with a majority of, lay members of the authority.) All licenses are granted subject to certain statutory conditions (sections 12–15), together with standard conditions developed by the HFEA for the particular procedure or with ones specific to the particular clinic or research project. Breach of a license condition may lead to a license being revoked (or varied) by a license committee (sections 18(1)(c) and (3) and 17(1)(e)). (Failure to follow the HFEA's Code of Practice may be taken into account by a license committee in determining whether the "person responsible" has breached a condition of the license or not carried out his duties under section 17 of the act (section 25(6)).

The license committees operate autonomously of the HFEA itself, in the sense that the full HFEA cannot grant a license and cannot direct a license committee to act in a particular way. To do so would be illegal and would undoubtedly lead to a successful application for judicial review to quash any decision reached. An appeal lies to the HFEA itself (section 20 and HFEA 1991, Part III) which, on the few occasions this has happened, sits as a small panel with a minimum of five members (with no overlap of members of the HFEA sitting at the two stages (section 20(3)). From the HFEA, an appeal lies on a point of law to the High Court, or in Scotland to the Court of Session (section 21). (There appears to be no provision covering an appeal in Northern Ireland.)

Clinics are licensed for up to three years to provide particular treatments, for example IVF (with or without donor eggs or sperm), AI with donor sperm, ICSI, and so on, with a named "person responsible" (usually the senior clinician) accountable to the HFEA for its operations and for conformity with the 1990 act and the HFEA's requirements as laid down in its Code of Practice (section 17). The *holder* of the license—known as the "nominal licensee"—is usually someone else, often a clinic manager (section 17(3)). The maximum period for a treatment or storage license is five years (schedule 2, paragraphs 1(5) and 2(3)).

By contrast, licenses for research are granted to individual projects, rather than to establishments, and there still has to be a "person responsible" who is accountable to the HFEA. Research licenses may only be granted for one of the eight purposes now permitted by the Act. The maximum period for a research project license is three years (schedule 2, paragraph 3(9)).

The licensing process for research on embryos is rigorous, reflecting their "special status" (Warnock Committee 1984, para. 11.17). A research project must have been approved by a local research ethics committee before the HFEA will consider an application for a license (Code of Practice 2001, para. 11.6). The License Committee will seek at least two independent peer reviews of the proposed project. The reviewers are asked to comment on, in particular:

- whether the proposed research falls under one or more of the research purposes permitted under the 1990 act;
- the potential importance of the research to the particular field;
- whether the research has previously been undertaken elsewhere;
- whether the use of human embryos is justified in furthering knowledge in the field;
- the suitability of the methods to be used for achieving the stated aims of the research;
- whether the proposed numbers of gametes or embryos are realistic and are likely to give meaningful results;
- the suitability of the proposed length of the study; and
- the suitability of the applicant's qualifications and professional background to undertaking research on human embryos.

A project can be licensed only if the committee is satisfied that the research is "necessary or desirable" for one of the stated purposes (schedule 2, paragraph 3(2)) and that the use of embryos is "necessary" (schedule 2, paragraph 3(6)). There is, therefore, a double hurdle: whether the use of human embryos is necessary, and whether the activity to be licensed (the research) is "necessary" or, if not, "desirable." The latter requires the HFEA to consider the merit and value of the research before it may grant a license.

If a license is granted, progress reports are required, and a final report must be provided to the HFEA, including the number of embryos used, the results and conclusions of the project, and any published work.

Licensing and Policy

The statutory arrangement has a curious consequence for the formulation of policy that may be required "on the hoof" by a particular license committee considering a novel application. In effect, the five members, rather than the full authority itself, may determine HFEA policy on a particular issue. The first applications for egg freezing (and subsequent use) and for the derivation of stem cells for research were decided in this way. It creates difficulties, including legal problems, for the HFEA later to decide that, in like circumstances, it is not HFEA policy to grant a license in a particular circumstance or for a specific procedure when a license committee has already done so. Issues of equality and fairness in exercising discretion in like cases arise. The introduction of a single license committee may help to provide consistency and continuity in decision making. Also, its constitution, with a chair and majority of lay members may go some way to allay any public concerns that scientists and medical professionals are determining the boundaries of ethical research.

Yet there are difficulties in ensuring that the HFEA formulates policy in these circumstances. The licensing and appeals structure makes it difficult for the full HFEA to consider a situation thrown up by an actual license application. The authority must not, and must not be seen to, instruct or direct a license committee on how to decide a particular application. Also, there may be an appeal to the HFEA if the decision goes against the applicant. Prior discussion might be regarded as tainting the decision-making process and lead to a successful judicial challenge for "procedural unfairness."

There is no doubt, however, that Parliament intended the HFEA to make policy within its area of competence. The authority has in recent years developed a system whereby it could maximize its policymaking role where novel questions arise in licensing applications. It is all a matter of logistics and sensitivity. It is now the practice to try to identify applications that have some novelty, which usually entails new techniques or procedures. With the appropriate anonymity, these are then referred to an appropriate committee, such as the Scientific and Clinical Advances Group or the Ethics and Law Committee (which in 2003 replaced, respectively, the Working Group on New Developments in Reproductive Technology and the Ethics Committee), and ultimately to the authority itself, for general advice on what the HFEA's policy should be. The advice is then considered by the license committee, which makes its own decision on the particular case in the light of that advice.

Policy

Policy formation is a matter for the authority, which is advised by its executive. It is a substantial part of its work. The Eleventh Annual Report of the authority, the most current available at the time of writing, identifies a number of policy issues that the HFEA is currently considering or has recently considered, including PGD, tissue typing, aneuploidy screening, embryo transfer, ICSI, donor information, and stem cell research (HFEA 2002a, 16–17).

However, the HFEA meets only on a monthly basis and only in ten months of the year, and therefore attends only to so much business. Equally, its size means that discussing every issue without some prior "sifting" of the issues would be difficult. To utilize the expertise and maximize the involvement of its members, the authority has since its inception operated with committees that undertake precisely this initial sifting. In formulating policy, perhaps the most important are the Ethics and Law Committee, the Regulation Committee, and the Scientific and Clinical Advances Group (all of which replaced other, earlier committees in 2003). Reports to the full authority from these committees allow the HFEA to consider policy choices in a practical way, knowing that the issues have been discussed by one (or more) of its committees at greater length and probably on a number of occasions. Ultimately, the authority may not adopt the approach put forward by the reporting committee, but the discussion is that much better informed as a result of the issue's prior consideration.

Sometimes, of course, policy issues are raised for the first time at full authority meetings and a choice may be made or, if time permits, a reference back to the appropriate committee will be made and the cycle of consideration within the authority begins.

In formulating policy within the HFEA, a number of sources of information, opinion, and argument are utilized. First, of course, there is the respective expertise of the individual members, whether clinician, scientist, lawyer, or layperson. The latter's "nontechnical expertise" as a member of the public should not be forgotten or underestimated when making moral or indeed scientific, choices.

Second, HFEA members are regularly briefed with the latest scientific and other published papers on reproductive technologies and reprogenetics. Sometimes the volume and complexity of the technical papers are a little overpowering. But it is essential to remain as fully informed as possible in making policy choices. Additionally, of course, relevant papers are provided when the members discuss a particular issue.

Third, the public's opinion on a particular issue may be sought. Public consultation documents have been used to aid the HFEA in formulating policy in a number of areas, for example, sex selection (HFEA 1993), donated ovarian tissue (HFEA 1994), payment to donors (HFEA 1998), cloning (HGAC/HFEA 1998), and PGD (HFEA 1999). Although the HFEA does not regulate according to public opinion, the views of the public are vitally important in its deliberations, particularly in areas of considerable moral controversy, such as cloning. It is fair to say that in one case, namely payment to sperm and egg donors, the consultation process contributed to a shift in the HFEA's initial policy response. Here, it was the professional response indicating the effect that a change of policy would have on the availability of sperm for donation that was particularly important.

Fourth, the HFEA interacts with other professional and governmental bodies. Examples of the former are the Royal College of Obstetricians and Gynaecologists, the British Fertility Society, and patient groups. Examples of the latter are, of course, the Department of Health, but also the Human Genetics Commission (HGC) (and its predecessors, the Human Genetics Advisory Commission and the Advisory Committee on Genetic Testing). Two of the most recent consultations, on cloning and PGD, have been with the HGC, and the HFEA's current policy on the availability and licensing of PGD is based on advice from a joint working group of the HFEA and HGC (as discussed below).

Multi-agency involvement has the obvious benefit of broader and greater consideration being given to particular issues. The HGC, of course, has a specific remit to advise the government in the field of human genetics. Its remit is both wider and narrower than that of the HFEA. One important difference is its constitution. It is a nonstatutory body. Its role is only advisory, and it cannot regulate, as the HFEA is able to do. It has no licensing powers and no teeth to enforce its views. In the area of reprogenetics, only the HFEA has the statutory power to control new developments and their implementation in clinical settings. Although there is no tension between the HFEA and HGC—the chairman of the HFEA is an ex officio member of the HGC—there is always the potential for turf disputes when multiple agencies have an interest in public policy formation and its implementation. Perhaps this potential would be even greater where two agencies both had overlapping legal powers.

REGULATING REPROGENETICS

Within its statutory jurisdiction, it is the HFEA that regulates reprogenetics through its licensing procedures. Of course, some techniques cannot be licensed because the 1990 act prohibits them (section 3(3)(d)). Since 1991 the HFEA has permitted or prohibited activity in a number of areas of reprogenetics:

- Sex selection of embryos is allowed only for serious medical conditions and not for social reasons (HFEA 2001, para. 9.9).
- Cloning of embryos for reproduction has never been permitted (and is now statutorily prohibited).
- Sperm sorting techniques should not be used (HFEA 2002, para. 9.10).
- Embryo splitting for treatment purposes is not permitted (HFEA 2002, para. 9.11).
- PGD is allowed only for serious inherited conditions.

In the last few years, two areas of reprogenetic developments have been especially prominent in public and other debates: PGD and cloning (including stem cell technology). The remainder of this chapter focuses on the HFEA's approach to regulating these developments.

PREIMPLANTATION GENETIC DIAGNOSIS
The Technique and Its Use

Preimplantation genetic diagnosis was a recognized technique before the 1990 act was enacted. Research projects to develop the technique were specifically contemplated in the 1990 act (schedule 2, paragraph 3(2)(e)). Since then, PGD has been utilized in the United Kingdom and elsewhere in the clinical context. It was developed as an alternative to prenatal diagnosis (PND) and termination of pregnancy.

PGD involves the creation of embryos and then the selection out of embryos found to carry a particular undesired genetic component, either at the gene level or at the chromosome level. It may also be used, and indeed was initially used, to sex embryos in order to avoid returning an embryo of a particular sex (usually male) where a sex-linked inheritable condition is present (such as hemophilia). PGD involves carrying out a biopsy of an embryo two to three days after fertilization, when the embryo is at the six- to ten-cell stage. Two cells are removed and subjected to a diagnostic technique to detect the abnormality, polymerase chain reaction (PCR) assay for single gene defects or fluorescent in situ hybridization (FISH) for chromosomal disorders.

As will be clear from this, PGD is not a technique deployed to overcome infertility problems. Rather, usually the couple is fertile but seeks access to the technology to avoid passing on a particular genetic condition. The latter is a feature of PGD as it has been used up to the present. It is not a screening technique, but it is used once a particular genetic condition is known to be in a family.

A new use of the technique has been advocated as a preimplantation genetic screening (PGS) procedure to determine the number of chromosomes in an embryo. The technique is the same, but the circumstances of its use are quite different. In aneuploidy screening, the purpose is to determine whether embryos that are to be returned to a woman undergoing infertility treatment have chromosome number abnormalities. It is thought that the latter may account for many instances of infertility. Thereby, only "healthy" embryos will be used, increasing the chances of implantation and reducing the risks of spontaneous miscarriage.

Thus, the use of PGS differs from that of PGD in that (1) it is part of an assisted reproduction program and (2) there will necessarily not be any background genetic risk—the obvious indicators are, in fact, maternal age (over 35 years) or a personal medical history of multiple miscarriage or failed IVF treatment.

Common to both PGD and PGS (or aneuploidy screening) is that the technique is intended to screen out *affected* embryos from use. The technique could, of course, be used to screen out *unaffected* embryos. This application would be rare, but it is conceivable. For example, it has been suggested that a congenitally deaf couple may seek to have a child similarly affected, as a child with normal hearing would be socially disadvantaged in the couple's living environment and quite possibly harmed by it. This situation raises rather different moral and public policy issues for a regulator, especially one that is legislatively bound to advance the "welfare of the child" (section 13(5)).

Finally, there is preimplantation tissue typing (human leukocyte antigen [HLA] typing), which, again, involves "selecting in" rather than "selecting out" embryos to provide a child who will be a tissue match, and therefore a possible tissue donor, for an existing child. In the well-known case in 2000 involving the Nash family in the United States, the parents sought HLA typing so that the child, when born, could be a bone marrow donor for an existing child who suffered from Fanconi anemia, a life-threatening condition,

Licensing PGD

Faced with the rapid developments in the uses of this technology, the HFEA had moved cautiously to license PGD, PGS, and HLA typing. In 1999 the HFEA adopted interim guidance allowing PGD. Also in 1999, a joint working party of the HFEA and HGC, while approving of PGD, was less than enthusiastic about making available PGS and HLA typing (HGAC/HFEA 1999). Nevertheless, faced with specific applications by clinics, in December 2001 the HFEA permitted PGS (aneuploidy screening) and, at the same time, it approved HLA typing in certain circumstances. As of August 31, 2002, nine centers were licensed for PGD and two for PGS. In February 2002, the HFEA licensed a clinic to carry out PGD for beta-thalassemia together with HLA typing so that the child could act be a compatible donor of stem cells from its umbilical cord to a sibling who suffered from the same life-threatening condition.

In 2002, the HFEA adopted revised and comprehensive guidance incorporating PGD, PGS, and HLA typing. The guidance contains detailed provisions concerned with information that should be provided to patients, procedures for reporting to the HFEA, and other matters concerned with safety. The main features of the licensing scheme are that individual practitioners are licensed to carry out embryo biopsies; PGD will be licensed only for specific genetic conditions that must be a "serious genetic condition," and both PGD with HLA typing and PGS (aneuploidy screening) will be licensed only in the specified circumstances set out in the guidance.

As with its earlier guidance, the HFEA's revised guidance recognizes that there should be a high level of regulation of these procedures. As a result, clinics may carry out PGD (or PGD with HLA typing) only for those conditions that are included by a license committee of the HFEA in the PGD Annex to their license. An application to vary the license must be made by a center that wishes to test for a genetic condition beyond those currently listed in the annex.

Preimplantation genetic diagnosis. PGD has been licensed for a number of genetic conditions. In doing so, the HFEA requires that there must be a "significant risk" of a "serious genetic condition." The HFEA guidance requires that the use of PGD be consistent with the current practice for terminations of pregnancy. Section 1(1)(d) of the Abortion Act of 1967 permits a termination, inter alia, when two doctors are of the opinion, formed in good faith, that "there is a substantial risk that if the child were born it would suffer from such physical or mental abnormalities as to be seriously handicapped."

While the interpretation and application of this provision are not without difficulty (Kennedy and Grubb 2000, 1424–28), there is no judicial guidance on what amounts to "a substantial risk" and "serious handicap." The HFEA looks to the Royal College of Obstetricians and Gynaecologists for guidance on abortion (HFEA 1996) and encourages clinics to apply it. Applying this criterion, the HFEA has licensed PGD for a number of serious genetic conditions, including a number of late-onset conditions such as adenomatous polyposis, but not yet Huntington disease. Once licensed for a particular condition, the HFEA leaves it to the clinicians involved to decide, in their clinical judgment, whether to offer PGD to a particular couple. The decision, however, should be made on the basis of the *patients'* perception of the condition and its impact on them and their family.

PGD with HLA typing. In its interim guidance in 2001, the HFEA was rather prescriptive in permitting HLA typing. It will not be widely available but, rather, will be permitted only in limited circumstances. The guidance lays down eight criteria that must be met. The most important are, perhaps, those that seek to constrain its availability to "desirable" situations. First, HLA typing will only be available for "severe or life-threatening" conditions that would justify PGD. Second, the embryos themselves must be at risk of the condition; that is, the recipient and the embryo must be at risk from the same genetic condition so that PGD is indicated. The effect of this criterion is that HLA typing becomes ancillary to the PGD procedure that will, in any event, be carried out in the interests of the future child. Third, the proposed recipient must not be a parent; the most likely recipient will be a sibling. Fourth, it must be a last resort: all other avenues of treating the recipient must have been explored. Finally, the intention must be to take only cord blood for treatment and not other tissue and organs. In this way the future child will not be exposed to any significant risk from the harvesting procedure. Any other procedure would require, in practice, the approval of the court, because it would not be in the medical interests of the donating child.[5] In 2004, the HFEA reviewed its guidance and adopted a more relaxed regulatory regime, on a case-by-case basis, no longer requiring, for example, that the donor child should itself be at risk from the condition to be treated in the recipient.[6]

PGS (aneuploidy screening). This procedure is, of course, designed to improve the chances of pregnancy occurring. It is not, in itself, intended to avoid a specific genetic inheritance. The guidance, therefore, lays down the categories of patient in whom aneuploidy screening may be advantageous and may therefore be made available: (1) women over thirty-five, (2) women with a history of recurring miscarriage, (3) women with several failed IVF attempts, and (4) women with a history of aneuploidy.

The Future of PGD

At the end of 2002, the HFEA's power to license HLA typing—and, by implication, PGD—was called into question in *R (On the Application of Quintavalle) v. HFEA*.[7] The claimant, a public interest group called CORE, argued that the HFEA had no power under the 1990 act to grant a license for HLA typing. CORE argued (1) HLA typing amounted to the "use" of an embryo and thus was illegal under the 1990 act unless authorized by a license, and (2) there was no power in the 1990 act to issue such a license. At first instance, Mr. Justice Maurice Kay agreed, but his decision was reversed on appeal.

The Court of Appeal agreed that PGD and HLA typing involved the "use" of an embryo because they both necessarily entailed a biopsy of the embryo. However, unlike the judge, the Court of Appeal concluded that the 1990 act allowed the HFEA to license both practices.[8]

The court examined the HFEA's licensing power, which, so far as relevant, allowed it to grant licenses that authorize, "in the course of providing treatment services," "practices designed to secure that embryos are in a suitable condition to be placed in a woman or *to determine whether embryos are suitable for that purpose*," if the practice was "necessary or desirable" for the purpose of providing treatment services (section 2(1)). First, the court examined the legislative history of the 1990 act and concluded that Parliament had contemplated PGD procedures, although not HLA typing, in 1990 and had intended to permit, rather than ban, PGD. Schedule 2, paragraph 3(2)(e) of the act permitted the HFEA to license research projects whose purpose was "developing methods for detecting the presence of gene or chromosome abnormalities in embryos before implantation." This was an explicit recognition of PGD. It was inconceivable that Parliament had intended research into PGD procedures to be permitted but not its subsequent use in treatment. When interpreting the act, the research and treatment provisions had to be reconciled.

Second, the court addressed the meaning of the statutory phrase "in the course of providing treatment services," which, in particular, requires that it should be "for the purpose of assisting women to carry children" (section

2(1)). In the light of the Parliamentary history, "treatment services" should not be interpreted as restricted to procedures where the intervention was designed to overcome the physical problems of infertility. Lord Justice Mance stated:

> To see the legislation as interested only in women's ability successfully to experience the physical process of pregnancy and birth would seem to me to invert the significance of the human wish to reproduce. Just as "placing an embryo in a woman" is only a first step towards a successful pregnancy, so pregnancy and the experience of birth are steps towards as expanded family life, not an end in themselves. (para. [127])

Thus, a broader meaning was appropriate, not limited to overcoming the physical problems of infertility or limited to selecting out genetic abnormalities that might threaten the viability of the unborn child. Instead, the court held that the act empowered the HFEA to license procedures that allowed a woman to "become pregnant and to bear children in the confidence that they will not be suffering from [hereditary] defects," or to produce a child with matching stem cells for the sick child. Thus, PGD and HLA typing fell within the statutory wording.

Third, the court held that the word "suitable" must take its meaning from the context. In the case of PGD and HLA typing, an embryo would be "suitable" only if it was free from the hereditary condition and, in the case of HLA typing, if it would be a match for the sick child. Thus, both PGD and HLA typing were practices designed "to determine whether embryos were suitable" for the purpose of assisting a woman to carry a child free of genetic disease or which would be a tissue match for a sibling.[9]

The Court of Appeal's judgment is a convincing endorsement of the HFEA's decision to allow HLA typing to proceed in limited circumstances. In April 2005, the House of Lords upheld and endorsed the Court of Appeal's decision and reasoning.[10] The HFEA had been publicly criticized by the House of Commons Science and Technology Committee for usurping Parliament's role.[11] Lord Phillips MR was clear that the HFEA had not done so:[12]

> Screening embryos before implantation enables a choice to be made as to the characteristics of the child to be born with the assistance of the treatment. Whether and for what purposes such a choice should be permitted raises difficult ethical questions. My conclusion is that Parliament has placed that choice in the hands of the HFEA.

As this comment and those of Lord Justice Schiemann[13] recognize, screening of embryos for "other characteristics"—that is, for social purposes or other nonmedical preferences—also falls within the HFEA's licensing powers. However, merely because the HFEA *can* license embryo selection for such characteristics does not mean that it will. Indeed, the PGD guidance discussed above makes plain that the HFEA will not allow selection other than for serious genetic conditions.

CLONING
The 1990 Act and Cloning

When the Warnock Committee reported in 1984, it recommended that the cloning of human embryos should be illegal (Committee of Inquiry into Human Fertilisation and Embryology 1984). Parliament accepted this recommendation (Committee of Inquiry into Human Fertilisation and Embryology 1987) and enacted section 3(3)(d) of the 1990 act, which states that "A license cannot authorize . . . (d) replacing a nucleus of a cell of an embryo with a nucleus taken from a cell of any person, embryo or subsequent development of an embryo."

Parliament, however, did not get it right, at least one can say that in retrospect. The 1990 act bans only a certain method of cloning involving the substitution of the nucleus of a cell *when part of an embryo*. The wording of section 3(3)(d) does not cover the "cell nuclear replacement" (CNR) technique that produced Dolly the sheep and that is the preferred technique for human cloning in the future. This technique involves the substitution of the nucleus of *an egg* with that of a nucleus taken from a somatic (adult) cell.

Relying on its wide remit over "embryos," the HFEA stepped in to regulate human embryo cloning. Creating an embryo for treatment or research purposes without a license from the HFEA is a criminal offense carrying a maximum penalty of two years' imprisonment. In 1998, the HFEA indicated that it would not license the creation of an embryo by cloning for the purposes of reproduction (so-called reproductive cloning) (HGAC/HFEA 1998). In effect, therefore, a ban on reproductive cloning was in force in the United Kingdom. The HFEA, however, left open the possibility that it would allow research projects that involve cloning with therapeutic or embryological aims (so-called therapeutic cloning). The position became unclear in 2001 when a public interest group challenged the HFEA's power to regulate either reproductive or therapeutic cloning.

The Quintavalle *Case*

In *R (On the Application of Quintavalle) v. Secretary of State for Health,*[14] the applicant was the director of the Pro-Life Alliance. In judicial review proceedings he sought a declaration that organisms created by CNR were not "embryos" within the meaning of section 1(1) of the Human Fertilisation and Embryology Act of 1990 and thus were not within the regulatory scheme of the Act. Mr. Justice Crane agreed, and held that the wording of section 1(1) defined "embryos" within the 1990 act as the products of fertilization. Since an organism produced by CNR was not the product of fertilization, it was not covered by the 1990 act, even though it could naturally be so described and such an interpretation was supported by expert opinion.

The judge's decision in *Quintavalle* threw the law and public policy in the United Kingdom into disarray as it made the CNR technique lawful but unregulated. The government was surprised by the decision not least because it had received legal advice to the contrary. However, academic analysis of the 1990 Act had since at least 1997 predicted the outcome reached by Mr. Justice Crane (Walsh and Grubb 1997).

The government responded in two ways. First, Parliament rapidly enacted the Human Reproductive Cloning Act of 2001 to make reproductive cloning by CNR a criminal offense (as discussed below). Second, the government immediately appealed the decision.

The Court of Appeal reversed the High Court decision, holding that the act had to be construed purposively.[15] The reasoning of the Court of Appeal was not without difficulty, tending as it did more toward judicial legislation than interpretation (Grubb 2002; Plomer 2002). Although Parliament had banned cloning only in the specific circumstances contemplated by section 3(3)(d) of the 1990 act, it had intended to bring within the remit (and regulatory framework) of the act any embryo, whether produced by fertilization or not. The statutory definition was to be seen as an inclusive, rather than exclusive, statement of the act's ambit of application. As a consequence, the procedure of CNR did involve the creation of an embryo within the 1990 act and therefore required a license from the HFEA. In February 2003, the House of Lords dismissed a further appeal by the Pro-Life Alliance and emphatically approved the reasoning of the Court of Appeal.[16]

In one sense, the House of Lords' decision was unnecessary because of speedy legislative intervention in the shape of the Human Reproductive

Cloning Act of 2001. However, what is important—perhaps crucial—is that the decision brought CNR embryos back within the regulatory framework of the 1990 act. It reaffirmed the HFEA's licensing powers over CNR embryos. The 2001 Act, in effect, abrogates the HFEA's licensing powers for reproductive cloning, but once again the HFEA has power to license embryo cloning for research or therapeutic purposes.

The Human Reproductive Cloning Act of 2001

Since the birth of Dolly there has been worldwide and almost universal opposition to the use of CNR to produce a human baby. Faced with the (theoretical) possibility of its happening in the United Kingdom after the High Court's decision in *Quintavalle,* within two weeks of the decision, Parliament passed the Human Reproductive Cloning Act of 2001, which makes it a criminal offense to place in a woman a cloned human embryo. The act came into force on December 4, 2001. Section 1(1) of the act provides that "A person who places in a woman a human embryo which has been created otherwise than by fertilisation is guilty of an offence." Proceedings for the offense may only be instituted by the DPP (section 1(3)), and the maximum penalty is ten years' imprisonment (section 1(2)).

The wording of the act is very clever. First, it obviates the argument accepted at first instance in the *Quintavalle* case that a CNR embryo is not an embryo under the 1990 act. It explicitly states that the crime covers "a human embryo which has been created otherwise than by fertilisation." And, of course, a CNR embryo is just such an entity.

Second, the wording avoids an even greater definitional problem. The 1990 act covers embryos produced "by fertilisation"; the 2001 Act covers all others—all those produced "otherwise than by fertilisation." As a consequence, there are no loopholes. Whatever technique is used—whether CNR or one yet to be developed—the 2001 act will apply. It therefore covers the currently unforeseen. It also avoids the need to provide a definition of a "cloned embryo," which is problematic. It is often thought that a cloned embryo is genetically identical to another person. Hence, for example, in seeking to ban cloning in the State of Victoria in Australia, the Infertility Treatment Act of 1995 defines "to clone" as "to form, outside the human body, a human embryo that is genetically identical to another human embryo or person" (section 3(1)). In fact, this would not cover an embryo produced by CNR, since that is not genetically identical to the person from whom the cell is taken to produce it; the enucleated egg, into which the nucleus of the source cell is placed, retains some of its own genetic material in its mitochondrial DNA. The resulting embryo is *almost* genetically identical to the source, but not quite. The wording of the 2001 act avoids this definitional difficulty.

However, the 2001 act is not comprehensive. It only prohibits "plac[ing] in a woman" a cloned embryo. It does not, on its face, prohibit the creation of such an embryo. This apparent lacuna is not a problem in reality since, following the Court of Appeal's decision in *Quintavalle,* the creation of such an embryo without a license from the HFEA would be a criminal offense under the 1990 act, punishable by up to two years' imprisonment (sections 3(1) and 41(2) and (4)). As was noted earlier, the HFEA has always indicated it will license cloning only as part of a research project and not with a view to reproduction.

Another difficulty concerns human-animal hybrids. Where such a hybrid is produced through fertilization using human and animal gametes, this may only be done with a license from the HFEA (section 4(1)(c)), which prohibits the mixing of human and live animal gametes. However, the 1990 act does not cover the case where the animal hybrid is produced through CNR: there is no "mixing" of gametes. Such a procedure would be regulated by the HFEA as the creation of an embryo only if that "embryo" is seen as a "human embryo" under the 1990 act. Also, placing it in a woman would then be a crime under the 2001 Act. Unfortunately, it is far from clear that such an embryo is a "human embryo": patently it is only biologically partly so. And, if an enucleated human egg has the nucleus of an animal cell placed in it, it will be far more animal than human in genetic terms. Even if the procedure is carried out the other way, there is no reason to think that a hybrid is anything other than a hybrid that cannot properly be described as human or animal. As such, the regulation and control of this remains without any legislation.

Stem Cells and "Therapeutic Cloning"

Stem cells. In recent years, a major contribution to the public's hope for medical miracles has come from claims about the future therapeutic potential of stem cell technologies. The scientific and medical interest in stem cells lies in understanding and harnessing the process of differentiation of these cells into specialized human tissues so as to develop cell-based therapies that can replace damaged or diseased tissue or particular cell functions. At present, the work is very much at the basic science stage. Scientists do not yet fully understand the processes of cell differentiation in humans, and work on this is being carried out in countries that allow embryo research. Therapies are still some distance in the future. It is, however, widely recognized that there is enormous potential for health applications in the future for stem cell technologies. They may result in therapies that cure genetically linked degenerative diseases, such as Parkinson disease and Alzheimer disease. Other diseases, such as diabetes, may become a thing of the past. The cloned embryos of an individual may be used to produce stem cells that, when introduced into the body, replace the damaged cells or tissue that cause the condition. Alternatively, they could be used to generate replacement tissue for that which is damaged—skin following severe burns injury, spinal tissue where an accident has damaged the spinal cord and led to paralysis, or cardiac tissue where heart disease has caused damage. It may even be possible to grow whole organs for transplantation. This may provide a solution to the worldwide shortage of organs for transplantation. Stem cells are found in the early embryo (embryonic stem cells), in the fetus, in the placenta and umbilical cord and in the tissues of adult bodies. However, at present its seems that embryonic stem cells (ES cells) may hold an advantage over those derived from the other sources. And the advantage of deriving stem cells from an embryo cloned from the patient is that they are exactly tissue-matched with that patient, overcoming the need to find a matched donor to avoid organ or tissue rejection by the patient.

Formulating public policy in the United Kingdom. The process of formulating public policy for research using cloned embryos and the linked issue of stem cell technologies began in 1998 in the joint Report of the HFEA/HGAC. The report recognized the scientific opinion that cloning techniques had great therapeutic potential if research proved successful and clinical applications were developed.

The report highlighted two possibilities. The first occurs where life-threatening and debilitating disease was caused by defects in the maternal mitochondrial DNA. CNR technology—here more accurately described as oocyte nucleus transfer—has the potential to avoid this by allowing a woman to have a child which was almost genetically hers but who would be free of the disease, because the "clean" mitochondria from the recipient egg would be inherited. This is not strictly an example of cloning, since the procedure involves inserting the nucleus of a woman's egg into a donor's egg stripped of its nucleus. The resulting egg (combining the clean mitochondrial DNA of the donor and her egg's own nuclear DNA) would then be fertilized using IVF techniques. The resulting child would have a unique genetic structure, with contributions from *three* parents—the mother, the egg donor, and the father.

The second possibility is the production of a cultured cell line for the purpose of cell or tissue therapy. This second possibility is, of course, what we now call therapeutic cloning, leading to the derivation and use of ES cells. The HFEA/HGAC's report was a first look at the ethical and policy implications of this emerging technology. The government did not immediately respond. Why it did not is unclear, given the extensive nature of the public consultation that preceded the HFEA/HGAC's report—193 responses were received. Certainly the controversial nature of cloning may have made the government feel uneasy. In addition, understanding of the science and potential of ES cell technology increased after the report. Instead of legislating immediately, the government set up an expert advisory group chaired by the Chief Medical Officer. That group's report, in June 2000, *Stem Cell Research: Medical Progress with Responsibility*,[17] supported the development of research (including cloning) involving ES cells to increase understanding of human diseases and disorders and of mitochondrial disease, and to develop treatments for these.

The 2001 regulations. The HFEA's power to grant licenses for the creation and use of human embryos in research is circumscribed in the 1990 act (section 11(1)(c) and schedule 2, paragraph 3). First, any proposed use of an embryo must be "*necessary* for the purpose of the research." Second, the purpose(s) of the project must fall within those permitted by schedule 2 to the 1990 act, and the activity licensed must be "necessary or desirable" for that purpose(s). There are five listed purposes in paragraph 3(2) of schedule 2:

- Promoting advances in the treatment of infertility;
- Increasing knowledge about the causes of congenital disease;
- Increasing knowledge about the causes of miscarriages;
- Developing more effective techniques of contraception;
- Developing methods for detecting the presence of gene or chromosome abnormalities in embryos before implantation.

Both the reports of HFEA/HGAC and of the Chief Medical Officer's Expert Group recognized that the listed purposes did not allow for research into the areas of development they had identified as most promising. As a result, it was recommended that the research purposes in the 1990 act be extended through delegated legislation, as contemplated in the 1990 act (HFEA/HGAC, para. 9.3; CMO Expert Group 2000, para. 5.10).

The government agreed (CMO Expert Group 2000). Following a rather difficult parliamentary debate, the Human Fertilisation and Embryology

(Research Purposes) Regulations of 2001[18] added three further research purposes. The HFEA now has the power to grant embryo research licenses for the purposes of:

(a) increasing knowledge about the development of embryos;

(b) increasing knowledge about serious disease; or

(c) enabling any such knowledge to be applied in developing treatments for serious disease.

The HFEA has now licensed a number of projects for the derivation of ES cells including, since 2004, cloning under both the original statutory purposes and, more recently, the extended purposes in the Regulations. The licensing process is essentially the same as for other embryo research except that the HFEA has decided to require applicants to justify why adult stem cells cannot be used; to provide details of the fate of ES cells; to place a sample in the MRC Stem Cell Bank; and not to pass on samples of ES cells to third parties other than through the Stem Cell Bank.

The wording of the regulations mirrors the enabling provision in schedule 2 of the 1990 act (paragraph 3(3)), but there remain linguistic problems that may well be exposed by public interest groups through litigation challenging the HFEA's jurisdiction to grant license for certain types of research. It is not clear, for example, whether all basic research on ES cells is covered by the new purposes. Such research may, if concerned with the processes of differentiation, be said to relate to "the development of embryos" (item (a)). However, if the research moves beyond that, but is not yet related to the development of treatments (item (c)), there is again a potential legislative lacuna.[19] Also, the regulations only contemplate research for embryological purposes or relating to serious diseases (and their treatment). The kind of situation contemplated by the HFEA/HGAC report, where tissue could be developed for use on a patient who has suffered injury through burns, is not covered. This was inevitable because the 1990 act does not permit Regulations to extend the HFEA's licensing power to cover the latter (schedule 2, paragraph 3(3)). Primary amending legislation alone could achieve this extension (although this was not the view expressed in the House of Lords when the draft regulations were debated).

Beyond the 2001 regulations. The controversy that surrounded the government's decision to introduce the 2001 regulations led to a political compromise. The regulations were passed by both Houses of Parliament, but the House of Lords would set up a select committee to look into the issues con-

nected with human cloning and stem cell research arising out of the regulations. The committee was chaired by the Bishop of Oxford and reported in
February 2002 (House of Lords Select Committee Report, 2001).

The committee made a number of detailed recommendations broadly
approving continued research using ES cells (including those derived from
cloned embryos) and the extension of the licensable purposes set out in the
2001 regulations. The Committee emphasized the need to be cautious, however. In particular, it supported the use of existing, surplus embryos to the
extent that was possible, rather than the creation (whether by cloning or otherwise) of embryos specifically for research.[20] Of course, the HFEA could
license the latter only where it was "necessary or desirable," neither of which
would be satisfied if the research could be done using existing, surplus
embryos. Research into the process of fertilization or the CNR technique
would be exceptional cases justifying the creation of embryos.

The derivation of ES cells is a matter for the HFEA and the licensing
process because the creation and/or use of embryos falls within the HFEA's
remit. How far does that regulatory regime extend? No doubt it permits the
HFEA, indeed requires the HFEA, to apply the consent provisions of the Act
to the creation and/or use of embryos for the purposes of research, including
ES cell derivation and study. Arguably, however, the subsequent or secondary
use of ES cells derived from embryos is not within the HFEA's regulatory
power. The reason for this is that once the ES cells are extracted from the
embryo, they no longer form part of an "embryo." Disaggregation of an embryo
will occur after about one to two days of being cultured to produce ES cells.
At this point the products of the embryo are beyond the licensing powers of
the HFEA. It is likely that a license condition on an embryo research license
could not lawfully extend to the use of ES cells that were no longer part of an
embryo. The conclusion must be that their subsequent use and storage is not
regulated by the 1990 act.[21] This was the view of the Chief Medical Officer's
Expert Group (2000 para. 3.11). Wherever the precise point in time may be,
clearly the HFEA's remit over "embryos" ends at some point in the time-line
starting with gametes and ending with stem cell use. Stem cells are immortal,
and the point must come where for practical reasons, if no other, the HFEA
will not be involved, and the 1990 act's regulatory regime can no longer have
any practical application.

In 2002, the government with the Medical Research Council set up a bank
for the storage of stem cell lines. The bank will be overseen by a steering committee and will be responsible for ensuring the purity and provenance of the

stem cell lines and monitoring their use. This development was endorsed by the House of Lords' Select Committee (2001 para 8.29), and the HFEA has indicated that it will be a condition on any license that entails deriving ES cells that they be deposited in the MRC bank. (Likewise the U.K. Research Councils have indicated that it will be a condition of any research grant.)

One final point on stem cells: At present, scientific endeavor has not moved beyond the research stage using stem cells. The time will come when research leads to the development of potential therapeutic applications—for many, that is the whole purpose of undertaking the research. When that happens, the clinical introduction of cell-based therapies in the United Kingdom will be subject to the current regimes that exist for the introduction of new medicinal products through clinical trials and licensing.[22]

THE FUTURE

The Status Quo

The framework established by the Human Fertilisation and Embryology Act of 1990 has been remarkably successful in regulating ART and reprogenetic developments in the United Kingdon. Apart from the recent embryo research regulations, the 1990 act has been amended only twice in two years. That is surprising ,given the nature of the area with which it deals and the scientific and clinical developments that have taken place in that time.

In her evidence to the House of Lords' Select Committee on Stem Cell Research, Dame Ruth Deech (until 2002 the chair of the HFEA) paid tribute to the draftsman of the 1990 act, who

> gave it sufficient flexibility to cope with new developments and yet made it robust enough to control the scientists and make matters acceptable and respectable . . . There is a clear framework, there are layers of enforceability starting with the primary legislation going through regulations, directions, and a Code of Practice, which have meant that we have been able to oversee progress on the medical and scientific fronts in a responsible and controlled manner. (House of Lords Select Committee 2001)

Perhaps the real beauty of the legislative framework lies in the broad discretion to regulate it conferred upon the HFEA. In 1990, Parliament made a number of fundamental choices to allow certain activities and not others—for example, to allow embryo research but not beyond fourteen days of development. Thereafter, it left the HFEA the discretion to regulate the permitted procedures through the licensing system. But, of importance, it did so not by naming the procedures but by defining the HFEA's jurisdiction in terms of the "creation," "use," and "keeping" of embryos or "keeping" and "use" of donated gametes. Thus, as Ruth Deech indicates, it allowed the HFEA to take control of developments in embryology and clinical treatments that were not even contemplated in 1990, including many developments in the field of reprogenetics.

Challenging the Status Quo

The tide may, however, be turning. Both the 1990 act and the HFEA are increasingly under scrutiny. Changes in the sociopolitical climate and in the increased recourse to litigation have shaken the solidity of the act and its regulator. A number of factors contribute to this situation.

Court challenges to the act and the HFEA's powers have increased in the past five years. It is no coincidence that th• HFEA's expenditure on professional fees (which includes legal fees) has risen dramatically, from £79,699 in 2000–2001 to £446,782 in 2001–2002 (HFEA 2002).

Most of these challenges have been to the terms of the act, but not all. Some cases have involved direct challenge to the HFEA's decision or application of its policy in a particular case. For example, in R (Assisted Reproduction and Gynaecology Centre and H) v. The Human Fertilisation and Embryology Authority,[23] the claimants sought judicial review of the HFEA's advice that a clinic should not transfer five embryos to a patient contrary to the HFEA's "3 embryo transfer" policy. (In 2001, the HFEA amended its policy to state that no more than two embryos should be transferred except in exceptional circumstances when three may be transferred.) In the end, the Court of Appeal held that the claimants' application was unarguable. The HFEA could not be shown to have reached an irrational conclusion having considered all the evidence including published evidence on the success rates of multiple transfers, the risk of multiple pregnancy, and the risk to the mother's health if that happened.

Two interesting points about the case. First, the challenge was brought not only by the patient but also by the clinic itself. The 1990 act resulted, in part, from an alliance between clinicians and scientists, on the one hand, and the government and Parliament on the other. Until 1990, there was little or no legal regulation of the clinical practice of any area of medicine, as opposed to the licensing of the practitioners themselves through, for example, the General Medical Council. The 1990 act changed that dramatically for clinicians involved in ART and for scientists engaged in embryo research. One can see the political dynamic of the time as being one of accepting the lesser of two evils, as the alternative to the 1990 act and a regulatory body such as the HFEA was, probably, the prohibition of some (perhaps many) of their activities such as embryo research. Thereafter, clinicians and scientists got along with the HFEA as an inevitable fact of life if they wished to pursue their professional work. They worked together, although tensions between clinicians and scientists and the HFEA have always been present. Professor Margot Brazier describes the system as being "built on consensus" (Brazier 1999, 167). We may be seeing the beginning of the breakdown of that consensus between clinicians and the HFEA, especially as the HFEA adopts a more aggressive stance as a regulator. It would be wrong to draw a conclusion from this one case, but it does seem likely that clinicians (and their clinics) may resort to legal action more in the future when the HFEA is perceived as constraining or trampling on their clinical judgment of what treatment is best for their patient.

The second interesting point to arise from the case concerns the Court of Appeal's strong statements about its own role when judicial review of the HFEA's decisions is sought. Mr. Justice Wall was clear:

> It is an area of rapidly developing science in which judicial review has a limited role to play. Disagreement between doctors and scientific bodies in this pioneering field are inevitable. The United Kingdom, through the Act, has opted for a system of licensing and regulation. The Authority is the body which is empowered by Parliament to regulate. Like any public body, it is open to challenge by way of judicial review, if it exceeds or abuses the powers and responsibilities given to it by parliament; but where, as is manifest here from an examination of the facts, it considers requests for advice carefully and thoroughly, and produces opinions which are plainly rational, the court, in our judgment has no part to play in the debate, and certainly no power to intervene to strike down any such decision. The fact that the Appellant may disagree with the Authority's advice is neither here nor there. (para. [65])

Mr. Justice Wall was, of course, considering a challenge to an exercise of the HFEA's discretionary powers. Here the warning is clear: rational decisions by the HFEA, even those that controvert a doctor's clinical judgment, are not ones with which the courts will interfere. Parliament has vested the power in the HFEA, and that is that.

Challenges to the scope and extent of the HFEA's powers are, however, another matter, as these entail the interpretation of a statute, which is ultimately a matter for the courts. In recent years, challenges to the terms of the 1990 act itself have increased. The Human Rights Acts 1998, and its incorporation of the European Convention on Human Rights, has raised public awareness of human rights issues, but it has also provided a real legal mechanism to challenge what was before beyond legal challenge.

In the context of reprogenetics and the 1990 act, the right to "private and family life" (Article 8) and the right to "marry and found a family" (Article 12) are easy legal pegs upon which to hang claims that a decision of the HFEA, denying treatment to a particular patient or to all those in a specific category of case, amounts to a breach of an individual's human rights and is therefore unlawful.[24] But the potential for legal challenge goes even further in that the very terms of the 1990 act can be reviewed by the court and, if contrary to the European Convention, the statutory provisions can be declared to be incompatible with the convention.[25] Thus, a court has ruled—indeed the government conceded—that the 1990 act breaches a child's right to private and family life under Article 8 when it declares him or her to be fatherless when born following posthumous treatment (the effect of section 26(6)(b)). Likewise, the absolute right of either gamete provider to prevent treatment with or storage of embryos because the act requires the prior consent of both gamete providers (the effect of schedule 3) is the subject of challenge under Articles 8 and 12.[26]

A further ingredient has been the (relatively) new phenomenon of litigation by public interest groups such as CORE and the Pro-Life Alliance. Their challenges to the powers of the HFEA to license PGD with tissue-typing and the creation and use of "embryos" produced through CNR have added to the litigation environment in which the HFEA now functions. In the first instance, CORE had no connection, direct or indirect, with the particular case, and yet the court did not doubt its standing to challenge the HFEA's powers. In the second instance, the challenge was entirely hypothetical, yet here too the court allowed the case to proceed. A few years ago, these cases would have been thrown out of court for lack of standing. The judges do not seem prepared to limit their access to the courts and, as a result, such groups are only likely to add to the increasing volume of litigation against the HFEA in future years.

CONCLUSION: SHIFTING SOCIOPOLITICAL CLIMATE

In its twelve-year history, the HFEA has not been the subject of sustained criticism by politicians. It has, of course, never attracted the praise of those whose personal views militate against embryo research, but equally, its competence and capacity to regulate has been relatively free from doubt. Even as recently as February 2002, the House of Lords' Select Committee on Stem Cell Research commented that "[t]he HFEA has an excellent record in ensuring that IVF clinics comply with the law" (para. 5.24). However, since then the political atmosphere seems to be changing.

In July 2002, the House of Commons Science and Technology Committee was highly critical of the HFEA's decision to license PGD with tissue typing (2002, para. 25).[27] The introduction of new developments of this kind went beyond the HFEA's competence and was a matter for Parliament. The HFEA was described in (no doubt deliberately) ungracious terms as an "unelected quango" (para. 26). The distrust of the HFEA as an effective regulator was barely disguised. Subsequently, in the House of Lords' debate on the *Report of the Select Committee on Stem Cell Research*, some members of the House of Lords did not disguise their dissatisfaction with the HFEA and its competence to regulate (House of Lords 2002, columns 1311–53).[28] The complaints go further and question the integrity of the 1990 Act over a decade after its enactment and led to calls for it, in the words of the House of Commons Science and Technology Committee, to "reconnect . . . with modern science" (2002, para. 28).

What has brought about this new scepticism of the HFEA's competence and the act's ability to cope with twenty-first century ART and reprogenetic science? Some of it, that concerning the HFEA, seems to stem from a number of high-profile incidents in fertility clinics reported in the media involving, for example, the mixup of sperm that resulted in a black baby being born to a white couple and the prosecution of an embryologist who misled patients into thinking that he had provided IVF treatment for them so that he could obtain the fees. Incidents of this sort have raised questions about the robustness of the HFEA's regulatory mechanisms, particularly its monitoring and inspection functions. It has to be recognized that the HFEA's regulatory procedures were developed in an entirely different age, if just over a decade ago, when inspection and monitoring of clinical practice were almost unheard of. Today, the situation is different. Inspection and audit are now routine parts of the regulation of health care delivery in the public and private sectors through the Commission for Health Improvement (NHS) and the National Care Standards Commission (private).[29] Recognizing the need to modernize its inspection and regulation processes, the HFEA has already put in place more robust, transparent, and intrusive inspection and audit procedures (HFEA 2002, 7).

As to the scepticism concerning the continued effectiveness of the 1990 act, there is a political perception that the recent legal challenges have shown the act to be creaking under the strain of coping with developments not foreseen in 1990. Of course, there is an element of truth in this. However, it is of the very nature of legislation that it must be interpreted and applied to new, often unforeseen, circumstances after its enactment. The real questions are, first, is the current act working, and second, would a new act fare any better.

In truth, the framework of the current Act does work. Of course, amendments to the 1990 Act will have to be made as legal challenges to the Act show up deficiencies or omissions. A good example of this will be the need to amend the Act to allow posthumous children to register their dead genetic father as a legal parent (currently prohibited by section 28(6) (b)).[30] By and large, however, the act "ensures a degree of public accountability. . . . [and] promotes high standards of medical practice" (Brazier 1999, 167). As the government observed in its response to the House of Commons' Report, "the 1990 Act is functioning reasonably well and provides a framework within which new advances can appropriately accommodated."[31]

We then return to the question of whether the broad discretion conferred on the HFEA—which makes the Act work—is acceptable. If it is not, decisions about the "dos and don'ts" of reprogenetics will still have to made somewhere by somebody. In reality, the decisions will have to be made by Parliament in the new act itself. There will be numerous, difficult policy choices to be made that may lead politicians, when faced with the task, to rue the day that the HFEA was not there to insulate them from the political controversy in which they would necessarily become directly embroiled. As Parliament would inevitably find, to cover every contingency, including those that are unforeseen, some decision-making discretion would have to be vested in a body like the HFEA.

NOTES

1. This remains the case following devolution of certain legislative powers and functions to the Scottish Parliament, National Assembly for Wales and the Northern Ireland Assembly.

2. Chapter 37. Hereafter all references to sections are to the 1990 act unless otherwise stated.

3. The excessively narrow circumstances in section 33 where information about donors, patients, or children born could be disclosed by the HFEA or clinics were extended by the Human Fertilisation and Embryology (Disclosure of Information) Act of 1992. Section 3A was added by the Criminal Justice and Public Order Act of 1994 (s156) and prohibits the use of fetal eggs in infertility treatment.

4. The Gene Therapy Advisory Committee (GTAC) assesses the ethical acceptability of individual proposals for clinical gene therapy research and the Genetics and Insurance Committee (GAIC) scrutinizes compliance of the ABI Code of Practice and agreed five-year moratorium on the use of genetic test results by insurance companies.

5. See, for example, *Re Y (Mental Patient: Bone Marrow Donation)* [1997] Fam 110 (bone marrow donation by incompetent adult).

6. See Human Fertilisation and Embryology Authority (HFEA), *Report on the Preimplantation Tissue Typing Review*, July 2004.

7. [2002] EWHC 2785 (Admin) and [2002] EWCA Civ. 667.

8. Importantly, as Lord Justice Mance pointed out (at para [110]), it is the "use" of the embryo—the biopsy—that is licensable, not the PGD testing itself, as the "use" of embryonic cells is not directly regulated by the 1990 act. The biopsy may, however, be licensed subject to conditions as to the testing that may subsequently take place: this is exactly the HFEA's regulatory regime as it operates through license conditions for PGD.

9. Curiously, unlike Lord Justices Schiemann and Mance, Lord Phillips MR thought that PGD/tissue typing procedures fell within the wording "designed to secure that embryos are in a suitable condition" at paras [43] and [48], when in fact this is more likely concerned with practices to maintain or protect its suitability rather than with tests to determine its suitability: see Mance LJ at para [126].

10. [2005] UKHL 28; [2005] 2 All E.R. 555.

11. *Developments in Human Genetics and Embryology,* Fourth Report of Session 2001-02, HC 791 (July 10, 2002) para 25.

12. At para [49].

13. *Per* Schiemann LJ at para [97]. And see now, Lord Hoffman in the House of Lords at paras. [28]–[29] and Lord Brown at para [62]. Contrast the more cautious views of Mance LJ at paras [132]–[134] and [144].

14. [2001] EWHC 918 (Admin); [2001] 4 All E.R. 1013.

15. [2002] EWCA Civ. 29; [2002] 2 All E.R. 625 (C.A.).

16. [2003] UKHL 13 and [2003] 2 All E.R. 113, discussed in A. Grubb, "Cloning (Cell Nuclear Replacement): The Scope of the Human Fertilisation and Embryology Act 1990" (2003) *Medical Law Review* 11:135.

17. *Stem Cell Research: Medical Progress with Responsibility: A Report from the Chief Medical Officer's Expert Group Reviewing the Potential of Developments in Stem Cell Research and Cell Nuclear Replacement to Benefit Human Health,* Department of Health, June 2000.

18. SI 2001/188.

19. For an interesting discussion of the scope of the Regulation, see House of Lords' Select Committee Report, *Stem Cell Research,* H.L. Paper 83(i), Session 2001–02, chap. 8, especially on this point paragraphs 8.9–8.15.

20. House of Lords' Select Committee Report, *Stem Cell Research,* H.L. Paper 83, Session 2001–02, paragraphs 4.28 and 5.14.

21. But note the view of Lord Justice Mance in *R (On the Application of Quintavalle) v. HFEA* [2002] EWCA Civ 667 at paras [109]–[110] that extracted embryonic cell mate-

rial is distinct from the embryo but that the licensing of its extraction (there for PGD) could be subject to conditions as to future testing.

22. Note the House of Lords' Select Committee recommendation that clinical studies should be overseen by a body such as GTAC, which oversees gene therapy trials; *op cit.*, paragraph 8.23. The government in its response rejected the suggestion, *op cit.*, paragraph 16.

23. [2002] *Lloyd's Rep. Med.* 148 (CA). Discussed in J. Laing (2002) *Medical Law Review* 10:209.

24. See *R v. Secretary of State for the Home Department, ex parte Mellor* [2001] EWCA Civ 472; (2001) 59 BMLR 1 (CA) (denial to a prisoner of access to artificial insemination justified under Art. 8(2) of the ECHR).

25. See *Rose v. Secretary of State for Health* [2002] EWHC 1593 (Admin); (2002) 69 BMLR 83 (Scott Baker J) (Art. 8 right to "private and family life" engaged when a child born by AI sought information about sperm donor—no decision on whether justified infringement under Art. 8(2)). The case involved a child born before the 1990 act came into force. The legislation currently prohibits disclosure of any information to a child about a donor (ss 33(1) and (2) read with s 31).

26. In *Evans v. Amicus Healthcare Ltd and others* [2004] EWCA Civ 727; [2004] 3 All E.R. 1025, the Court of Appeal held that a gamete provider's right to "private and family life" protected under Article 8 of the European Convention on Human Rights was not infringed where she was unable to use an embryo for her treatment due to the withdrawal of consent by the male gamete provider. The court held that any breach of her right was justified as a proportionate legislative response to protect the right of the other gamete provider under Article 8 not to become a father against his wishes.

27. *Developments in Human Genetics and Embryology,* Fourth Report of Session 2001–02, HC 791 (10 July 2002) para 25.

28. *Hansard,* HL, cols 1311–1353 (5 December 2002).

29. Their functions, together with that of the Audit Commission, are to be subsumed within a single body, the Commission for Healthcare, Audit and Inspection (CHAI).

30. See now, Human Fertilisation and Embryology (Deceased Fathers) Act 2003.

31. *Government's Response to the Report from the House of Commons Science and Technology Committee: Developments in Human Genetics and Embryology* (November 2002), para 34. Cm 5693.

REFERENCES

Brazier, M. 1999. Regulating the reproduction business? *Medical Law Review* 7:166.

Chief Medical Officer's Expert Group. 2000. *Stem Cell Research: Medical Progress with Responsibility. Report from the Chief Medical Officer's Expert Group Reviewing the Potential of Developments in Stem Cell Research and Cell Nuclear Replacement to Benefit Human Health.* Department of Health, U.K.

Code of Practice. 2001. 5th ed., para. 11.6.

Committee of Inquiry into Human Fertilisation and Embryology. 1984. *Report of the Committee of Inquiry into Human Fertilisation and Embryology.* Cmnd 9314.

Committee on Standards in Public Life. 1995. *First Report of the Committee on Standards in Public Life* (chaired by Lord Nolan). Cm. 2850-I.

Department of Health. 2000. *Government Response to the Recommendations made in the Chief Medical Officer's Expert Group Report "Stem Cell Research: Medical Progress with Responsibility."* August. Cm 4833.

Grubb, A. 2002. Regulating cloned embryos? *Law Quarterly Review* 118:358.

Grubb, A. 2003. Cloning (cell nuclear replacement): The scope of the Human Fertilisation and Embryology Act 1990. *Medical Law Review* 11:135.

Her Majesty's Government. 1987. *Human Fertilisation and Embryology: A Framework for Legislation.* Cm 259.

———. 2002. *Government's Response to the Report from the House of Commons Science and Technology Committee: Developments in Human Genetics and Embryology.* Cm 5693.

House of Commons. 2002. *Developments in Human Genetics and Embryology.* Fourth Report of Session 2001-02, HC 791 (July 10).

House of Lords. 2002. *Hansard,* HL, cols 1311–1353 (December 5).

House of Lords' Select Committee Report. 2001. *Stem Cell Research.* H.L. Paper 83(i), Session 2001–02.

Human Fertilisation and Embryology Authority (HFEA). 1993. *Sex Selection: Public Consultation Document,* January 1993.

———. 1994. *Donated Ovarian Tissue in Embryo Research and Assisted Conception.* July.

——— 1996. *Termination of Pregnancy for Fetal Abnormality.*

———. 1998. *Consultation on the Implementation of Withdrawal of Payment to Donors.* February.

———. 1999. *Consultation Document on Preimplantation Genetic Diagnosis.* November.

———. 2002a. *Eleventh Annual Report and Accounts.*

———. 2002b. *Sex Selection: Choice and Responsibility in Human Reproduction.*

Human Fertilisation and Embryology Authority (Licensing Committees and Appeals) Regulations. 1991. SI 1991/1889.

Human Genetics Advisory Commission (HGAC) and Human Fertilisation and Embryology Authority (HFEA). December 1998. *Cloning Issues in Reproduction, Science and Medicine: A Report from the Human Genetics Advisory Commission and the Human Fertilisation and Embryology Authority.* December.

———. 1999. *Report of Working Party on Preimplantation Genetic Diagnosis.* November.

Interim Licensing Authority for Human In Vitro Fertilisation and Embryology. 1991. *The Sixth Report of the Interim Licensing Authority for Human In Vitro Fertilisation and Embryology.*

Kennedy, I., and A. Grubb. 2000. *Medical Law.* 3rd ed. Butterworths, London.

Laing, J. 2002. *Medical Law Review* 10:209.

Plomer, A. 2002. Beyond the HFE Act 1990: The regulation of stem cell research in the UK. *Medical Law Review* 10:132.

R v. Secretary of State for the Home Department, ex parte Mellor [2001] EWCA Civ 472; (2001) 59 BMLR 1 (CA).

Rose v. Secretary of State for Health [2002] EWHC 1593 (Admin); (2002) 69 BMLR 83 (Scott Baker J).

Walsh, P., and A. Grubb. 1997. I want to be alone. *Dispatches* 7:1.

Any opinions or views expressed here are personal and should not be attributed to the HFEA.

CHAPTER EIGHT

The Evolution of Public Policy on Reprogenetics in Canada

PATRICIA A. BAIRD

The cultural attitudes and values broadly espoused by a society influence how a country's public policy evolves to deal with the choices posed by new technologies. It is useful to remember that, despite sharing a language and a 3,000-mile-long border, Canada and the United States have quite different histories. As a result, the cultures and values of the two countries differ more than is immediately apparent. These differences, which are deeply embedded in what might be called the national worldview, have led to a distinctive shaping of public policy regarding new reproductive technologies in Canada.

The formative nature of some of the culture differences has been described well in Seymour Martin Lipset's classic book, *Continental Divide* (1990), which teases out some of the most fundamental differences in the relationship of government to the governed in Canada and the United States. Lipset notes that Canadians' attitude in general is that government is there to act in the public interest, whereas U.S. citizens have, in general, a greater mistrust of government—government is something to have as little of as possible. As Lipset writes, "One society leans toward communitarianism—the public mobilization of resources to fulfill group objectives—the other sees individualism—private endeavour—as the way an 'unseen hand' produces optimum, socially beneficial results."

Most commentators converge in the view that Canadians tend to be less highly individualistic in their worldview, with the relationship of the individual to the collectivity therefore being construed differently from the more individualistic stance in the United States. In Canada, there appears to be a common understanding that individuals are embedded in networks of relationships and are not isolated entities, concerned to protect their own interests against the encroachment of others. People are connected in families and communities and through many different social bonds, and they recognize they cannot enjoy rights and interests in isolation.

A principle evidently of much more importance to Canadians than to U.S. citizens is solidarity. Solidarity is the core concept on which the health care system rests, and why health care is universally available. Solidarity is not the same as justice. Solidarity emerges from an emotional bond and fellow-feeling, a sense of "we're all in it together" (d'Oronzio 2001). This is something many Europeans identify with, but it is less well received in the United States, where individual autonomy and individual freedom are emphasized. Nevertheless, it is the collective emotional togetherness that I call solidarity that has allowed the Canadian publicly supported health care system to evolve the way it did. The health care system reflects the fact that most Canadians think individuals should be treated equally in the face of illness and disease; the provision of universal health care is a tangible way for a society to express mutual support and caring for its members. The difference in how the individual relates to the collective means there is not as strong a place for the market in some facets of Canadian lives, and there is a prevailing view that medical care should be provided on the basis of need, not on the basis of ability to pay.

This attitudinal difference is also behind the fact that Canada has a much narrower range of income distribution. In fact, it has chosen tax and social policies that have a redistributive effect. Over the past decade Canada has ranked in the top half-dozen countries in the world for high life expectancy and low infant mortality. The United States, on the other hand, exhibits the largest income gap between rich and poor among wealthy nations, and its health indicator ranking on life expectancy and infant mortality is much lower than Canada's—far lower than one would expect for its wealth (Marmor and Sullivan 2000; Wilkinson 1996).

There are also significant differences between the two countries in religious attitudes. Canadians adhere more to hierarchical denominations—the big three are the Anglican, Catholic, and United Churches. Americans are more likely than Canadians to be fundamentalist Christians, to believe in God and the devil, and to enjoin a more literal reading of the Bible. Christian fundamentalism in Canada does not have the same media presence, numbers, or political influence as in the United States. This may be why the debate about embryo research and reproductive technologies in Canada has not been as polarized and divisive (*Globe and Mail* 2003).

Another relevant part of the social context that influences public policy development is that Canada is a federated state. This makes things more interesting, but certainly more complex. The United Kingdom, for example, did not have to take into account other levels of government when the Human Fertilisation and Embryology Authority (HFEA) was put into place (HFEA 1991). In Canada, although health research and public health education are under the jurisdiction of the federal government, which transfers funding to the provinces to partially subsidize health care services, the provinces themselves are responsible for health care delivery, and they have jurisdiction over hospitals and health professions. (Royal Commission on New Reproductive Technologies 1993, chap. 4). This fact leads to some differences from province to province in precisely what is funded or covered in the tax-supported provincial health care system. For example, although all provinces cover diagnostic investigations of infertility, in vitro fertilization (IVF) is paid for by public insurance only in Ontario, and only for blocked fallopian tubes. Like elective cosmetic plastic surgery, medical practice using reproductive technologies (ARTs) has developed outside the public system, in comparison with other aspects of medical care, which are seen as necessary by provincial health care funding policies.

A ROYAL COMMISSION ON NEW REPRODUCTIVE TECHNOLOGIES

By the end of the 1980s, concerns from many sources, including women's groups, legal and medical professional groups, religious groups, and others, led to calls for the appointment of a royal commission as a constructive way to deal with the complex issues raised by new reproductive technology use. In Canada, a royal commission is an instrument of public policymaking that is set up by the government as an independent body, at arm's length from the government. Its role is to consult widely and do necessary research before making recommendations to the federal government about how to deal with the given policy area in its mandate in a way that is in the public interest. The Royal Commission on New Reproductive Technologies was set up by the federal government at the end of 1989. It was asked to recommend policies on how reproductive technologies should be dealt with in the public interest in

Canada. The mandate, reproduced in the final report, is worth quoting at length:

The Royal Commission on New Reproductive Technologies will be established under Part I of the *Inquiries Act* and will inquire into and report on current and potential medical and scientific developments related to new reproductive technologies, considering in particular their social, ethical, health, research, legal and economic implications and the public interest, recommending what policies and safeguards should be applied. The Commission will examine, in particular,

1. implications of new reproductive technologies for women's reproductive health and well-being;
2. the causes, treatment and prevention of male and female infertility;
3. reversals of sterilization procedures, artificial insemination, in vitro fertilization, embryo transfers, prenatal screening and diagnostic techniques, genetic manipulation and therapeutic interventions to correct genetic anomalies, sex selection techiques, embryo experimentation and fetal tissue transplants;
4. social and legal arrangements, such as surrogate childbearing, judicial interventions during gestation and birth, and 'ownership' of ova, sperm, embryos and fetal tissue;
5. the status and rights of people using or contributing to reproductive services, such as access to procedures, 'rights' to parenthood, informed consent, status of gamete donors and confidentiality, and the impact of these services on all concerned parties, particularly the children; and
6. the economic ramifications of these technologies, such as the commercial marketing of ova, sperm and embryos, the application of patent law, and the funding of research and procedures including infertility treatment.

The commission's report on this wide-ranging mandate was made available in December 1993.

The commission undertook its task by consulting very broadly. The commission held widely publicized open hearings across the country in which more than 550 people participated. In addition, more than 500 written briefs were received. Since it is difficult or intimidating for some people to be present at public hearings, toll-free telephone lines were set up to allow easy input, and more than 6,000 people called. Because these avenues provide input that is self-selected, the commission also surveyed more than 15,000 randomly selected Canadians regarding issues in its mandate. People with personal experiences with the technologies could request nonpublic sessions with the commission, and more than 500 people took advantage of this opportunity.

The commission made a vigorous effort to bring the issues to the attention of the public and raise Canadians' awareness of the choices involved. It held informational meetings and a large search conference, as well as televised round tables and debates. It distributed more than 50,000 newsletters and 250,000 information kits, brochures, speeches, and other pieces of information. In all, more than 40,000 individuals were directly involved with its work. Some, such as those representing labor unions or religious groups, gave the commission input on behalf of many other people they had consulted. As a result, by the time its work was completed, the commission had received more input and interaction with the public than had any other royal commission to that time (Royal Commission 1993, chap. 6).

At the same time, the Royal Commission on New Reproductive Technologies set up an extensive research and evaluation program. Through this program the commission sought to discern what was actually occurring across the country by gathering data from both clinics and patients. It extensively examined the issues, with projects and analyses in many disciplines, including the social sciences, ethics, law, and medicine. It also analyzed the experience of other countries in studying the technologies and dealing with the issues they raise. More than 300 researchers at some fifty institutions participated in this extensive research program, and fifteen volumes were published summarizing the research findings.

Through these two streams of work, public consultations and research and analysis, the commission was able to provide for the first time a comprehensive picture of infertility and of new reproductive technology use in Canada, and substantive social, ethical, and legal analysis of the implications of using, or not using, the technologies.

The commission made its decisions about policy recommendations in the light of both the research findings and the broad-based input from the public, using explicit principles to guide the choices it made. The ethical orientation the commission adopted was an ethic of care that gave priority to the mutual care and connectedness between people and their communities. Within that orientation, the commission relied on eight guiding principles, on the ground that it was useful not only to have an ethical perspective that fostered care and community but also to have explicit guiding principles of special relevance to its mandate, to have a framework for addressing issues when conflicts arose.

Each principle shed a different kind of light on the options available and helped to ensure socially just policies. The eight guiding principles were individual autonomy, equality, respect for human life and dignity, protection of the vulnerable, noncommercialization of reproduction, appropriate use of resources, accountability, and balancing individual and collective interests. This approach was not, of course, a panacea, but the commission found that it led to a more complete canvassing of the issues and a more thorough consideration of how the issues affected various individuals and groups in society (Royal Commission 1993, chap. 3).

The commission's two-volume final report set out the science and the social and ethical issues raised by the science in a clear and comprehensive way. The commissioners outlined their thinking and reasoning for coming to the recommendations they made. The report was deliberately written to be accessible to the general reader because it was felt important that as many Canadians as possible become aware of the issues and participate in policymaking.

THE ROYAL COMMISSION'S RECOMMENDATIONS

In brief, the commission recommended that the Canadian government, as guardian of the public interest, should do two things: put boundaries around the use of new reproductive technologies and put in place a system to manage them within those boundaries. The management system was intended to apply not just to the immediate future but to all new and future reproductive technologies and their attendant social issues in a flexible, responsive, ongoing way (Baird 1995).

The commission also recommended legislation to prohibit several aspects of new reproductive technologies:

- certain kinds of human embryo research (reproductive cloning, making hybrids with or transferring to other species);
- using eggs from female fetuses for implantation;
- selling human eggs, sperm, embryos, fetuses or fetal tissue; and
- paying for or acting as an intermediary for surrogacy arrangements.

The commission's ethical analysis had suggested that these activities should not be done, and public support for those proscriptions was clearly in evidence from the consultations with the general public and various groups.

At the same time, the commission strongly recommended that the Canadian government establish a national regulatory body, with licensing required for the provision of new reproductive technologies to people. It said that Canada should not continue with the harmful and inequitable patchwork of standards and uses that it had documented across the country, with clinics and practices ranging from exemplary to harmful. A strong consensus had emerged from the consultations that a regulatory body was needed. The commission stated that a national approach was essential because technologies have social implications that are not containable within the boundaries of a single province. For example, allowing commercial surrogacy in one province conveys a view that the practice is acceptable—and that view cannot be contained within one province's boundaries. Permitting sixty-three-year-olds to have IVF in one province but not another would encourage reproductive tourism.

The commission recommended that a national regulatory body be set up to license and regulate the provision of services to people. It recommended that the body be kept at arm's length from government because it had heard a strong message from across the country that it should be separate from Health Canada. The commission recommended that women should normally make up at least half of the regulatory body's membership and that the body should include people with a broad range of experiences and perspectives, including ethics, law, and social sciences. The commission report said members did not have to be reproductive medicine experts; they could get expert input. There had been a preponderance of input from the public that self-regulation by the medical profession alone was not appropriate or sufficient in this field. The report said it was important that the members of the regulatory body not feel they were representing particular constituencies or stakeholders to whom they were accountable, as that was judged to be a recipe for stalemate. It was strongly recommended the members come from diverse experiences and backgrounds and wear a "citizen's hat" in making their judgments. They should be there as parliamentarians—to make judgments in the interest of the public, not of special groups. Attention should be paid to any issues of conflict of interest when members were appointed. To ensure openness and transparency, the report recommended that license hearings be public, and that the national regulatory body report annually to Canadians through Parliament on what was occurring in Canada in uses of reproductive technology.

The report recommended that it be compulsory in Canada to have a license from the regulatory body to provide certain services to people, and that obtaining and keeping the license would be conditional on complying with certain clearly specified conditions. The report noted that an advantage of a regulatory body was that the minimum could be embodied in legislation: although the law would require a license to provide services to people, the policies and rules to be complied with to retain the license could be shaped in such a fashion as to be responsive to change, without the necessity of changing the law. Having the flexibility to respond quickly to the implications of new technology was judged to be important in a field where knowledge changes rapidly, for it usually takes many years to change legislation.

RESPONSE BY THE FEDERAL GOVERNMENT

The commission reported in December 1993. A year and a half later, in July 1995, the federal minister of health called a press conference. In it she asked for a voluntary moratorium on nine practices, saying that the provincial governments supported the moratorium and that a further response was being worked on (Government of Canada 1995). The nine items she enumerated were human embryo cloning; commercial preconception or "surrogacy" arrangements; buying and selling of eggs, sperm and embryos; egg "donation" in exchange for IVF services; ectogenesis; retrieval of eggs from fetuses for donation or research; formation of animal-human hybrids; germline genetic alteration; and sex selection for nonmedical reasons.

Commentators across the country found this a totally inadequate response. As one editorial put it, "in spite of a broad public consensus on the need for federal leadership, the Minister's handling of this pressing issue has been disgracefully lame" (*Ottawa Citizen,* 1995). The media quoted clinic directors who said they were not going to abide by it (*The Province* 1995).

Two different committees were formed to give advice to the minister, and in June 1996, the *Act Respecting New Reproductive Technologies*—Bill C-47— was introduced to Parliament. It received its first and second reading, but when a federal election was called in 1997, the bill died on the order paper. Bill C-47 was believed by many to be inappropriate. It addressed only prohibitions, very similar to the earlier call for a moratorium, but it did not address the other side of the coin—the licensing and regulatory aspects that are needed to ensure that access to technologies is offered according to appropriate standards and in an accountable way. The commission had heard almost unanimously from all sectors that a regulatory body was needed.

In May 2001, the federal health minister sent new proposed legislation governing assisted reproduction to the Parliamentary Standing Committee on Health. He asked the committee to examine it and report back to him by January 2002, after which the legislation, with any changes, was to be put before the House. There had been extensive consultation with provincial governments, and it was proposed to make available the option to provinces, if they wished, of putting in place an "equivalency agreement" for other than the prohibitions.

One of the main stated purposes of the legislation was to protect the health and safety of Canadians. It would put in place an oversight licensing agency, and the legislation also took into account the information needs of people using ART by setting up a registry. The legislation applied to the activities used to help some people have children and the use of human embryos in research. The written consent of gamete donors was an important feature in both areas.

The standing committee reported back on its review of this legislation in December 2001 (Standing Committee on Health 2001), and five months later the minister of health introduced Bill C-56, *An Act Respecting Assisted Human Reproduction*, in the House of Commons (Bill C-56, 2002). This bill had its first reading on May 9, was debated at second reading on May 21, 22, and 24, 2002, and was approved in principle by a vote of 170–63. As is usual procedure, it was then referred back to the House of Commons standing committee for a clause-by-clause analysis, which the committee finished before the end of the year, referring the slightly amended bill back to Parliament. The bill, newly numbered C-13, came before the House for debate in January 2003. This bill was passed by the House of Commons in October 2003 but died on the order paper. The bill was reintroduced, renumbered as Bill C-6, *An Act Respecting Assisted Human Reproduction and Related Research*, in February 2004. This latest version of the legislation was finally passed by the Senate on March 11, 2004, and shortly afterward, on March 29, 2004, it received royal assent and became law.

THE CURRENT LEGISLATION

The legislation prohibits some activities and makes other activities subject to control under regulations, requiring a license to carry them out. The legislation created the Assisted Human Reproduction Agency (AHRA) of Canada to license facilities for research and for provision of assisted reproduction. The legislation prohibits making human embryos by nuclear transfer cloning or by embryo splitting. It permits embryo research in licensed facilities, including research on stem cells taken from existing embryos that are in excess of treatment needs. It does not permit making embryos for research other than for improving or providing instruction in assisted reproduction procedures. It permits reimbursement of expenses, but not payment, to gamete donors. It permits licensed facilities to facilitate noncommercial surrogacy. Penalties depend on whether terms and conditions of a license have been contravened, or whether a prohibition has been violated, so that penalties range from a fine of up to $100,000 to 10 years' imprisonment and a $500,000 fine. The legislation is to be revisited in three years, so that if the situation changes, the bill can be amended. For example, if in the future the use of cells from clonal embryos appears to offer a lifesaving therapy that is not possible in any other way, the ban on making clonal embryos for research could be reconsidered. It would require broad public consultation and debate at that time.

COMMENTS ON THE LEGISLATION

The development of policies to deal with reprogenetics in Canada has been a long, time-consuming process. In my view, it is much more important at this stage to get a regulatory system established than to delay the implementation of such a system by quibbling over details. Many of the people now using ARTs do so without the benefit of fully disclosed information on risks and benefits, without good data collection or appropriate record keeping, and so without reliable information on the outcomes of treatment. The important outcome of the legislation is that licensing of these activities will be mandatory. Changes can be made when an overall system is in place. In a fast-moving field, it is difficult to respond in a timely way with legislation, whereas the rules with which those applying for licenses must comply can be changed rapidly as necessary. It would be preferable to keep specific legislated prohibitions to the minimum necessary and address the need for control in the conditions of license. Another reason to do so is that the language of prohibition legislation may inadvertently prohibit something it did not intend to prohibit, or leave out an application that becomes possible.

The legislation in Bill C-13 is more balanced than the earlier Bill C-47 was, because it addresses not just prohibitions but ensuring access to safe and beneficial technology use. Canadians using these technologies need to be confident that the technologies are provided in a regulated environment, with assurance that standards of service provision, information disclosure, and record keeping are being met. At this time, the system outlined in Bill C-13 is starting to be put in place, and it is likely to meet these criteria. The national regulatory body could also provide an ongoing focal point for public participation and input, as technological capacities continue to grow rapidly, posing new policy choices.

IMPEDIMENTS TO GOVERNING ASSISTED HUMAN REPRODUCTION

Why has it taken so long in Canada to put in place mechanisms to oversee reproductive technology?

One impediment was the timing. A national initiative was proposed at a time when the federal government was completely focused on the referendum regarding the separation of Quebec from Canada. It made national leadership on any front more complex and difficult. Obviously, if a national body is proposed at a time when the population in Quebec is voting whether or not to separate, such an initiative could be used to make a case that the federal government is encroaching on Quebecers' terrain. Even though that phase is past, federal-provincial jockeying for territory is a permanent feature of the Canadian political landscape.

A second impediment was also related to timing: the new regulatory body was proposed at a time when budgetary restraint to get the national debt under control was at the top of everyone's agenda. The early 1990s was a period of increasing debt load. The federal debt then was in excess of $500 billion, and the interest payments on the debt took a substantial proportion of all tax revenues, leaving government with less room to move. Committing itself to reducing the debt, the government began downsizing the governmental bureaucracy. In this climate a national initiative, the new regulatory body, was proposed that no department had budgeted for, and consequently there were no identified funds to set it up. To become funded and implemented, it had to compete with other priorities and displace something else that was already funded. Doing anything new in a time of budgetary restraint and downsizing is extremely difficult. As government staffing was reduced, individuals were moved to new positions frequently and so did not get to know a portfolio in depth or come to understand its policy implications. Thus, there was a lacuna in the knowledge base, and appropriate policy initiation by policy champions within the government bureaucracy was not being realized.

A third impediment to implementation was the broad reach of the commission's mandate and the scope of the policy recommendations. Included were issues as diverse as donor insemination, the use of fetal tissue, legal reform, sex education, and environmental policy. Because the recommended policy responses did not all fit neatly into one department but involved ministries such as Justice, Health, Environment, and Education, the proposed national regulatory body and national regulation were left without a readily identifiable champion in government.

To the multiministerial scope of the effort was added another structural difficulty. In a federal-provincial nation, different levels of government are involved, and the decision-making authority for implementing some aspects may be diffused and not clearly located. Yet the commission judged it inappropriate to simply leave the provinces to deal with the issues in a fragmented way, and so it elected to bring together under one umbrella all the initiatives it recommended. The use of these technologies involves national concerns that cut across social, ethical, legal, medical, economic, and other considerations, as well as a great number of institutions. The commission judged that a national regulatory response was needed to safeguard the individual and societal interests involved, but in the ensuing years, the federal government had less leverage in health care, the context in which reproductive technologies are delivered. The cutbacks in federal contributions to health care over several years left the federal government unable to take a strong leadership role. The provinces, for their part, saw the federal government as wanting to call the tune but not pay the piper. Now that the federal government has increased the money it transfers for funding health care, it is in a better position to implement a national policy.

Another impediment to timely policy implementation had to do with the education of the public. The science involved in ART is complex, and the social issues emanating therefrom cannot be reduced to simple messages.

A central impediment to policy implementation is the public's diffuse interests versus the highly focused interests of professional players in the field (Marmor and Christianson 1982). Groups such as medical professional organizations, researchers, and infertility groups are often well organized and have a large personal stake in policy decisions. Their interest is concentrated, and they have a disproportionate influence on policy. They may be able to skew policy, and it is in their interest to do so. For example, some of the commission's recommendations were seen as a threat to self-regulation and autonomy by some medical professionals, who made a strong representation against them to political decision makers. Of course, the preferences and priorities of individuals with concentrated interests may be quite different from those of the general public, but the diffuse nature of the public interest means that it is unlikely to be mobilized on these issues. The individuals who are affected in this case are all of us who have a stake in the kind of community we live in. Most Canadians do not want to see a society where young women can be induced to take health risks to sell their eggs or induced to conceive in order to hand over the baby at birth for money. Interest groups are more likely to influence policy decisions than those holding diffuse public interests, even though the latter are far more numerous. There may be an analogy here to getting significant health care reform enacted in the United States. It is the same sort of problem: those who would benefit from reform are diffuse and without an organized voice or resources. The opponents—medical professional groups, insurers—are well organized, well funded, and have a large personal stake in policy decisions.

Any topic that is turned over to a royal commission by definition concerns issues that cannot be easily solved through existing structures and mechanisms, and because it is always easier for governments to do nothing than to act, a royal commission may be used as a temporizing device to avoid action. My closing comment on impediments to policy implementation is to urge the longer view. Significant policy change in a large and multicultural society such as Canada does not happen overnight. Policy learning goes on over periods of years, and advocacy coalitions take time to come together to press for action (Sabatier 1987). In addition, the federal government must assume a leadership role as a legitimate policy broker and must have the political will to act. It has been said that the recommendations of royal commissions take an average of six years to be implemented, if they are implemented at all. In the decades since the Royal Commission on the Status of Women reported in 1970, most of the 167 recommendations made have now been implemented, but had we looked at the situation in the first few years following the report, we would have felt quite despondent (Status of Women Canada 1995)..

WIDENING THE FRAME OF DEBATE

Most debate on reproductive technology focuses on weighing harms and benefits to individuals. This is a dangerously incomplete framing. Looking at issues simply as a matter of personal reproductive technology choice, although it brings a lens to bear on individual autonomy and reproductive freedom, tends to exclude other issues from consideration. A shift from framing as individual choice to framing as social effects—how the uses of technology affect others and society at large—is needed. Individual choices in reproduction are not isolated acts; they affect the child, other people, and future generations. Viewing the use of reproductive technology as only a personal matter inappropriately minimizes the potentially serious social consequences.

Reproductive technology uses also affect the health care system. Overall, the costs resulting from assisted reproduction are substantial. For example, the cost of multiple gestations after assisted reproduction at just one hospital in the United States was $3 million in one year in the early 1990s (Callahan 1994). The cost is high because complications after IVF are frequent, with a small percentage of women having ectopic pregnancies and about 25 percent having a miscarriage (HFEA 2000, 15; Holst 1991). Another factor generating costs is that more than four out of ten live-born children after IVF are from a multiple pregnancy (HFEA 2000, 11). They are more likely to be born prematurely and to need expensive neonatal intensive care (Bergh et al. 1999). Children born prematurely also use more medical, educational, and social services over time. In countries with publicly supported health care and social systems, these expenses have to be absorbed by the publicly supported systems, even if the original procedure was done in a private clinic. Currently in Canada, the profits from IVF are being privatized and the costs socialized, so society has a legitimate interest it needs to protect. In addition, the wider consequences of how these technologies are applied must be considered, because we all have a stake in the type of community that we live in. We do not want it to be one where the use of technology commodifies children, commercializes family formation, exploits women who are less advantaged, or increases social injustice.

Many issues arising from reproductive technology use cannot be resolved in the framework of individual autonomy and reproductive choice, because this framework leads us to overlook the collective and transgenerational consequences (Baird 2000). The use of scientific technology focused on individual wishes may result in social harms because individual interests differ from the public good at times. It is analogous to the case of the tragedy of the commons, where ranchers sharing grazing land or fishers sharing a fishing ground have an incentive to overgraze or overfish because doing so benefits the individual, even though the community is harmed. The aggregate effect of individually beneficial choices may harm the long-term common good, and the cumulative impact of individual choices can result in an unethical system. In public policymaking, it is inappropriate to subordinate every consideration to the question of whether a technology helps someone have a child. Public policymaking differs from individual decision making: if there is a conflict between the total social good and the good of an individual, public policy must uphold the public interest (Lamm 1999).

All members of the public have a stake in how we use reproductive technologies. Even though individuals who use the technologies directly are in a minority, how those technologies are used influences social values, and consequently society has a legitimate role in deciding if there should be some limits. The far-reaching nature of these choices means that more voices must be involved in making decisions. The decisions should not be taken preemptively by a clinical facility or a group of scientists who ignore the wishes of the rest of the community. Not just those who are knowledgeable in biology or science but sociologists, humanists, and citizens with a variety of life experiences should have their perspectives represented, their voices heard.

CONCLUSION

In the United States, the debate over how reproductive technologies should be used seems to be conducted largely in terms of individual freedom to make choices, and the burden of proof appears to be on anyone wanting to restrict that freedom. Thus, the likelihood of concrete harm must be demonstrated before limits can be put in place. In Canada, potential harms and social harms and consequences seem to weigh more, perhaps because of the different way such issues are framed and viewed. That difference in how the debate is framed may stem from the cultural differences in the way the individual is seen in relationship to the collective. However, framing the issues in the public dialogue in a way that allows multiple perspectives to be taken into consideration, not just an individual's desire to have a child, can effect change. Policy in the public interest is more likely to be achieved if reproductive technology use is viewed as a matter not solely of personal choice but one with larger social implications.

NOTE

Much of the preceding material was covered in an invited presentation to the President's Council on Bioethics, Washington, DC, June 20, 2002.

REFERENCES

Baird, P. A. 1995. Proceed with care: New reproductive technologies and the need for boundaries. *Journal of Assisted Reproduction and Genetics* 12:491–98.
———. 2000. Should human cloning be permitted? *Annals of the RCPSC* 33:235–37.

Bergh, T., A. Ericson, T. Hillensjö, et al. 1999. Deliveries and children born after in-vitro fertilisation in Sweden 1982–95: A retrospective cohort study. *Lancet* 354:1579–85.

Callahan, T. L., J. E. Hall, S. L. Ettner, et al. 1994. The economic impact of multiple-gestation pregnancies and the contribution of assisted-reproduction techniques to their incidence. *New England Journal of Medicine* 331:244–49.

d'Oronzio. J. C. 2001. Keeping human rights on the bioethics agenda. *Cambridge Quarterly of Health Care Ethics* 10:231–40.

Globe and Mail. 2003. The abortion debate, and where it rests. Editorial. January 21, A16.

Government of Canada. 2002. Bill C-56, *An Act Respecting Assisted Human Reproduction.* News release. www.hc-sc.gc.ca/english/protection/reproduction/index.htm (accessed December 18, 2002).

———. 1995. Health minister calls for moratorium on applying nine reproductive technologies and practices in humans. News release no. 1995–57. July 27. Ottawa.

Holst, N., J. M. Maltau, F. Forsdahl F, et al. 1991. Handling of tubal infertility after introduction of in vitro fertilization: changes and consequences. *Fertility and Sterility* 55:140–43.

Human Fertilisation and Embryology Authority. 1991. *First Annual Report.* London: HFEA.

———. 2000. *Ninth Annual Report.* London: HFEA.

Lamm, R. D. 1999. Redrawing the ethics map. *Hastings Center Report* 29, no. 2: 28–29.

Lipset, S. M. 1990. *Continental Divide: The Values and Institutions of the United States and Canada.* New York: Routledge.

Marmor, T. R., and J. B. Christianson. 1982. *Health Care Policy: A Political Economy Approach.* Beverly Hills, CA: Sage.

Marmor, T. R., and K. Sullivan. 2000. Canada's burning! Media myths about universal health coverage. *Washington Monthly* 32:15–20

Ottawa Citizen. 1995. Baby trade untouched. July 28, A10.

The Province (Vancouver). 1995. Baby talk. Editorial. August 1, 1995, A12.

Royal Commission on New Reproductive Technologies. 1993. *Proceed with Care: Final Report of the Royal Commission on New Reproductive Technologies.* Ottawa: Canada Communications Group—Publishing.

Royal Commission on the Status of Women in Canada. 1970. *Report of the Royal Commission on the Status of Women in Canada.* Ottawa.

Sabatier, P. A. 1987. Knowledge, policy-oriented learning, and policy change. *Knowledge: Creation, Diffusion, Utilization* 8, no. 4: 649–92.

Standing Committee on Health. 2001. *Assisted Human Reproduction: Building Families.* Ottawa: Public Works and Government Services Canada—Publishing.

Status of Women Canada. 1995. *Royal Commission on the Status of Women: An Overview, 25 Years Later.* Ottawa: Status of Women Canada.

Wilkinson, R. G. 1996. Income distribution and health. In *Unhealthy Societies: The Afflictions of Inequality,* 72–109. New York: Routledge.

PART FOUR

Regulating Reprogenetics in the United States

CHAPTER NINE

A Brief History of Public Debate about Reproductive Technologies

Politics and Commissions

KATHI E. HANNA

Over the past thirty years, society has faced a steady progression of advances in medically assisted reproduction and genetics that have been simultaneously considered everything from miraculous to immoral, depending on one's point of view. In vitro fertilization (IVF) and other assisted reproductive technologies, prenatal diagnosis, preimplantation genetic diagnosis, fetal tissue transplantation, prospects for germline gene transfer, human embryo research, and now human cloning have increased the need for public discussions about difficult public policy choices. Many of these choices, although lumped under "bioethics," are in fact social issues of considerable importance for policy. They have significant implications for choices regarding research funding, legislative prohibitions, regulations, moratoria, health care financing, and reimbursement. They can even enter campaign politics in critical election years.

Underlying many of the debates over these issues is a concern for the sanctity of human life and the relative importance of an individual life when weighed against the importance of many lives. Thus, often two "good things" are in conflict, such as a societal incentive to ameliorate disease through embryonic stem cell-based therapy and an individual's belief that the destruction of an embryo is the equivalent of murder. How to set boundaries and a course for proceeding as a society in this web of ethical complexity has become extremely contentious.

Controversy over science and technology, especially over those matters pertaining to reproduction and genetics, entails unique clashes between expertise and ignorance, encompassing ideals about rationality and progress and challenging our traditional notions of legitimacy and authority. Who gets to decide these important issues when so many are affected and there is no central authority? In the absence of a single authoritarian church or other mechanism with which to handle these issues in a pluralistic democracy, U.S. society increasingly finds itself turning to its government for the resolution of knotty ethical issues. The need has not been so much to find moral solutions to complex policy issues but to identify the moral problems and define the trade-offs among alternative moral principles (Hanna 1991). Beginning in the early 1990s, the need to discuss these issues at the national level has been increasingly recognized. In calling for a forum for such discussions in the early 1990s, former senator Mark Hatfield said, "in public policy, if there is a vacuum, government eventually will fill it, right or wrong, good or bad. We just can't let difficult bioethical matters evolve at will; we ought to help direct them" (U.S. Congress, Office of Technology Assessment (OTA) 1993).

Pluralism and democracy do not provide a very efficient set of processes through which to resolve such complexity. Government involvement in the area of reproductive science policy has demonstrated that, in general, we adjust the system in incremental ways through a variety of convoluted processes. This approach to governance, called "the science of muddling through" by economist Charles Lindblom (1959, 1979), is by no means unique to reproductive technology. It has long been the hallmark of U.S. public policymaking. However, it is particularly germane to our national response to reproductive technology, for several reasons: (1) rather than engaging in rational research and assessment of all possible solutions to a complex set of problems, it allows policymakers to concentrate only on measures that differ incrementally from existing policies; (2) the issues to be addressed are continually redefined until a response that is most amenable to solution is identified; and (3) as a result, a "suitable solution" does not exist, only a series of endless assaults on the problem(s) (within the realm of feasibility).

With this strategy toward public policy and decision making, it is a wonder that the government ever gets anything done. And sometimes that is the point. Inaction is action. Incrementalism results in decision making that is sometimes merely therapeutic, aimed at soothing some existing shortcomings and not at promoting future social goals (Lindblom 1959, 1979). It serves a useful purpose when society is critically divided on issues that cross scientific, technical, legal, social, political, and spiritual boundaries.

Since 1974, numerous federal commissions, committees, and panels have been created in the United States using public funds to deliberate about a wide variety of complex biomedical and ethical issues. Among such issues, those pertaining to reproductive technology and genetics have consistently appeared as foci of concern. Some commissions were created because of a public policy need for a mechanism or forum to articulate common values and foster consensus on bioethical issues in the face of growing cultural and religious heterogeneity. Others, specifically those created by the Department of Health and Human Services (DHHS) to provide advice on defined topics, were assigned explicit tasks, with clear end results anticipated by public decision makers. In many cases, these commissions were asked to handle political "hot potatoes" in response to a crisis (for example, the discovery that in the 1940s and 1950s the U.S. government had sponsored research studies that included injecting plutonium into human subjects, and the announcement that Dolly the sheep had been cloned). In some cases, the appointment of a commission gives policymakers time to gather their own information, strategize, and gauge public perceptions. This is not to belittle the value of national discourse on highly contentious issues: buying time is an important and rarely acknowledged role played by appointed commissions and committees.

Bioethics commissions offer an opportunity for mediating points of view among parties with differing levels and types of knowledge, and they offer the opportunity in an environment that ideally is one step removed from the political arena. At their best, they do more than just choose among competing alternatives; instead, they engage in an evolving public process with room for a plurality of viewpoints.

In recent years, these discussions have become increasingly public as a result of the Freedom of Information legislation (5 U.S.C. § 552) and requirements for open meetings through the Federal Advisory Committee Act (P.L. 92-463, 5 U.S.C., App.). These statutes have required that advisory groups accommodate the need of the public to have access to proceedings and files. That accommodation, while essential, can be a painful and prolonged process, especially when the public is polarized on an issue such as abortion, which permeates every discussion about reproductive technology. The degree of opposition sometimes appears to make a compromise or rational adjudication of differences impossible, and even open discourse is sometimes inhibited. Nevertheless, federally sponsored deliberations about sensitive social and scientific issues must now be conducted in broad daylight.

Reviewing the history of federal efforts to address issues in reproductive technology is instructive in many ways. It sheds some light on what makes some bodies more influential than others, elucidates the factors that both converge and intervene to enhance or subvert intent, and underlines the growing role of politics and public opinion in setting the agenda for discussion. Most important, it highlights the limited role that reason plays in resolving contentious issues surrounding reproduction and the meaning of life. Not only are these deliberative bodies conducting their work in an environment charged with disagreement about the proper path to take, but they can often face internal conflict among the members of the body, resulting in conclusions that are carefully crafted to reach internal consensus and not always transparent to those not sitting in the room.[1] To appreciate the role of public discourse in public policy, one has to appreciate and accept the reality that in the end, politics usually trumps all. This is not to denigrate deliberate and scholarly attempts to parse difficult social and moral issues but rather to acknowledge the power of representative government. Commissions and other advisory committees clearly add value to the national discussion and, given the right timing and circumstances, can produce recommendations that can be readily implemented, and in a few cases are.

A BRIEF HISTORY OF PUBLIC DELIBERATION
ABOUT REPRODUCTIVE TECHNOLOGIES

The U.S. government's forays into the realm of bioethics have had lasting impacts on the way society conducts biomedical research and delivers medical care. Five national bodies devoted specifically to bioethics, including reproductive technologies, have been established by Congress or the president since 1974:

- the National Commission for the Protection of Human Subjects of Biomedical and Behavioral Research (National Commission; established by the National Research Act of 1974, P.L. 348)
- the President's Commission for the Study of Ethical Problems in Medicine and Biomedical and Behavioral Research (President's Commission; P.L. 95-622, 1978)
- the Biomedical Ethics Advisory Committee (BEAC; established as a congressional body through P.L. 98-158, 1985)
- the National Bioethics Advisory Commission (NBAC; established by Executive Order 12975, signed by President Clinton on October 3, 1995)
- the President's Council on Bioethics (PCB; established by Executive Order 13237, signed by President George W. Bush on November 28, 2001)

A sixth federal initiative, the Ethics Advisory Board (EAB), was established by the secretary of the Department of Health, Education and Welfare (DHEW) in 1978 in response to a recommendation of the National Commission to ensure federal-level review of research involving IVF. Another department-level group was impaneled to review human fetal tissue transplantation research, and still another to suggest standards for human embryo research. In most cases, Congress or the president or his agents delegated to these bodies the task of considering bioethical problems that the legislative or executive branch was having problems resolving. Each of these efforts, described below, existed in unique circumstances that contributed to their success or failure. While these bodies often covered a wide range of topics, the discussion is limited to events directly related to the focus of this book.

The National Commission

The National Commission was established with the signing of the National Research Act of 1974, which originated from a bill sponsored by Senator Edward M. Kennedy. Congressional debate dated back to 1968 concerning the abuse of human research subjects. Congressional interest was piqued by a series of research scandals, including the Tuskegee syphilis trials (Heller 1972; Tuskegee Syphilis Study Ad Hoc Advisory Panel 1973) and the Willowbrook hepatitis experiments (see Faden and Beauchamp 1986). These controversies were the capstone to a landmark article published by Henry Beecher in 1966 that presented twenty-two examples of "unethical or questionably ethical studies" published in major medical journals. The article was influential largely because it showed that abuses were occurring in research conducted by mainstream investigators (Rothman 1991) and signaled to Congress that biomedical researchers were not adequately policing themselves and that some sort of oversight was necessary. These events marked the beginning of a national focus on the ethics of human research.

In 1973, the Senate Labor and Public Welfare Committee began a series of hearings on human experimentation (Jonsen 1998). Interest was intensified by controversy over NIH-funded research involving aborted fetuses (Cohn 1973). In 1972, allegations about experiments with fetuses both in and ex utero created controversy (fueled by the greater societal debate about elective abortion) over the use of fetal tissue in research. During the debate a number of bills were circulated, including one that would have created a National Human Experimentation Board. However, lacking support for such a measure, a compromise was reached. The proposal for a national oversight board was dropped in exchange for an agreement that DHEW would issue regulations governing research with human subjects (ACHRE 1995). DHEW quickly developed regulations, which were issued in May of 1974 (39 *Federal Register* 18914–18920), and the National Research Act was signed in July of that year.

The National Commission was created as a part of DHEW, although it operated relatively independently. At the top of its agenda was research using the human fetus. Within four months of assuming office, the commissioners were mandated to report on the subject, with the proviso that the presentation of their report to the secretary of DHEW would lift a moratorium that Congress had imposed on federal funding of research using live fetuses. In July 1975, the National Commission submitted its conclusions and recommendations in its report, *Research on the Fetus,* which formed the basis for DHEW regulations issued later that year on research involving fetuses, pregnant women, and human IVF. Those regulations, 45 CFR 46, SubPart B, remain in place today, although they have not been widely adopted by other federal agencies. *Research on the Fetus* was an impressive piece of work, presaging many more reports that laid a foundation for current human subject regulations in the United States.

In its findings, the National Commission did not define the "personhood" of the fetus; however, it did recognize the genetic heritage and vulnerability of the fetus and affirmed that it should be treated respectfully and with dignity, regardless of its life prospects. The commission also affirmed the legitimacy and importance of fetal research for improving the health of fetuses both in the present and in the future.

Interestingly, before the National Commission came into being, DHEW had proposed rules regarding research involving the human fetus (McCarthy 1992). The rules generated a storm of controversy and resulted in heated debate in Congress. The bureaucrats who had prepared the regulations had examined the literature and put together well-thought-out and articulated regulations, and were surprised by the ensuing debate. What the National Commission eventually recommended was virtually the same as that originally written by the bureaucracy, but this time the same substance was received with praise and approval from all sides. In politically sensitive areas of debate, sometimes the messenger is more important than the message.

The National Commission operated from 1974 until 1978, issuing ten reports, culminating in the seminal *Belmont Report* (National Commission 1978), which identified three fundamental ethical principles applicable to research with human subjects—respect for persons, beneficence, and justice—which translated respectively into provisions for informed consent, assessment of risk and potential benefits, and selection of participants. The *Belmont Report* was important primarily because it linked desired ethical standards and practices and existing concerns to fundamental ethical principles. It laid great emphasis on autonomy, elaborated and extended the notion of informed consent, recognized the special vulnerability of specific populations (including children, prisoners, and the mentally infirm), and fleshed out details of review through institutional review boards (IRBs), which are now embodied in federal research regulations. (Much has been written about the impact of the *Belmont Report* and the subsequent regulatory framework that was created for the protection of human subjects—a topic of considerable ongoing debate, but not directly relevant to this chapter [see, for example, IOM 2003, NBAC 2001].)

Congress and the executive branch found the work of the National Commission useful. It produced reports that were tailored to executive branch needs. Its work involved policies, programs, and regulations of the federal government, which gave it a clear and more utilitarian focus. It also enjoyed the advantage of being the first of its kind, the standard bearer to which all future commissions would be compared. When its charter expired, it recommended that a successor body be created, but with broader authority to address issues beyond protection of human participants in research. Issues regarding the safety of recombinant DNA were being debated on Capitol Hill, and termination of treatment was rapidly becoming a national issue in the wake of the Karen Ann Quinlan case and other court challenges to medical authority. The debate about a coherent national health plan was on one of its periodic upswings. Congress concurred that a more general mandate for a national bioethics organization was in order and created the President's Commission.

The President's Commission

The President's Commission was established by Section III of Public Law 95-622. The congressional language specified several tasks, as it had for the National Commission, but also gave the President's Commission the authority to undertake studies at the request of the president or on its own initiative. Congress was explicitly excluded from providing additional topics to be addressed, to avoid the use of the commission for special interests. If there was consensus within Congress that certain issues should be addressed, the commission had the authority to pursue those topics if it concurred.

With elevation to presidential stature, the scope of the commission was broadened to the entire federal government, so that it could make recommendations to multiple agencies. In addition, its scope was extended beyond human subjects research protections to include medical practice. Appointment powers resided with the president. Like the National Commission, the legislation creating the body had a forcing clause, but unlike the National Commission, the President's Commission's reports made few specific recommendations to which federal agencies were required to respond.

The strategy pursued by the President's Commission was to attain consensus among the commissioners. The explicit goal of unanimous agreement does not imply that other views were ignored, but rather that the commissioners came to hold positions that diverged from those staked out by interest groups. This political phenomenon of consensus building persists in areas of long-standing public controversy (Hanna 1991; Nelkin 1992; Wolf 2003).

The President's Commission operated from 1980 until 1983 and issued eleven reports, including one on genetic screening and counseling, building on the previous work of the National Academy of Sciences (National Academy of Sciences 1975; President's Commission 1983) and one on human gene therapy, entitled *Splicing Life* (President's Commission 1982). The gene therapy report served to ground a potentially explosive discussion and to thwart legislation under consideration. The genetic screening report correctly identified issues but languished amid federal inaction until the discovery of the gene for cystic fibrosis eight years later rekindled a national debate (OTA 1992).

Had the commission continued to exist beyond 1983, it might have been drawn further into the political mainstream concerning health policy issues. On balance, the President's Commission left an impressive legacy. Many of its reports had an immediate impact on policy, others were sleepers that anticipated issues to emerge later in the 1980s, and most of its reports are still widely cited by scholars in bioethics and in related public policy debates. The issue of whether any commission has real impact is not easily resolved and often depends on who one asks (Gray 1995). The greater complexity of the President's Commission's mandate compared with the National Commission's and the increasing presence of interest group politics, however, foreshadowed an impending storm.

A two-year debate about reestablishing the President's Commission began in November 1982, when *Splicing Life* was released at a hearing before Albert

Gore, Jr., then a member of the House of Representatives. The hearing focused on the implications of human genetics, particularly gene therapy. *Splicing Life* emphasized the distinction between genetically altering somatic cells, which would not lead to inherited changes, and genetically altering germ cells (sperm, egg cells, and their precursors), which would induce inherited changes. This distinction permitted policymakers and others to clearly understand that some cases of gene therapy would not be morally different from any other treatment, clearly pointing to some cases where gene therapy might be technically preferable—and morally equivalent—to other treatments. The report steered the debate away from vague speculations about playing God and how to thwart the technological imperative and toward prudent policies of research protocol review and processes to formulate policy.

The President's Commission recommended that the National Institutes of Health (NIH) review progress in gene therapy through its Recombinant DNA Advisory Committee (RAC), and that NIH consider the broad implications of commencing gene therapy. The RAC accepted this recommendation in April 1983 and began to debate the merits of the new technology and to assess its social implications, later drafting "Points to Consider in the Design and Submission of Human Somatic Cell Gene Therapy Protocols," adopted in 1986 as the keystone document in public oversight of the new technology (Fletcher 1990; Murray 1990).

The report also noted that there was a need for public debate, which could be mediated by an ad hoc commission on genetics or by a standing federal bioethics commission. Rep. Gore was impressed with the report and by the process that produced it. He subsequently introduced legislation to create a president's commission on human genetic engineering, favoring permanent oversight of advances in human genetics and reproduction. This became the seed for legislation to create the Biomedical Ethics Board and Advisory Committee (described below), with a broader mandate than human genetics, as Gore became convinced that a broader mandate would be more useful.

During this same period in the Senate, there were several separate proposals to re-establish the President's Commission, to give the Institute of Medicine a mandate to do studies in bioethics, and to have the congressional Office of Technology Assessment also conduct such work.

Continuation of the President's Commission was unacceptable to several conservative senators. Their principal objections were grounded in displeasure over the Commission's recommendations regarding termination of treatment at the end of life, especially those pertaining to withdrawal of nutrition and hydration. Senate conservatives wanted bioethics brought under direct congressional scrutiny. Three senators sent informal inquiries to the IOM and OTA asking if either institution could do the work, and if so, whether they wished to do so. The response of each was equivocal because of the political perils of such an endeavor (Hanna, Cook-Deegan, and Nishimi 1993). The end result was the creation of an entirely new agency, the Biomedical Ethics Board and Biomedical Ethics Advisory Committee. The bill the proposal was attached to passed both chambers but was vetoed by President Reagan, for reasons unrelated to the bioethics provisions. It was reintroduced in the 99th Congress, vetoed again, but then passed in a veto override by strong House and Senate majorities (P.L. 99-158).

The Biomedical Ethics Advisory Committee

The Biomedical Ethics Advisory Committee (BEAC) was a fourteen-member group whose multidisciplinary membership was appointed by the Biomedical Ethics Board, comprised of twelve members of Congress—three each from the majority and minority parties of the House and Senate. It took almost a year for the four party leaders of the House and Senate to appoint the twelve members of the congressional board, which then took on the responsibility of appointing the fourteen members of BEAC, the operational arm. The appointment process was painstakingly long, nearly two and a half years. It took another year to appoint the two lay representatives, an exercise that deepened the mistrust that had been building up for several years among members of the congressional board (Hanna, Cook-Deegan, and Nishimi 1993).

The BEAC finally met in September 1988, less than a week before its authorization expired. The committee adopted rules of operation and elected a chairman and vice chairman. The BEAC had the authority to hire an executive director and staff and was directly responsible for carrying out the studies of topics in biomedical ethics mandated by legislation or specified by the congressional Board. As the BEAC began to take flight, the congressional board to which it was tethered was sinking deeper and deeper into the abortion debate.

The BEAC was required to prepare at least three reports on specified topics, as well as to provide annual reports. The first mandated report, on the implications of human genetic engineering, stemmed from the original Gore bill proposing an extension of the President's Commission (H.R. 98-2788). The deadline for the second report, on fetal research, expired before BEAC members were appointed. The fetal research mandate was reinstated in the

Omnibus Health Extension Act of 1988 (P.L. 100-607), with the deadline delayed until November 1990. A third mandate focused on AIDS research and treatment.

The structure, never stable, began to disintegrate in March 1989, when the Senate board members were unable to elect a chairman and found themselves in a partisan logjam along pro-choice–antiabortion lines. A pivotal meeting took place at the peak of an acrimonious Senate debate to confirm former senator John Tower as secretary of defense. Partisan tensions were high and tempers short. The BEAC's existence faltered over vote counts on its board. The National Right to Life Committee was frustrated at having only five of thirteen BEAC members in the antiabortion camp, by its own count. On the pro-choice side of the board, there was concern that nothing could be issued from the BEAC that did not pass muster with the National Right to Life Committee. Both antiabortion and pro-choice factions thus regarded the bicameral structure with great suspicion because the opposite faction controlled part of it. The BEAC died in the cross-fire, and the office was closed at the end of September 1989, having never issued a report. Alex Capron, chair of the ill-fated committee, has written that the politics of abortion was strong enough to interfere with all other topics planned for consideration, including genetics, on which the membership gave no sign of dividing along abortion politics lines (Capron 1997). The BEAC stands as the exemplary "wrong approach" to creating a deliberative body for review of controversial issues. Because its fate was controlled by elected officials operating in a highly contentious atmosphere, it was doomed almost from the outset. Fifteen years later it is even harder to contemplate a successful bipartisan effort emerging from Congress to create such a body, with the rise of the politics of "wedge" issues and an evenly split Congress.

Deliberative Bodies Established at the Departmental Level

In 1975, the former DHEW announced it would fund no proposal for research on human embryos or on IVF unless the proposal had been reviewed and approved by a federal ethics advisory board. IVF was still an experimental technique: Louise Brown, the first IVF baby, was born in 1978. The human subjects regulations that resulted from the National Commission's work required review of such work by an Ethics Advisory Board (EAB), to be appointed by the DHEW Secretary. In 1977, NIH received an application from an academic researcher for support of a study involving IVF. After the application had undergone scientific review within NIH, it was forwarded to the EAB appointed by Joseph Califano, then secretary of DHEW. At its May 1978 meeting, the EAB agreed to review the research proposal.

With the increased public interest that followed the birth of Louise Brown that summer, Secretary Califano asked the EAB to study the broader social, legal, and ethical issues raised by human IVF. On May 4, 1979, in its report to the secretary, the EAB concluded that federal support for IVF research was "acceptable from an ethical standpoint" provided that certain conditions were met, such as informed consent for the use of gametes, an important scientific goal "not reasonably attainable by other means," and not maintaining an embryo "in vitro beyond the stage normally associated with the completion of implantation (14 days after fertilization)" (DHEW EAB 1979, 106, 107). No action was ever taken by the secretary with respect to the board's report; for other reasons, DHEW dissolved the EAB in 1980. Considerable opposition emanated from the Roman Catholic Church about the morality of IVF, which contributed to paralysis regarding reconstitution of the EAB (Congregation 1987).

Because it failed to appoint another EAB to consider additional research proposals, DHEW effectively forestalled any attempts to support IVF research, and no experimentation involving human embryos was ever funded pursuant to the conditions set forth in the May 1979 report or through any further EAB review.

The Office of Technology Assessment's May 1988 report on infertility forced a reexamination of the EAB (OTA 1988). A subsequent House hearing focused on the absence of the EAB. Assistant Secretary of Health Robert Windom promised to reestablish an EAB, and a new charter was published but never signed in the waning months of 1988, following the election of President Bush (Windom 1988). The first Bush administration did not support reestablishing an EAB, thus extending a twelve-year lapse in a federal mechanism for the review of controversial research protocols. This would continue until 1993, when the NIH Revitalization Act effectively ended the de facto moratorium on IVF and other types of research involving human embryos by nullifying the regulatory provision that mandated EAB review. However, the controversy over embryo research was nowhere near ended.

NIH's Human Embryo Research Panel. Because the NIH Revitalization Act of 1993 effectively ended the de facto moratorium on IVF and other types of research involving human embryos, then NIH director Harold Varmus convened a Human Embryo Research Panel (HERP) to develop standards for determining which projects could be funded ethically and which should be considered "unacceptable for federal funding."

The panel of scientists, ethicists, legal scholars, and lay representatives worked in an environment of heightened scrutiny by the antiabortion lobby, which inundated NIH with petitions and at times created a hostile setting for the panel's meetings (all of which were conducted in public) and for the panelists individually. Panel members received threatening letters and phone messages, and security at meetings was heightened (Hall 2003). HERP submitted its report to the Advisory Committee to the NIH Director (ACD) in September 1994. In addition to describing areas of research that were acceptable and unacceptable for federal funding, the panel made the controversial recommendation that under certain conditions, embryos could be created for research purposes.

Acting on this submission, the ACD formally approved the HERP recommendations (including a provision for the deliberate creation of research embryos) and transmitted them to NIH Director Harold Varmus on December 1, 1994. Before Varmus could even consider the recommendations and prepare his public response, on December 2 the White House, preempting Varmus, intervened to clarify an earlier endorsement of embryo research, with President Clinton stating in a press release, "I do not believe that Federal funds should be used to support the creation of human embryos for research purposes, and I have directed that NIH not allocate any resources for such requests."

Varmus proceeded immediately to implement those HERP recommendations not proscribed by the president's clarification, concluding that NIH could begin to fund research activities involving "surplus" embryos. Before any funding decisions could be made, however, Congress attached a rider to that year's DHHS appropriations bill that stipulated that none of the funds appropriated could be used to support any activity involving "1) the creation of a human embryo or embryos for research purposes; or 2) research in which a human embryo or embryos are destroyed, discarded, or knowingly subjected to risk of injury or death greater than that allowed for research on fetuses *in utero* under 45 CFR 46.208(a)(2) and section 498(b) of the Public Health Service Act (42 USC 289g(b))." Additional legislative riders have been inserted into subsequent annual DHHS appropriating statutes, enacting identically worded provisions into law. Thus, to date, no federal funds have been used for research that directly involves the deliberate creation or destruction of a human embryo, and the removal of the requirement for EAB review became moot. This issue would resurface in 1998 when the issue of human embryonic stem (ES) cells was addressed by NBAC. However, HERP was prescient in its view to the future of embryo research. It considered the possibility of successful isolation of ES cells well in advance of the actual accomplishment, and suggested that it might be scientifically important to create human embryos for research purposes for which clear clinical potential could be seen (NIH 1994).

Human Fetal Tissue Transplantation Research Panel. During the 1980s, DHHS was grappling with another related and controversial issue. In 1988, Assistant Secretary Windom initiated a moratorium on the use of fetal tissue in transplantation research funded by the federal government. He requested that NIH convene a panel to advise him about the technical stakes and ethical implications of such research, specifically whether the moral issues surrounding the source of such tissue (elective abortions) could ethically be separated from the use to which such tissue is put (for example, treatment of Parkinson disease or diabetes). NIH complied and scheduled a meeting for September 1988, following many months of wrangling among NIH, the DHHS secretary's and assistant secretary's offices, and the White House. The initial, unrealistic expectation was that an ad hoc advisory panel would make recommendations after a single meeting, but the issues proved far too complex and divisive (Childress 1991). The panel met to hear testimony from disease groups, researchers, and those opposed to the research. They voted on a set of specific recommendations, and found a majority in favor of permitting such research as long as three conditions were met in addition to IRB approval: (1) the decision to donate tissue was kept separate from and made only after the decision to abort; (2) the process for abortion was not altered in any way; and (3) the informed consent of both parents was obtained in cases when the fathers could be contacted. The majority of the panel argued that they did not have to directly engage in questions about the morality of abortion, since the practice was legal (Childress 1991).

Two separate dissenting statements argued that the abortion issue should not be sidestepped. One statement dissented from the majority on three grounds: (1) that the process of using fetal tissue was inherently suspect because it would give women an altruistic incentive to perform an immoral act (i.e., elective abortion); (2) that such research fostered complicity in the practice of elective abortion because it would necessarily entail close collaboration with those performing abortions; and (3) that permission from the mother and father was illegitimate, since the parents had abandoned the fetus by seeking the abortion. A report was issued with a compilation of recommendations and vote tallies, accompanied by two dissenting statements; several separate assenting statements were signed by subgroups of the majority, taking issue with points made in the dissenting statements and going further into justifications for the recommendations, thus providing a glimpse of how the panel had reached its conclusions in the main report (Advisory Committee to the Director 1988). Panel members voted 19-2 to recommend continued funding for fetal tissue transplantation research under guidelines designed to ensure the ethical integrity of any experimental procedures (Adams 1988; Duguay 1992; Silva-Ruiz 1998). In November 1989, after the transition from the Reagan to the Bush administration, DHHS Secretary Louis Sullivan extended the moratorium indefinitely, based on the position taken by the minority-voting panel members that fetal tissue transplantation research would increase the incidence of elective abortion (Goddard 1996; Robertson 1990). Attempts by Congress to override the secretary's decision were vetoed by President Bush or were not enacted into law.

In October 1992, a consortium of disease advocacy organizations filed suit against Secretary Sullivan, alleging that the Hyde Amendment (banning federal funding of abortion) did not apply to research or transplantation involving fetal tissue. The plaintiffs argued, moreover, that applying a fetal tissue transplantation research ban was beyond the department's statutory authority under the law. The suit was preempted on January 22, 1993, when the new administration shifted national biomedical policy and directed Clinton's DHHS secretary Donna Shalala to remove the ban on federal funding for human fetal tissue transplantation research. In March 1993, the NIH published interim guidelines for research involving human fetal tissue transplantation (OPRR 1994). Provisions to legislate these safeguards were promptly proposed in Congress and included in the NIH Revitalization Act of 1993, which President Clinton signed into law on June 10, 1993. The interim guidelines became final and still govern research in this area. The initial recommendations of the 1988 panel served as the basis for the final guidelines. The involvement of health advocacy and disease-focused groups was critical in ensuring that such research could go forward under stringent oversight. This phenomenon would also play a critical role in the debate over ES cell research.

The National Bioethics Advisory Commission

The National Bioethics Advisory Commission (NBAC) was established by President Clinton in 1995 to provide advice and make recommendations concerning bioethical issues arising in the context of government research programs. It was the first such presidential-level body to be constituted since the expiration of the President's Commission in 1983. Its original mandate called on the commission to address human subjects protections and issues emerging from genetic technologies. Four months into its existence, and within days of the published report of Dolly, the cloned sheep, President Clinton instituted a ban on federal funding related to attempts to reproduce human beings through cloning. In addition, he asked NBAC to address within ninety days the ethical and legal issues surrounding the subject of cloning human beings. The commission began its discussions fully recognizing that any effort in humans to transfer a somatic cell nucleus into an enucleated egg involves the creation of an embryo, with the apparent potential to be implanted in utero and developed to term. Thus, the federal restrictions on use of federal funds to create an embryo would apply.

Early in its deliberations, the NBAC noted that while the creation of embryos for research purposes alone always raises serious ethical questions, as witnessed by the controversy that followed the HERP recommendations, the use of somatic cell nuclear transfer to create embryos for research purposes raised no new issues. However, the unique and distinctive ethical issues raised by the use of somatic cell nuclear transfer to create children do raise new concerns, for example, serious safety issues, individuality, family integrity, and treating children as objects. Consequently, the commission focused its attention on the use of such techniques for the purpose of creating an embryo that would then be implanted into a woman's uterus and brought to term. It also expanded its analysis of this particular issue to encompass activities in both the public and private sector (NBAC 1997).

To arrive at its recommendations concerning the use of somatic cell nuclear transfer techniques to create children, the NBAC also examined the longstanding religious traditions that guide many citizens' responses to new technologies and found that religious positions on human cloning are pluralistic in their premises, modes of argument, and conclusions (NBAC 1997, vol. 2). In the end, the public policies recommended with respect to the creation of a child using somatic cell nuclear transfer reflected the commission's best judgments about both the ethics of attempting such an experiment and its view of the traditions regarding limitations on individual actions in the name of the common good. The commission concluded that the use of this technique to create a child would be a premature experiment that would expose the fetus and the developing child to unacceptable risks. It argued that this in itself might be sufficient to justify a prohibition on cloning human beings at that time, even if such efforts were to be characterized as the exercise of a fundamental right to attempt to procreate.

The commission concluded that there should be imposed a period of time in which no attempt would be made to create a child using somatic cell nuclear transfer, so that a further national discussion could ensue. The NBAC made an immediate request to all firms, clinicians, investigators, and professional societies in the private and non-federally funded sectors to comply voluntarily with the intent of the federal moratorium.

The NBAC further recommended that federal legislation be enacted to prohibit anyone from attempting, whether in a research or clinical setting, to create a child through somatic cell nuclear transfer cloning. However, it warned that any regulatory or legislative actions undertaken to effect the foregoing prohibition on creating a child by somatic cell nuclear transfer should be carefully written so as not to interfere with other important areas of scientific research. In a nod to the possibility that embryonic stem cells might be derived and provide promising new therapies, the NBAC wrote that no new regulations were required regarding the cloning of human DNA sequences and cell lines, since neither activity raised the scientific and ethical issues that arise from the attempt to create children through somatic cell nuclear transfer. In less than two years, the NBAC would have to go back to these issues.

Despite several efforts in both chambers to legislate a ban on human cloning to produce a child, no laws have been passed, in part because of the inability of Congress to disentangle human cloning for reproductive purposes from cloning to derive ES cells for the purpose of research.

The NBAC's Stem Cell Report

The scientific reports of the successful isolation and culture of ES cells and embryonic germ (EG) cells renewed the long-standing controversy about the ethics of research involving human embryos and cadaveric fetal material. Again, President Clinton turned to the NBAC for advice on the promise of these research developments, as well as to address the ethical concerns. The commission reiterated its previous position that creation of an embryo using somatic cell nuclear transfer for the purpose of isolating ES cells raises questions similar to those raised by the creation of research embryos through IVF, and it reemphasized that at the current time, federal funds need not be used for such research. The president also asked the NBAC to provide advice on the creation of human-nonhuman chimeras using somatic cell nuclear transfer, which would raise unique concerns.

The NBAC noted that conscientious individuals can come to different conclusions regarding both public policy and private actions in the area of stem cell research, observing that differing perspectives cannot easily be bridged by any single public policy. The commission added that "the development of public policy in a morally contested area is not a novel challenge for a pluralistic democracy such as that which exists in the United States. We are profoundly aware of the diverse and strongly held views on the subject of this report and have wrestled with the implications of these different views at each of our meetings devoted to this topic. Our aim throughout these deliberations has been to formulate a set of recommendations that fully reflects widely shared views and that, in our view, would serve the best interests of society" (NBAC 1999, iii).

In its recommendations, the commission stopped short of endorsing the use of somatic cell nuclear transfer to create an embryo for the purposes of deriving stem cells. Instead it recommended that "at this time," federal funding for the use *and* derivation of ES and EG cells should be limited to two sources of such material: cadaveric fetal tissue and embryos remaining after infertility treatments. The commission left open the possibility that these sources might prove insufficient and that the need for cloning to derive superior cell lines should be revisited after sufficient scientific work had been conducted to justify that further step.

The commission advanced the public policy debate by taking a head-on approach to the perennial issue of the "moral status of the human embryo." Rather than trying to define it, which it admitted no federal body could or should do adequately, it wrote:

> Although we believe most would agree that human embryos deserve respect as a form of human life, disagreements arise regarding both what form such respect should take and what level of protection is required at different stages of embryonic development. Therefore, embryo research that is not therapeutic to the embryo is bound to raise serious concerns and to heighten the tensions between two important ethical commitments: to cure disease and to protect human life. For those who believe that the embryo has the moral status of a person from the moment of conception, research (or any other activity) that would destroy the embryo is considered wrong and should not take place. For those who believe otherwise, arriving at an ethically acceptable policy in this arena involves a com-

plex balancing of a number of important ethical concerns. Although many of the issues remain contested on moral grounds, they co-exist within a broad area of consensus upon which public policy can, at least in part, be constructed. (NBAC 1999, 67)

Immediately on release of the report, President Clinton—as he did with HERP—again made clear his view that his advisory committees were truly advisory. In a tersely worded press release he commended NBAC for the "thoroughness with which they engaged in this discussion and the national dialogue that they facilitated, seeking the views and opinions of virtually every segment of our society, including scientists, patients, scholars from most of the major religions in the United States, lawyers, philosophers, ethicists and the public."

In the background, a federal policy was already being crafted. When the question arose of whether to provide federal funding for human ES cell research using IVF embryos remaining from infertility treatments, the NIH director sought the opinion of Harriet Rabb, DHHS general counsel, regarding the effect of the prohibition in the current appropriations rider. Rabb reported to Varmus that the legislation did not prevent NIH from supporting research that uses ES cells derived from this source because the cells themselves do not meet the statutory, medical, or biological definition of a human embryo (NIH 1999).[2]

Having concluded that NIH may fund internal and external research that utilizes ES cells but does not create or actively destroy human embryos, NIH delayed actual funding until such time as an ad hoc working group would be able to develop guidelines for the conduct of ethical research in this area. But time ran out. Before any grants could be funded, the infamous 2000 election results produced a new administration, and therefore new policies. In August 2001, President George W. Bush announced that NIH could fund research using ES cells, but only if the lines had been derived prior to August 9, 2001. Thus, in his view, the federal government could not be considered complicit in the destruction of the embryos. In his printed statement, the president said, "As a result of private research, more than 60 genetically diverse stem cell lines already exist. I have concluded that we should allow federal funds to be used for research on these existing stem cell lines 'where the life and death decision has already been made.' This allows us to explore the promise and potential of stem cell research without crossing a fundamental moral line by providing taxpayer funding that would sanction or encourage further destruction of human embryos that have at least the potential for life."[3] As of this writing, the number of cell lines that are actually available for this area of research remains in dispute, and several universities are deriving their own ES cell lines using private funds. The fact that such activity has not been legislated as illegal (despite attempts by conservative factions in Congress to do so) speaks to the unspoken public compromise, which is to allow the work to proceed in the private sector beyond the grasp of the federal government and out of sight of groups that oppose such research.

The President's Council on Bioethics

At the end of the Clinton administration, the charter for the NBAC was allowed to expire in anticipation that the next president, whoever he might be, would want his own set of advisors and most likely a different charter. In November 2001, President George W. Bush named a new body, called the President's Council on Bioethics (PCB).

The council's charter allows it to consider a range of bioethical matters connected with specific biomedical and technological activities, such as embryo and stem cell research, assisted reproduction, cloning, uses of knowledge and techniques derived from human genetics or the neurosciences, and end-of-life issues.

In its first report, *Human Cloning and Human Dignity: An Ethical Inquiry,* ten members of President Bush's Bioethics Council recommended a four-year moratorium on "cloning-for-biomedical-research." They also called for "a federal review of current and projected practices of human embryo research, preimplantation genetic diagnosis, genetic modification of human embryos and gametes, and related matters, with a view to recommending and shaping ethically sound policies for the entire field." The advocates of the moratorium argued that a moratorium "would provide the time and incentive required to develop a system of national regulation that might come into use if, at the end of the four-year period, the moratorium were not reinstated or made permanent." Further, they argued that "in the absence of a moratorium, few proponents of the research would have much incentive to institute an effective regulatory system."

Seven members of the eighteen-member council (one abstained) voted for "permitting cloning-for-biomedical-research now, while governing it through a prudent and sensible regulatory regime." They advocated allowing research to go forward only when the necessary regulatory protections to avoid abuses and misuses of cloned embryos had been put in place. "These regulations might touch on the secure handling of embryos, licensing and prior review of research projects, the protection of egg donors, and the provision of equal access to benefits." The divide in the council's vote undermined its impact in the scientific and policy communities and highlighted the problems created when a national body fails to come to consensus (Hall 2002). Like its predecessor, the NBAC, the PCB failed to persuade Congress to pass a ban on cloning to create a human being. To the credit of both bodies, however, it was not for lack of trying. Congress, in its endless political machinations, failed to successfully distinguish in a single piece of legislation cloning for the purposes of creating a human being from cloning to create, for example, ES cell lines for research.

In January 2004, the PCB issued a report, *Monitoring Stem Cell Research,* which took a distinctly different tack, providing a descriptive overview of the status of the science and the regulatory framework for the science currently being conducted, without making recommendations. Members of Congress on both sides of the aisle and an increasingly sophisticated patient advocacy community have kept up pressure for reconsideration of the current policy limiting public funds to approved cell lines. One can only speculate that the public airing of PCB's internal fallout over its cloning report and rising public support for ES cell research might have tempered the council's approach to its work. Compared with the NBAC, which operated at arm's length from the White House, the PCB continues to have close ties to administration officials and is likely to be influenced by such close relationships.

OBSERVATIONS

The National Commission, the President's Commission, and the EAB, BEAC, NBAC, and PCB were all national responses to the need for a mechanism to address contentious issues in the practice of medicine and the conduct of biomedical research. This would suggest that policymakers recognize the need for a federal effort comprised of diversely trained individuals to monitor the interface between ethics and medicine. At their best, these bodies inform legislators, regulators, adjudicators, health care providers, scientists, and the lay public about principles to be considered when making difficult decisions in medicine and biomedical research. Although there are pitfalls attendant on centralization of such discussions in one entity (the tendency to lose flexibility in interpretation and the potential for capture by political interests), such centralization brings authority to the process that is rarely achieved without it. In all the examples provided in this chapter, with the exception of the BEAC—which was never given a chance to succeed—the advisory groups established themselves as authoritative sources on complex issues. That does not guarantee influence, however. For better or for worse, members of Congress and the executive branch will assign different weight to a group that they have created. Thus, for example, DHHS took seriously the advice of the fetal tissue panel and the human embryo research panel.

And, although national commissions allow debates about contentious issues to go forward in a somewhat less politicized way than is possible on the floor of Congress or on centerstage at the White House, the political stakes in the issues addressed are increasingly high. In the area of reproductive technology, abortion is the issue lingering at the door, and it is an issue that is increasingly used purely for political purposes. Any advisory group facing the issue of abortion either directly or indirectly knows that whatever message it tries to convey will be lost in the clamor of antiabortion versus pro-choice politics.

In its 1993 report, *Biomedical Ethics in Public Policy,* the OTA identified six key elements that influence the success of such deliberative bodies: (1) the charge (which will influence its authority or lack thereof); (2) the appointment process; (3) the bureaucratic location; (4) reporting requirements (to whom and how shall the group report and in what manner); (5) budget and staffing; and (6) targeted audience(s). A key consideration concerns the mission of the organization, whether it is to address broad policy issues and offer guidance, such as the National Commission or the President's Commission, or make functional recommendations regarding specific procedures or protocols, such as the EAB.

The Role of Mandate

It is my view that the role of commissions or panels discussing bioethics is not to identify the controlling moral principle but rather to identify what is known, clearly define the controversy, and develop a reasoned approach to some type of public resolution. No commission has ever been so authoritative as to have fully altered public policy, as it should be, as they are advisory panels, not elected officials or government employees. These bodies are most successful when they actually perform the function of developing and analyzing relevant information and deriving useful policy options based on empirical, rather than abstract, analysis. This is a useful exercise, and one that many policymakers do not have the luxury to engage in. Thus, one of the principal contributions to be made by such a body is educative. Although two commissions have addressed the issue of human cloning, the approach each took to its analysis and the outcomes reached are somewhat different, and one can learn something and expand one's thinking from reading both reports. When no single answer is adequate to resolve a complex question, hearing from more than one group is essential.

In addition, to be truly useful, a commission must deal not only with substance but also with process in addressing its mandate. If procedural questions (beyond the legal ones) are not addressed, the discussion takes place in a vacuum. One of the reasons the National Commission's work has been so influential is its focus on developing principles and practices for research ethics. As another example, the NIH Human Embryo Research Panel developed a schema to assist the NIH in making funding decisions, which would have been a useful tool had the research been allowed to go forward.

There seems to be an advantage in providing a mandate that allows for consideration of a wide range of issues in health care and biomedical research. Once a broadly charged group has gained credibility with a variety of constituencies by doing a good job of addressing one topic, it can use its credibility to more efficiently and effectively take on new and perhaps more controversial topics. On the other hand, sunset clauses should always be considered. There is some danger in allowing a commission to become a self-perpetuating body in search of a mission. This has yet to become an issue in the United States.

Appointment Process, Composition, and Consensus

The mandate of a body will affect its appointment process. If the mandate is very narrow, it is easier to select individuals with narrow ideological views for membership, diminishing the chances for a broad and open discussion. On the other hand, if the mandate is created in response to specific topical needs, then the membership will likely reflect specific areas of expertise. This diversity of expertise works well if it is not tempered by extremes in ideology. The processes of a body deliberating such complex social issues should be part socialization (appreciation of the problems rooted in experience) and part theory (ethical, legal, and philosophical). This requires that such a deliberative body should be composed of both theoreticians and practitioners. Although ethics "experts"—persons with formal training in philosophy, moral theory, or theology—bring to a commission's deliberations a familiarity with how past moral dilemmas have been resolved and general strategies for resolving them, this expertise is useful only when combined with active fact finding and real-world experience. Some credit the successes of previous boards and commissions to a multidisciplinary and multi-experiential group of individuals (OTA 1993).

In addition, while appointing members solely on the basis of their direct alliance with special interests, such as the antiabortion lobby, might be viewed as an important goal of those special interests, such an approach is short term and likely to create gridlock or divisiveness. Ideology is not a useful basis for forming a bioethics committee. It does not mean that one not appoint any members with strongly held views; it does mean that one not allow special interests to nominate, vet, or approve the candidates. Appointments should be cognizant of interests but not interest groups, distinguishing between beliefs and organizations. Moreover, there is no way of predicting which way people will move on issues with which they are not familiar. Appointing members because it is believed that their views are predictable on all issues can backfire. I have witnessed members of a group completely reverse their position on a given topic once they had the time and opportunity to hear all sides of an argument and process the facts available.

Achieving consensus is a goal of most deliberative bodies appointed by the government, but it cannot or should not always occur. It is more likely to occur if panelists are answerable to interest groups and therefore may refrain from changing their stated views to honor outside commitments, even if convinced by the force of arguments. This would preclude a consensus that would otherwise form among hypothetical "reasonable persons." If common ground cannot be found, then the utility of a national commission process may be greatly reduced for policymakers, although the process of attempting to reach consensus, even when impossible, can be instructive in identifying stakeholders and highlighting controversy. On some issues there is little common ground to cultivate, as is the case now for issues related to abortion, cloning, and stem cell research.

CONCLUSION: IN THE END, IT'S A PUBLIC PROCESS

Although the United States has a spotty and erratic history of systematically addressing contentious issues in bioethics, the outcomes have not been so poor that we should throw up our hands and give up. True, for those who believe in rationality, there is the disappointing message that chance, fate, and just plain politics lurk behind every policy decision, no matter how thoughtful the tendered analysis, and especially when human reproduction is the topic under discussion. And those who believe that such bodies can only succeed if they proceed in a pure scholarly fashion should consider Friedrich Nietzsche's admonition that "scholars who become politicians are usually assigned the comic role of having to be the good conscience of state policy" (1980 [1878]). Public policy is not for the pure, although one hopes that those who engage in it are of good conscience.

Although advisory committees always face the danger of being abused for political purposes, perhaps a worse fate is being irrelevant. Those groups that have maintained their intellectual integrity, relying on logic, scholarship, and sound judgment, and that remain sensitive to democratic values need not face that fate (Bulger, Bobby, and Fineberg 1995).

A look back at these deliberative bodies shows that they can and have played an important role in enhancing the legitimacy and power of the lay public. Several bodies, including HERP and the NBAC, actively sought ways to engage the public in their discussions. Engaging the public can provide decision makers not necessarily with the right decision, but with a more enlightened framework within which to make a decision. Arrogance serves no group well, especially when so much is at stake.

Harold Shapiro, chair of NBAC, is fond of the terms "national conversation" and "national discussion" to describe the important role played by commissions. An important lesson to be learned from this concept is that difficult moral decisions made in a modern pluralistic society require that all those with a vested interest in the outcome be brought into the discussion at some point. One test that can be applied is asking whether the deliberations and recommendations will hold up over time, and the answer may have to do with who sits around the table or who is heard by those who sit there. Nonetheless, even when the right people are brought to the table and every effort is made to be fair, open, and impartial, political forces can always intervene to negate their efforts. This is the frustrating consequence of a representative government.

A central lesson learned from this chronology of national efforts is that there will always be tensions between various factions on issues that we all care about, such as those raised by reproductive technologies. These require difficult and complicated discussions, which can be especially challenging when they must be conducted in the light of day. Discussions not conducted in public view, however, should be discounted. If a panel believes that an issue is too sensitive for public discussion, it should not discuss it at all, as irresponsible as that might seem. If the issue is that volatile, it is more than likely politicized as well, and it will be raised and debated by Congress.

Those appointed to public bioethics bodies are constantly looking for a framework in which to deliberate. Religion is no longer an acceptable mechanism for resolving disputes, despite the desire in some circles of American society to make it so. Some people resort to the law, but laws can be wrong or ambiguous. Others turn to procedural approaches, that is, if we follow a process that everyone agrees is correct, then we should come up with an answer that we can agree on or accept. No single approach is sufficient or satisfactory. The true test for any public deliberative body should be, was the process ethically defensible? Did it stimulate dialogue instead of confrontation? Did it recognize new constituencies and try to determine who stands to get hurt? Answering yes to these questions may be as close as a society can get to the truth. In some highly contested areas, we may have to settle for the politics of the second best because there may not be a best. And what is best by scientific or medical standards may not be the best political option (Hanna 1991).

NOTES

1. I have spent a lot of time in rooms with many of these organizations, first as an observer of the President's Commission for the Study of Ethical Problems in Medicine and Biomedical and Behavioral Research and the Human Fetal Tissue Transplantation Research Panel in the 1980s, and subsequently as a consultant/staff member to the NIH Human Embryo Research Panel and the National Bioethics Advisory Commission in the 1990s. In addition, I was on the staff of the congressional Office of Technology Assessment when the Bioethics Advisory Committee floundered in Congress in the late 1980s. As such, much of what I describe in this chapter I observed firsthand. I have tried to supplement my observations with those of others. Some readers might be troubled by the lack of scholarly evidence behind my observations and assertions, and I do not pretend to have any to offer. There are excellent scholarly analyses available on the role and effectiveness of commissions. It is not my attempt here to offer anything other than my own insights.

2. Memorandum from Harriet Rabb to Harold Varmus, January 15, 1999.

3. The White House, Office of the Press Secretary, August 9, 2001.

REFERENCES

Advisory Committee on Human Radiation Experiments (ACHRE). 1995. *Final Report.* Washington, DC: U.S. Government Printing Office.

Adams, A.M. 1988. Background leading to meeting of the Human Fetal Tissue Transplantation Research Panel consultants. *Report of the Human Fetal Tissue Transplantation Research Panel,* vol. 2, A3–A5. Bethesda, MD: National Institutes of Health.

Advisory Committee to the Director. 1988. *Report of the Human Fetal Tissue Transplantation Research Panel.* Bethesda, MD: National Institutes of Health.

Beecher, H. K. 1966. Ethics and clinical research. *New England Journal of Medicine* 274, no. 24: 1354–1360.

Bulger, R. E., E. M. Bobby, and H. V. Fineberg, eds. 1995. *Society's Choices.* Washington, DC: National Academies Press.

Capron, A. M. 1997. An egg takes flight: The once and future life of the National Bioethics Advisory Commission. *Kennedy Institute of Ethics Journal* 7, no. 1: 63–80.

Childress, J. 1991. Deliberations of the Human Fetal Tissue Transplantation Research Panel. In *Biomedical Politics,* ed. K. E. Hanna, 215-48. Washington, DC: National Academies Press.

Cohn, V. 1973. Live-fetus research debated. *Washington Post,* April 10, A-1.

Congregation of the Doctrine of the Faith. 1987. *Instruction on Respect for Human Life in Its Origin and on the Dignity of Procreation.* Vatican City.

Duguay, K. F. 1992. Fetal tissue transplantation: Ethical and legal considerations. *CIRCLES: Buffalo Women's Journal of Law and Social Policy* 1:36.

Ethics Advisory Board, U.S. Department of Health, Education and Welfare. 1979. *Report and Conclusions: Support of Research Involving Human In Vitro Fertilization and Embryo Transfer.* Washington, DC: U.S. Government Printing Office.

Faden, R. R., and T. L. Beauchamp. 1968. *A History and Theory of Informed Consent.* New York: Oxford University Press.

Fletcher, J. C. 1990. Evolution of the ethical debate about human gene therapy. *Human Gene Therapy* 1:55–68.

Goddard, J. E. 1996. The National Institutes of Health Revitalization Act of 1993 washed away many legal problems with fetal tissue transplantation research but a stain remains. *Southern Methodist University Law Review* 49:375–99.

Gray, B. H. 1995. Bioethics commissions: What can we learn from past successes and failures? In *Society's Choices,* ed. R. E. Bulger, E. M. Bobby, and H. V. Fineberg. Washington, DC: National Academies Press.

Hall, S. S. 2002. President's Bioethics Council delivers. *Science* 297:322–24.

Hanna, K. E. 1991. *Biomedical Politics.* Washington, DC: National Academies Press.

Hanna, K. E., R. M. Cook-Deegan, and R. Y. Nishimi. 1993. Finding a forum for bioethics in public policy, *Politics and the Life Sciences* 12:205–19.

Heller, J. 1972. Syphilis victims in U.S. study went untreated for 40 years. *New York Times,* July 26.

Institute of Medicine. 2003. *Responsible Research: A Systems Approach to Protecting Research Participants.* Washington, DC: National Academies Press.

Jonsen, A. R. 1998. *The Birth of Bioethics.* New York: Oxford University Press.

Lindblom, C. E. 1959. The science of muddling through. *Public Administration Review* 19:79–99.

———. 1979. Still muddling, not yet through. *Public Administration Review* 39:517–29.

Mann, T. 1945. Address delivered at the Library of Congress, May 29.

McCarthy, C. 1992. Personal communication, December 4, Washington, DC.

Murray, T. H. 1990. Human gene therapy, the public, and public policy. *Human Gene Therapy* 1:49–54.

National Academy of Sciences. 1975. *Genetic Screening: Procedural Guidance and Recommendations.* Washington, DC: National Academies Press.

National Bioethics Advisory Commission. 1997. *Cloning Human Beings,* vols. 1 and 2. Rockville, MD: National Bioethics Advisory Commission.

———. 1999. *Ethical Issues in Human Stem Cell Research,* vols. 1-3. Rockville, MD: National Bioethics Advisory Commission.

———. 2001. *Ethical and Policy Issues in Research Involving Human Participants.* 2 vols. Bethesda, MD: National Bioethics Advisory Commission.

National Commission for the Protection of Human Subjects of Biomedical and Behavioral Research, U.S. Department of Health, Education and Welfare. 1975. *Research on the Fetus.* Washington, DC: U.S. Government Printing Office.

———. 1978. *The Belmont Report: Ethical Principles and Guidelines for the Protection of Human Subjects of Research.* Washington, DC: U.S. Government Printing Office. Reprinted in the *Federal Register,* April 19, 1979.

National Institutes of Health. Ad Hoc Working Group of the Advisory Committee to the Director. 1999. *Draft Guidelines for Research Involving Pluripotent Stem Cell Research.* Bethesda, MD: NIH.

———. 1994. Human Embryo Research Panel. *Report of the Human Embryo Research Panel.* 2 vols. Bethesda, MD: NIH.

Nelkin, D., ed. 1992. *Controversy: Politics of Technical Decisions.* New York: Sage.

Nietzsche, F. 1980 [1878]. "Scholars as Politicians." In *Sämtliche Werke: Kritische Studienausgabe*, vol. 2, 301. Ed. Giorgio Colli and Mazzino Montinari. Berlin: de Gruyter.

Office for Protection from Research Risks (OPRR). 1994. *Human Subjects Protections: Fetal Tissue Transplantation—Ban on Research Replaced by New Statutory Requirements.* April 29.

President's Commission for the Study of Ethical Problems in Medicine and Biomedical and Behavioral Research. 1982. *Splicing Life.* Washington, DC: U.S. Government Printing Office.

———. 1983. *Screening and Counseling for Genetic Conditions.* Washington, DC: U.S. Government Printing Office.

President's Council on Bioethics. 2002. *Human Cloning and Human Dignity: An Ethical Inquiry.* Washington, DC: President's Council on Bioethics.

———. 2004. *Monitoring Stem Cell Research.* Washington, DC: President's Council on Bioethics.

Robertson, J. A. 1990. Reproductive technology and reproductive rights. In the beginning: The legal status of early embryos. *Virginia Law Review* 76:437–517.

Rothman, D. J. 1991. *Strangers at the Bedside: A History of How Law and Bioethics Transformed Medical Decision Making.* New York: Basic Books.

Silva-Ruiz, P. F. 1998. Section II: The Protection of Persons in Medical Research and Cloning of Human Beings. *American Journal of Comparative Law* 46:151–63.

Tuskegee Syphilis Study Ad Hoc Advisory Panel. 1973 (April). *Final Report of the Tuskegee Syphilis Study Ad Hoc Advisory Panel.* Washington, DC: U.S. Department of Health, Education and Welfare, Public Health Service.

U.S. Congress, Office of Technology Assessment (OTA). 1988. *Infertility: Medical and Social Choices.* Report no. OTA-BA-358. Washington, DC: U.S. Government Printing Office.

———. 1992. *Cystic Fibrosis and DNA Tests: Implications of Carrier Screening.* Report no. OTA-BA-532. Washington, DC: U.S. Government Printing Office.

———. 1993. *Biomedical Ethics in U.S. Public Policy.* Report no. OTA-BP-BBS-105. Washington, DC: U.S. Government Printing Office.

Windom, R. E. 1988. Memorandum to James B. Wyngaarden, March 22. In *Report of the Human Fetal Tissue Transplantation Research Panel,* vol. 2, A3. Bethesda, MD: NIH.

Wolf, R. 2003. The art of building consensus, and avoiding controversy. *International Studies Review* 5, no. 2: 273.

CHAPTER TEN

Possible Policy Strategies for the United States

Comparative Lessons

ALISON HARVISON YOUNG

My "marching orders" for this chapter came in the form of a number of questions: Why is there such a lack of regulation in the area of reprogenetics in the United States? What sorts of strategies might be employed to replace the numerous and frequently overlapping advisory bodies with more effective and broader regulation? Could regulatory bodies be used in the United States to deal with *speculative* harm?

These are huge and daunting questions. They are also important questions that highlight the differences, often profound, between the legal and political culture of the United States, on the one hand, and that of Canada, the United Kingdom, and many other jurisdictions, on the other. In this chapter I emphasize the importance of taking cultural considerations into account in designing legal solutions. To use an agricultural metaphor, however successfully avocados may be grown in California, they can't be grown in Scotland! I argue that a broad, national regulatory framework like that provided by the British Human Fertilisation and Embryology Authority (HFEA) or the one recently enacted in Canada's Bill C-6, the Assisted Human Reproduction Act,[1] is unlikely to be an effective or politically viable approach in the U.S. context. Nevertheless, there are important roles to be played by the state and by existing institutions, such as contract law, private law, professional self-regulation, and ethical guidelines. In addition, certain practices might appropriately be addressed by legal prohibitions, such as human reproductive cloning or germline alteration. These are the practices that seem to attract a high level of national and international consensus as being unacceptable.

From the outset, we should recognize that U.S. culture has historically tended to be suspicious of government and the potentially intrusive power of the state. This position is closely related to the dominant discourse of individual rights and liberalism (Harvison Young 1998), which places a high value on individual construal of the good life and sees state intervention as justified only to address real harm, and then (at least in principle) as minimally as possible. Canadian culture, however, is more collectivist or communitarian in nature and sees the state as a benevolent force, expecting the state to be the architect of broad solutions to social challenges.

Although the literature, particularly the feminist literature, is replete with powerful indictments of many aspects of new reproductive technologies (NRTs), the starting premise tends to be quite different from that in Canada. In other words, government intervention in the United States tends to be seen as a last resort, or at least as minimalist. As Cass Sunstein has said, "American law generally treats private preferences as the appropriate basis for social choice" (1986, 1129). The right to make individual choices in privacy comes first and foremost. More frequently than in Canada, controversies in the United States play out in the context of an individualist, rights-oriented framework. This is illustrated by the fact that courses and conference topics in this area tend to have titles such as "Reproductive Rights." On the other hand, as a Canadian teaching in the United States a few years ago, I called my University of Pennsylvania course "Regulation and NRTs." During the first class, I asked my students what sorts of issues interested them. The answers were generally framed in terms of rights: rights of access to NRTs by the disabled and by gays and lesbians, rights to know your biological parents, rights to abortion, rights to autonomy, rights to procreate, and so on. These answers stood in stark contrast to those I had received a year earlier at McGill University, where student after student spoke of the need to control and regulate the technologies and their applications. In the United States, the Canadian approach to issues relating to NRTs is likely to seem startlingly foreign. The executive summary of the final report of the Royal Commission on New Reproductive Technologies outlines the Canadian approach this way: "Government, as the guardian of the public interest, must act to put boundaries around the use of new reproductive technologies, and must put in place a system to manage, not just for now, but, equally important, in an ongoing way" (Royal Commission 1993).[2] This statement, which echoes throughout the Royal Commission's report, articulates two fundamental premises that set Canada apart from the United States. The first is the notion of a "public interest." The second is the view that government has a broad and active role in protecting and promoting that public interest. There is little talk of rights; indeed, the comments on rights in the report are rather dismissive.

In the United States, the discourse concerning the role of the state in general, and with respect to new reproductive technologies in particular, is different. First, the individual rights discourse plays a central role. Second, the rationale for and extent of regulation in the United States are more minimalist. Richard Schultz has explained the Canadian penchant for regulation by demonstrating that unlike in the United States, the functions of regulation in Canada go beyond mere economic efficiency, embracing social and political objectives in what would be strictly economic regulation in the United States (Schultz 1980).

These differences are not unique to the arena of new reproductive and genetic technologies. Comparative studies of the nature of regulation in Canada and the United States reveal the extent to which it is informed by basic ideology. Legislation in the United States tends to be drafted with a view to constraining regulators and tends to provide detailed instructions on what, how, when and where to regulate. In addition, it is very frequently rationalized in terms of correcting market deficiencies, such as the lack of consumer information. In other words, it is greatly concerned with minimalist government intervention. The Canadian preference, on the other hand, is for broad legislative mandates conferring substantial discretionary authority on the regulators (Nemetz et al. 1986).

It should not be surprising, then, that the general approach to regulation is reflected in attitudes toward regulation in the field of reprogenetics. Although the U.S. academic literature is rich on the subject of reprogenetics, with an especially rich feminist literature on the potential harms involved, this literature tends to be suspicious of state intervention, and it is rare that solutions are seen in terms of a state response in the collective interest. Indeed, the issues themselves are often framed in terms of reproductive rights, which are evocative, at least in the U.S. culture, of issues of individual rights, such as access by same-sex couples or disabled persons to various technologies. When government action is proposed in the United States, it is generally quite specific, such as regulation to govern the safe storage of sperm.[3] Accordingly, the difference between the wide-ranging, top-down approach reflected in the

Royal Commission report can be striking. As U.S. political scientist Rosalind Pollard Petchesky writes,

It is almost unthinkable that any politician in the U.S. today would be found denouncing the commercialization of biomedical technologies, including infertility treatments, on the ground that it "commodifies human beings" and is therefore "ethically unacceptable." Much less are we accustomed to hearing about government's responsibility to regulate commercial interests on behalf of "quality control" and "the public interest." . . . We in the U.S. live in a society in which the very concept of a "public" that public servants have a duty to guard is pretty much obsolete-as opposed to various particular and private interests (e.g., "women," now cast by the media as one among many "special interest groups"). In other words, the tradition of solidarity and social security that is deeply embedded in the political cultures of many European social democracies as well as Canada's, and briefly flickered during our New Deal and Great Society eras, has quite gone out of memory in the U.S. (Petchesky 1996)[4]

REGULATING REPROGENETICS IN THE UNITED STATES

One of the difficulties with the area of reprogenetics is that the subjects covered embrace a wide range of concerns and issues. Some, such as the safe storage of sperm, are clearly health and safety issues. Some, such as the use of and access to fertility drugs, may already be covered by regulatory bodies, such as the Food and Drug Administration (FDA). Others, such as issues relating to human reproductive cloning or germline alteration, may be dealt with by prohibitions. Many of these issues, in both Canada and the United States, cut across the lines of legislative jurisdictional competence, adding a level of complexity absent in unitary states such as the United Kingdom. Finally, many of the issues, including some of the most controversial ones, invoke matters of choice, autonomy, and privacy, which have been understood in the United States as deeply individualized matters with respect to which state intervention is generally seen as suspect.

The field of reprogenetics would be even less likely than most in the United States to attract significant support for broad-based regulatory control because much of it concerns issues that are typically characterized and understood as matters of individual choice. A good example is access to genetic testing. In addition, many aspects of reprogenetics (such as the storage of embryos or gamete donation and the question of compensation for donors) attract more social controversy than consensus—precisely the circumstances in which a liberal state should be very restrained about imposing particular visions of the good. Even in Canada, with a more collectivist culture, the absence of social consensus on many issues has been a major obstacle to legislation.

These are some of the reasons why I believe that attempting to create a regulatory body like the U.K.'s HFEA in the United States would be a little like trying to grow avocados in Scotland. Having said this, however, I do believe that there are strategies that can be deployed to improve the level of regulation considerably. These strategies should be understood as complementary; none is entirely adequate in itself.

CONSUMER INFORMATION AND PROTECTION

One of the great ironies in the United States is that, despite cultural attitudes rejecting intrusive state authority, there are huge quantities of regulation in many areas. The premise of such legislation, however, is usually informed by those same cultural and political norms. The sphere of consumer protection legislation provides a useful illustration. In the United States, consumer protection may be understood as predicated less on a paternalistic concept of protecting the consumer from exploitation and more on the idea that a flow of full information from the supplier to the consumer is a necessary condition for an effective marketplace. In other words, while U.S. culture might be very hostile to the notion of banning in vitro fertilization (IVF) in certain circumstances, it would be more receptive to the notion that a prospective consumer is entitled to full disclosure of all the risks and likely benefits. In fact, Congress did pass a bill in the early 1990s that established criteria for the reporting of success rates of fertility centers. During a sabbatical in the United States a few years ago, I reviewed a few annual cycles of these reports, but I found the reporting and data structure to be unwieldy and unlikely to be very useful for those considering treatment. This would seem, however, to be a useful strategy to explore, as there has already been some legislation of risk disclosure in other contexts, and the idea that information is crucial has been accepted. In addition, reporting can provide a vehicle for transparency and public scrutiny. Thus, there is at least the potential for the principle of adequate and free-flowing information to serve as a basis for a much broader system of regulation than was previously imagined, and one that is certainly applicable to areas beyond assisted conception. This was hinted at a few years ago by the psychologist for a fertility institute in Philadelphia, who remarked that the most powerful form of regulation for his clinic was the desire not to be the subject of front-page news for something gone wrong.

HARNESSING THE INSTITUTIONS OF PRIVATE LAW

To say that the legal and ethical consequences of modern reproductive technology are numerous and diverse is an understatement. Seldom has the law been confronted with such urgent demands and such an apparent need to respond to, if not actually to control, technological change. There is still great controversy as to what role, if any, the law should play in resolving this debate, and because reproductive technologies are evolving rapidly, there is a real danger that formal laws may become obsolete very quickly.

It is important to consider the resources that are available through a number of existing legal institutions that have some regulatory roles and could be more effectively harnessed. These include traditional institutions such as contracts and torts, as well as extrajudicial regulatory regimes such as ethical codes and guidelines, professional self-regulation, and other informal norms that may emerge in clinical settings. These institutions may be augmented, altered, or supplemented by statutory changes. Such changes might, for example, impose certain terms for contracts of certain sorts, or alter or impose standards or duties of care. In addition, the media and educational forums should not be forgotten as ways of informing the public and helping to ensure transparency and accountability on the part of service providers. These approaches do not appear to be exclusive of one another. But neither would any of them be a sufficient means in and of itself to address or regulate all aspects of NRTs.

Contractual Principles

The role that contracts should play in matters such as surrogacy has been a controversial subject over the years (Brinig 1995). In 1985, the Ontario Law Reform Commission produced a report that recommended that surrogacy contracts be enforceable as contracts subject to preconception judicial approval. This report has had a generally hostile reception (Royal Commission 1993). In Quebec, a provision has been added to the Civil Code of Quebec (Art. 541 C.C.Q.) stating that agreements to procreate for another are absolutely null and void. Even in the United States, the contractual model has fallen into considerable disfavor as far as these issues are concerned, and few if any states would treat a surrogacy contract as an ordinary enforceable contract.

In the famous *Baby M* case (537 A.2d 1227 (N.J.1988)), the gestational mother or surrogate (who was also the genetic mother) changed her mind in the course of the pregnancy and fought to keep the child. Ultimately, the New Jersey Supreme Court found the contract to be contrary to public policy and therefore unenforceable, although at first instance the contract had been held to be valid and enforceable. Nevertheless, custody was granted to the Sterns, the commissioning parents (Mr. Stern was also the genetic father), with access granted to Mary Beth Whitehead, the gestational mother, on the basis that this was in the best interests of the child.

The publicity surrounding cases like this one has generated a strong reaction against the view that contractual notions should have any normative relevance in this area whatsoever. Yet it seems clear that ordinary people continue to conduct their lives—even in relation to such matters—in ways that presuppose the moral relevance of notions of agreement, consent, and autonomy. For example, a former student of mine practicing in Montreal in the early 1990s informed me that she had been asked by a senior partner in her law firm to draft a surrogacy agreement. All the parties knew, she said, that the contract would not have any legal force or effect. Nevertheless, the parties were apparently all of the view that sitting around a table and discussing all aspects of the arrangement would maximize the chances of a full understanding of what was involved and minimize the risk of conflict.

So what role should contracts play? It does not necessarily follow from treating contract as morally relevant that such contracts be enforceable. Indeed, there is even a persuasive argument to be made that a provision such as Article 541 in the Civil Code of Quebec creates an incentive for the commissioning couple (usually better educated and wealthier) to treat the gestational mother (usually less educated and less affluent) well, because they know that if she decides to keep the child, the contract will not assist them. But the values underlying contractual principles do play significant roles as social ordering devices (Trebilcock 1991; Trebilcock et al. 1994). Acknowledging the moral relevance of contractual principles is not an all-or-nothing proposition. As Trebilcock and colleagues (1994) have suggested, some aspects of an agreement may well be subject to formal regulation. Prices may be regulated, legal advice may be mandatory, or certain remedies (such as specific performance) may be proscribed for certain matters. Indeed, some agreements (as with surrogacy in the Civil Code of Quebec) may justifiably be treated as legally null and void. But the point is that by recognizing the existence of, as it were, a marketplace of services within which some people will operate, the legislator may exercise a certain level of control through the incentives and disincentives that actually exist.

A more subtle argument about the institution of contract that is more significant in the United States than in Canada I will mention only briefly. A number of authors have written on the relatively broad regulatory impact of contract law. Anthony Kronman (1980), for example, has written on the various ways in which contract intersects with distributive justice and with regulatory control. He argues (for example) that usury laws and minimum wage laws are examples of contractual regulation that may be effective redistributive tools. In short, the private institution of contract law performs some of the functions that Canadians think of as falling within the realm of public law. The pervasiveness of the institution of contract law and its regulatory potential is not something that should be dismissed. Rather, the harnessing of contract is something that we should include in any arsenal of potential strategies.

Tort Liability

An in-depth analysis of the possible role and implications of tort law in regard to NRTs is beyond the scope of this chapter. For present purposes, however, it is worth emphasizing that tort law provides an institution with preexisting norms and infrastructures that could be used, modified, and harnessed by a regulatory regime that might limit some aspects of tort liability and create or expand others.

It is interesting to note that tort law has already begun to provide a forum for some NRT issues in the United States. The defendants have usually been service providers or brokers. In *Stiver v. Parker* (975 F.2d 261 (1992)), the surrogate mother sued the broker, an attorney, and the physicians involved for damages sustained when her child was born with severe birth defects. The birth defects were allegedly caused by exposure to a disease carried by the contracting father's semen, which had not been tested prior to the insemination attempt.[5]

One of the concerns that might be raised about the application of tort law to NRTs is that women might find themselves as defendants in tort actions brought by commissioning couples alleging, for example, that a mother's drug use or nutritional habits during pregnancy breached duties of care owed to them, or to the child in the event that it was subsequently born alive (*Montreal Tramways v. Leveillé*, [1933] S.C.R. 456). This concern points to yet another reason to favor of a regulatory regime. It would be very easy to establish certain classes of persons or actions that would give rise to liability, and a bar on tort actions against the mother would be defensible in light of her potential vulnerability. Similarly, the exposure of the more powerful players such as brokers, lawyers, and doctors to potential tort liability could serve as a significant deterrent to inappropriate or negligent conduct. A regulatory regime could also establish certain standards of care the breach of which would amount to breaches of statutory duties giving rise to exposure to liability.

In short, tort law should be seen as one means of regulating conduct that can play an important role in any regulatory scheme. Interestingly, tort law has tended to be identified with a "nonregulatory" climate such as exists in the United States, and has fallen into disfavor for that reason. Tort law in and of itself cannot be an adequate form of regulation of NRTs. It is not proactive but reactive in nature; it does not discuss, articulate, and establish guidelines in advance so as to help set practice but operates by civil sanction after the fact, often in a climate where there was uncertainty about the appropriate standards to begin with. However, it may prove to be an important device to ensure compliance with the regulatory standards of the players who have the most to gain or lose in financial terms, and for whom the financial risks are well worth minimizing.

Ethical Codes and Guidelines

One of the recurring themes since the release of the Royal Commission's final report on new reproductive technologies in 1992 has been the inadequacy of professional self-regulation as a response to the challenges posed by NRTs. An unfortunate by-product of this has been a tendency to neglect the positive role that ethical codes and guidelines can play as one of several regulatory devices. Again, a full discussion of the role that ethical codes and guidelines might play is beyond the scope of this chapter. It suffices for present purposes to underline some of the reasons to ensure they are not neglected.

The central reason for ensuring that codes and guidelines are not neglected is that they provide a framework of standards for the service providers closest to the issues, such as the physicians, lawyers, hospitals, and psychologists involved. This occurs at a few levels. First, the periods of development of ethical codes and guidelines provide the opportunity for discussion and debate of the issues in the home context, as it were, of the service providers. This can be difficult and controversial, as was recently the case with the development of the Tri-Council Code of Ethical Conduct for Research Involving Humans

(1997). Nevertheless, the very process of attempting to promulgate such a policy is likely to stimulate discussion and sensitize the players to the existence of the ethical issues involved. To the extent that the media report these debates, public involvement and response may in turn influence the development of codes and guidelines. For the institutions involved in the development of such codes, the process may provide a more open and transparent opportunity for discussion than normally arises.

Second, ethical codes and guidelines serve an important purpose by necessitating the creation of institutional structures—however informal—for their consideration, interpretation, and application. Although the existence of codes and guidelines may not predetermine the outcome of a particular matter, it is likely to ensure a discussion of the issues. In addition, the issues (such as a maximum age for ovum recipients or the number of embryos that may be implanted) are addressed in real-world settings, often in individual cases. This aspect of a regulatory schema is most likely to be of the bottom-up variety: new issues are likely to come into view through work on the individual, actual case. Recognizing the significance of these institutions as potential resources and sources of information will be crucial to the credibility of any regulatory structure. Depending on the structure of these bodies, their existence (especially in conjunction with a licensing form of regulation) could be an essential mechanism in promoting the accountability of the service providers and in necessitating a high degree of communication with the regulator.

EDUCATION AND THE MEDIA

Agencies play an educational role. In Canada, a good example is the Canadian Human Rights Commission (1985). Education concerning the risks of certain practices and their legal status can be very important, as is having a structure that encourages and provides a forum for public debate and input. The educational arm of regulatory agencies can go into communities, help organize panels, and participate in the ongoing dialogue among the various stakeholders. This function is important not only for disseminating information but for receiving it as well. To the extent that the content of regulatory norms depends on some degree of public consensus, their perceived legitimacy will also depend on the body's ability to discern and interpret that consensus.

A federal schema could perform a valuable educational role in fostering public discourse. By facilitating conferences or seminars in different parts of the country on particular issues, a federal body could help develop uniform standards across the country, at least in areas where consensus might emerge. The United States has achieved national standards successfully through "model" and "uniform" codes in a number of regulatory areas. In light of the complex constitutional issues that arise in a federal state, the federal role as leader and facilitator is very important. It could spearhead the development of model forms of regulation to complement those areas outside federal legislative jurisdiction. In countries as large and diverse as Canada and the United States, this will not always result in identical legislation across the country, but it is safe to say that it will exercise an influence in this direction, especially with respect to less controversial matters. This vision, of course, is predicated on the notion of education as at least partly as discourse, of promoting real communication and interchange between the various stakeholders who may not so much fundamentally disagree as approach the issues from vastly divergent perspectives.

In imagining alternatives to the simple prohibition of certain specified approaches, then, one can devise a multiplicity of means that combine formal with informal norms, traditional with less traditional institutions, and top-down with bottom-up forms of regulatory norms. Many of these roles avoid the problems arising out of the division of powers because they foster a less exclusively command-oriented view of the federal government's role.

The Canadian impulse, more so than in the United States, has been to dismiss the significance of the law of tort and contract as potentially effective modes of regulation. But as I have discussed elsewhere (Harvison Young and Wasunna 1998), these have regulatory relevance in a number of ways. First and most obviously, tort standards of care do affect the conduct of service providers. Although the influence tends to be felt only *after* harm has transpired, it serves to prevent similar harm in the future. In addition, standards of care may be affected by statutory provisions or by practices. This means that strategies to inform and improve standards of care can be useful. As well, the publicity arising out of particular tort litigation, especially in the United States,[6] can heighten public awareness of the potential problems.

Contract law is, on the face of it, even more relevant to the notion of regulation because it is by definition prospective, forcing a consideration of all the issues in advance of any trouble. Some states have adopted a combined contract plus regulation model to deal with surrogacy arrangements by which the arrangement is judicially approved in advance. It is important to realize that the adoption of some contract norms need not mean a rigid application of the rules relating to widgets and real property. For example, specific performance need not be a part of such a scheme, and indeed, many jurisdictions provide for a post-birth "cooling-off" period during which a birth mother may change her mind (as in adoption statutes).

PROFESSIONAL AND VOLUNTARY BODIES

Much ink has been spilled on the subject of the inadequacy of various self-regulatory bodies, whether professional bodies or others such as hospital ethics advisory committees. As a strategic matter, however, these bodies should not be dismissed, for they are necessary (though not sufficient) elements in a broad regulatory strategy, for a number of reasons. Chiefly, they may provide institutional frameworks that can provide for the integration of norms within certain settings. Additionally, they may provide settings in which previously voluntary norms can be implemented as requirements.

CONCLUSION

Any analysis of policy strategies must take into account the legal, historical and political culture. The situation is more complex in federal states such as the United States and Canada, where issues of division of power, especially in matters pertaining to areas that cut across health, the integrity of the family, and drug and safety regulation, make the project of regulating nationally even more challenging. In light of this and the foregoing discussions, a broad and comprehensive regulatory structure such as that in place in the United Kingdom pursuant to the HFEA act would seem to be an unlikely solution. There are, however, a number of other policy avenues that can be and should be creatively explored.

NOTES

The Honorable Madam Justice Alison Harvison Young was appointed to the bench in November 2004. The conference to which she contributed this work occurred prior to her appointment.—*Eds.*

1. Assisted Human Reproduction Act, S.C. 2004, c. 2 (Bill C-6). Bill C-6 sets out a series of prohibited activities, but it also provides for the establishment of a national regulatory agency, the Assisted Human Reproduction Agency (sections 21–39).

2. On March 29, 2004, Bill C-6 received royal assent; however, the portions of the act establishing the Assisted Human Reproduction Agency and other sections prohibiting certain activities are not yet in force. Bill C-6 was enacted following a very protracted

discussion that began when the Royal Commission on New Reproductive and Genetic Technologies was established in 1989. The Royal Commission report was issued in 1993. The first attempt to legislate, Bill C-47, *An Act Respecting Human Reproductive Technologies and Commercial Transactions Relating to Human Reproduction*, was introduced in June 1996 but died on the order paper in April 1997 when an election was called. This bill proposed a series of prohibited practices but did not establish a regulatory agency.

3. Another reason for the patchwork aspect of U.S. regulation in reprogenetics is that legislation tends to arise as a response to particular controversies. This is especially evident in the area of surrogacy, with respect to which there is widely varying state legislation ranging from total prohibition to adoption-like regulation to nothing at all. Prohibitive legislation tends to be enacted as an immediate political response to highly publicized cases of the "Baby M" sort rather than as a proactive regulatory approach.

4. Petchesky also correctly cautions against oversimplification of the difference in political discourse or rhetoric in the two countries:

> If the rhetoric of individual choice and privacy seems to prevail in the U.S. political landscape, it is also the case that our religious and right-wing anti-abortionists have frequently invoked ideas of social responsibility, care, and human dignity to advocate a ban on abortion technologies, not only in the name of "fetal rights" but to protect alleged community interests in "the family" and "truewomanhood."

5. For a more recent example, see *Perry-Rogers v. Obasaju*, 282 A.D.2d 231 (N.Y. App. Div. 2001), in which the defendant fertility clinic implanted the fertilized embryos from a third party into the uterus of the plaintiff along with the plaintiff's own embryos, resulting in the plaintiff giving birth to the third party's biological child as well as her own. See also *Huddleston v. Infertility Center Of America Inc.*, 700 A.2d 453 (Pa. Super. Ct. 1997), in which a surrogacy business was found to be in special relationship to its client-participants and the child that the surrogacy undertaking creates.

6. I am thinking here of the publicity surrounding the 1995 scandal at the Asch Clinic in Irvine, California, where physicians had used (surplus) ova from one woman to treat another (whose own ova had been used unsuccessfully for IVF) without the knowledge or consent of either. By the time this was revealed, both women had given birth to children.

REFERENCES

Brinig, M. F. 1995. A maternalistic approach to surrogacy: Comment on Richard Epstein's enforcement of surrogate contracts. *Virginia Law Review* 81:2377.

Canadian Human Rights Act. 1985. R.S.C. 1985, c. H-6. s.16(2).

Harvison Young, A. 1998. New reproductive technologies in Canada and the United States: Same problems, different discourses. *Temple International and Comparative Law Journal* 12:43–85.

Harvison Young, A., and A. Wasunna. 1998. Wrestling with the limits of law: Regulating new reproductive technologies. *Health Law Journal* 6:239–77.

In the Matter of Baby M. 1988. 537 A.2d 1227 (N.J.1988).

Kronman, A. 1980. Contract law and distributive justice. *Yale Law Journal* 89:472.

Nemetz, P., et al. 1986. Social regulation in Canada: An overview and comparison with the American model. *Policy Studies Journal* 14:580, 586.

Ontario Law Reform Commission. 1985. *Report on Human Artificial Reproduction and Related Matters.* Toronto: Ontario Ministry of the Attorney General.

Petchesky, R. 1996. Women's rights, social rights and biomedical free trade zones. In *Governing Medically Assisted Human Reproduction*, ed. L. Weir. City: Publisher.

Schultz, R. The development of regulation in Canada. Address at the Management Institute Montebello Conference, Seminar on Regulatory Purpose and Policy (1978). Reprinted by McGill Center for Study of Regulated Industries (1980) (available from the author).

Sunstein, C. 1986. Legal interference with private preferences. *University of Chicago Law Review* 53:129.

Royal Commission on New Reproductive Technologies. 1993. *Proceed with Care: Final Report of the Royal Commission on New Reproductive Technologies.* Ottawa: Minister of Government Services.

Trebilcock, M. 1991. Economic analysis of law. In *Canadian Perspectives on Legal Theory*, ed. R. F. Devlin. Toronto: Edward Montgomery.

Trebilcock, M., M. Martin, A. Lawson, and P. Lewis. 1994. Testing the limits of freedom of contract: The commercialization of reproductive materials and services. *Osgoode Hall Law Journal* 32:613.

Tri-Council Working Group. 1997. Code of Ethical Conduct for Research Involving Humans: The Medical Research Council of Canada, The Natural Sciences and Engineering Research Council of Canada, The Social Sciences and Humanities Research Council of Canada.

CHAPTER ELEVEN

The Development of Reprogenetic Policy and Practice in the United States

Looking to the United Kingdom

GLADYS B. WHITE

The development of reprogenetics policy in the United States is in a state of flux. The most recent and perhaps most influential development in this area comes in the form of the 2004 report of the President's Council on Bioethics, *Reproduction and Responsibility: The Regulation of New Biotechnologies.* Early in this report, which is described by the council as a diagnosis of the clinical and regulatory status of reprogenetics in the United States, there is a careful delineation of what has and what has not been achieved over the course of a more than two-year effort on the part of the council. In the letter of transmittal accompanying the report to the president of the United States, Council Chair Leon Kass writes the following:

> The Council finds that our regulatory institutions have not kept pace with our rapid technological advance. Indeed, there is today no public authority responsible for monitoring or overseeing how these technologies make their way from the experimental to the clinical stage, from novel approach to widespread practice. There is no authority public or private that monitors how or to what extent these new technologies are being or will be used, or that is responsible for attending to the ways that they affect the health and well-being of the participants or the character of human reproduction more generally. Our existing regulatory institutions, such as the FDA or local institutional review boards, do not at the present time oversee this area, and the welcome ethical standards promulgated by the professional societies are somewhat limited in scope and not binding on individual practitioners. (President's Council on Bioethics 2004, xvii)

Despite this sweeping admission of all that is arguably not up to snuff in the United States, it is nevertheless surprising that the Council states early in the report that

> thinking about regulating new reproductive biotechnologies [is] extremely complicated in ways largely peculiar to the U.S. Although the Council has heard presentations on regulatory schemes used in other countries, this document does not deal with them. We are eager, first of all, to disclose and assess what is going on in our own country and, given the noted peculiarities of American law and political culture, there is good reason to doubt whether foreign practices can serve directly as models for what we can and should do here. In any event, there is no consensus among those nations which have chosen to regulate in this domain. (2004, 12)

The argument I present in this chapter counters what appears to be a facile conclusion on the part of the President's Council, namely, that there are no "foreign practices which can directly serve as a model for what we can and should do here." I argue here that important lessons can be learned and strategies can reasonably be adopted from the practices put in place in the United Kingdom to deliver assisted reprogenetic services. These strategies can be utilized, and in one case have been utilized, even in the absence of overarching legislation like that establishing the British Human Fertilisation and Embryology Authority (HFEA). The four key strategies I discuss are (1) licensing of infertility treatment centers, (2) public consultation, (3) scientific review and approval of innovative practice *before* new services are offered to patients, and (4) specific and explicit attention to the welfare of the child born as a result of assisted reproductive technologies (ARTs).

In addition to discerning what kinds of lessons can be learned from the U.K. experience, it is important to keep in mind that human reproduction is a feature of the human condition. It neither results from nor is contained by the legal or regulatory structure of particular nations. Human reproduction is at its essence biological, even when technological assists are employed. It is also worth noting that prohibitions in one country need not limit the reproductive options of its citizens, who may simply go elsewhere to seek reproductive assistance. The Diane Blood case, in which Ms. Blood sought to be inseminated with the sperm from her deceased husband, was refused permission to do so in the United Kingdom, and then went to Belgium to have the procedure completed, is a demonstration of this reality (*BBC News* 2004.). The use of reprogenetic techniques is a global enterprise, and therefore it is shortsighted and ultimately futile to ignore or insulate ourselves from what other countries are doing. In addition, inasmuch as we are citizens of the world, parents and their children could at any time be seeking health care abroad and marrying and reproducing with someone who has been born as a result of ART provided in a country other than our own. Therefore, ensuring the inherent safety of assisted techniques generally is an ethical imperative. We in the United States have a much greater ethical responsibility to ensure that safety is a worldwide common denominator of reprogenetic practices than we have to define or limit ourselves to any uniquely U.S. American version of what is safe in this important area of medical practice.

WHY LICENSE INFERTILITY TREATMENT CENTERS IN THE UNITED STATES?

Individuals and couples who seek out infertility services in the United States generally learn of the availability of such services through referral by a personal physician or through media advertising. Because in most states, services are paid for out of pocket (Massachusetts is a notable exception), there is no robust third-party payer who is looking over the shoulder of health care providers as they diagnose, treat, or bill patients. Therefore, the provision of infertility treatment services, including newer reprogenetic techniques, cleaves more closely to a consumer or commercial model of service exchange than it does to more traditional models of the provision of medical or health care. This means that those who are the recipients of care in this area of medical practice carry heavy responsibilities for educating themselves about diagnostic and treatment alternatives and identifying quality care providers and centers. Because the diagnosis and treatment of infertility are interdisciplinary and multifaceted, a team of practitioners and a center with necessary laboratory facilities are almost always involved. There are no clear or simple strategies that patients can use to assess or predict the quality of care that they are apt to receive in a given center, and this quality varies.

Although the Fertility Clinic Success Rate and Certification Act of 1992 (P.L. 102-493) is generally cited as the important and overarching legislation that ensures quality of services across the more than 350 infertility treatment centers in the United States, the United States still has an essentially voluntary system for reporting infertility treatment success rates and inspecting the laboratory and reproductive practice aspects of each center (U.S. Centers for Disease Control and Prevention [CDC] 2003). The most recent national summary of ART success rates notes that not all centers in the United States have reported and that pregnancies and live births resulting from artificial insemination or the treatment of women to induce ovarian stimulation are not included at all. The omission of the use of ovarian stimulation alone is significant, because dramatic cases of multiple gestation, such as the McCaughey septuplets, born in 1996, resulted from ovarian stimulation alone. In another instance, in 2004 a twenty-nine-year-old woman from Pennsylvania delivered sextuplets as a result of using fertility drugs; she and her husband were already the parents of three-year-old twins, who may also have resulted from infertility treatment (CNN 2004). I address this issue later in the chapter in the context of thinking about the welfare of children born as a result of maternal infertility treatment.

Aside from the voluntary and incomplete nature of the ART success rate reporting structure in the United States, other structural problems result from the lack of a comprehensive system of oversight. For example, there are no mandatory regulations or guidelines stipulating who may open an infertility treatment center or how long a center may operate without achieving even one live birth (White 1998). In the 1994 *Fertility Clinic Success Rate Report*, one-third of centers reporting cryopreservation of embryos had never had a live birth from such embryos (Wilcox et al. 1996). In addition, there are no regulations or guidelines that specify the range of services that may be offered at a specific center given the available personnel and facilities, when or if innovative practices may be offered clinically to patients, and the need for careful descriptive material that distinguishes standard offerings from those that are available only in the context of a research protocol.

In the United Kingdom, as stipulated in the HFEA act, infertility treatment centers must be licensed before they can open their doors and begin to provide services to the public. The HFEA awards licenses (1) for infertility treatment, (2) for storage, and (3) for research. Infertility treatment centers are periodically inspected and licenses are awarded or reissued after an assessment of the facilities, interviews with staff members, examination of consent forms, validation of success rates, ensuring that there are protocols for channeling patient complaints, and even checking the temperature and level of the cryoprotectant fluid (White 1998). In the case of license reissue, a report is developed indicating necessary improvements that must be made for the license to be retained. The act of licensing and then displaying evidence of a license to the health-consuming public attests that certain necessary conditions have been met for the delivery of care, and patients and their families have these assurances as soon as they walk in the door. There is no comparable licensing or "Good Housekeeping Seal of Approval" equivalent that clearly indicates to patients in the United States that the center from which they seek care has met even minimal safety standards. It is almost impossible for infertility patients in the United States to competently come to this conclusion on their own. Therefore, the licensing of infertility treatment centers in the United States is clearly important. A 1996 study trip to the United Kingdom revealed that those few centers that had been shut down by the HFEA merely moved to the United States and resumed operations here (White 1998).

The absence of a system for licensing all infertility treatment centers in the United Sates places an unacceptable burden on those who need care, because they have no real opportunity to obtain a composite assessment of the features of care or the safety of services in a specific center or geographic location. A licensing process that clearly identified quality centers meeting even minimal standards of safety would allow individuals and couples to spend their resources wisely and make discriminating judgments about the best places to seek care. It would also be a good idea to identify centers of excellence in the provision of reprogenetic services in the United States. Those practice groups that excel in this specialty could be recognized, which would likely improve the quality of care delivered overall. Canada has recently adopted this strategy; the Assisted Human Reproduction Act of 2004 stipulates in part that an agency is to be formed that will be responsible for the issuance and review of licenses, the collection and analysis of health reporting information, inspections, and the enforcement of other stipulations of the act. From this time forward, all activities in Canada that involve the use of reprogenetic material will require a license that is held by those sites offering the procedures.

WHY CONSULT THE AMERICAN PUBLIC
ABOUT REPROGENETIC PRACTICES?

Until recently, the requirement to consult the public about controversial matters relating to human reproduction and the provision of genetic services had been a distinguishing and unique feature of the activities of the U.K.'s HFEA alone. The HFEA has consulted the British public about sex selection, donated ovarian tissue, cloning issues, and preimplantation genetic diagnosis, to name a few topics. Early in the process of establishing the HFEA there was recognition of the importance of educating and "bringing the public along" about the science, ethics, and social implications of infertility treatment, so that all would understand the state of the art as a specialty practice within medicine and have a chance to register their opinions. The United States has been slower to appreciate the necessity of either educating the public or seeking public opinion or support. A number of factors probably account for this lacuna, including the idea that reprogenetic issues are the purview of scientists and physicians and too technical for the public to understand, and the expectation that these topics would be viewed only through the lens of abortion politics as yet another referendum with only pro-choice or pro-life options. Therefore, any public survey that appears to touch on the status of the human embryo in any way is viewed as having predictable results. Finally, the American disinclination to consult the public is related to the belief that the strategies used in the diagnosis and treatment of infertility are private matters between physicians and patients, and public points of view are therefore irrelevant.

There are important ethical reasons, however, to consult the public about the development and use of advances in reprogenetics. These reasons include the following: (1) Human reproduction is an essential human experience, and the technical features of assisted technologies have dramatic implications for patients. (2) An unsafe practice in assisted reproduction is not limited to one occasion; instead, the outcomes reverberate from generation to generation. (3) The public must be knowledgeable enough to make judgments about aspects of reprogenetic medical practice and decide when and how these issues should be addressed in public law. (4) The opinions of the public are valid on their own and may reasonably shape the prioritization and development of reprogenetic technologies. Scientists, physicians, attorneys, and other highly educated individuals are not the only experts in this area. Human reproduction is the common denominator of a much wider human experience.

In the United States, two years ago, a new organization named the Genetics and Public Policy Center was funded by the Pew Charitable Trusts and established as part of the Phoebe R. Berman Bioethics Institute at Johns Hopkins University. The center serves as an independent and objective source of credible information on genetic technologies and genetic policies for the public, media, and policymakers. Reprogenetics has been one of the center's initial areas of focus, and a high priority has been placed on public consultation. Most recently, the center has conducted a consultation on preimplantation genetic diagnosis and developed a report, published in 2004, containing policy issues and options on this topic. Public consultation is an important activity in the United States and should continue across a broad range of topics that are relevant to the use and development of reprogenetic services. Public consultation goes hand in hand with public education.

WHY REVIEW AND APPROVE INNOVATIVE PRACTICE?

There is much to learn from the British approach and the work of the HFEA, because it ensures some regularity in the ways in which innovations are evaluated and then offered to patients. New approaches to the diagnosis and treatment of infertility must be reviewed and approved by the national scientific advisory group within the HFEA, and the infertility treatment center must be licensed to offer a new intervention to patients. Any innovation must be consistent with the nationally defined Code of Practice and assessed in terms of whether it serves the best interests of the eventual child. In the United States, the President's Council on Bioethics identifies this problem but does not suggest or develop a more effective strategy for changing the status quo. Note the following:

> A key area of concern for the Council is the ease and speed with which experimental technologies and procedures (such as intracytoplasmic sperm injection (ICSI) or preimplantation genetic diagnosis (PGD)), move into clinical practice, even in the absence of careful clinical trials regarding their efficacy and their long-term effects on children born with their use. It would be useful for consumers and policy makers to understand more fully how each clinic manages the process of introducing new technologies and practices and what safeguards are employed. Such information would include the human subject protections in place; the extent to which technologies are first tested in animals; the standards that must be satisfied before a given procedure is deemed fit for clinical use and the measures taken to evaluate safety and efficacy. (2004, 214)

Recently, another innovation may have made its way into clinical practice in the United States, once again demonstrating the need for a more systematic approach to even the initial use of a new therapeutic technique. The May 2004 issue of *Fertility and Sterility* reports the use of a new technique in Turkish infertility clinics known as round spermatid injection, or ROSI. This variation on intracytoplasmic sperm injection makes use of round immature spermatids extracted from the testes, which are then mixed with oocytes to create embryos in vitro. The Turkish experience consisted of 143 attempts to make embryos by ROSI, two-thirds of which did not develop at all after fertilization. Eleven embryos that did appear to be viable were transferred to the uteruses of women, but no pregnancies resulted. Chromosomal tests conducted on the embryos created in the lab revealed chromosomal abnormalities, including missing chromosomes and fragmented DNA (Benkhalifa et al. 2004, 1283).

There is no information available about the extent to which ROSI has been offered to patients in the treatment of infertility in the United States, and there is no way of knowing how or if patients have been informed about the possible availability of this technique. Research results in Turkey, however, indicate that it should not be used. It will be up to the professional community in the United States to ensure that it is not used. No professional guidelines pertaining to this technique, however, have appeared to date.

The President's Council on Bioethics acknowledges that "institutional review boards do not at the present time oversee this area, and the welcome ethical standards promulgated by the professional societies are somewhat limited in scope and not binding on individual members" (2004, xvii). Individuals, couples, and their progeny who have used or experienced reprogenetic technologies in the United States have generally done so as consumer-patients, not as research subjects or participants. The council knows that innovative reprogenetic practices do not appear initially in the United States in the form of clinical trials, yet in their recommendations they repeatedly refer to "enforcement mechanisms." The recommendations that refer to enforcement are non sequiturs, because there is absolutely no enforcement structure in place in the United States. In contrast to the status quo here, new diagnostic and therapeutic techniques are available in the United Kingdom initially only in the context of approved and licensed research protocols that are offered widely to the public only when the Scientific Affairs committee of the HFEA determines that they are effective and safe. This provides a much better system of quality control to British citizens seeking reprogenetic services.

In the conclusion to the report, the President's Council states that "as a whole, the present system of regulation advances a number of goods and values. It allows for the robust and innovative practice of medicine, permitting physicians' wide latitude to employ novel approaches in their efforts to help patients overcome infertility and experience the joys of parenthood. It promotes the safety and efficacy of products for their intended use and provides an extensive system of protections for human subjects participating in clinical trials" (2004, 172). Yet the current system in the United States is a patchwork of voluntary laboratory inspections and reporting requirements that does not ensure safety for patients. A formal, mandatory mechanism for research review and approval of infertility treatment techniques is needed. In addition, we should be able to identify what interventions are offered where.

For reasons known only to the members of the President's Council, the council has chosen to err on the side of allowing wide freedom in the very heterogeneous delivery of reprogenetic medical services in the United States, with unacceptable consequences in terms of ensuring basic levels of safety and protection from risks. There is not even an alert mechanism to sound a warning should a safety problem arise.

The HFEA has recently noted a problem with the temperature of the cryoprotectant used in some infertility treatment centers in the United Kingdom (discussed on the Web site, www.hfea.gov.uk). The HFEA conducted a review of the small number of incidents in which inadequate temperatures led to the loss of stored patient materials. It quickly developed strict new guidelines to protect the safety of frozen sperm, oocytes (eggs), and embryos stored at fertility clinics throughout the country. This sort of alert and response is currently impossible in the United States.

WHY PAY ATTENTION TO THE WELFARE OF THE CHILD BORN AS A RESULT OF REPROGENETIC TECHNIQUES?

Let us compare the two perspectives, from the United States and the United Kingdom. The President's Council explains that "our main focus is on the well-being of children who might be conceived and born with the aid of new reproductive and genetic technologies, and on the possible implications of these biotechnologies for future reproduction considered more broadly" (2004, 8). In contrast, the 1990 act establishing the HFEA states that before offering anyone treatment, a clinic must "take account of the welfare of any child who may be born as a result of that treatment (including the need of that child for a father), and of any other child who may be affected by the birth."

Although both the President's Council on Bioethics and the HFEA assert a sincere desire to take into account the welfare of the child born as a result of reprogenetic practices, only the United Kingdom demands that this be a formal part of the assessment and treatment process. There is no formal assessment tool used to ascertain the welfare of the eventual child born as a result of ART in the United States. The increased incidence of multiple births in particular has a dramatic effect on the welfare of the child: it has been demonstrated repeatedly that the prematurity and low birth weights accompanying multiple births, and supermultiples in particular (quadruplets and above), are potentially life-threatening and disadvantageous to neonates (White and Leuthner 2001).

There are at least two ways in which the treatment of infertility can result in multiple births. First, in the case of in vitro fertilization (IVF), limiting the number of embryos transferred to the uterus is a way of exerting some control over the size of the pregnancy. Even if only one or two embryos are transferred, spontaneous blastomere splitting could occur, resulting in twins, but generally speaking, the number of embryos that implant is smaller than the actual number transferred. The HFEA has limited the number of embryos transferred in IVF to two. (A few years ago, the limit was three embryos, but continued concern over multiple births led the agency to reduce the number.) This limit is legal and binding. In the United States, for many years, there was no professional guidance suggesting that the number of embryos transferred via IVF should be limited. The issue was considered to be a matter of professional judgment on the part of the physician and was not necessarily even discussed with the patient. The U.S. view was that the doctor knows best and should have the prerogative of transferring a large number of embryos to enhance the chances of achieving a pregnancy. In some centers, all embryos resulting from successful fertilization via IVF were transferred so that there would be no lingering concerns about spare or leftover embryos. Today there are professional guidelines, not necessarily binding on the physician, that stipulate that more modest numbers of embryos should be transferred, and that the physician should factor in the age and other characteristics of both the patient and the embryos (American Society of Reproductive Medicine 2004).

The objective of limiting multiple births becomes more complex when ovarian stimulation of the woman is used as the method of infertility treatment, because there is not the same opportunity to count out and transfer a certain number of embryos as a way of achieving some control. When ovarian hyperstimulation regimens are used, there is no way of predicting how successful this intervention will be or how many of the resulting oocytes will be fertilized in vivo through intercourse. It is possible to view the number of ripening follicles by sonography, and if it appears that the woman may ovulate in large numbers, she can be counseled to skip intercourse that cycle. But this kind of monitoring is imprecise and uncertain. Many recent cases of large multiple births in the United States have resulted from the use of ovarian stimulation alone rather than IVF. Practice guidelines for the use of ovarian stimulation in the United States urge caution about repeated use of this therapy in younger women, but these guidelines are not always observed. In addition, obstetrician-gynecologists who are not necessarily specialists in the treatment of infertility may prescribe ovarian stimulation, and these outcomes are not included in reports on infertility treatments from the CDC or the Society for Assisted Reproductive Technology. The high numbers of multiple births associated with infertility treatment are probably the most serious negative consequence of treatment in terms of the welfare of the neonate and the growing child, owing to the serious risks and burdens associated with both premature birth and low birth weight at delivery.

CONCLUSION

There is no higher priority than ensuring the safety of reprogenetic technologies, both in the United States and in the world. In the United States, the President's Council on Bioethics takes a modest and fundamentally inadequate approach to this issue. This attitude is illustrated well in the comment, "we must be sure that changes to the present system are not worse than doing nothing. The appeal of doing nothing in this arena is, frankly, rather great" (2004, 185). The reluctance of the council to consider approaches to oversight and quality control that have been effectively used in other countries around the world, notably the United Kingdom, results in recommendations that do little to alter the status quo.

Because human reproduction is a significant feature of human biological experience and because one generation's reproductive choices, including the utilization of reprogenetic techniques, will affect subsequent generations, any inadequacies with respect to safety are unacceptable. As I have argued in this chapter, some of the features of the HFEA can and should be adopted here.

A first and important step is to license infertility treatment centers and reissue these licenses based on periodic inspections. Licensure is necessary to ensure minimum levels of safety and quality in the delivery of services. Second, public consultation, a feature of the work of the HFEA for more than ten years and initiated recently in the United States by the Genetics and Public Policy Center at Johns Hopkins University, needs to be continued and expanded in an effort both to educate the public in an ongoing way and to take the pulse of the public on these matters. Public engagement is not for the purpose of achieving consensus on reprogenetic matters but rather to educate the public and create a space for discussion that is not immediately filled by the abortion wars.

Third, a more systematic method for the review of innovation in both the diagnosis and treatment of infertility must be developed and utilized. New techniques that are clearly experimental do not routinely make their appearance in the form of a research clinical trial and therefore do not necessarily benefit from institutional review board oversight. Spontaneity and novelty are not appropriate features in the delivery of infertility services. Instead, safety and effectiveness should be the priorities, for the benefit of the parents and even more so in the interest of the health and welfare of the resulting child. The welfare of the child is of paramount value. It trumps clinical and research interests and the procreative rights of parents. If a particular intervention or pattern of care is not good for the resulting child, that alone renders it unacceptable in the treatment of infertility.

REFERENCES

American Society for Reproductive Medicine. 2004. http://www.asrm.org..

BBC News. 2004. Diane Blood registers sons. June 6. http://newsvote.bbc.co.uk/mpapps/pagetools/print/news.bbc.co.uk/1/hi/england/Nottingham.

Benkhalifa, M., S. Kahraman, A. Biricik, S. Serteyl, E. Domez, Y. Kumtepe, and M. B. Qumsiyeh. 2004. Cytogenetic abnormalities and the failure of development after round spermatid injections. *Fertility and Sterility* 81:1283–88.

CNN. 2004. Pennsylvania mom delivers sextuplets. May 11. www.cnn.com/2004/US/Northeast/05/11/sextuplets.ap/index.html.

Genetics and Public Policy Center. 2004. Genetic testing of embryos to pick "savior sibling" okay with most Americans: New survey explores attitudes on preimplantation genetic diagnosis (PGD). Media advisory, May 3. www.dnapolicy.org.

Human Fertilisation and Embryology Act of 1990. 1990. http://www.hfea.gov.uk.

Parens, E., and L. P. Knowles. 2003. Reprogenetics and public policy: Reflections and recommendations. *Hastings Center Report* July-August: S1–S24.

President's Council on Bioethics. 2004. *Reproduction and Responsibility: The Regulation of New Biotechnologies.* Washington, DC. www.bioethics.gov/reports/reproductionandresponsibility/index.html.

Toronto Star. 2003. Backbench MP plots to block bill on cloning. June 10.

U.S. Congress, Office of Technology Assessment. 1988. *Infertility: Medical and Social Choices.* Report no. OTA-BA-358 (May). Washington, DC: U.S. Government Printing Office.

U.S. Centers for Disease Control and Prevention, National Center for Chronic Disease Prevention and Health Promotion (Atlanta, Georgia); American Society for Reproductive Medicine, Society for Assisted Reproductive Technology (Birmingham, Alabama). 2003. *2001 Assisted Reproductive Technology Success Rates: National Summary and Fertility Clinic Reports.* December. www.cdc.gov/reproductivehealth/ART01/index.htm.

Weiss, R. 2004. New fertility technique may produce genetic abnormalities. *Washington Post,* May 24, A-10.

White, G. B. 1998. Crisis in assisted conception: The British approach to an American dilemma. *Journal of Women's Health* 7, no. 3: 321–28.

White, G. B., and S. R. Leuthner. 2001. Infertility treatment and neonatal care: The ethical obligation to transcend specialty practice in the interest of reducing multiple births. *Journal of Clinical Ethics* 12, no. 3: 223–30.

Wilcox, L. S., J. L. Kiely, C. L. Melvin, and M. C. Martin, Society for Assisted Reproductive Technology and the American Society for Reproductive Medicine. 1996. Assisted reproductive technology in the United States and Canada: 1994 results generated from the American Society for Reproductive Medicine/Society for Assisted Reproductive Technology Registry. *Fertility and Sterility* 66:697.

CHAPTER TWELVE

Reprogenetics and Public Policy

Reflections and Recommendations

ERIK PARENS AND LORI P. KNOWLES

At the first of the discussions that led eventually to the writing of this chapter, a respected clinician-researcher in the world of reprogenetic medicine referred to his field as "one big embryo experiment." The phrase nicely captures what this chapter is about. It is about the ethical issues and policy challenges that arise in the context of researchers and clinicians doing new things with embryos. The range of such activities is wide and growing, from studying embryos for the sake of basic knowledge about developmental biology, to using them as sources of embryonic stem (ES) cells that can be coaxed to cure disease, to creating, selecting, and altering them for the sake of producing children. This chapter focuses on the last set of aims and emphasizes the need for improved public oversight—a need that grows more urgent as reproductive and genetic medicine converge to produce the new field of reprogenetics (Andrews 1999; Bonnicksen 1998; Silver 1997).

For a variety of reasons, research involving the use, creation, alteration, and storage of gametes and embryos is subject to little regulation in the United States. This situation is potentially dangerous. Unlike older in vitro fertilization (IVF) techniques, many new reprogenetic techniques make structural changes to cells,[1] and with structural changes come concerns about the safety of the children produced by the technology. Further, both older and newer techniques raise concerns about the safety of the women who donate the eggs and the women in whom the fertilized eggs are implanted—the egg donors and the gestating mothers.

But the concerns that are expressed in relation to reprogenetics have to do not only with safety. Just as important is the well-being of children produced by these techniques—and the well-being of the families and the society into which those children are born. Are we in danger of allowing a market mentality to colonize childbearing, as it has already colonized so much of our lives? Could the proliferation of techniques that increasingly enable us not just to have children but to choose characteristics unrelated to their health exacerbate our tendency to think of children as the objects of our making? Could these techniques lead us to think of ourselves as mechanisms that are valued for our individual parts or traits rather than as individuals who are valued for being unique wholes? Could it aggravate some forms of unfairness, or complicity with unjust norms? (Buchanan et al. 2000; Little 1998; Mehlman and Botkin 1998). Put positively, what can we do to increase the chances that these techniques will be used in ways that further the happiness of children, families, and ultimately our society as a whole?

The answers to these questions must be pursued within a framework of fundamental beliefs and commitments to such values as liberty, equality, solidarity, and justice. They are likely to be complex and will sometimes reveal deep disagreements. But such disagreement should not stand in the way of trying to talk together about matters of such great importance.

We, the authors of this chapter, cannot help but have views of our own about some of these contested questions. But our primary purpose is not to defend those views. Rather, we wish chiefly to establish that our society needs to find better ways to grapple with—and regulate—reprogenetic activities. The future of reprogenetic practice is too important to be decided solely by the marketplace. We call for the creation of an oversight structure that will make possible a thorough and transparent policy discussion of reprogenetics and effective regulation of those facilities involved in reprogenetic research and services.

The chapter is divided into five parts: In the first part, we delineate what we mean by reprogenetics. In the second part, we identify some of the ethical concerns that commentators have broached in relation to reprogenetics, and we argue that questions about well-being must be part of the policy conversation. The third part describes the historical roots of our current oversight situation. Reproductive medicine and genetics have long been overseen separately, and with very different degrees of care. The politics of abortion have largely prevented any effective oversight of reproductive medicine. But as reproductive medicine and genetics converge, the current state of affairs does not allow us as a society to anticipate and contemplate the emerging reprogenetic picture in all of its complexity.

To shed light on what a better approach to reprogenetics policy in the United States might look like, the fourth part briefly explores the weaknesses and strengths of the regulatory approaches adopted by the United Kingdom and Canada. The final part sketches a proposal for an oversight body that could respond to the technological and ethical realities of reprogenetics in the United States.

WHAT IS REPROGENETICS?

In this chapter we define reprogenetics broadly, as the field of research and application that involves the creation, use, manipulation, or storage of gametes or embryos. We also define embryo broadly, adopting the definition that Congress uses in its ban on funding for embryo research: "any organism . . . that is derived by fertilization, parthenogenesis, cloning, or any other means from one or more human gametes or human diploid cells" (National Bioethics Advisory Commission [NBAC] 1999). Of course, there are alternative definitions that reflect the choices a society makes (Green 2001).

The techniques used to create, use, and manipulate embryos for reproductive purposes can also be put to nonreproductive purposes. For example, the somatic cell nuclear transfer (SCNT) or cloning technique can be used, in principle, for the reproductive purpose of creating a child or for the nonreproductive purpose of creating a source of ES cells (and ultimately transplantable tissue). Because the reproductive and nonreproductive uses of embryos are inextricably entwined, we must consider them together if we want to understand and anticipate the implications of our "big embryo experiment."

This broad understanding of reprogenetics—all interventions involved in the creation, use, manipulation, or storage of gametes and embryos—delimits a fairly distinct class of interventions. Reprogenetic research and practice include interventions aimed at creating embryos, whether for reproductive or therapeutic purposes and whether by traditional means such as IVF or by newer means such as SCNT or intracytoplasmic sperm injection (ICSI). Also included are interventions aimed at altering gametes or embryos, whether by the traditional techniques of recombinant DNA or by the newer techniques involving cellular surgery or the use of artificial chromosomes. (Interventions aimed at transferring genes to somatic cells to cure individuals of disease are plainly excluded.)

The scope of reprogenetics, and correspondingly of this chapter, could have been broadened still further to include surrogacy arrangements and prenatal testing. Ultimately, following the example set by the mandate of the United Kingdom's Human Fertilisation and Embryology Authority (HFEA), it excludes all interventions on embryos and fetuses inside a woman's body (*Human Fertilization and Embryology Act* 1990). Research on and treatment of embryos and fetuses that are in a woman's body are regulated to differing extents by regulations applicable to human subjects research and by statutory and common law. Also, a conception of reprogenetics broad enough to encompass these other domains would be unwieldy.

Alternatively, the scope of the reprogenetics could have been limited to those techniques that involve emerging technologies. This narrower conception of reprogenetics, however, would have made it impossible to contemplate the bigger reprogenetic picture—the ways in which reproductive and genetic technologies are converging. Of course, future discussions may identify different ways of delimiting the scope of reprogenetics. Such discussions should be encouraged.

Reprogenetics in Action

The past few years have provided several opportunities to notice the very different purposes to which we can put our growing capacity to do things with gametes and embryos—to notice the very different ways in which reproductive research and practice converge with genetic research and practice.

- In September 1998, news broke about a technology that can sort sperm according to the weight of the chromosomes they carry, with an accuracy rate of approximately 85 percent (Fugger et al. 1998). The company that developed this technology markets it to couples that desire to select the sex of their children. As of January 2004, approximately 419 children had been born using this technique (MicroSort 2006).
- Molly Nash had Fanconi anemia. Her parents wanted to have a second child who would not have Fanconi syndrome, and who also could be a histocompatible donor to Molly—a source of compatible cord blood. To help the Nashes have such a child, clinician-researchers used preimplantation genetic diagnosis (PGD), or the genetic diagnosis of embryos created in a laboratory, to identify suitable embryos for transfer to Molly's mother's uterus. A child who was both free of disease and histocompatible with Molly was born in August 2000 (Verlinsky et al. 2001).

- In March 2001, researchers at the Institute for Reproductive Medicine and Science at Saint Barnabus, New Jersey, announced that an experimental technique had helped approximately twenty women become pregnant. These women had previously been unable to conceive because of defects in their eggs' cytoplasm, the ooplasm. The researchers performed "ooplasm transplantation" by injecting healthy ooplasm from donor eggs into defective ones. Because the ooplasm contains tiny organelles called mitochondria, and because each mitochondrion contains a small loop of DNA, ooplasm transplantation entails the transfer of genetic material from one egg to the other. The researchers announced they had achieved the first successful "germ-line modification" and that it had resulted in apparently healthy babies (Barritt, Brenner, Malter, et al. 2001).

- To date, much of the public and policy conversation about research on ES cells has focused rather narrowly on the moral status of embryos and the potential of ES cells to be put to the therapeutic purpose of creating transplantable tissue. If the ES cells were created through SCNT techniques, they could be used to generate transplantable tissue that was fully histocompatible with the person who received it. Largely missing from this discussion has been a recognition that, in theory, ES cell research could be combined with both SCNT and gene transfer techniques for the reproductive purpose of creating either healthy or "enhanced" embryos—and children (Weiss 2003; Zwaka and Thompson 2003).

These four examples suggest some of the ways in which reproductive and genetic technologies are coming together to increase our capacity to prevent or cure disease—and to create children with traits we desire, some of which are related to health, others of which may not be. IVF can help prospective parents have a child—whatever child they get in the genetic lottery. The newer techniques go one step further: they promise to help prospective parents choose what kind of child they get, or at least to increase the chances that their children will have some traits rather than others. Some of those traits will be related to the health of someone other than the child—like Molly Nash's brother, Adam. Other traits, someday, may be related not to anyone's health but to some perceived advantage (Tang et al. 1999).

It is altogether too early in our understanding of the genetics of complex traits to know how far the project of enhancing offspring can go, in good part because complex traits appear to involve extremely complex interactions among many genes and environmental factors (Gordon 1999; Pinker 2003). But even if adding genetic material (whether genes or artificial chromosomes) to embryos to enhance human traits does not prove feasible, we are likely to learn enough about genotype-phenotype relationships that some entrepreneurial individuals will promise that they can at least increase a prospective parent's chances of having a child with some desired trait, even if the child is created merely through IVF and PGD rather than through SCNT and gene transfer. We are just beginning to explore what that new power may mean for the well-being of children, parents, and society as a whole (Buchanan et al. 2000).

WHAT'S AT STAKE?

The convergence of reproductive and genetic technologies raises complex and sometimes profound ethical questions that call out for informed policy, publicly and transparently developed. Some of these questions are about tangible harms; others, however, are about nontangible harms. In the first category fall concerns about the safety of the women who provide oocytes, as well as concerns about the safety of the gestating mothers and of the children produced. The second category encompasses broader concerns about human well-being. Although some of the reprogenetic technologies are increasingly thought to be within the purview of the Food and Drug Administration, the FDA is not mandated to consider well-being concerns.

Well-being concerns are not all equally persuasive for all commentators. It is not our goal here to defend them all, however—or to defend exactly our way of articulating or organizing them. Delineating a representative range of these concerns is enough to establish the need for a transparent policy discussion of reprogenetics. That discussion will allow us to accept or reject the various concerns that commentators have broached. Yet given the concerns, we should not forgo that discussion and leave regulation to the market alone.

Safety

In reproductive medicine, more so than in most other areas of medical practice, the line between clinical innovation and human experimentation is fuzzy: "patients" in reproductive medicine sometimes can be subjected to the high levels of uncertainty and risk commonly associated with being a research subject (NBAC 2001). Consequently, reprogenetics raises concerns about the

safety of the women, children, and tissue providers who are involved in reproductive medicine. As in all scientific experimentation, it is important to be
realistic about the nature of scientific uncertainty. Although researchers and
clinicians are often confident that they can predict what the outcomes of a particular technique will be, in fact we often cannot reliably predict the outcomes. We must expect the unexpected. At the very least, we need adequate
testing and record keeping to approach the standard of scientific research
mandated in other areas of research.

The newer reprogenetic techniques raise a number of unresolved safety
concerns. The potential health risks to children who might be created by
means of cloning technologies have been widely publicized. In addition, it
remains unknown how safe and effective ooplasm transplantation is. There is
some evidence to suggest that ooplasm transplantation may involve an
increased risk of aneuploidy (that is, having an atypical number of chromosomes), although the clinical data are too incomplete to support any clear conclusions (Barritt, Willadsen, et al. 2001). But safety concerns are not limited to
the newer reprogenetic technologies. Insofar as traditional IVF often results in
multiple births, babies born by such methods are at increased risk of "prematurity, low birth weight, infant death, and lifelong disability" (New York State
Task Force on Life and Law 1998, xiii). Recent studies have suggested that
children produced by means of ICSI may be at an increased risk of aneuploidy
(Hansen et al. 2002; Powell 2002).

Reprogenetic technologies often require a supply of eggs from either the
patient or donors (who actually often sell their eggs or provide them in
exchange for fertility services). New technologies like ooplasm transplantation and ES cell research will only increase the demand for oocytes. The risks
to women who provide eggs are associated primarily with the drugs used to
induce superovulation. Severe ovarian hyperstimulation syndrome is a rare
but life-threatening event. A potential increase in the risk of ovarian cancer is
also thought to be associated with superovulation. In addition to the drug-
related risks, there are some surgical risks, including possible "puncture of
the fallopian tubes, infection or bleeding" (National Conference of State Legislatures 2001, 33). Traditional assisted-reproductive techniques also put gestating women at increased risk of preeclampsia, diabetes mellitus, bleeding,
and anemia (Institute for Science, Law and Technology Working Group 1998).
In addition to the risks associated with the drugs and surgical techniques,
women and children are at increased risk of developing the infections that
accompany tissue (including egg or sperm) transplantation.

In discussing safety-related risks, it is important to remember that the couples seeking to have children with these techniques are often more than willing to bear them. There is, however, an ethical consensus that parents have a prima facie obligation to shield their prospective children from preventable impairments (Buchanan et al. 2000; Murray 1996). Needless to say, an obligation to shield children from reprogenetically induced, preventable impairments must be balanced against the parental right to try to create a child. In other words, parents must balance their desire to create a child with their desire to shield the child from preventable harms.

How best to balance those competing values and desires is open to debate, and oversimplified generalizations about what individuals want and what they owe each other are not adequate to help us understand the complex relationships and motivations that are inherent in good family life. Everyone can agree, however, that there is a need for good data about the real risks inherent in these technologies.

Unfortunately, experimental reprogenetic techniques have been rapidly introduced to the market "without sufficient prior animal experimentation, randomized clinical trials, or the rigorous data collection that would occur in federally funded studies" (Institute for Science, Law and Technology1998). In fact, ooplasm transplantation was advertised on the Internet before the FDA intervened to collect information and conduct hearings on the technique's safety and efficacy (FDA 2002). Without good data, no one can give meaningful informed consent to engage in such activities, no matter how important the aim of having a child.

Well-Being

Public policy in the field of reprogenetics is more challenging than in some other domains because, even if all the safety concerns were addressed, other vital concerns would remain. Given the depth and complexity of the desire to have a biologically related child, the techniques used to gratify that desire can raise equally deep and complex questions about human well-being.

Arguably, many well-being concerns are facets of the same fundamental worry that using technology to produce "better" children will drive us toward making the fundamental mistake of treating children—and the rest of us—as commodities rather than as persons (Radin 1987). Whereas we think it appropriate to give a price to commodities, we think it is a category mistake to give a price to children; to do so is to miss that the sort of being we're dealing with is "priceless" (Knowles 1999; Murray 1996). To the extent that reprogenetic practices promote the view that the value of gametes, embryos, or children depends on their particular traits, those practices will raise similar concerns.

Skeptics sometimes claim that such concerns conceal nothing more than fear of the new (Harris 1992). Very likely they are a sign of fear, but they can also reflect a desire to affirm the intrinsic value of the diversity of human forms. Well-being concerns are in part about the fact that reprogenetic technologies are being used not by persons who aim to shape themselves, but rather by parents who aim to shape their children. Using reprogenetic means for this goal may exacerbate parents' tendencies to think of children as the objects of their making and to have unrealistic expectations of their children. Well-being concerns are also in part about the belief that in using reprogenetic means to shape children, we are expressing a problematic conception of what it is to be a human being (Turner 1998). The worry is that in using these means we will lose sight of the fact that children are wholes that cannot be reduced to the sum of their traits if we are to understand adequately what they are.

Another source of concern is the prospect that we might someday use reprogenetic means to enhance children's traits. If we presume that access to such enhancements is unequal, then there is reason to worry that parents who already purchase social advantages will be able, in effect, to purchase genetic capacities to use those advantages—thereby potentially increasing the gap between the haves and the have-nots (Resnik, Steinkraus, and Langer 1999; Walters and Palmer 1997). Imagine that the teenager already blessed with social advantages like enrollment in Stanley Kaplan prep courses was in addition outfitted at birth with a reprogenetic form of Ritalin, thus endowing the capacity to be especially good at exploiting social advantages like the prep courses. That children with advantages are already using psychopharmacological agents in just that way is hardly an argument for permitting reprogenetic means to achieve more of the same. Nor can we regard the decision to use reprogenetic means as a "private choice," for such choices would generate pressures on others to follow suit. Some parents will no doubt fervently want to acquire such advantages for their prospective children, yet if they obtain them, other parents will likely feel pressured, perhaps even obligated, to purchase the same services for their children (Wertheimer 1987).

If we assume instead that all parents have equal access to new enhancements for their children, concerns about justice still do not disappear. Some commentators argue that if we approved general use of reprogenetic enhancements, we might then begin to use reprogenetic means to solve complex social problems and in so doing undermine our commitments to equality and diversity; prospective parents might use the technology to increase the chances that their children would more successfully live up to dominant ideals, which at least in some cases would be unjust (Little 1998). Imagine an intervention that increases the chances that a child will have the pale pigmentation currently valorized in the West: although we might readily imagine why parents would want to insulate their children from the norm that values pale pigmentation, we might nonetheless worry that using reprogenetics to deal with discrimination leaves the unjust norms in place.

Still other concerns center on the well-being of the women who will provide the eggs, whether for research or for reproduction. As has been articulated in parallel fashion in the debate over the ethics of commercial surrogate pregnancy (Arneson 1992; Macklin 1996; Satz 1992), these women seem to be candidates for coercion and exploitation. The potential for exploitation is aggravated when the phenotype of the woman providing the eggs is irrelevant. In such cases the woman may be especially vulnerable to economic coercion. Although high prices are reportedly sometimes offered for college women's eggs, researchers will likely seek a cheaper source of oocytes for techniques such as therapeutic ES cell research and ooplasm transplantation. Many of the women who undergo hyperstimulation and surgical removal of oocytes for research purposes would likely do so because they need the money, yet they would likely not be as well placed to protect themselves. Just as we do not encourage the buying and selling of organs because such a market could exploit the poor, we should be wary of a market in human reproductive materials (Stempsey 1996).

There are other long-standing questions about the effects such commercialization of reproduction will have on us as a society (Arrow 1972). One reason many argue that commercialization of human reproduction should be avoided is that they object to putting a price on something priceless, to rendering it open to comparison and bargaining (Radin 1987). Some also argue that we lose something important by replacing gift relationships with market exchanges (Murray 1987). Although markets already exist in a number of human "goods" intimately tied to our personhood, such as human labor and human beauty, there need not be markets in all such goods. We need these issues to be part of the discussion that informs reprogenetics policymaking, rather than fatalistically accept the colonization of children-and family-making by the market.

The Controversy over Well-Being

In the U.S. public policy debate, concerns such as the ones mentioned above have often been viewed by some commentators with skepticism, if not derision. They are frequently referred to as "symbolic," "speculative," "vague," and sometimes "religious" (Robertson 1995).

Yet even ardent critics of these concerns still accord them weight. For example, John Robertson, one of the strongest proponents of procreative liberty, acknowledges that "at a certain point . . . a practice such as cloning, enhancement, or intentional diminishment of offspring may be so far removed from even pluralistic notions of reproductive meaning that they leave the realm of protected reproductive choice" (Robertson 1994, 41). Robertson understands that if we are to place limits on procreative liberty, then there is no way around the difficult work of taking well-being concerns seriously.

Similarly, Dr. Charles Strom, who used PGD to help Molly Nash's family produce a histocompatible sibling without Fanconi anemia, recognizes that PGD could also be used to test for non-health-related traits, and he appears to have concerns about some of those uses. He told a *New York Times Magazine* reporter that reprogenetics research of the sort he himself conducts has "all been forced into the private sector . . . where there are no controls." He added, "There should be limits. It is up to us, as a society, to decide what they are" (Belkin 2001, 36). It is important to note that Strom's call for controls and limits is not based on concerns about safety alone.

It will not be easy to fully articulate the limits that should be placed on these technologies. But if we are to have any limits, then we as a society will have to find a language in which to articulate them.

Though making public policy based on well-being concerns will be difficult, it will not be without precedent. We already allow questions about the well-being of individual children to guide some reproductive decisions. For example, the state considers the well-being of children in adoption decisions (Daniels et al. 2000). Before prospective parents are permitted to adopt a child, they are required to provide evidence that they would be good parents. What constitutes a good parent is far from obvious, and making such judgments is difficult, but that does not prevent us from making such determinations.

Indeed, the New York State Task Force on Life and the Law in 1998 suggested that physicians are "entitled to consider the welfare of any child who might be born" as a result of reproductive and genetic procedures. Although the task force staunchly supports procreative liberty, it does, in the name of child welfare, identify circumstances that may warrant refusing prospective parents access to assisted-reproductive services. Consequently, despite a general reluctance to address well-being issues in reproductive policy, there are precedents for defining limits to procreative liberty in the name of child welfare in public policy (Shanley 2001). Similar judgments could be made to define limits to the circumstances in which reprogenetic technologies are used.

There's no denying that we hold dear different and sometimes competing fundamental values, including liberty, equality, solidarity, and justice. When those values come into conflict, we in the United States generally prefer to allow individuals to resolve the conflict themselves—to exercise their individual liberty and choose for themselves. But we do not always leave it to individuals alone to resolve conflicts between values. For example, we have decided as a matter of public policy that people cannot buy and sell other people. In this case, equality trumps freedom. Similarly, we prohibit a market in organs because such a market would undermine some values that we esteem even more than we esteem an individual's liberty to buy and sell what she wants. We have decided instead to rely on the altruism of donors, even though donors do not meet the demand for organs, because doing so furthers the ethical commitments of our society (Murray 1995).

Absent systematic regulation, reprogenetic technologies are limited mainly by the constraints of the market and the piecemeal constraints of professional self-regulation. The extent to which reproductive decisions, materials, and techniques should be left to the marketplace should be part of our public policy discussion. Though no one would dare place an ad for a kidney, much less a child, in a college newspaper, ads are placed in university papers to induce young women with particular traits to sell their eggs for use in IVF (Frase-Blunt 2001; Lefer 1999, 38). And, as mentioned earlier, it is now possible in the United States to purchase an increased chance that you will get a baby with the sex you prefer.[2] Most countries with similar cultures have prohibited sex selection that is unrelated to disease prevention (Steinbock 2002). Indeed, many countries hold that markets in human reproductive tissues, technologies, and services are simply "blocked exchanges" (Andre 1995), or "hors du commerce" (Loiseau 2000). The United Nations' *Universal Declaration on the Human Genome and Human Rights* asserts that civilized societies must avoid putting a price on human reproduction.

Embryo Research

Most Western industrialized countries share a view that embryos in petri dishes are neither persons nor mere property (Knowles 2000). Insofar as embryos could become persons if they were transferred from petri dishes into wombs, they deserve our respect; how much respect the entity deserves depends in part on how far along the developmental path it is. The farther along the path it is, the more respect it deserves. We express that respect with prohibitions and limits that restrict the uses for which and conditions under which research on embryos may be conducted (National Institutes of Health [NIH] 1994). But many think that some research is acceptable. Long before reproductive specialists were creating and manipulating embryos to produce children, they had to conduct experiments on embryos, which no one would have dreamed of implanting in a woman. IVF would never have got off the ground without embryo experimentation.

Yet even if many people agree that at least some embryo research is ethically permissible, many questions remain about what it means for us to use embryos to serve our purposes. Will a given technique or manner or purpose of embryo research express appropriate respect for these entities? Or will it incline us to think of embryos as "mere stuff," to put to whatever purposes we see fit? Will our activities involving embryos incline us to treat these entities as mere instruments for pursuing other goals—and will doing so affect how we understand our relationships to each other and, ultimately, our relationships to the rest of the natural world? All of those questions are ultimately about the well-being of individuals and of our society as a whole.

Other countries have struggled to think about these issues at a policy level and to make clear the ethical commitments that underlie their embryo research policies. We must do the same. The overall task, therefore, is to design an oversight system that allows debate about both safety and well-being to inform responsible reprogenetics policy.

PUBLIC POLICY, REGULATION, AND REPROGENETICS

The current public policy stance regarding reprogenetic technologies is a compromise and a patchwork, derived from deep divides in American politics and the accidents of scientific progress. It is riddled with redundancies, inconsistencies, gaps, and inefficiencies. The political division that has hampered public policy on reprogenetics is rooted in the vitriolic U.S. debate over abortion. Given the polarizing dynamics of this debate, much of the public policy conversation about embryo research and reproductive policy has consisted of pro-choice and antiabortion activists shouting past each other. Unsurprisingly, many policymakers have chosen to avoid entering that fray, and therefore they have not been able to agree that some embryo research is acceptable for some purposes but not for others. As a result, almost all embryo research has been driven into the private sector. The natural secrecy of the private sector can have two results: it can impede the progression of the science, given the need for confidentiality (Blumenthal et al. 1996), and it can reduce the public's role in deliberating about the direction of the science. For the bulk of such work to go on in the "shadowlands" of the private sector (Annas 1998) is both potentially dangerous for participants and incompatible with the ideal of conducting such work in the light of forthright public deliberation.

The second reason we lack a productive public conversation about reprogenetics has to do with the historical fact that until recently, reproductive medicine and genetic medicine were separate lines of inquiry, pursued by professionals with training in independent scientific and medical fields. Even if genetic and reproductive technologies were not already converging, the redundancies, inconsistencies, gaps, and inefficiencies in the current systems of oversight for genetic and, especially, for reproductive medicine would call out for reform. But genetic and reproductive technologies are converging. A new system to oversee reprogenetic research and services is needed, therefore, for functional reasons, because the old categories of "genetics" and "reproductive" research do not reflect the new technological realities. The ooplasm transplantation protocol is a prime example of an intervention that does not fit cleanly into either of the old categories: the purpose is reproductive, but achieving it entails a genetic change.

Converging Lines of Research

In the mid-1970s, when research into reproduction and genetics was getting off the ground in earnest, the two fields appeared largely unrelated. Reproductive medicine had begun to promise that IVF could help infertile couples have children. There really was no genetic medicine as such, just genetics researchers dreaming of curing terrible diseases. The possibility of genetically modifying gametes and embryos was quickly dismissed, on the ground of an apparent consensus that U.S. society would never embark on making such changes. The ethical and technical barriers, it was regularly asserted, were simply too high.

At that time, the two fields were overseen in quite different ways. Gene transfer research underwent intense regulatory oversight and became the subject of a well-developed policy conversation about its purposes; reproductive medicine has received much less careful attention.

Genetics. The NIH's Recombinant DNA Advisory Committee (the RAC) was created in 1974 in part to be a forum for better public conversation about genetics research. In the beginning, the RAC was a forum to discuss concerns about the safety of splicing foreign genes into microorganisms. In 1982, the report *Splicing Life*, produced by the President's Commission for the Study of Ethical Problems in Medicine and Biomedical and Behavioral Research, argued that the RAC's purview should be expanded to include gene transfer protocols in humans and that its membership should be expanded to include, among others, lay public participants, and ethicists. In 1985, when the RAC adopted guidelines for researchers proposing to embark on gene transfer experiments in humans, it was responsible for making recommendations to the NIH director about protocol approval and for promoting a public conversation about the purposes of such research. It became, therefore, a place to discuss questions about both safety and well-being. Even though researchers in the private sector were not required by law to put their protocols before the RAC, they did so voluntarily—at least until 1996.

In 1996, NIH director Harold Varmus announced that he would eliminate the RAC. He argued that because the basic issues surrounding gene transfer research had been resolved, RAC oversight was redundant (NIH 1996). When observers responded that the RAC was needed more than ever because of the prospect of germline modification and genetic enhancement, Varmus revised his recommendation to eliminate the RAC. He left it standing but took away its power to approve protocols, opting instead to rely on a system of institutional review board (IRB) and FDA oversight.

While there are redundancies and even some inconsistencies between RAC and FDA oversight of genetics research, together at least they provide mechanisms for broaching both safety and well-being issues. Further, most genetics research carried out in the private sector is overseen by the FDA, and private sector genetics research is often voluntarily taken before the RAC if researchers or their sponsors think they are broaching a "novel issue."

Unfortunately, however, the RAC's guidelines describe its mandate in terms of the technology that was around in the 1980s; it considers only those interventions that involve recombinant DNA. Thus the ooplasm transplantation protocol technically fell outside of the RAC's purview, even though it involved inheritable genetic modifications, because the protocol employed cellular surgery rather than recombinant DNA. It was only that technological detail that kept the protocol, which the researchers themselves called the first successful "human germline genetic modification," from being subject to RAC scrutiny (Juengst and Parens 2003). And thus that research was conducted without public conversation, under the supervision only of the researchers and their institution's IRB.

The lack of a comprehensive, informed oversight system means that researchers in reprogenetics risk violating two critical moral obligations, one to individuals and one to society. The first is the researcher's obligation to avoid harming individuals. Clinician-researchers are obliged to refrain from offering techniques to produce children until the techniques have been shown to pose minimal risks to such children. But many reprogenetic techniques have not yet been shown to pose such minimal risks. In the ooplasm transplantation protocol, the researchers acknowledged that the long-term effects of the intervention were simply not known (Cohen et al. 1998; Templeton 2002). Indeed, two of the fourteen fetuses they produced had Turner syndrome (Barritt et al. 2000). (One spontaneously aborted and the other was selectively aborted.) Turner syndrome is not an uncommon genetic disorder, and the Turner syndrome births may not have been caused by the procedure—or they may have. Researchers and clinicians in the United States and abroad expressed concern that such risks were taken with little understanding of the long-term health consequences (Templeton 2002). Similar safety concerns have surrounded the use of ICSI (American Society for Reproductive Medicine [ASRM] 2000). The potential danger of such procedures calls out for a public system of oversight that relies on more than the discretion of individual researchers and their institutions.

Second, since scientists are members of a democratic community who share resources (and all researchers in the United States benefit directly or indirectly from our extraordinary scientific infrastructure), they are obliged to subject their research to public scrutiny, especially if the research promises to affect future children and thus the future of our society. That obligation is embodied in the RAC. But the ooplasm transplantation protocol ran afoul of the spirit of this obligation. The decision to make inheritable genetic modifications in the human genome should not be left to individuals. It should be made at a policy level after public discussion about both safety and well-being concerns (Frankel and Chapman 2002).

Reproductive medicine. In contrast to genetic research, reproductive research in the United States goes on with relatively little public scrutiny. The National Conference of State Legislatures recently summed up the current system of regulation in the United States when it wrote, "A substantial proportion of research and innovative therapy in reproductive medicine need not be subject to peer review, may not conform to current standards for informed consent, and may be offering services that have never been fully evaluated for safety and efficiency" (National Conference of State Legislatures 2001, 28). This minimalist approach is in stark contrast to that taken in much of the rest of the democratic world (Cohen 1997; Annas 1998).

The history of the oversight of reproductive medicine is heavily influenced by the dynamics of the abortion debate. Those dynamics make policymakers reluctant to engage in a discussion about embryo research. In the late 1970s, the Ethics Advisory Board (EAB), which was appointed by the Carter administration, endorsed the idea of federal support for embryo research. According to EAB guidelines, federally funded embryo research had to be reviewed by the EAB. Thus, when under Presidents Carter, Reagan, and George H. W. Bush funding for the EAB was denied, the result was a de facto ban on federally funded embryo research. The *Health Research Extension Act* of 1985 precluded embryo research not intended to benefit the particular embryo (P.L. 99-158, 1985). In 1993, however, with the arrival of the Clinton administration, Congress nullified the EAB-approval requirement and temporarily ended the ban (P.L. 103-43, 1993).

Also in 1993, NIH director Harold Varmus created the Human Embryo Research Panel (HERP) to give him advice regarding what kinds of embryo research NIH ought to fund. In 1994, HERP endorsed funding for embryo research, including funds for some creation of embryos. Presciently, HERP argued that if ES cells were ever isolated in humans, ES cell research would be one form of embryo research that should be eligible for federal funding. Although Clinton rejected HERP's recommendation with respect to funding the creation of embryos for research, he otherwise endorsed the HERP report. In 1995, in reaction to HERP and Clinton, Congress passed the Dickey-Wicker amendment, which precludes federal funding of embryo research through annual NIH Appropriation Acts.[3] Consequently, where embryo research goes on, it does so without public money or scrutiny—in the private sector.[4]

Another part of the explanation for the current lack of oversight of reproductive medicine is that many new interventions in the field are considered "innovative application"—not research—by those who offer them. And because they are presented as innovative clinical practice rather than as research, oversight of them is left to the discretion of the individuals or institutions offering them.

Moreover, because most insurance companies still do not pay for infertility services, they have not insisted on scrutinizing the results of reproductive research in the way they scrutinize other forms of medical research. And because patients often accept that the failure rate of reproductive interventions is high, malpractice litigation has not effectively brought legal scrutiny to the field (National Academy of Sciences 2002).

None of this is to say that reproductive research and services go on without any oversight or regulation. Virginia and New Hampshire have comprehensive legislation regarding assisted reproduction (Institute for Science, Law, and Technology 1998), and many states have laws regulating some aspects of, or techniques used in, embryo research (Walters 2003). At the federal level, the 1992 *Congressional Fertility Clinic Success Rate and Certification Act* (FCSRCA) requires clinics offering assisted reproduction technologies to disclose pregnancy success rates to the Centers for Disease Control. And laboratories that perform the diagnostic tests related to assisted reproduction, such as semen or hormonal analysis, must be certified under the federal *Clinical Laboratories Improvement Act* (CLIA) (New York State Task Force 1998).

Professional organizations in reproductive medicine have also set practice standards. The American Society for Reproductive Medicine (ASRM) set practice standards for IVF, GIFT, and related procedures in 1998. The ASRM also created guidelines for gamete and embryo donation in 1998, and revised them in 2002. Members of ASRM's Society for Assisted Reproductive Technologies (SART), who account for as many as 90 percent of the providers of reproductive services, comply with FCSRCA, allow inspections, run accredited embryology laboratories, and follow the ethical guidelines of ASRM.

Finally, the FDA has asserted its jurisdiction over cloning and ooplasm transplantation on grounds that such interventions create "products" analogous to the biological products already within its mandate (gene therapy products, for example) (Zoon 2001). Given that the FDA's mandate is limited to the consideration of issues related to safety and efficacy, therefore leaving out concerns about well-being, it would be best if technologies like cloning and ooplasm transplantation did not fall exclusively within the FDA's mandate.

Presidential bioethics advisory commissions have taken up both the safety and well-being issues raised by certain technologies involving embryos—cloning and stem cell research—but only on an ad hoc basis. The modus operandi of President Clinton's National Bioethics Advisory Commission was to respond to the president's specific requests, which made it difficult to consider the full reprogenetic picture. President Bush's President's Council on Bioethics (PCB) in 2002 issued an advisory report on the use of cloning technology, but, like NBAC, its resources and mandate are limited, it will likely be replaced with a change in presidents, and its role is purely advisory. Consequently, the NBAC and PCB reports will likely join the thoughtful, articulate advisory reports that form part of this country's academic bioethics work, but not part of its public policy.

In sum, many groups, commissions, and federal agencies have commented on or asserted authority over various aspects of reproductive services and research, yet there is, at best, a patchwork system of oversight. There is no standing body to promote public conversation about issues of safety and well-being that arise in the context of new reproductive technologies.

Embryonic stem cells: A critical moment. We are at a critical and perhaps a propitious juncture in the development of reprogenetics and in the history of the debates over embryo research. Research on ES cells occurs at the convergence of reproductive and genetics technologies. That convergence brings promise and peril, which may prove vivid enough to make both sides of the abortion debate contemplate a compromise regarding embryo research.

It is widely known both that research on ES cells holds the promise of producing transplantable tissue for people in desperate need and that isolating ES cells entails the destruction of embryos. It is less widely known that ES cells also could be crucially involved in the creation of embryos; ES cells could ultimately be used to create healthy children and, at least in principle, to create genetically enhanced children.

ES cells have three remarkable properties. The first is their pluripotentiality—their capacity to be coaxed to develop into many tissue types. The second is their "immortality"—their capacity to proliferate indefinitely in an undifferentiated form. Because of their immortality, if a researcher wanted to insert genes into cells, ES cell lines provide an unlimited supply of "targets." Finally, ES cells are extraordinarily malleable; that is, it is easier to insert genes where you want them in ES cells than in other kinds of cells (Gordon 1999). The combination of immortality and malleability not only makes ES cells superb targets for gene insertions, it also makes them excellent vehicles for producing inheritable genetic modifications.

If researchers were to perform gene transfer on ES cells and then employed cloning to transfer an ES cell's nucleus into an egg, they could move from creating transplantable tissue to creating altered embryos. Those alterations could be aimed at producing healthy embryos—or "enhanced" embryos. In this respect, then, ES cell research is part of the bigger reprogenetic picture.

In 1998, when James Thomson and his colleagues isolated human ES cells, President Clinton asked the NBAC to provide advice regarding ES cell research. NBAC delivered a report in late summer of 1999. Given the medical promise of the research, NBAC argued, an exception should be made to the statutory ban on federal funding of embryo research to permit federal agencies to fund research involving the derivation of human ES cells. Thus a second high-level government panel followed HERP in arguing that some embryo research ought to be publicly funded.

Clinton rejected his own ethics advisory commission's advice, however, opting instead to accept the legal opinion of the Department of Health and Human Services' general counsel, Harriet Rabb, that the Dickey-Wicker amendment applied to research on embryos and that ES cells were not embryos (Rabb 1999). Dickey-Wicker also states that federal funds may not be used for research "in which a human embryo or embryos are destroyed," and ES cell research entails the destruction of embryos. But Rabb opined that the letter of the law permitted federally funded researchers to use ES cells as long as they did not derive them. Derivation could be left to researchers in the private sector. In August 2001, President George W. Bush employed the same use-derivation distinction but stipulated that federally funded researchers could use only ES cells that had been derived with private money before August 9, 2001.

By relying on the use versus derivation distinction, the Clinton and Bush administrations squandered an opportunity to make a distinction instead between acceptable and unacceptable purposes for embryo research. Everyone who has used IVF has been the beneficiary of one sort of embryo research. And if anyone ever benefits from the ES cell research that the federal government now funds, that person will be the beneficiary of another form of embryo research.

If we want to enjoy such benefits, we should forthrightly support continued embryo research. In giving our support, we must recognize that the embryo research enterprise, which requires a destruction of human embryos, does entail a moral cost—as do many things we desire. Many would allow, for example, that slaughtering animals for food and allowing medical students to dissect cadavers have their costs, even though they are justifiable. In thinking about embryo research, we must work out how we can both respect embryos and, under some circumstances and for some purposes, benefit from the things

we can do with them. We need to figure out the difference between the purposes of the embryo research we want to endorse and the purposes of that we
reject. Hiding behind distinctions like the one between use and derivation
makes no sense for those who wish to face the bigger reprogenetic picture in
all of its complexity.

The basic point here is that ES cells in particular, and embryos in general,
can be put to many different purposes. Adequate responses to those purposes
will require more than the blanket yes of the advocates or the blanket no of the
critics. To their credit, some people in the antiabortion camp have already, in
light of the therapeutic possibilities opened up by ES cell research, begun to
modulate their blanket no to embryo research. Senator Orrin Hatch, who is
opposed to abortion, has stated that ES cell research is a form of embryo
research he can support, and he supports a bill that would permit the use of
embryos in therapeutic cloning research. As antiabortion advocate Tony
Blankley wrote in the *Washington Times,* "The imminent private sector
exploitation of [ES cell research] will force intellectually honest right-to-lifers
to abandon our cherished illusion of moral clarity on this issue" (Blankley
2000). Similarly, pro-choice supporters like George Annas and Lori Andrews
have suggested that there ought to be limits on what we can do with embryos
(Annas, Andrews, and Isai 2002).

These are perhaps but preliminary calls for compromise, and they might
prove ephemeral. If they are to lead to any genuine accord, with substantive
consequences for promoting some forms of research and constraining others,
they must receive some institutional support. We must create a governmental
body that will, among other things, facilitate systematic and nuanced policy
deliberation about the wide variety of health and non-heath-related things we
can do with embryos.

The Role of Government in Reprogenetics

There will be little disagreement about the claim that safety concerns warrant government oversight. Many people from within infertility medicine
believe that we need improved government oversight to protect participants/
consumers (Annas et al. 2002). Many of those same people would probably
also agree that there ought to be some form of public discussion about how
this new research and practice will affect the well-being of us all.

Two objections, however, can be raised against attempting to promote
broad-based public deliberation about questions of well-being and against

attempting, through political and moral deliberation, to develop a common framework of values within which public policy on reprogenetics could be formulated.[5] First, questions about possible future consequences are necessarily based on claims that are more tentative than the scientific knowledge and empirical data that policymakers often wish to have on hand before making decisions. But in fact, making public policy decisions under conditions of uncertainty and incomplete knowledge is a familiar problem, and the remedy is not policy inaction. What are required are open and reasonable deliberation, a sense of humility in the face of very complex questions, a willingness to listen and learn, and the flexibility and honesty to make corrections to policy when initial assumptions or beliefs turn out to be mistaken.

Second, some have argued that public deliberation and public policy should be limited to procedural and technical questions. This is primarily because, they believe, opening the public sphere up to issues as difficult and controversial as what constitutes human well-being would be dangerous in a pluralistic democracy (Calabresi and Bobbitt 1978). It would be dangerous partly because it would be a source of conflict, and partly because policies or laws informed by a particular conception of human well-being could threaten the liberty of those who hold different beliefs about human well-being.

This second viewpoint is important as a caution against the possible misuse of public deliberation, but it does not provide a compelling reason to forgo the process of deliberation altogether. Even in so contentious and sensitive an area as human reproduction and family life, public policy cannot and should not be limited to procedural issues alone. Doing so suggests that all human relationships are characterized only by rational, voluntary contract and self-interested exchange. In this realm, public policy cannot and should not be limited to the negative, protective functions of providing for individual security and the prevention of harm, as important as these are. The function of public policy even in a democratic, pluralistic society is also positive; it is to promote the enjoyment of liberty and rights, to promote social justice, and to promote the well-being of its citizens.

Liberty itself is an aspect of human well-being. Liberty and autonomy cannot flourish in a society in which the individual is merely protected from harm; they can flourish only where the individual also is supported in her human dignity and worth—where she is educated and is provided with equal opportunities to develop personal talents and abilities. It would be supremely ironic if, out of concern for the protection of individual liberty and diversity of opinion, we hobbled the primary democratic vehicle we have that creates a context within which liberty itself can prosper and be most meaningful. That vehicle is the process of fair and open public deliberation about the conditions of justice and liberty in our polity, and the conditions of human well-being in our society. Contrasting visions of human well-being are the lifeblood of politics and are always at work, even though sometimes they are so "self-evident" to so many that we do not notice them at all. We should not fear this aspect of political discourse and deliberation, we should embrace it and put it to good use.

One of the government's responsibilities is to promote the public welfare, and how reprogenetic technologies are developed and disseminated will affect the public welfare. Some of those effects will be relatively narrow: among these more contained consequences might be legal dilemmas regarding the identities of children and responsibilities of parents, questions regarding the care and support of children, and issues surrounding the medical treatment decisions of children produced by these new techniques (Annas 1998). Other effects will be broader: reprogenetics might transform the meaning of having a child, being a member of a family, and being a member of a community.

Our government has an interest in influencing the development and dissemination of technologies with this kind of power. Given that the current system of reprogenetics oversight is potentially dangerous, out of step with the reality of the convergence of reproductive and genetic medicine, and sometimes subverts genuine public conversation, it is time to contemplate new reprogenetic policy mechanisms. It is, of course, ambitious to try to describe mechanisms that are less dangerous, that reflect current technological developments and are capable of facilitating a conversation about the bigger picture. Such a task could not possibly be accomplished in one fell swoop by any single group. We are at the beginning of a long process, and this chapter merely points in one direction we might go to create safer and better-informed oversight of reprogenetic research and practice.

INTERNATIONAL REGULATION OF REPRODUCTIVE GENETICS

There are several possible regulatory vehicles that might allow for better oversight of reprogenetics, and each strategy has strengths and weaknesses. Our overarching recommendation in this chapter is for comprehensive regulation of reprogenetic techniques in both the private and public sphere. That recommendation is guided, in part, by an analysis of the regulatory strategies of other countries, in particular those of the United Kingdom and Canada. In spite of the close cultural ties between those countries and our own, differences in culture and political tradition make wholesale importation of either of their regulatory schemes both impossible and inappropriate. Nonetheless, it is informative to consider what in these countries has worked and what has failed.

The United Kingdom

In 1984, the Committee of Inquiry into Human Fertilisation and Embryology headed by Dame Mary Warnock (the Warnock Committee) issued a detailed report outlining the results of a two-year consultation process on embryo research and assisted human reproduction. The Warnock Report reviewed the ethical issues associated with new reproductive techniques and stated the committee's opinions (both majority and minority opinions, in some cases) about what policymakers ought to adopt in designing oversight.

The Warnock Report covered many issues, including some controversial topics that generated significant disagreement, such as the moral status of the human embryo and the acceptability of human embryo research. Ultimately, the report articulated a number of opinions about the acceptability of human embryo research, the need for limits and restrictions to certain practices, and the need for a centralized oversight body that could create and implement public policy and adapt to technological developments.

The government adopted the recommendations of the Warnock Report and drafted legislation aimed at regulating the storage and use of gametes and embryos in treatment and research. The legislation, the *Human Fertilisation and Embryology Act* of 1990, established a national oversight body called the Human Fertilisation and Embryology Authority. The HFEA has the status of a "quango"—a body in an arm's-length relationship to the government that is housed outside the Department of Health yet is accountable to the Secretary of State. To ensure that it is not overloaded with scientist and clinician voices, the act stipulates that membership is interdisciplinary.

The HFEA is responsible, through various committees, for licensing and monitoring clinics and laboratories involved in gamete or embryo storage, creation, or use, and section 5 of the act sets out the purposes for which licenses will be required (falling under the rubric of licenses for treatment, storage, or research). In addition, the HFEA functions as an information resource for patients, clinics, and clinicians alike. It achieves this, in part, by establishing and publishing a code of practice "giving guidance about the proper conduct of activities carried on in pursuance of a license under the Act." Through the setting of standards and the provision of licenses, the HFEA provides both quality control and assurances that ethical conduct in embryo research is maintained.

The act also details the situations in which consents must be obtained. Through a series of detailed and mandatory consent procedures, it attempts to ensure that patients consider some later contingencies and how they would respond to them. If the couple divorces, for example, to whom do stored IVF embryos resolve? Consequently, in the face of disagreements and unforeseen circumstances, the parties involved will have already articulated their wishes with respect to dispositional authority, discard, or storage of their gametes or embryos, and unnecessary litigation can be avoided. Not all contingencies can be foreseen, of course, but the system has proven quite effective.

Because research, storage, and treatment involving gametes and embryos are to be monitored, committees of the HFEA have been formed to approve protocols that use gametes and embryos in research and medicine. Consequently, the HFEA has responsibility for licensing novel applications with embryos and gametes and, therefore, fulfills a policymaking function. When a novel application that raises questions of well-being comes before a committee, the protocol is sent to the full HFEA for discussion and approval. Thus the smaller licensing committee does not make policy decisions that should be subject to broader discussion and approval. Finally, in addition to its licensing and monitoring functions, the HFEA maintains an information registry on the gametes, embryos, patients, and children that have been involved in licensed activities.

The authority of the HFEA to grant licenses is limited by the purposes described in section 11 of the act. The decision to articulate the purposes of embryo usage rather than specific techniques has ensured that the act can incorporate novel techniques that were not envisaged when the act was drafted. In addition, if new techniques and applications emerge that fall outside the HFEA's statutory authority, the act allows Parliament to expand the range of purposes that are placed under the HFEA's authority, thereby ensuring that new purposes do not call for new oversight agencies and preserving the integrity of the system. The act has been drafted in sufficiently general terms, however, that it remains almost unchanged more than a decade after its inception.

One reprogenetic development that the act could not incorporate, as initially written, was the isolation of ES cells. The response was a good, if not painless, example of well-informed democratic policymaking in the face of rapid scientific advance (Masood 1999).[6] The government spearheaded a public and policy debate about whether and when ES cell research and cloning techniques are valuable enough to be permitted for some purposes, and about what those purposes might be (Masood 1999). In 1998, both the HFEA (together with the Human Genetics Advisory Commission) and an independent expert group formulated policy recommendations.

The independent expert group recommended that ES cell research be allowed for specific therapeutic purposes and that cloning techniques be permitted for the creation of research embryos that might lead ultimately to autologous transplantation techniques (Chief's Medical Officer's Expert Group 2000). In addition, the group's report (known as the Donaldson Report) recommended that future review of approved ES cell protocols be conducted to determine whether the research has proven fruitful and merits continued use of human embryos. The Donaldson Report was accepted in its entirety by the government, which drafted additional purposes to add to the act by way of regulation. These amendments were accepted in a free (nonpartisan) vote by parliamentarians. Consequently, these new reprogenetic techniques now fall under the oversight of the HFEA, maintaining a comprehensive, coherent oversight of reproductive genetics.

The HFEA has been a model law for many countries attempting to craft regulation in this area, including Canada, Australia, and France. It is important to note, however, that the United Kingdom is not mired in a divisive abortion debate, and that fact probably helps explain the public acceptance (for the most part) of the oversight system's decisions.

The support in the United Kingdom for the HFEA extends to the scientific and regulatory communities, which appear to have worked out a nonadversarial relationship. When a clinic cannot be licensed due to insufficiencies in its standards or its protocols, the HFEA works with that clinic to ensure that it understands what is required for it to successfully apply for a license. Despite the comprehensive and highly centralized regulation, the United Kingdom remains committed to scientific freedom and arguably has one of the most liberal embryo research policies in the world.

There are a number of lessons to be gleaned from the experience in the United Kingdom. First, recommendations for Congress should be framed in general terms outlining suggested restrictions, conditions, and limits on the use, storage, and creation of embryos and gametes. Second, acceptable and unacceptable purposes of embryo research should be articulated rather than specific techniques. Third, a mechanism for adding to or adapting the enabling legislation in the face of new developments or information should be incorporated into the legislation. Fourth, a detailed informed consent procedure should be considered as a way of preventing unnecessary litigation and respecting patient autonomy. Fifth, the oversight authority should be responsible for developing a code of practice as a means of educating researchers, clinicians, and patients. And finally, the respect the HFEA enjoys is partly the result of its ability to make scientifically informed and coherent decisions. This ability derives from its members' considerable expertise and the wide discretion accorded them. Similarly, any U.S. oversight authority should possess an expertise not likely shared by the members of Congress and should be granted significant discretion in making its decisions.

Canada

The Canadian policy experience in overseeing human reprogenetic technologies has followed a slightly more tortured path than the British experience. Its different experience is partly the result of Canada's diversity of opinions about reprogenetics, the depth and effort put into the public consultation process, and the constitutional and political division of powers between the federal and provincial governments.

In 1989, a Royal Commission on New Reproductive Technologies was established by the federal government to consult the public on issues related to "new reproductive technologies." The commission was charged with developing a substantive analysis of the technologies' implications for Canadian citizens and society, and with making recommendations to the government for public oversight. More than 40,000 Canadians were directly involved in the commission's public consultation process.

In 1993, the commission released its findings in a two-volume report, with fifteen volumes of supporting material and discussion (Royal Commission on New Reproductive Technologies 1993). The report articulated an "ethic of care" that should govern this area of research and practice and eight detailed principles that informed its recommendations. The commission made specific recommendations with respect to prohibitions and restrictions that should apply to embryo research. In addition, it recommended the establishment of a national regulatory body responsible for mandatory licensing of treatment and research involving gametes and embryos. Like the HFEA, the commission recommended that the regulatory body be at arm's length from the government. In addition, the body was to be constituted with a membership of at least 50 percent women.

These recommendations were followed three years later by a voluntary moratorium on nine unacceptable practices (Connor 1995), which was widely regarded as unsuccessful. In 1997, a first legislative bill was introduced into parliament as an attempt to act on the commission's recommendations. That bill, Bill C-47 (*An Act Respecting Human Reproductive Technologies and Commercial Transactions Relating to Human Reproduction*) sought to criminalize a number of activities already subject to the voluntary moratorium and came under intense criticism for its failure to establish a licensing scheme or national regulatory body. The bill died when an election was called in 1997. In May 2002, after extensive consultations with the provinces, a second bill— this time entitled the *Assisted Human Reproduction Act* (AHRA)—was introduced to parliament (*An Act Respecting Assisted Human Reproductive Technologies and Related Research*). It passed in March 2004.

Like the counterpart British act, the AHRA purports to govern the creation, use, and storage of embryos and gametes in both treatment and research. However, unlike the British act, it also bans commercial transactions in human reproductive tissues (sperm and eggs) and commercial surrogacy. One of the guiding principles of the AHRA is the prohibition of commercial exploitation of human reproduction. Interestingly, the AHRA enshrines the guiding principles of the act within the act itself rather than in a preamble, as is more common. Placing the principles within the preamble means that they are not strictly enforceable as part of the act and can be used primarily to clarify or interpret the meaning of the act. But if the principles are affirmed in the AHRA itself, they must be taken into account when interpreting or implementing a section of the act or its supplementing regulations.

Also like the British act, the AHRA outlines the restrictions, conditions, and prohibitions on uses of gametes and embryos. Both Canada and the United Kingdom have prohibited modifying the human germline, sex selection for other than medical reasons, and creating human-nonhuman chimeras. It is worth noting that all these activities have taken place or have been attempted in the United States in the absence of legal prohibitions and comprehensive oversight.

The AHRA follows the British lead in establishing a national oversight body that has an arm's-length relationship to the government. As detailed in section 24 of the act, the Agency is responsible for licensing and monitoring facilities and for maintaining an information registry. In addition, it must communicate to and consult with the public and set conditions to maintain a license under the act. The Canadian act, again like the British act, explicitly requires the oversight body to carry out a public consultation and information function, aimed not only at the lay public, but also at stakeholders such as clinicians and patients. Clearly, the blueprint for the Canadian AHRA was Britain's HFEA of 1990.

There are lessons to be learned from both the British and Canadian experiences, not the least of which is that the road toward coherent oversight is long and often tortuous. But the public conversation that forms the bedrock of that process is rich, informative, and important for individuals and society alike. The ability to oversee reprogenetic research and practice from a national perspective provides both scientific quality control and greater certainty that ethically unacceptable activities are not being conducted with gametes and embryos behind a veil of secrecy in the private sector.

A POLICY PROPOSAL

There are many obstacles to any serious political initiative to regulate reprogenetics research—and human embryo research in general. Surely one of the greatest obstacles is the fear each side in the abortion war will have of losing any ground. Many people would prefer the status quo to any risk of a setback.

But some people have begun to take such risks. And if our society is to submit reprogenetic innovations to public oversight, others must take such risks as well. Developments in, for example, PGD, ooplasm transfer, cloning, and ES cell research invite us to step back and contemplate the bigger reprogenetic picture. Thoughtful people should accept that invitation and begin to think broadly and boldly: they should design a system that can foster the discussion of safety and well-being concerns—and can ensure that new reprogenetic techniques that raise those concerns do not slip through the regulatory cracks.

First Steps toward Public Discussion

We make three recommendations.

First, to bring embryo research into the light of public deliberation, Congress should lift the current ban on federally funded embryo research. We cannot have responsible oversight of reprogenetics research and practice, or of embryo research generally, if we do not first acknowledge that we already support those activities in a wide variety of ways. The United States has already embarked on one big embryo experiment. If we do not forthrightly accept that fact by allowing the federal government to oversee research and practice involving embryos, then the market will be the only mechanism to distinguish acceptable from unacceptable purposes of those activities.

Second, to take action toward regulatory oversight in the United States, a commission must consolidate and translate the many documents that have already been written on this topic, solicit views from the diverse U.S. constituencies that are or should be engaged with this topic, and synthesize this material to make legislative recommendations about statutory authority for an oversight body. The work of the commission, referred tohere as the Reprogenetics Technologies Advisory Commission (RTAC), would be similar in some respects to that of the Royal Commission in Canada, although the audience for this body would be Congress. The advisory commission would, in part, engage the public, stakeholders, and expert constituencies in consultation; articulate the ethical commitments that must guide such a regulatory effort; and draft the terms of reference for embryo research, including the limits, restrictions, and prohibitions to be written into legislation. That commission would then report its findings in the form of recommendations to Congress for a legislative initiative.

Third, in formulating its recommendations, the commission should carefully consider the possibility of creating a standing federal entity, a Reprogenetics Technologies Board (RTB), to facilitate reasoned and systematic public and policy deliberation about the purposes of reprogenetic research and practice. The board's authority would extend to the public and private sectors, and it would factor concerns about safety and well-being into policymaking and license-granting decisions. The board would, in important respects, resemble the United Kingdom's HFEA.

Drawing from the lessons learned in the United Kingdom and Canadian experience, it will be important, first, that the Reprogenetics Technologies Advisory Commission's recommendations for Congress be framed in general terms; it should only outline its suggested restrictions, conditions, and limits on the use, storage, and creation of embryos and gametes. Second, in defining the RTB's purview, the recommendations (and the eventual legislation) should articulate acceptable and unacceptable purposes of embryo research rather than specific techniques. Third, recognizing that it is impossible to keep pace with scientific and technological developments, the legislative initiative should incorporate a mechanism for adding to or adapting the enabling legislation in the face of new developments or information. Fourth, the board should be granted significant discretion, since its members will need to develop an expertise not likely shared by the members of Congress. Fifth, a detailed informed consent procedure should be considered to enable patients to contemplate what they want done with their embryos and gametes in unexpected circumstances, such as death and divorce; such procedures would be aimed both at preventing unnecessary litigation and respecting patient autonomy. And finally, the board should be responsible for developing a code of practice as a means of educating researchers, clinicians, and patients.

There are many possible obstacles to the creation of a new federal oversight board for reprogenetics. First, there is an open question about the constitutionality of any federal regulation of scientific research that occurs in the private sector. To date, there is no clear indication that Congress cannot implement such regulation; indeed, that it can has already been assumed in the bill recently passed by the House to ban all cloning. Yet the possibility remains that the federal oversight board envisioned here would face a constitutional challenge.

Second, the recommendations will likely face opposition from the entrenched participants in the abortion debate. The recommendation to lift the embryo research ban will raise deep concerns among anti-abortion advocates, who are likely to argue, starting from the premise that embryos are persons, that all embryo research is immoral and that none should be publicly funded. And at least initially, the prospect of any mechanism to oversee reprogenetics research and practice will raise deep concerns among pro-choice advocates, who may argue that accepting limits on the things researchers and clinicians can do with embryos is the first step down a slippery slope to limiting a woman's right to choose. Yet some people committed to the anti-abortion position now acknowledge that embryos in petri dishes are not persons, and agree that there are some things researchers ought to be permitted to do with embryos. Similarly, some committed to the pro-choice position now acknowledge that procreative liberty is not absolute, and agree that there are some things researchers and practitioners ought not to be permitted to do with embryos.

If any of these recommendations are to be taken seriously, then certainly, both sides of the abortion battle will have to believe that their concerns will be taken seriously. Thus, if the advisory commission were to be appointed (much less if it were to recommend the creation of a standing board along the lines of the HFEA), then moderate representatives from all sides would have to be involved. Members of the commission would have to be appointed by a bipartisan committee, with representation from both the House, the Senate, and a variety of stakeholders. Possibly the former chair of the NBAC and the current chair of the President's Commission on Bioethics could jointly help to nominate members.

Ongoing Discussion and Oversight

Even though the notion of creating an HFEA-like body in the United States will encounter resistance (Palmer and Cook-Deegan 2003), the time may be right. Others before us have called for regulatory action on some of the topics touched on in this chapter. These proposals have often focused on reproductive medicine, however, missing some of the larger concerns of reprogenetics, and they have typically sought mechanisms to ensure the safety of participants, neglecting well-being concerns.

For example, in 1996 the now-defunct National Advisory Board on Ethics in Reproduction (NABER) recommended that "serious and timely consideration be given in the United States to the establishment of a standing federal regulatory body to license infertility centers. This body would have responsibility and sufficient support for surveillance of infertility centers around the country for the purpose of regulating and accrediting the provision of services of assisted reproduction" (NABER 1996, 301). In a 1996 editorial in *Fertility and Sterility*, Howard Jones, founder of the Jones Institute of Reproductive Medicine (in Norfolk, Virginia), endorsed NABER's recommendation and claimed that it was also supported by the ASRM and SART. Jones cited a November 1995 news release issued jointly by the ASRM and SART which states that "such an independent licensing authority might oversee and validate the clinical and laboratory practice of ART, and function independent of and be funded separately from The American Society for Reproductive Medicine and The Society for Assisted Reproductive Technology." The consumer advocacy group RESOLVE also endorsed the idea (Aronson and Zieselman 1996).

Thus, there appears to be some support in the provider-consumer community for the idea of a licensing authority to improve safety, efficiency, and accountability in reproductive medicine. A number of groups have also called for better oversight in reprogenetics. A working group convened by the American Association for the Advancement of Science called for a body to consider not only the safety but also the well-being issues raised by attempts to produce "inheritable genetic modifications" (Frankel and Chapman 2002).[7] The National Conference of State Legislatures, which is concerned about consumer safety, has called for improved oversight of reproductive services (New York State Task Force 1998). The National Research Council report on cloning technology specifically suggested that a HFEA-like body be created to govern reproductive genetics. More recently, in 2002, the President's Council on Bioethics called for a moratorium on "research cloning," in large part to allow Congress to develop regulatory oversight in this area.

What follows are some preliminary thoughts on how an HFEA-like oversight board might look in the United States. In accordance with our own advice, we frame our proposal in general terms. A different view of the board might of course emerge from the advisory commission we have recommended.

Scope. The RTB's scope of authority would be articulated in the legislation that creates it, as called for by the advisory commission. The legislation should indicate that the RTB would grant licenses, monitor and inspect facilities, create a code of practice, consult with the public, and keep an information registry. The legislation would articulate those purposes, related to both treatment and research, involving the creation, use, manipulation, and storage of gametes and embryos for which licenses may be granted by the RTB. The RTB would be empowered to make licensing decisions in light of concerns about both safety and well-being.

In addition, an important function of the legislation is to articulate those practices that are unacceptable and therefore may not be the subject of a license. Both the British and Canadian acts forbid, for example, reproductive cloning and use of an embryo past fourteen days of development. Which practices should be identified as unacceptable would be part of the deliberations of the advisory commission.

The RTB's authority would extend to both the public and private sectors. At least with respect to safety concerns, a system of regulatory separation is arbitrary. It defies commonsense to protect participants in federally funded research from bodily harm, but not to protect those in privately funded research from the same. Respect for the safety and dignity of persons does not change with their location. In accordance with this line of reasoning, the NBAC in 2001 recommended the creation of a new federal-level body to oversee all human subjects research.

Membership. The RTB should be composed of persons from inside and outside the scientific community. The United Kingdom's HFEA has seventeen members and a staff of approximately forty-five. The Canadian agency will seat thirteen members, at least half of which must be women. Given the volume of work required to oversee reprogenetics in the United States, the RTB should have approximately seventeen members, and should be well staffed and funded. According to the act establishing the HFEA, at least half of the

HFEA's members must not be involved in medicine or science; neither the chair nor deputy chair is allowed to be a physician or scientist; the chair represents the "lay non-scientific opinion on these matters" (Deech 2000). This seems an appropriate balance of expertise for the RTB as well. In addition, a minimum of 50 percent of the RTB members should be women.

Such a body should be as independent and insulated as possible from the undue influence of election politics, consumer or business advocates, and pro- or antiabortion activists. For it to have moral authority, it must represent a wide range of perspectives and interests. Its membership would need to draw upon researchers, clinicians, consumers, lawyers, ethicists, and others. Yet every effort must be made to enable members to speak as individuals, with particular views, rather than as defenders of a given group's agenda. Striking this balance will be crucial and very difficult, but not impossible.

Functions. A body such as the RTB can be thought of as fulfilling three intimately related functions. The first would be to make policy regarding the things people do with gametes and embryos, from basic embryo research to reprogenetics services, by applying and interpreting the purposes, principles, and strictures of the enabling legislation. This policymaking function would be accomplished by granting (or denying) licenses for laboratories and clinics to carry out the research and clinical activities described in the legislation. The enabling legislation will probably flatly prohibit some activities, but other activities will likely be left partly to the RTB's discretion. Thus the licensing might, for example, make it possible to sell PGD to prospective parents seeking to test for disease-related traits but not to test for traits unrelated to disease (such as height, if testing for such traits became technically feasible). The licensing would be analogous to that performed by the HFEA in the United Kingdom. Also like the HFEA, the RTB would monitor and inspect premises and activities carried out under a license and maintain a register of information about donors, treatments, and children born from those treatments.

The second function of the RTB is to set standards for those activities by creating a code of practice. Such a code might detail informed consent procedures, for example, or delineate the proper handling of embryos that are to be transferred to a woman's uterus in the course of IVF. The code would necessarily change over time, of course, but at any given time it would establish a uniform standard for everyone offering reproductive services covered under the legislation. The code would also articulate the general guiding principles, which might build on the established U.S. principles of justice, beneficence, and autonomy.

A third and fundamentally important function of the RTB would be to engage in public consultation and promote public conversation about emerging issues in embryo research generally and reprogenetics more particularly. This responsibility to promote public conversation—indeed to create new constituencies committed to exploring this fascinating and important new arena of endeavor—is essential. In effect, we are calling not merely for the creation of a regulatory body, but for richer and more nuanced democratic deliberation about these vital issues. But one note of caution must be sounded here. Public consultation and transparency of political process are both important, and public consultation must not stand in the way of action. Public consultation should be immediate and ongoing, but so too must be the creation of policy.

The Bigger Picture

The convergence of reproductive and genetic medicine will lead to a vast increase in our capacity to relieve suffering and distress. It may also eventually increase our capacity to shape our children. Thus that convergence raises questions not only about the safety of children, but also about the well-being of those children and of the society they will join. Asking questions about the well-being of the participants in this endeavor is as important as asking questions about their safety. As Harold Shapiro, chair of President Clinton's National Bioethics Advisory Commission, has stated, "One of our greatest responsibilities is to consider the full implications of our new knowledge not only for relieving human suffering and distress but for the social and cultural institutions that are as critical as DNA to supporting our individual and collective lives" (Shapiro 1999, 223).

To deal with the emerging field of reprogenetics, to address those questions and implications, and to fulfill that responsibility, we need a new structure for oversight and regulation and transparent public policy discussion. The preliminary suggestions offered in this chapter about the shape that structure might take are not as important as the underlying recommendation that we begin quickly and formally to grasp and respond to the bigger reprogenetic picture.

It is easy to view reprogenetics as a train that has left the station. The speed of the science and the passion of the pro-market and antiregulatory advocates can convince one that calls for thoughtful oversight and regulation in this area are futile. But while this train certainly is not going to return to the station, it would be a terrible mistake to act as if its destination were foreordained.

Ruth Deech, formerly the chair of the Human Fertilization and Embryology Authority, recently recounted hearing a lecture by the great British infertility specialist Robert Edwards in the early days of IVF. According to Deech, Edwards asserted that to have an authority like the HFEA to make policy and to regulate research involving embryos was to bring "Nazism and Stalinism into the bedroom" (Deech 2000, 14). But as Deech replies, civilized societies have always exerted some control over reproduction, whether by crafting rules to govern incest, or the appropriate age of marriage, or abortion, or contraception, or adoption.

The situation today is significantly more complex than in the early days of IVF. Assisted reproduction now encompasses a multifaceted arena of scientific research, some of which is not even devoted primarily to reproduction. We should be relieved to learn that the fundamental ethical questions regarding the ethics of producing children are not new, even as we acknowledge that the technological possibilities render ever greater the need for careful oversight and regulation. To respond to that need, we should ask ourselves what we can do to increase the chances that we are creating a society into which good parents will want to bring children.

AUTHORS' NOTE

This chapter was originally published in 2003 as a special supplement to the *Hastings Center Report*, the journal of The Hastings Center. Where details in the international situation have changed, these are reflected in chapter 6 of this book. Developments continue in the area of human embryonic stem cell research. Individual states in the United States have enacted stem cell funding laws to compensate for the lack of progress that has been made to change U.S. federal policy (Knowles 2006). To date there has been little effort to incorporate questions of wellbeing into regulatory initiatives in the United States.

NOTES

1. This is the case with respect to ooplasm transplantation (Barritt et al. 2001). Indeed, when the U.S. researchers announced the ooplasm transplantation, their colleagues here and abroad expressed alarm about the possible health consequences (Austin 2001).

2. For example, via the MicroSort method.

3. The law states that no DHHS funds can be used to "create a human embryo or embryos for research purposes; or for research in which a human embryo or embryos are

destroyed, discarded, or knowingly subjected to risk of injury or death greater than that allowed for research on fetuses in utero."

4. IRB review of such research in the private sector is voluntary.

5. We thank Bruce Jennings for his insights on this question.

6. The House of Lords subsequently overturned a challenge to the HFEA's authority.

7. The scope of the AAAS recommendations is narrower than ours, however, since it speaks only to the alteration of gametes and embryos, whereas we seek to address the creation, use, and storage of gametes and embryos. Our recommendations are also more expansive in that they suggest the creation of a federal-level body that both makes policy and grants licenses. Whereas the AAAS report looks primarily to the RAC as a model body, our report looks first to the HFEA.

REFERENCES

Act Respecting Human Reproductive Technologies and Commercial Transactions Relating to Human Reproduction. 1997. Bill C-47. Ottawa, Ontario, Canada: Public Works and Government Services.

Act Respecting Assisted Human Reproductive Technologies and Related Research. 2002. Bill C-13, second reading October 9, 2002, reprinted as amended by the Standing Committee on Health as a working copy for the use of the House of Commons at Report Stage and as reported to the House on December 12, 2002. http://www.parl.gc.ca/37/21parlbus/chambus/house/bills/government/c-13/c-13_1/90187BE.html.

American Society for Reproductive Medicine. 1998. *Revised Minimum Standards for In Vitro Fertilization, Gamete Intrafallopian Transfer, and Related Procedures: A Practice Committee Report.* http://www.asrm.org/media/practice/revised.html.

———. 2000. *Does Intracytoplasmic Sperm Injection (ICSI) Carry Inherent Genetic Risks?* Birmingham, AL: American Society for Reproductive Medicine.

———. 2002. *2002 Guidelines for Gamete and Embryo Donation: A Practice Committee Report: Guidelines and Minimum Standards. Fertility and Sterility* 77, no. 6, suppl. 5.

Andre, J. 1995. Blocked exchanges: A taxonomy. In *Pluralism, Justice and Equality,* ed. D. Miller and M. Walzer, 171–97. Oxford: Oxford University Press.

Andrews, L. 1999. *The Clone Age: Adventures in the New World of Reproductive Technology.* New York: Henry Holt.

Annas, G. 1998. The Shadowlands: Secrets, lies, and assisted reproduction. *New England Journal of Medicine* 339:935–39.

Annas, G. J., L. B. Andrews, and R. M. Isasi. 2002. Protecting the endangered human: Toward an international treaty prohibiting cloning and inheritable alterations. *American Journal of Law & Medicine* 28:151–78.

Arneson, R. J. 1992. Commodification and commercial surrogacy. *Philosophy and Public Affairs* 21, no. 2: 132–64.

Aronson, D. D., and K. M. Zieselman. 1996. A consensus for regulation? *Fertility and Sterility* 66:862–63.

Arrow, K. J. 1972. Gifts and exchanges. *Philosophy and Public Affairs* 1:343–62.

Austin, K. 2001. New germline-changing IVF procedure could easily have transferred severe disease. *BioMedNet News,* May 17. http://news.bmn.com/report.

Barritt, J. A., C. A. Brenner, H. E. Malter, and J. Cohen. 2001. Mitochondria in human offspring derived from ooplasmic transplantation. *Human Reproduction* 16: 513–16.

Barritt, J. A., C. A. Brenner, S. Willadsen, and J. Cohen. 2000. Spontaneous and artificial changes in human ooplasmic mitochondria. *Human Reproduction* 15 (spec. suppl. 2): 207–17.

Barritt, J. A., S. Willadsen, C. Brenner, and J. Cohen. 2001. Epigenetic and experimental modifications in early mammalian development: Part II. Cytoplasmic transfer in assisted reproduction. *Human Reproduction Update* 7:428–35.

Belkin, L. 2001. The made-to-order savior. *New York Times Magazine,* July 1.

Blankley, T. 2000. The fountain of youth? Moral dilemmas of embryo research. *Washington Times,* April 26.

Blumenthal, D., M. Causino, E. Campbell, and K. S. Louis. 1996. Relationships between academic institutions and industry in the life sciences: An industry survey. *New England Journal of Medicine* 334:368–73.

Bonnicksen, A. 1998. Transplanting nuclei between human eggs: Implications for germline genetics. *Politics and the Life Sciences* 17:3–10.

———. 2002. *Crafting a Cloning Policy: From Dolly to Stem Cells.* Washington, DC: Georgetown University Press.

Buchanan, A., D. Brock, N. Daniels, and D. Wikler. 2000. *From Chance to Choice.* Cambridge: Cambridge University Press.

Calabresi, G., and P. Bobbitt. 1978. *Tragic Choices.* New York: W. W. Norton & Co.

Chief Medical Office's Expert Group. 2000. *Stem Cell Research: Medical Progress with Responsibility. A Report from the Chief Medical Officer's Expert Group Reviewing the Potential of Developments in Stem Cell Research and Cell Nuclear Replacement to Benefit Human Health.* London: Department of Health, August 16.

Cohen, C. 1997. Unmanaged care: The need to regulate new reproductive technologies in the United States. *Bioethics* 11, no. 3–4: 348–65.

Cohen, J., R. Scott, M. Alikani, T. Schimmel, S. Munne, J. Levron, and L. Wu. 1998. Ooplasmic transfer in mature human oocytes. *Molecular Human Reproduction* 4:269–80.

Committee of Inquiry into Human Fertilisation and Embryology. 1984. *Report of the Committee of Inquiry into Human Fertilisation and Embryology.* London: HMSO.

Connor S. 1995. Marleau right to be cautious on reproductive technologies. *Toronto Star,* August 4.

Daniels, K. R., E. Blythe, D. Hall, and K. M. Hanson. The best interests of the child in assisted human reproduction: The interplay between the state, professionals, and parents. *Politics and the Life Sciences* 19:33–44.

Deech, R. 2000. Assisted reproductive techniques and the law. *Medico-Legal Journal* 69, pt. 1: 13–24.

Food and Drug Administration. 2002. CBER hearings. May 9-10. www.fda.gov/ohrms/dockets/ac/cber02.htm.

Frankel, M. S., and A. R. Chapman. 2002. *Human Inheritable Modifications: Assessing Scientific, Ethical, Religious, and Policy Issues.* Washington, DC: American Association for the Advancement of Science.

Frase-Blunt, M. 2001. Ova-compensating? Women who donate eggs to infertile couples earn a reward—but pay a price. *Washington Post,* December 4.

Fugger, E. F., S. H. Black, K. Keyvanfar, and J. D. Schulman.1998. Births of normal daughters after MicroSort sperm separation and intrauterine insemination, in-vitro fertilization, or intracytoplasmic sperm injection. *Human Reproduction* 13:2367–70.

Gordon, J. W. 1999. Genetic enhancement in humans. *Science* 283:2023–24.

Green, R. M. 2001. *The Human Embryo Research Debates: Bioethics in the Vortex of Controversy.* Oxford: Oxford University Press.

Hansen, M., J. J. Kurinczuk, C. Bower, and S. Webb. 2002. The risk of major birth defects after intracytoplasmic sperm injection and in vitro fertilization. *New England Journal of Medicine* 346:725–30.

Harris, J. 1992. *Wonderwoman and Superman: The Ethics of Human Biotechnology.* New York: Oxford University Press.

Health Research Extension Act. 1985. P.L. 99-158.

Human Fertilisation and Embryology Act. 1990. United Kingdom (c. 37).

Human Fertilisation and Embryology (Research Purposes) Regulations. 2001. Statutory Instrument no. 188.

Human Genetics Advisory Committee and Human Fertilisation and Embryology Authority. 1998. *Cloning Issues in Reproduction, Science and Medicine.* www.doh.gov.uk/hgac/papers/paperd1.htm.

Institute for Science, Law, and Technology Working Group. 1998. ART into science: Regulation of fertility techniques. *Science* 281:651–52.

Jones, H. 1996. The time has come. *Fertility and Sterility* 66:1092.

Juengst, E., and E. Parens. 2003. Germ-line dancing: Definitional considerations for policy makers. In *Human Genetic Modifications across Generations: Scientific, Ethical, Religious and Policy Issues,* ed. A. Chapman and M. Frankel, 20-36. Baltimore, MD: Johns Hopkins University Press.

Knowles, L. P. 1999. Property, patents and progeny: Selling our selves. *Hastings Center Report* 29, no. 2: 38–40.

———. 2000. *International Perspectives on Human Embryo and Fetal Tissue Research. Background Paper for Ethical Issues in Human Stem Cell Research,* H1–H22. Rockville, MD: National Bioethics Advisory Commission, January.

———. 2006. State-sponsored human stem cell research: Regulatory approaches and standard setting. In *States and Stem Cells: Policy and Economic Implications of State-Sponsored Stem Cell Research,* ed. A. D. Levine, 75–111. Princeton, NJ: Policy Research Institute for the Region.

Lefer, D. 1999. An ad for smart eggs spawns ethics uproar. *Daily News* (New York), March 7.

Little, M. O. 1998. Surgery, suspect norms, and the ethics of complicity. In *Enhancing Human Traits: Ethical and Social Implications,* ed. E. Parens, 162–76. Washington, DC: Georgetown University Press.

Loiseau, G. 2000. Typologie des choses hors du commerce juridique RTD civ (1, Janvier–Mars): 47.

Macklin, R. 1996. What is wrong with commidification? In *New Ways of Making Babies: The Case of Egg Donation,* ed. C. Cohen. Bloomington: Indiana University Press.

Masood, E. 1999. Expert group to look at UK cloning law. *Nature* 400:4.

Mehlman, M. J., and J. R. Botkin. 1998. *Access to the Genome: The Challenge to Equality.* Washington, DC: Georgetown University Press.

MicroSort. Web site. www.microsort.com/results.html (accessed July 2006).

Murray, T. H. 1987. Gifts of the body and the needs of strangers. *Hastings Center Report* 17, no. 2: 30–38.

———. 1995. Organ vendors, families, and the gift of life. In *Organ Transplantation: The Human and Cultural Context,* ed. S. J. Youngner, R. Fox, and L. J. O'Connell, 101-25. Madison: University of Wisconsin Press.

———. 1996. *The Worth of a Child.* Berkeley and Los Angeles: University of California Press.

National Academy of Sciences. 2002. *Scientific and Medical Aspects of Human Reproductive Cloning.* Washington, DC: National Academies Press.

National Advisory Board on Ethics in Reproduction. 1996. Report and recommendations on oocyte donation by the National Advisory Board on Ethics in Reproduction (NABER). In *New Ways of Making Babies: The Case of Egg Donation,* ed. C. Cohen, 237–93. Bloomington: Indiana University Press.

National Bioethics Advisory Commission. 1999. *Ethical Issues in Human Stem Cell Research.* Rockville, MD: National Bioethics Advisory Commission.

———. 2001. *Report and Recommendations of the National Bioethics Advisory Commission.* Vol. 1 of *Ethical and Policy Issues in Research Involving Human Participants.* Bethesda, MD: National Bioethics Advisory Commission.

National Conference of State Legislatures. 2001. *Genetics Policy Report: Reproductive Technologies.* Washington, DC: National Conference of State Legislatures.

National Institutes of Health. 1986. *NIH Guidelines For Research involving Recombinant DNA Molecules.* Section I-B. *Definition of Recombinant DNA Molecules.* Bethesda, MD: National Institutes of Health.

———. 1994. *Report of the Human Embryo Research Panel.* Bethesda, MD: National Institutes of Health.

———. 1996. NIH proposal to abolish Recombinant DNA Advisory Committee. *BioLaw* 11, no. 10: U.225–31.

New York State Task Force on Life and the Law. 1998. *Assisted Reproductive Technologies: Analysis and Recommendations for Public Policy.* New York: New York State Task Force on Life and the Law.

NIH Reauthorization Act. 1993. 45 CFR 46.201-207.

NIH Revitalization Act. 1993. P.L. 103-43.

Palmer, J. G., and R. Cook-Deegan. 2003. National policies to oversee inheritable genetic modifications research. In *Designing Our Descendants: The Promises and Perils of Genetic Modifications,* ed. A. R. Chapman and M. S. Frankel, 275–95. Baltimore, MD: Johns Hopkins University Press.

Pinker, S. 2003. Better babies? Why genetic enhancement is too unlikely to worry about. *Boston Globe,* June 1.

Powell, K. 2002. Seeds of doubt. *Nature* 422:656–58.

President's Commission for the Study of Ethical Problems in Medicine and Biomedical and Behavioral Research. 1982. *Splicing Life: A Report on the Social and Ethical Issues of Genetic Engineering with Human Beings.* Washington, DC: Government Printing Office.

President's Council on Bioethics. 2002. *Human Cloning and Human Dignity: An Ethical Inquiry.* Washington, DC: President's Council on Bioethics.

Rabb, H. 1999. Memo from Harriet Rabb to Harold Varmus. In statement of Harold Varmus, M.D., Director, National Institutes of Health, before the Senate Appropriations Subcommittee on Labor, Health and Human Services, Education and Related Agencies, January 26. http://freedom.house.gov/library/technology/stemcell.asp.

Radin, M. J. 1987. Market inalienability. *Harvard Law Review* 100:1849–1937.

Resnik, D. B., H. B. Steinkraus, and P. J. Langer. 1999. *Human Germline Gene Therapy: Scientific, Moral, and Political Issues.* Austin, TX: R. G. Landes.

Robertson, J. A. 1994. *Children of Choice: Freedom and the New Reproductive Technologies.* Princeton, NJ: Princeton University Press.

———. 1995. Symbolic issues in embryo research. *Hastings Center Report* 25, no. 1: 37–38.

Royal Commission on New Reproductive Technologies. *Proceed with Care: The Final Report of the Royal Commission on New Reproductive Technologies.* Ottawa: Canadian Government Publishing, 1993.

Satz, D. 1992. Markets in women's reproductive labor. *Philosophy and Public Affairs* 21, no. 2: 107–31.

Shanley, M. L. 2001. *Making Babies, Making Families.* Boston: Beacon Press.

Shapiro, H. 1999. Reflections on the interface of bioethics, public policy, and science. *Kennedy Institute of Ethics Journal* 9, no. 3: 209–24.

Silver, L. 1997. *Remaking Eden: Cloning and Beyond in a Brave New World.* New York: Avon.

Steinbock, B. 2002. Sex selection: Not obviously wrong. *Hastings Center Report* 32, no. 1: 23–28.

Stempsey, W. E. 1996. Paying people to give up their organs: The problem with commodification of body parts. *Medical Humanities Review* 10, no. 2: 45–55.

Tang, Y.-P., E. Shimizu, G. R. Dube, C. Rampon, G. A. Kerchner, and M. Zhuo. 1999. Genetic enhancement of learning and memory in mice. *Nature* 401:63–69.

Templeton, A. 2002. Ooplasmic transfer: Proceed with care. *New England Journal of Medicine* 346:773–75.

Turner, R. C. 1998. Do means matter? In *Enhancing Human Traits: Ethical and Social Implications,* ed. E. Parens, 151-61. Washington, DC: Georgetown University Press.

Verlinsky, Y., S. Retchitsky, W. Schoolcraft, C. Strom, and A. Kuliev. 2001. Preimplantation diagnosis for Fanconi anemia combined with HLC matching. *Journal of the American Medical Association* 285:3130–33.

Walters, L. 2003. Research cloning, ethics, and public policy (letter). *Science* 299:1661.

Walters, L., and J. G. Palmer. 1997. *The Ethics of Human Gene Therapy.* New York: Oxford University Press.

Weiss, R. 2003. Scientists replace stem cell genes. *Washington Post,* February 10.

Wertheimer, A. 1987. *Coercion.* Princeton, NJ: Princeton University Press.

Zoon, K. 2001. *Letter to Sponsors / Researchers—Human Cells Used in Therapy Involving the Transfer of Genetic Material by Means Other Than the Union of Gamete Nuclei.* Washington, DC: U.S. Food and Drug Administration, July 6. www.fda.gov/cber/ltr/cytotrans070601.htm.

Zwaka, T. P., and J. A. Thomson. 2003. Homologous recombination in human embryonic stem cells. *Nature Biotechnology,* February 10. doi:10.1038/nbt788.

Index